9/13

2

RACE AND JUSTICE

Wrongful Convictions of African American Men

Marvin D. Free, Jr.
Mitch Ruesink

LYNNE
RIENNER
PUBLISHERS

BOULDER
LONDON

Published in the United States of America in 2012 by
Lynne Rienner Publishers, Inc.
1800 30th Street, Boulder, Colorado 80301
www.rienner.com

and in the United Kingdom by
Lynne Rienner Publishers, Inc.
3 Henrietta Street, Covent Garden, London WC2E 8LU

Library of Congress Cataloging-in-Publication Data
Free, Marvin D.
   Race and justice: wrongful convictions of African American men /
   Marvin D. Free, Jr. & Mitch Ruesink.
   Includes bibliographical references and index.
   ISBN 978-1-58826-810-5 (hbk.: alk. paper)
   1. Discrimination in criminal justice administration—United States.
2. Judicial error—United States. 3. African American criminals.
I. Ruesink, Mitch. II. Title.
   HV9950.F744 2012
   364.3'496073—dc23   2011034705

British Cataloguing in Publication Data
A Cataloguing in Publication record for this book
is available from the British Library.

Printed and bound in the United States of America

The paper used in this publication meets the requirements
of the American National Standard for Permanence of
Paper for Printed Library Materials Z39.48-1992.

5 4 3 2

Contents

Tables

Preface

It is inevitable that even in the optimal situation some innocent individuals will be declared guilty in a court of law. Until recently, however, the assumption that held sway was that wrongful convictions were both infrequent and the result of the failure of individual actors in the criminal justice system to carry out their assigned responsibilities properly. Few attributed this failure to properties inherent in the criminal justice system. As the science of DNA progressed, however, and as numerous miscarriages of justice surfaced, those previous assumptions were called into question. Psychological studies of eyewitness accounts further raised issues regarding the infallibility of such accounts. As cases of wrongful convictions began to accumulate and the mass media started publicizing these cases, interest in wrongful convictions accelerated. Yet, the data on wrongful convictions remain largely fragmented and incomplete. Although some flagrant miscarriages of justice (e.g., the Tulia, Texas, drug bust and the abuse of prosecutorial power in Dallas, Texas) receive considerable attention from the media, numerous other cases of wrongful conviction receive meager exposure. Moreover, the current preoccupation of the media with economic and global issues makes it doubtful that this topic will dominate the news for the foreseeable future.

Although numerous books on wrongful convictions exist, none has exclusively focused on the wrongful conviction of African American men. By focusing on this racial minority, our intention is not to dismiss the impact that wrongful convictions have had on other marginalized groups in society. Rather, the exclusive focus on a single racial minority is meant to provide the reader with an appreciation of a group that is disproportionately impacted by the criminal justice system. Whether one analyzes arrest, conviction, or incarceration data, the overrepresentation of African Americans becomes immediately apparent. Numerically, the bulk of those found in these statistics are male rather than female, although both genders are disproportionately found in criminal justice statistics. Since the number of known wrongful conviction cases is substantially larger for the male African American population, this study limits its investigation to African American men.

1

Wrongful Convictions in the United States

It is better that ten guilty escape than one innocent suffer.
—*English jurist Sir William Blackstone (1723–1780)*

It is hard to envision a criminal justice system that never produces erroneous convictions, yet for many years few questioned the US criminal justice system. When a wrongful conviction was detected, it was typically attributed to a failure of some of the actors within the system to carry out their assigned responsibilities correctly. After all, it was reasoned, because defendants are presumed to be innocent until proven guilty, the system was more inclined to release guilty individuals than to convict innocent ones. This reasoning, however, ignores some very important facts. First, public defenders frequently believe that their clients are guilty, if not of this crime then of some other crime (Blumberg 1967; McIntyre 1987). Second, prosecutors share this view of the defendant's guilt as do many jurors (Christianson 2004). Further complicating the problem is the financial inability of many defendants to afford adequate legal representation. Moreover, many defendants are not only destitute but disproportionately drawn from racial and ethnic minorities, because they frequently inhabit the areas of the city in which police surveillance is most heavily concentrated. To the extent that the dual stigma of poverty and minority status contributes to the stereotypic perception that they are criminals, receiving a verdict of not guilty becomes more problematic. And because many wrongfully convicted individuals have prior criminal records (whether justified or not), the presumption of innocence becomes more tenuous. Thus, wrongful convictions are a reality in the US criminal justice system. What remains open to debate is the relative frequency with which these miscarriages of justice occur.

1

The chapter begins with a succinct review of the study of wrongful convictions in the United States. This is followed by a discussion of the estimated prevalence and incidence of wrongful convictions as well as a critique of these estimates. The chapter then examines factors frequently attributed to wrongful convictions and the effect of race on the conviction of innocent persons. A discussion of the focus and scope of the study is found at the end of Chapter 1.

A Selective Overview of the Study of Wrongful Convictions

Empirical investigations of wrongful convictions in the United States can be traced back to 1932, when Edwin Borchard published *Convicting the Innocent: Sixty-five Actual Errors of Criminal Justice*. Since that time other books with similar themes followed, including *Court of Last Resort* (Gardner 1952), *Not Guilty* (Frank and Frank 1957), *The Innocents* (Radin 1964), and *Wrongful Imprisonment: Mistaken Convictions and Their Consequences* (Brandon and Davies 1973). What Richard Leo (2005, 204) describes as "the beginning of the modern era of the study of wrongful conviction[s]" began in 1987 with Hugo Bedau and Michael Radelet's seminal article in the *Stanford Law Review*. In "Miscarriages of Justice in Potentially Capital Cases," Bedau and Radelet provide evidence that the problem of wrongful conviction is more prevalent than previously thought and raise the specter that wrongfully convicted individuals have been executed. They document at least 350 wrongful convictions that occurred in capital trials in the United States from 1900 to 1985. Although Stephen Markman and Paul Cassell (1988) have been critical of their findings, the sheer volume of erroneous convictions suggests that the problem is potentially much more serious than previously envisioned.

Interest in wrongful convictions was further piqued as a result of DNA testing. In 1989 Gary Dotson's 1979 rape conviction was overturned after a DNA sample absolved him of any wrongdoing. His case represents the first time that a convicted individual had been exonerated on the basis of DNA evidence (Gross et al. 2005). More cases of wrongful conviction were soon forthcoming. An early study by the United States Department of Justice (1996) identified twenty-eight cases in which convicted individuals were exonerated through DNA evidence. According to the Innocence Project (2011), the number of DNA exonerations for the United States currently stands at 267.

In addition to DNA testing, the problem of the wrongful conviction of innocents received substantial press coverage when in 2000 the governor of the state of Illinois imposed a moratorium on executions, given the increasing number of wrongful convictions being discovered at that time (Huff 2002). At the time of the moratorium more death row inmates had been exonerated than had been executed since capital punishment was reinstated in Illinois during the 1970s (Leo 2005). Moreover, according to the Center on Wrongful Convictions (2009a),

> In the quarter century between restoration of the Illinois death penalty and Governor George Ryan's blanket clemency order, 298 men and women were sentenced to death in Illinois. Of those, 18 have been exonerated—a rate of 6%, the highest exoneration rate of the 38 states with death penalties on their books.[1]

Innocence projects have furthered our understanding of the significance of the problem of wrongful convictions, although the data are fragmented and limited in scope. The earliest innocence project was initiated by Barry Scheck and Peter Neufeld in 1992 at Yeshiva University's Benjamin N. Cardozo School of Law. According to their website, "The project is a national litigation and public policy organization dedicated to exonerating people through DNA testing and reforming the criminal justice system to prevent future injustice" (Innocence Project 2009b). The Center on Wrongful Convictions at Northwestern University's School of Law also boasts a multifunctional innocence program. Structured around three components, the Center on Wrongful Convictions provides not only legal representation but research and community service to raise public awareness and to promote reform within the criminal justice system (Center on Wrongful Convictions 2009b). Today approximately forty law schools in the United States have programs that focus on the exoneration of innocent individuals (Zalman 2006).

Arguably, the most extensive body of information on wrongful convictions is available at Hans Sherrer's Forejustice (2011) website. With an international list of over three thousand wrongfully convicted individuals, this database represents the largest enumeration of wrongful convictions. The website also provides the user with a link to *Justice Denied*, a magazine devoted exclusively to those who have been wrongfully convicted. Printed at least four times annually, *Justice Denied* is published by the Justice Institute, a nonprofit organization in Seattle, Washington.

A steady stream of recent books has further stimulated interest in the problem of the conviction of innocents. For example, *Presumed Guilty: When Innocent People Are Wrongly Convicted,* by Martin Yant, was published in 1991. Michael Radelet, Hugo Bedau, and Constance Putnam in 1992 documented over four hundred wrongful convictions in potentially capital cases. Four years later C. Ronald Huff, Arye Rattner, and Edward Sagarin published *Convicted but Innocent: Wrongful Conviction and Public Policy,* which further highlighted the problem of failed justice. Innocence Project founders Barry Scheck and Peter Neufeld (along with Jim Dwyer) published *Actual Innocence: Five Days to Execution and Other Dispatches from the Wrongly Convicted* in 2000. A collection of readings appeared in 2001. Edited by Saundra Westervelt and John Humphrey, *Wrongly Convicted: Perspectives on Failed Justice* examined the causes of wrongful convictions and the demographic characteristics of those wrongly convicted. Additionally, Westervelt and Humphrey included case studies and a section that proposed ways to ameliorate the situation. Some other notable books on wrongful convictions include Stanley Cohen's (2003) *The Wrong Men: America's Epidemic of Wrongful Death Row Convictions* and Scott Christianson's (2004) *Innocent: Inside Wrongful Conviction Cases.*

Estimating the Prevalence and Incidence of Wrongful Convictions

Determining the frequency and number of cases in which individuals have been wrongly convicted is problematic at best. Because investigations of wrongful convictions in the United States typically concentrate on the most serious offenses, given the potential for severe sanctions (including the possibility of death in capital-eligible cases), less serious cases go largely undetected. To the extent that these less serious crimes may result in suspended sentences or probation, the wrongly convicted defendant may lack the incentive to pursue a legal remedy. The defendant's limited financial resources may further result in an acceptance of an erroneous guilty verdict (Gross et al. 2005). And because wrongfully convicted defendants may possess a prior criminal record, there is often little outcry from the public. Nor can an estimate of wrongful convictions rely on statistics derived from successful appeals: innocence alone does not guarantee a successful appeal and a successful appeal does not necessarily demonstrate *factual innocence,* given that convictions may be overturned on the basis of procedural errors alone. Thus, estimates of wrongful convictions that rely on known cases of wrongful conviction will tend to understate the scope of the problem.

To avoid these pitfalls some researchers have derived their estimates by surveying individuals who work within the criminal justice system. These estimates, however, are based on perceptions that are of unknown validity. There are few prosecutors, for example, willing to acknowledge that they have convicted innocent persons. It is therefore reasonable to assume that criminal justice personnel are conservative in their estimates of the number of cases of failed justice. With these caveats in mind, a brief review of research in this area follows.

The number of known wrongful convictions varies considerably from study to study. Many researchers have focused exclusively on wrongful capital convictions. While these are the most egregious miscarriages of justice, death sentences comprise only a miniscule amount of all felony sentences.[2] As previously noted, Bedau and Radelet in 1987 identified 350 capital cases involving erroneous convictions. Their study, however, examined only a fraction of the 7,000-plus executions that occurred during the twentieth century. This figure was revised to at least 416 cases involving wrongful conviction in 1992 (Radelet et al.). Combining data from DNA exonerations, a sample of capital sentences, and information obtained from the Innocence Project, D. Michael Risinger (2007) estimates that between 3.3 percent and 5 percent of all capital rape-murder convictions in the 1980s involved innocent defendants. In an examination that includes capital cases from 1970 to 1992, William Holmes (2001) suggests that more than 106 individuals were erroneously convicted of capital crimes in the United States. Using more recent data, Samuel Gross and colleagues (2005) uncovered 340 convictions of innocents from 1989 through 2003.

Other researchers have concentrated on exonerations that resulted from DNA testing. As noted previously, the earliest of this research dates back to the 1996 Department of Justice study, which analyzed 28 wrongful convictions overturned by DNA evidence. Four years later, Scheck, Neufeld, and Dwyer (2000) documented 62 cases in which convicted individuals were later found to be innocent through DNA testing. Today there are 267 cases in which DNA evidence has culminated in the exoneration of convicted innocents (Innocence Project 2011).

Surveys of criminal justice professionals typically disclose a small percentage of cases that are thought to have resulted in the wrongful conviction of an innocent person. In *Convicted but Innocent: Wrongful Conviction and Public Policy,* Huff and colleagues (1996) report on the results of a questionnaire mailed to Ohio criminal justice personnel (judges, prosecutors, public defenders, sheriffs, and chiefs of police) and state attorneys general. Of those who responded, 72 percent believed that wrongful convictions constituted less than 1 percent of all criminal cases in the United States. An additional 20 percent of those surveyed felt that innocent individuals had been wrongly convicted 6 to 10 percent of the time. A more recent survey of judges, defense attorneys, prosecutors, and police from

Ohio suggests similar perceptions (Ramsey 2007). Inquiring about the frequency of system errors that result in wrongful conviction, Robert Ramsey found that his respondents believed that wrongful convictions occur at a rate of 0.5 to 1 percent in felony cases in their own jurisdictions and at a slightly higher rate (1 to 3 percent) for the United States as a whole. A replication of the Ohio survey using criminal justice personnel in Michigan revealed almost identical estimates (Zalman, Smith, and Kiger 2008). Respondents estimated a wrongful conviction rate of less than 0.5 percent in their own jurisdictions and a wrongful conviction rate of 1 to 3 percent for the country overall, although defense lawyers perceived more wrongful convictions than judges, prosecutors, and police officials. While these estimates suggest the perception that relatively few cases result in wrongful conviction, even if only 0.5 percent of all cases culminate in a wrongful conviction, in a given year there will be approximately five thousand wrongful felony convictions.

Criminal Justice System Factors
Associated with the Conviction of Innocents

Although wrongful convictions are commonly the result of the coalescence of multiple factors, the most frequently cited contributor to false convictions is *witness error*. Since Edwin Borchard's observation in 1932 that witness error was present in over half of his wrongful convictions, researchers have found that witness error is a prominent factor in the conviction of innocents. According to the Innocence Project (2009c), witness error is a factor in over three-fourths of DNA exonerations. Nor are individuals employed by the criminal justice system unaware of this problem. Witness error (primarily witness misidentification) was perceived to be the number one reason for wrongful conviction by 78.6 percent of the criminal justice personnel surveyed in a recent study (Huff et al. 1996, 67). While most witness error is not deliberate (Huff et al. 1996),[3] a number of factors can contribute to misidentification. As Mitch Ruesink and Marvin Free (2005, 4–5) note:

> Psychological factors, including exposure time, amount of light, distance from observer, level of violence, and post-event factors (e.g., eyewitnesses given leading information) can influence the perceptions of eyewitnesses. Misidentification is also more likely when the observer and the observed are of different races. Empirical research demonstrates that cross-racial identifications are most problematic when white eyewitnesses are attempting to identify African American subjects (Rutledge

2001). Systemic factors associated with misidentification include lineups that contain only one person who looks like the alleged perpetrator and lineups in which the suspect is of a different racial group than others in the lineup. Finally, societal and cultural factors such as personal prejudice, expectations based on past experience, and stereotypes may affect what we "see."

Police and *prosecutorial misconduct* are present in a number of the known wrongful conviction cases as well. A study of DNA exonerations by the Innocence Project disclosed the presence of police misconduct in half of their cases. Similarly, prosecutorial misconduct was present in 42 percent of the wrongful convictions (Scheck et al. 2000, 246). Moreover, a recent national examination of the judicial system found that prosecutorial misconduct led to charge dismissals, conviction reversals, or reduced sentences in over two thousand cases. Yet a number of questionable prosecutorial practices did not result in any action being taken. According to Steve Weinberg (2003a), "In thousands more cases, judges labeled prosecutorial behavior inappropriate, but allowed the trial to continue or upheld convictions using a doctrine called 'harmless error.'"

The organizational culture of the police and district attorney's office can produce a climate in which the probability of wrongful convictions is enhanced if expedience and winning at all costs is emphasized. Perhaps nowhere was this more apparent than in the Dallas County District Attorney's Office (DCDAO), where prosecutors are alleged to have stated, "Anyone can convict a guilty man; it takes a real prosecutor to convict an innocent one" (cited in Huff et al. 1996, 43). This climate of permissiveness has not gone unnoticed. Since Texas began allowing postconviction DNA testing in 2001, Dallas County has had the most exonerations of any county in the United States. Consequently, a conviction integrity unit has been established to review old conviction cases for prosecutorial misconduct, and District Attorney Craig Watkins, an African American, has been hired to oversee the process. Moreover, in 2008 CBS's *60 Minutes* featured a story on the DCDAO; and in 2009 Investigation Discovery, a sister station to the Discovery Channel, televised six episodes of *Dallas DNA,* which examined the convict integrity unit of the DCDAO and DNA exonerations in Dallas County (Barta 2008; Emily 2009).

Police and prosecutorial misconduct can manifest itself in a myriad of ways. Police, for example, may "coach" the witness during the lineup; use unscrupulous methods (e.g., brutality, threat, force, or deceit) to obtain a confession; "plant" evidence; mishandle physical evidence; or threaten potential witnesses for the suspect. Prosecutorial misconduct may involve improper behavior during the grand jury proceedings; dismissal of potential jurors because of their race, ethnicity, or gender; harassment or bias toward the defendant or defense attorney; use of known false or misleading evidence; suppression of exculpatory evidence; withholding information that the witness testifying against the accused was offered immunity (or other rewards) for testifying; and use of improper closing arguments (Gershman 1991; Huff et al. 1996; Weinberg 2003a). Other examples of prosecutorial misconduct include the use of inappropriate or inflammatory comments during trial; the mischaracterization of the facts or evidence of the case; mishandling the evidence; and "threatening, badgering, or tampering with witnesses" (see Davis 2007, Chapter 7, for a more complete discussion). Additionally, the likelihood of a wrongful conviction is enhanced when the police and prosecutors fail to adequately investigate other possible perpetrators of the crime and ignore evidence that fails to support their views (Humphrey and Westervelt 2001).

False confessions represent another factor that is associated with the conviction of innocents. Duress, coercion, intoxication, diminished capacity, mental impairment, a misunderstanding of the law, fear of violence by the police, actual harm by the police, the threat of a harsh sentence if a confession is not given, and a misunderstanding of the situation have all been found to be associated with the admission of guilt by an innocent. The extent to which false confessions contribute to wrongful convictions varies in the research. The Innocence Project (2009d) reports that false confessions (in the form of an incriminating statement, confession of guilt, or a guilty plea) are a factor in one-fourth of all DNA exonerations. On the other hand, a 2003 report examining forty-two wrongful murder convictions in Illinois since 1970 noted that 59.5 percent of the convictions "rested in whole or part on false confessions" (Warden et al. 2003).

The *use of informants/snitches* is another leading contributor to wrongful convictions. In over 15 percent of all DNA exonerations, testimony from informants or jailhouse snitches was a factor in the erroneous conviction (Innocence Project 2009e). In many of these cases the jury was unaware that the informant/snitch had been paid to testify against the defendant or had been released from prison in exchange for the testimony and therefore had an incentive to lie. The Center on Wrongful Convictions suggests that the problem of using testimony from snitches is even more acute. An examination of 111 death row exonerations since the reinstatement of capital punishment in the 1970s revealed that 45.9 percent of the wrongful convictions were the result "in whole or part on the testimony of witnesses with incentives to lie—in the vernacular, snitches" (Warden 2004, 3), thus making the testimony of snitches the main cause of conviction in known wrongful conviction capital cases.

Moreover, racial disparity in drug enforcement may be exacerbated by the use of police informants in minority communities. According to Alexandra Natapoff (2009), a law professor at Loyola University in Los Angeles and expert on criminal snitching, because the police focus attention on the communities where their informants reside, high-crime urban communities, which are typically overrepresented by people of color, tend to come under closer scrutiny than their more affluent (and more white) suburban counterparts.[4] And because police informants commonly have an incentive to lie, they are often unreliable sources of information. The overexposure of urban minority inhabitants means that "false accusations, mistaken warrants, erroneous raids, and wrongful convictions associated with snitches will be more frequent in communities in which the practice is prevalent" (113).

Ineffective defense counsel represents yet another possible factor contributing to the conviction of innocents. Again, research is inconclusive regarding the extent to which this problem is responsible for wrongful convictions. Whereas ineffective defense counsel contributed to only 2.8 percent of the wrongful capital convictions examined by Bedau and Radelet in 1987, it was present in 27 percent of DNA exonerations (Scheck et al. 2000, 246). Ineffective defense counsel can be influenced by a number of factors, including insufficient funding, lack of mechanisms for monitoring the quality of legal representation provided to the defendant, an unmotivated defense counsel, the presumption of guilt that pervades the criminal justice system, and the difficulty of proving the presence of ineffective counsel on appeal (Bernhard 2001).[5]

Unvalidated or improper forensic science is the second most common factor leading to the conviction of innocent defendants based on DNA exonerations (Innocence Project 2009f). Unvalidated or improper forensic science includes

> the use of forensic disciplines or techniques that have not been tested to establish their validity and reliability; testimony about forensic evidence that presents inaccurate statistics, gives statements of probability or frequency (whether numerical or non-numerical) in the absence of valid empirical data, interprets nonprobative evidence as inculpatory, or concludes/suggests that evidence is uniquely connected to the defendant without empirical data to support such testimony; or misconduct, either by fabricating inculpatory data or failing to disclose exculpatory data. (Innocence Project 2009f)

In 2003 the US Department of Justice estimated skewed testimony, sloppy work, and tainted evidence by the Federal Bureau of Investigation may have been present in three thousand cases tried prior to 1997 ("Errors at F.B.I." 2003). Contaminated evidence, mislabeled blood samples, falsified DNA data, inflated statistical matches of DNA evidence, and questionable testimony by forensic experts or laboratory managers have been reported in several states as well (Tanner 2003). In 2008 the Wayne County, Michigan, prosecutor began a three-year investigation of cases that may have been tainted by inaccurate forensic evidence examined by the Detroit Police Department Forensic Services division. Although the investigation is focusing primarily on cases in which firearms evidence led to a conviction, the cases may number in the thousands (Lundberg 2008).

Nor is the military exempt from criticism regarding its crime laboratories. The US Army Criminal Investigation Laboratory, which examines over three thousand criminal cases annually, has recently come under scrutiny for its lax supervision and its failure to notify defendants when discrepancies were later detected. Particularly problematic is the work of one of its star laboratory analysts, Phillip Mills, who was employed there for almost thirty years. A three-year review of his cases revealed numerous problems. Because 83 percent of the evidence that he had examined had been destroyed in accordance with military policy at the time, only 388 cases were subject to retesting. However, reanalysis disclosed that in over half of the DNA cases that could be retested, the laboratory officials disagreed with Mills's conclusions. As a result of Mills's errors, 67 suspect files were subsequently withdrawn from the national DNA database. In 2008, when the study was finally concluded, the army was supposed to forward its findings to David Leta, a federal prosecutor, so that he could determine if Mills's conduct was a violation of federal law. Although military officials claim to have forwarded this report as required, Leta apparently never received it and only learned about the report when investigative journalists from McClatchy newspapers contacted him in 2011 about the investigation. Since the $1.4 million spent on retesting Mills's evidence, the US Army Criminal Investigation Laboratory has implemented over 100 changes and modifications to its practices (Taylor and Doyle 2011).

Perhaps one of the least recognized factors in wrongful convictions is *plea bargaining* by innocent defendants.[6] Plea bargains may look especially attractive to an innocent defendant with a prior criminal record or one who does not qualify for a public defender (Huff et al. 1996). Because innocence projects are more likely to devote their limited resources to cases involving extended sentences or the death penalty, plea-bargained cases are unlikely to receive much exposure.

Wrongful Convictions and African Americans

The effect of race in wrongful convictions has been investigated by some researchers. For instance, racial prejudice as a factor in wrongful convictions is emphasized in Chapters 5 and 6 of *In Spite of Innocence* (Radelet et al. 1992). Huff and colleagues (1996) note that African Americans and Hispanics are disproportionately found among the wrongfully convicted. They suggest that witness misidentification (particularly in cases in which the witness and the accused are of different races) and prejudice by the police and prosecutors, along with a myriad of other factors, contribute to this disparity. An entire chapter in *Wrongly Convicted* (Westervelt and Humphrey 2001) is devoted to a discussion of racial bias and wrongful convictions. Talia Harmon (2004), after comparing eighty-two capital cases in which inmates were exonerated with a matched group of executed inmates, concludes that defendant race and victim race are predictive of case outcome. The regression models also suggested the possibility of an indirect relationship between the combination of defendant and victim race, strength of evidence, and case outcome. In their examination of exonerations from 1989 through 2003, Samuel Gross and colleagues (2005) document racial disparities, particularly in cases of rape and in cases involving individuals who committed the crime while a juvenile. Although their data do not permit a determination of the reasons for the observed disparity, they speculate that because many of the rape cases were interracial, cross-racial misidentification and racial bias and discrimination probably contributed to the miscarriages of justice. They further note the potential impact of "a dual system of juvenile justice in this country, one track for white adolescents, a separate and unequal one for black adolescents" (551). Additionally, a study of forty-two wrongfully convicted women by Ruesink and Free (2005) revealed numerous racial differences. Exonerated African American women were more likely to have been wrongly incarcerated for drug offenses and murder, whereas their white counterparts were more likely to have been wrongly incarcerated for child abuse. Geographical differences were also detected: two-thirds of the wrongful convictions of African American women were from southern jurisdictions. Further, the primary reason(s) for wrongful conviction varied by race. Perjury by criminal justice officials was present in 53 percent of the African American cases. In contrast, only 4 percent of the white cases involved perjury by criminal justice officials. Nevertheless, the authors caution against generalizing beyond their sample as the large number of cases from the Tulia (Texas) drug bust inevitably skewed some of the findings involving black women. Similarly, the Wenatchee (Washington) child-abuse scandal accounted for seven of the fifteen child-abuse cases for white women, therefore disproportionately impacting that subsample.

It should be evident from this succinct overview that the literature has observed racial differences in studies of wrongful conviction. Typically, though, the discussion of race is subordinate to the discussion of other variables. As the literature suggests, marginalized groups come under greater scrutiny by the criminal justice system than nonmarginalized groups. In particular, individuals of lower socioeconomic status are more likely than others to become entrapped in the criminal justice system. According to Jeffrey Reiman and Paul Leighton (2010) in their now classic book, *The Rich Get Richer and the Poor Get Prison: Ideology, Class, and Criminal Justice,* lower-class individuals are more likely than their middle- and upper-class counterparts to be arrested, charged, and convicted. They are additionally more likely to receive harsher sentences. Furthermore, the offenses typically attributed to the lower class are more likely than those attributed to the middle and lower class to be labeled as violations of the criminal statutes by society. While few scholars would dismiss the importance of socioeconomic status in any discussion of the criminal justice system, it is important to note that much of the data analyzed in the book uses race as a proxy for social class. In other words, their discussion of the significance of social class is at least partially influenced by race. Yet a computer-generated search of books failed to disclose any publications that exclusively focused on an enumeration of wrongfully convicted African American men.

Why This Study Focuses on African American Men

That minorities in general, and African Americans in particular, are over-represented at every stage of the criminal justice system is irrefutable. Although approximately 12 percent of the US population is black, African Americans eighteen years of age and older accounted for 27.8 percent of all adults arrested in 2009 (Federal Bureau of Investigation 2010, Table 43C). For African Americans under the age of eighteen the disparity was even more pronounced. During that same year black juveniles represented 31.3 percent of all juvenile arrests (Federal Bureau of Investigation 2010, Table 43B). And although the Uniform Crime Reports does not provide a race x gender breakdown, males were disproportionately arrested, accounting for 74.7 percent of all arrests in 2009 (Federal Bureau of Investigation 2010, Table 42). Gender disparity is even greater in the offense categories typically discussed in the wrongful conviction literature. Almost 90 percent of all arrests for murder and nonnegligent manslaughter, 98.7 percent of all arrests for forcible rape, and 88.2 percent of all arrests for robbery involved males (Federal Bureau of Investigation 2010, Table 42).

African Americans are additionally overrepresented in other areas of the criminal justice system. Marc Mauer and Ryan King (2007) of the Washington, DC–based Sentencing Project report that blacks are 5.6 times more likely than whites to be incarcerated. More recently, Ashley Nellis and Ryan King (2009, 3) found that "racial and ethnic minorities serve a disproportionate share of life sentences." Nationally, almost half of all inmates serving a life sentence are African American. Racial disparity is even more evident when life-without-parole (LWOP) sentences are examined. Blacks accounted for 56.4 percent of the LWOP population. Further, blacks constitute 42 percent of the inmates on death row and 35 percent of all executions since the reestablishment of capital punishment in 1976 (Death Penalty Information Center 2011).

Yet none of these disparities matters if the figures reflect actual differences in offending patterns. Studies that have investigated the extent to which the racial differences in offending can explain racial disparity have been unable to justify the higher rates for African Americans. An examination of national data for 1979, for example, revealed that 20 percent of the racial disparity could not be accounted for after controlling for racial differences in criminal activity (Blumstein 1982). This figure increased to 24 percent when 1991 prison data were utilized (Blumstein 1993). Even more troubling are the findings of Michael Tonry and Matthew Melewski (2008). Using 2004 incarceration data, they concluded that 39 percent of the incarceration rate for African Americans remains unexplained after racial differences in offending are considered. With a substantial amount of the racial disparity unexplained by legally relevant factors, an investigation of the false conviction of African American men represents a chance to further understand the dynamics involved in this area of the criminal justice system.

Focus and Scope of the Book

The research reported in this book has three objectives, the first of which is to enumerate the *known* cases of wrongful conviction involving African American men during a specified time period. Because earlier empirical investigations of wrongful convictions have not exclusively focused on this segment of the population, this research is largely exploratory in nature. A second objective of the study is to describe qualitatively and quantitatively the defining characteristics of these cases relying primarily on data available electronically and in print. The third objective is to go beyond citing mere statistics in examining the cases. Instead, the narratives attempt to portray (to the extent the data permit) those who have experienced a miscarriage of justice in a more personal light.

Chapter 2 commences a discussion of wrongfully convicted African American men. Factors contributing to wrongful convictions are enumerated and discussed. Table 2.1 discloses the names, charges, and jurisdiction of known cases of wrongfully convicted African American men since 1970 that appeared in the electronic and print media by 2008. This chapter also highlights some of the more flagrant miscarriages of justice that have recently been acknowledged.

Four chapters focus on wrongful convictions according to the most serious offense for which the defendant was charged. Chapters 3 and 4 focus on wrongful convictions involving violent offenses by analyzing wrongful convictions for murder/attempted murder and rape/sexual assault, respectively. The chapters examine the extent to which the previously identified factors in wrongful convictions are present in these cases. Further, the impact of victim characteristics (age, gender, and race) in the wrongful conviction of innocents is explored. Chapter 5 analyzes drug-related cases that resulted in erroneous conviction of innocent defendants. This chapter focuses on recent drug busts in Tulia, Texas; Hearne, Texas; and Mansfield, Ohio, in which African Americans were apparently singled out for differential treatment. Finally, Chapter 6 scrutinizes wrongful convictions in cases that involve robbery and other offenses not previously examined.

The book concludes in Chapter 7 with a summary of the results of this study. Suggestions for future research and a brief discussion of issues surrounding the topic of wrongful convictions are additionally examined in the last chapter. Two appendixes appear at the back of the book. Appendix A provides an elaboration of the methodology used in this research, and Appendix B provides the reader with a short narrative of each of the cases included in the investigation.

It is equally important to note the limitations of this investigation.[7] Because many wrongful convictions are unknown, the cases identified in this study may not be representative of all wrongfully convicted black men. Consequently, only descriptive statistics are reported in this book. Nor is the book meant to theoretically examine the larger issues of institutional racism and marginalization. Because this would involve a sociological and historical overview of race relations in the United States and an examination of the development and enforcement of criminal statutes, it is beyond the scope of this book. It should further be acknowledged that because this is an exploratory study, it should not be construed as the "final word" on the subject. Rather, the authors' purpose in conducting this investigation is that the findings might inspire additional research in this area that will permit the use of inferential statistics and the testing of competing theoretical models.

Notes

1. The current number of states with capital punishment statutes is the fewest since 1978. On March 9, 2011, Illinois abolished the death penalty, making it the sixteenth state (plus the District of Columbia) to prohibit the death sentence. According to the Death Penalty Information Center ("Illinois Governor Signs Bill" 2011), other states are also considering this option. Currently thirty-four states, the US government, and the US military authorize the use of capital punishment for select offenses.

2. For example, in 2004 over one million adults were convicted of a felony in state courts. An additional 66,518 individuals were convicted in federal courts (US Department of Justice 2007, 1 and 2). Yet only 138 convicted felons were sentenced to death during 2004 (US Department of Justice 2006, 14).

3. Samuel Gross and colleagues (2005) suggest that whether misidentification is accidental or deliberate may vary by offense. Their examination of 340 contemporary wrongful convictions disclosed that false rape convictions were more likely the result of mistaken identity, whereas false murder convictions were more likely the result of deliberate misidentification.

4. A study of search warrants in San Diego found that these warrants were issued disproportionately for African American and Hispanic residents living in predominantly minority communities. Although these groups constitute less than one-third of the city's population, they accounted for over 80 percent of all warrants and 98 percent of the warrants seeking cocaine. Further, the warrants targeting African Americans and Hispanics were less likely than those targeting whites to result in the discovery of contraband. Whereas two-thirds of the warrants involving whites were successful in locating contraband, most of the warrants involving African Americans and Hispanics failed to disclose the presence of contraband. According to Natapoff (2009, 113), "One reason for this disparity is that 80 percent of warrants were based on confidential informants."

5. In 1984, in *Strickland v. Washington,* the US Supreme Court diminished the probability of appealing a decision on grounds of ineffective counsel. According to this decision, the appellate court must be convinced that a different verdict would have been rendered if the defense counsel had pursued the case more diligently. The difficulty associated with making this determination is alluded to by Justice Marshall in his dissent. "Seemingly impregnable cases can sometimes be dismantled by good defense counsel. On the basis of a cold record, it may be impossible for a reviewing court confidently to ascertain how the government's evidence and arguments would have stood up against rebuttal and cross-examination by a shrewd, well-prepared lawyer" (from *Strickland v. Washington* 1984, 710; cited in Bernhard 2001, 232–233).

6. Josh Bowers (2008) from the University of Virginia School of Law takes exception to the view that plea bargains are responsible for false convictions. He contends that false guilty pleas are the result of errors during arrest, charging, and/or trial rather than the result of plea bargaining itself. Bowers further asserts that most individuals who accept plea bargains are recidivists who engage in petty crimes and who therefore tend to have an advantage during plea-bargaining negotiations, given the potentially high pretrial process costs and the need for prosecutors to prioritize their workload. Although the criminal justice system is biased toward these individuals, Bowers argues that plea bargains often result in release, thereby mitigating the earlier discriminatory processes.

7. Richard Leo and Jon Gould (2009) are very critical of the use of the narrative method utilized in this research. They argue that "scholarship based on stories about wrongful conviction tends to oversimplify causation" (16). Leo and Gould further contend that this approach "tends to portray causation as unidimensional . . . even though we know that cases of wrongful conviction have multiple sources" (16). Although their concerns are valid *if the purpose of the investigation is to ascertain dimensions of causality,* this study has no such aspirations. While the cases are arranged throughout this book according to the role of a particular factor (e.g., eyewitness error) in the miscarriage of justice, the purpose is to highlight the importance of that factor in that particular instance. Further, a perusal of the accompanying discussion and relevant tables typically discloses that *multiple* factors are present in the false conviction. These factors, moreover, are referred to as contributing to, rather than causing, the wrongful conviction. Thus, the criticisms leveled at the narrative method in general by Leo and Gould appear to be irrelevant to this investigation.

2

Meet the
Wrongfully Convicted

Our justice system should punish the guilty,
free the innocent and have the wisdom to know the difference.
—*William S. Sessions, former FBI Director*

Using the procedures described below, this investigation uncovered 343 cases in which African American men had been wrongfully convicted. Before examining some of the more egregious instances in which justice failed, however, a discussion of the methodology employed in the study is warranted.

Locating the Cases

Given the fragmented nature of data on wrongful convictions, multiple databases were consulted in the preparation of this research (see Appendix A for an elaboration of each of these databases). Four databases provided the bulk of the cases included in the final data set used in this analysis. The most extensive enumeration of wrongful convictions can be found at the Forejustice website. Global in scope, this website contains a list of over three thousand innocent individuals from ninety-four countries. The Center on Wrongful Convictions, located at the Northwestern University School of Law, enumerates over seven hundred cases of wrongful convictions in the United States from the twentieth century to the present. A third major source of information on wrongful convictions is provided by the Innocence Project, which is affiliated with the Benjamin N. Cardozo School of Law at Yeshiva University in New York City. The last major database can be found at the website of the Death Penalty Information

Center, whose enumeration includes 130 wrongful convictions from 1973 through 2008, the cutoff date for the research.

As alluded to in Chapter 1, the Dallas, Texas, district attorney's office has had a higher rate of overturned convictions over the years than any other prosecutor's office in the United States.[1] Because many of the reversed convictions involved African American men, special attention was devoted to a series of stories about prosecutorial misconduct in the Dallas area published in the *Dallas Morning News*. Its online counterpart, dallasnews.com, was also consulted in the process of identifying relevant cases for inclusion in this study. Both sources contained invaluable information of a more personal nature that was often unavailable elsewhere.

During the course of this investigation, it became evident to the investigators that there had been numerous wrongful convictions resulting from questionable drug raids in cities such as Tulia, Texas; Hearne, Texas; and Mansfield, Ohio. Because the incident in Mansfield, Ohio, was too recent to ensure inclusion in the databases utilized in this study, additional information on this drug bust was pursued using various websites as well as personal correspondence with individuals familiar with the drug bust.

This study limits its analysis to known wrongful convictions involving African American men that occurred since 1970. The investigation further restricts the cases to known wrongful convictions that were identified by the media through 2008. A final sample of 343 individuals was identified using these parameters. Table 2.1 discloses the names of these wrongfully convicted individuals, their charges, and the location of their trials.

Identification and Categorization of Variables Associated with Wrongful Conviction

Using factors found in earlier wrongful conviction research, this study classified the contributors to wrongful convictions according to eight categories (see Appendix A for additional information on the selection of these variables). The variables examined in this study include: (1) witness error, (2) police misconduct, (3) prosecutorial misconduct, (4) false confessions, (5) the use of informants/snitches, (6) forensic errors, (7) perjury by criminal justice officials, and (8) insufficient evidence to support a conviction. Further, where appropriate, incompetency of the defense counsel is noted.

Information contained in the databases consulted in this research permitted the inclusion of other potentially relevant variables. Through a careful analysis of the data it was possible to ascertain (1) the state that had

Table 2.1 List of Known Wrongfully Convicted African American Men by State, 1970–2008 (N=343)

Name	State	Charge(s)
Medell Banks, Jr.	AL	Murder
Melvin Todd Beamon	AL	Murder
James "Bo" Cochran	AL	Murder, robbery
Freddie Lee Gaines	AL	Double murder
Dale Mahan	AL	Rape, kidnapping
Ronnie Mahan	AL	Rape, kidnapping
Walter McMillian	AL	Murder, rape
William Ward	AL	Manslaughter
Freddie Lee Wright	AL	Double murder, robbery
Christopher McCrimmon	AZ	Triple murder, robbery, aggravated robbery, burglary
Andre Minnitt	AZ	Triple murder, robbery, aggravated robbery, burglary
Eugene Allen	CA	Murder
Herman Atkins	CA	Rape, forcible oral copulation, robbery
Timothy Atkins	CA	Murder, robbery
Damon Auguste	CA	Rape, sodomy
Clarence Chance	CA	Murder
Tony Cooks	CA	Murder
Frederick Daye	CA	Rape, kidnapping, robbery, motor vehicle theft
Antoine Goff	CA	Murder
Ernest (Shuhaa) Graham	CA	Murder
Willie Earl Green	CA	Murder
Harold Hall	CA	Double murder, rape
Charles Harris	CA	Drug related
Albert Johnson	CA	Sexual assault (2 counts)
Troy Lee Jones	CA	Murder
Jason Kindle	CA	Robbery
Dwayne McKinney	CA	Murder, robbery
Oscar Lee Morris	CA	Murder, robbery
Aaron Lee Owens	CA	Double murder
Benny Powell	CA	Murder
Elmer "Geronimo" Pratt	CA	Murder
John Tennison	CA	Murder
Mark Reid	CT	Sexual assault, kidnapping
James Tillman	CT	Sexual assault, kidnapping, robbery, assault, larceny
Bradford Brown	DC	Murder
James Adams	FL	Murder
Larry Bostic	FL	Sexual battery, robbery

continues

Table 2.1 *continued*

Name	State	Charge(s)
Anthony Brown	FL	Murder
Joseph Green (Shabaka) Brown	FL	Murder, rape, robbery
Timothy Brown	FL	Murder
Willie Brown	FL	Murder
Kevin Coleman	FL	Murder
Alan Crotzer	FL	Sexual battery, kidnapping, burglary, aggravated assault, robbery, attempted robbery
Johnny Frederick	FL	Murder
Joseph Nahume Green	FL	Murder
Robert Earl Hayes	FL	Murder, rape
Rudolph Holton	FL	Murder, rape
David Keaton	FL	Murder, robbery
Anthony Ray Peek	FL	Murder
Derrick Robinson	FL	Murder
Gary Siplin	FL	Theft (including swindling/fraud, deception, grand larceny)
Frank Lee Smith	FL	Murder, rape
Gilbert Stokes	FL	Murder
Arthur Teele, Jr.	FL	Threaten to assault or cause bodily harm
Delbert Lee Tibbs	FL	Murder, rape
Jerry Frank Townsend	FL	Murder (6 counts), rape (1 count)
Larry Troy	FL	Murder
Jerry Banks	GA	Double murder
Earl Patrick Charles	GA	Double murder, robbery
Robert Clark	GA	Rape, kidnapping, robbery
Douglas Echols	GA	Rape, kidnapping, robbery
Clarence Harrison	GA	Rape, kidnapping, robbery
Calvin Johnson, Jr.	GA	Rape (2 counts), sodomy, burglary
Walter McIntosh	GA	Double murder
Gary Nelson	GA	Murder, rape
Samuel Scott	GA	Rape, kidnapping, robbery
Robert Wallace	GA	Murder
John Jerome White	GA	Rape, aggravated assault, burglary, robbery
Willie "Pete" Williams	GA	Rape, kidnapping, sodomy
Kenneth Adams[a]	IL	Double murder, rape
Randy Boss	IL	Murder
Revell Boss	IL	Murder
Marcellius Bradford	IL	Murder, rape, robbery, aggravated kidnapping
Robert Brown	IL	Murder
Ronnie Bullock	IL	Deviate sexual assault, aggravated kidnapping
LaVale Burt	IL	Murder
Dean Cage	IL	Criminal sexual assault
Perry Cobb	IL	Double murder, robbery
Michael Evans	IL	Murder, rape, kidnapping

continues

Table 2.1 *continued*

Name	State	Charge(s)
Sammie Garrett	IL	Murder
Hubert Geralds	IL	Murder
Michael Glasper	IL	Robbery
Harold Hill	IL	Murder, rape
Madison Hobley	IL	Felony murder (7 counts), aggravated arson (7 counts), arson
Dana Holland	IL	Aggravated criminal sexual assault (1st case), attempted murder, robbery (2nd case)
Elton Houston	IL	Murder
Stanley Howard	IL	Murder, attempted armed robbery
Verneal Jimerson[a]	IL	Murder, robbery, kidnapping
Henry Johnson	IL	Murder
Juan Johnson	IL	Murder
Richard Johnson	IL	Rape, robbery
Ronald Jones	IL	Murder, rape
Carl Lawson	IL	Murder
Lloyd Lindsey	IL	Murder (4 counts)
Alton Logan	IL	Murder
Marcus Lyons	IL	Criminal sexual assault (2 counts), unlawful restraint
Jerry Miller	IL	Rape, kidnapping, robbery
James Newsome	IL	Murder, robbery, armed violence
Calvin Ollins	IL	Murder, robbery, kidnapping, sexual assault
Larry Ollins	IL	Murder, robbery, sexual assault
Leroy Orange	IL	Murder (4 counts), concealment of a homicidal death (4 counts), robbery, aggravated arson
Aaron Patterson	IL	Double murder
Marlon Pendleton	IL	Rape, robbery
Anthony Porter	IL	Double murder, armed robbery, unlawful restraint, unlawful use of weapons (2 counts)
Willie Rainge[a]	IL	Double murder, rape
Donald Reynolds	IL	Criminal sexual assault, attempted criminal sexual assault, robbery, attempted robbery
Lafonso Rollins	IL	Rape (4 counts), robbery
Omar Saunders	IL	Murder, robbery, kidnapping, sexual assault
Steven Smith	IL	Murder
Paul Terry	IL	Murder, rape, aggravated kidnapping, deviate sexual assault, indecent liberties with a child
Franklin Thompson	IL	Murder
Darby Tillis	IL	Double murder, robbery
Billy Wardell	IL	Criminal sexual assault, attempted criminal sexual assault, robbery, attempted robbery
Dennis Williams[a]	IL	Double murder, rape
John Willis	IL	Sexual assault (multiple counts), robbery
Dan Young, Jr.	IL	Murder, rape
Harold Buntin	IN	Rape, robbery
Keith Cooper	IN	Robbery

continues

Table 2.1 *continued*

Name	State	Charge(s)
Larry Hicks	IN	Double murder
Larry Mayes	IN	Rape, robbery, unlawful deviate conduct
Christopher Parish	IN	Robbery
Charles Smith	IN	Murder, robbery
James Hall	IA	Murder
Terry Harrington	IA	Murder
Curtis McGhee, Jr.	IA	Murder
William Gregory	KY	Rape, attempted rape, burglary
David Alexander	LA	Murder, robbery
Gene Bibbins	LA	Rape, burglary
Dan L. Bright	LA	Murder, robbery
Dennis Brown	LA	Rape, burglary, crimes against nature
Clyde Charles	LA	Aggravated rape
Allen Coco	LA	Rape, burglary
Shareef Cousin	LA	Murder
Harry Granger	LA	Murder, robbery
Travis Hayes	LA	Murder
Willie Jackson	LA	Attempted aggravated rape, robbery
Rickey Johnson	LA	Aggravated rape
Curtis Kyles	LA	Murder
Dwight Labran	LA	Murder
Ryan Matthews	LA	Murder
Johnny Ross	LA	Rape
John Thompson	LA	Murder
Calvin Williams	LA	Murder
Kevin Williams	LA	Robbery ($15 taken)
Michael Williams	LA	Aggravated rape
Calvin Willis	LA	Aggravated rape
Ronald Addison	MD	Murder, gun possession
Michael Austin	MD	Murder, robbery
Cornell Avery Estes	MD	Murder
Anthony Gray, Jr.	MD	Murder, rape
Eric D. Lynn	MD	Murder
Leslie Vass	MD	Robbery
Bernard Webster	MD	Rape, daytime housebreaking
Laurence Adams	MA	Murder, robbery
Christian Amado	MA	Murder
Ulysses Rodriguez Charles	MA	Aggravated rape, robbery, unlawful confinement, entering a dwelling armed with intent to commit a felony

continues

Table 2.1 *continued*

Name	State	Charge(s)
Stephen Cowans	MA	Armed assault with intent to murder, home invasion, assault & battery by means of a dangerous weapon, robbery, assault & battery on a police officer, assault by means of a dangerous weapon, unlicensed possession of a firearm
Shawn Drumgold	MA	Murder
Frank Grace	MA	Murder
Donnell Johnson	MA	Murder
Lawyer Johnson	MA	Murder
William Johnson	MA	Assault
Bobby Joe Leaster	MA	Murder
Neil Miller	MA	Rape, robbery
Marvin Mitchell	MA	Forcible sexual intercourse of a minor (2 counts), unnatural sexual intercourse of a minor (2 counts)
Marlon Passley	MA	Murder
Guy Randolph	MA	Aggravated sexual assault
Louis Santos	MA	Murder
Nathaniel Hatchett	MI	Kidnapping, carjacking, armed robbery, criminal sexual conduct
Eddie Joe Lloyd	MI	Murder, rape
Dwight Love	MI	Murder
Claude McCollum	MI	Murder, rape
Vidale McDowell	MI	Murder
Walter Swift	MI	Rape, robbery
David Brian Sutherlin	MN	Rape
Kennedy Brewer	MS	Murder, rape
Levon Brooks	MS	Murder, rape
Arthur Johnson	MS	Rape, burglary
Cedric Willis	MS	Murder, robbery, rape, aggravated assault
Joseph Amrine	MO	Murder
Antonio Beaver	MO	Robbery
Johnny Briscoe	MO	Rape, sodomy, burglary, robbery, stealing, armed criminal action
Darryl Burton	MO	Murder
Eric Clemmons	MO	Murder
Lonnie Erby	MO	Rape, kidnapping, robbery, sodomy, armed criminal action, sexual abuse, attempted rape, attempted robbery, felonious restraint, stealing
Larry Johnson	MO	Rape, sodomy, kidnapping, robbery
Steven Toney	MO	Rape, sodomy

continues

Table 2.1 *continued*

Name	State	Charge(s)
Riky Jackson	PA	Murder
Vincent Moto	PA	Rape, robbery, involuntary deviate sexual intercourse, criminal conspiracy
Edward Ryder	PA	Murder
Drew Whitley	PA	Murder
Harold Wilson	PA	Triple murder
Tyrone James	SC	Murder
Warren Douglas Manning	SC	Murder
Perry Mitchell	SC	Criminal sexual contact
Winfred Peterson	SC	Murder
Clark McMillan	TN	Rape, robbery
Dennis Michael Allen[d]	TX	Drug related
James Ray Barrow[d]	TX	Drug related
Landis Barrow[d]	TX	Drug related
Leroy Barrow[d]	TX	Drug related
Mandis Barrow[d]	TX	Drug related
Troy Benard[d]	TX	Drug related
Clarence Lee Brandley	TX	Murder, rape
Fred Brookins, Jr.[d]	TX	Drug related
A. B. Butler	TX	Rape, kidnapping
James Levi Byrd	TX	Robbery
Kevin Byrd	TX	Rape
Charles Allen Chatman	TX	Aggravated rape
Tim Cole	TX	Rape
Armenu Jerrod Ervin[d]	TX	Drug related
Wiley Fountain	TX	Rape
Michael Fowler[d]	TX	Drug related
Jason Paul Fry[d]	TX	Drug related
Larry Fuller	TX	Rape
Lenell Geter	TX	Robbery
James Curtis Giles	TX	Aggravated rape
Willie Hall[d]	TX	Drug related
Cleveland J. Henderson[d]	TX	Drug related
Mandrell L. Henry[d]	TX	Drug related
Eugene Henton	TX	Sexual assault
Christopher Jackson[d]	TX	Drug related
Antrone Lynelle Johnson	TX	Rape
Eliga Kelly, Sr.[d]	TX	Drug related
Johnnie Earl Lindsey	TX	Rape
Joseph Corey Marshall[d]	TX	Drug related
Vincent Dwight McCray[d]	TX	Drug related
Thomas Clifford McGowan	TX	Burglary, aggravated sexual assault

continues

Table 2.1 *continued*

Name	State	Charge(s)
Billy Wayne Miller	TX	Aggravated sexual assault
Joe Welton Moore[d]	TX	Drug related
Arthur Mumphrey	TX	Aggravated sexual assault
Kenneth Ray Powell[d]	TX	Drug related
Ricardo Rachell	TX	Aggravated sexual assault
Anthony Robinson	TX	Sexual assault
Benny Lee Robinson[d]	TX	Drug related
Billy James Smith	TX	Aggravated sexual assault
Donald Wayne Smith[d]	TX	Drug related
Ben Spencer	TX	Murder, aggravated robbery
Josiah Sutton	TX	Rape, carjacking
Ronald Gene Taylor	TX	Aggravated sexual assault
Timothy Wayne Towery[d]	TX	Drug related
Keith Turner	TX	Rape
James Waller	TX	Rape
Patrick Waller	TX	Rape, aggravated kidnapping, aggravated robbery
Calvin Washington	TX	Murder, rape
Kareem White[d]	TX	Drug related
Jason Jerome Williams[d]	TX	Drug related
Joe Sidney Williams	TX	Murder, rape
James Lee Woodard	TX	Murder, rape
Harry Miller	UT	Robbery
Marvin Anderson	VA	Rape, sodomy, robbery, abduction
Darrell A. Copeland	VA	Firearm related (felon in possession of firearm)
Russell Leon Gray	VA	Murder
Troy D. Hopkins	VA	Murder
Julius Earl Ruffin	VA	Rape, sodomy
Lindsey Scott	VA	Rape
Teddy Thompson	VA	Robbery
Phillip Leon Thurman	VA	Rape, abduction, assault
Earl Washington, Jr.	VA	Murder, rape
Troy Webb	VA	Rape, kidnapping, robbery
Arthur Lee Whitfield	VA	Rape (2 counts), sodomy, robbery
Benjamin J. Harris III	WA	Murder
Jarrett Adams	WI	Sexual assault
Dimitri Henley	WI	Sexual assault
Anthony Hicks	WI	Rape, robbery

Notes: a. Defendants known as the Ford Heights Four.

     b. Defendants part of the well-publicized Central Park jogger incident in New York City in the late 1980s that led to the coining of a new word, "wilding," used to refer to predatory youth.

     c. Defendants involved in the Mansfield, Ohio, drug bust scandal.

     d. Defendants involved in the Tulia, Texas, drug sting involving perjured testimony from a white undercover sheriff's deputy.

jurisdiction over the case, (2) the specific offense(s) for which the defendant was charged, (3) the sentence, (4) the year the defendant was convicted, (5) the year the defendant was released (if applicable), and (6) the year the defendant was cleared (if applicable). If any of this information was unavailable from the four primary databases, additional computer searches were conducted to locate the missing data. Moreover, because victim race has frequently been found to be related to the outcome of criminal justice cases,[2] the race of the victim in violent crimes was examined. Additional victim characteristics, including gender and age, were analyzed in cases involving crimes against the person. Both qualitative as well as quantitative data were utilized to better understand the circumstances surrounding the wrongful conviction.

Data collection proved to be tedious and labor intensive, especially when the research involved older cases. In many of these cases electronic links to additional information were no longer accessible. Regardless of age, descriptions of the events surrounding the cases were sometimes contradictory and frequently incomplete. To reconcile differences and to locate supplemental data, both print and electronic media were utilized. When telephone numbers and email addresses for individuals associated with the cases (e.g., journalists and attorneys) could be ascertained, the researchers attempted to verify missing data through personal correspondence. Although telephone conversations and emails provided some additional information, numerous telephone calls were unreturned or, when returned, resulted in no new accumulation of information. Consequently, the narratives in this study vary in their completeness.

The Sample

Table 2.2 provides an overview of the cases. Because organizations that represent wrongfully convicted clients typically focus their limited resources on those cases in which defendants received harsh sanctions, and because harsh sanctions tend to accompany convictions involving the most serious offenses, most known cases of wrongful convictions, regardless of the race of the defendant, involve serious crimes. This overabundance of serious crimes is particularly evident in the sample of wrongful convictions examined here. Although arrests of blacks for murder comprised less than 1 percent of all black arrests for 2008 (Federal Bureau of Investigation 2009, Table 43), murders (N=174) account for slightly over one-half of the cases identified in this research.[3] Similarly, forcible rape arrests constituted less than 1 percent of all 2008 black arrests (Federal Bureau of Investigation 2009, Table 43), yet rape and sexual assault wrongful convictions (N=109) represent 31.8 percent of the known wrongful conviction cases. More to the point, whereas the combined arrests for murder and rape/sexual assault accounted for less than 1 percent of the total black arrests in 2008, these offenses constitute almost 83 percent of the known cases examined in this study.

**Table 2.2   Descriptive Statistics of Sample of
Wrongfully Convicted African American Men (N=343)**

Number of wrongful convictions according to most serious offense

Offense	Number of Cases	% of N
Murder and attempted murder	174	50.7
Rape/attempted rape, sexual assault, sexual battery	109	31.8
Drug-related[a]	40	11.7
Robbery	15	4.4
All others	5	1.5
Total	343	100.1

Top 5 states according to most serious offense

	Murder	Rape	Drugs	Robbery	Miscellaneous
1	IL (36)	TX (20)	TX (24)	1T[b]: IN (2)	1: FL (2)
2	FL (18)	IL (10)	OH (15)	1T: NC (2)	3 states with 1
3	CA (15)	3T: LA (9)	CA (1)	1T: TX (2)	
4	NY (11)	3T: NY (9)		9 states with 1	
5T	LA (10)	GA (7)			
5T	MA (10)				

Top 10 states according to number of wrongful convictions

1	TX (52)	4T: FL (22)	7: LA (20)	10T: NC (11)
2	IL (47)	4T: NY (22)	8: MA (15)	10T: VA (11)
3	OH (26)	6: CA (21)	9: GA (12)	

Sample summary

There are 31 states and the District of Columbia with at least one known wrongful conviction (AL, AZ, CA, CT, DC, FL, GA, IL, IN, IA, KY, LA, MD, MA, MI, MN, MS, MO, NJ, NM, NY, NC, OH, OK, PA, SC, TN, TX, UT, VA, WA, and WI).

There are 19 states with *no* known wrongful convictions (AK, AR, CO, DE, HI, ID, KS, ME, MT, NE, NV, NH, ND, OR, RI, SD, VT, WV, and WY).

Notes: a. Thirty-nine of the 40 drug-related cases are attributable to the Tulia, TX, or Mansfield, OH, drug busts.

  b. "T" indicates a tie.

Of the total black arrests in the United States in 2008, 15 percent were for drug abuse violations (Federal Bureau of Investigation 2009, Table 43). In this investigation, the 40 known wrongful convictions in which the most serious offense involved a violation of a drug law comprise almost 12 percent of the total cases. Although this percentage approximates the figure found in the 2008 arrest statistics, 39 of the 40 drug-related cases in the sample are attributable to two drug raids.

The last offense category examined separately in this study is robbery. In 2008, black arrests for robbery totaled 56,948, or 1.9 percent of the total arrests of blacks in the United States (Federal Bureau of Investigation 2009, Table 43). The 15 wrongful convictions in which robbery was the most serious offense account for 4.4 percent of the cases in this investigation. Consequently, robbery is somewhat overrepresented among the wrongful conviction cases.

Table 2.2 further identifies the states with the most wrongful convictions of blacks by offense type. Texas appears in the top five states in three offense categories (rape, drugs, and robbery), whereas Illinois, New York, and Louisiana each appear in the top five states in two offense categories (murder and rape). Although California is the third most common state for wrongful convictions involving murder and the third most common state for drugs, the latter ranking is based on a single wrongful conviction involving drugs.

Of the thirty-one states and the District of Columbia represented in this study, Texas (N=52) and Illinois (N=47) have the largest number of wrongful convictions involving blacks. Five additional states (Ohio, Florida, New York, California, and Louisiana) have 20 or more cases. Rounding out the top ten states are Massachusetts with 15 cases, Georgia with 12 cases, and North Carolina and Virginia with 11 cases apiece. When a comparison is made between those states with at least 20 black wrongful convictions and the 2008 estimated US population, the sample appears to be representative of the United States. Five of the seven states with at least 20 known black wrongful convictions are from the five most populated states in the United States. Moreover, the two remaining states contain a substantial black population. Of Ohio's 11,485,910 inhabitants, 12 percent are classified by the US Census Bureau as black, whereas 32 percent of Louisiana's 4,410,796 inhabitants are classified as black (US Census Bureau 2009). Additionally, many of the states with no known black wrongful convictions have small black populations. Of the nineteen states with zero cases, nine (Idaho, Maine, Montana, New Hampshire, North Dakota, Oregon, South Dakota, Vermont, and Wyoming) have black populations that comprise 3 percent or less of that state's total population. An additional five states (Alaska, Colorado, Hawaii, Nebraska, and West Virginia) have black populations that represent less than 5 percent of their inhabitants (US Census Bureau 2009).

Caution should be exercised, nevertheless, when interpreting these descriptive statistics, because the known cases of wrongful convictions involving blacks probably constitute only a fraction of the actual number of such cases. Furthermore, some states have been more carefully scrutinized than others. Although there is at least one innocence project in every state (excluding programs in Oregon and Tennessee that are currently being reorganized), most of the projects are of recent origin and do not have the capacity to process the myriad of requests (truthinjustice 2009). Moreover, the presence of the Center on Wrongful Convictions in Illinois and the Cardozo Innocence Project in New York increases the likelihood of the discovery of wrongful convictions in those states.

Witness Error and the Conviction of Innocents

A recurring theme found in the wrongful conviction literature involves the conviction of innocents as a result of the misidentification of suspects by witnesses. The Innocence Project (2009c), for example, found that witness error was present in over three-fourths of the DNA exonerations. Although most witness errors are not deliberate (Huff et al. 1996), cross-racial identification appears to be more problematic. In particular, John Rutledge (2001) found that white subjects were more likely to misidentify black subjects than white subjects.[4] The following cases illustrate some of the problems associated with witness misidentification in the wrongful conviction of African American men.

Clyde Charles

In 1981 a young white nurse reported that she had been raped during the early morning hours near Houma, Louisiana. She described her assailant as a clean-shaven black man with short hair who was wearing a dark jogging jacket with stripes. At the time of his arrest, Charles was wearing a dark jogging jacket with white stripes. However, contrary to her initial description, he sported an Afro haircut, a mustache, and a goatee. The arresting officer immediately took Charles to the hospital where the victim was receiving medical attention. In an interview with PBS's *Frontline* (2000), Charles describes what happened next:

[The officer] asked me to get out of the car. I asked, "Get out of the car for what?" He just said, "Nigger, get out of the car." I got out of the car. He put me in front of the car, on the emergency ramp, with my hands cuffed behind my back in a profile position. . . . Suddenly, out of my perimeter view, I saw them roll a white female out there in a wheelchair. Every time I tried to face her, they smashed my head back with their hands. I kept hearing the police officer say, "Make sure he's the one, make sure you identify him right." From my perimeter view, I saw her shaking her head, saying that I'm the one that committed the crime.

In 1982 an all-white jury comprised of ten women and two men found Charles guilty after deliberating for three and a half hours and sentenced him to life imprisonment. Proclaiming his innocence, Charles's requests for DNA testing went unheeded for almost ten years. It was only after the Innocence Project offered legal counsel that an examination of his DNA was approved. After the results of the test came back negative, he was finally released from Angola State Prison on December 17, 1999.

Herman Atkins

In another case of apparent mistaken identity, Herman Atkins was sentenced to over forty-five years in prison for the rape and forced oral copulation of a white woman in a shoe store in Lake Elsinore, California. Atkins was additionally convicted of burglary. The victim, a twenty-three-year-old white woman, was working alone in the store late at night when she was forcibly raped repeatedly and made to perform oral sex in the stock room. When offered a book of mug shots, the victim was unable to identify her assailant. However, she later noticed a wanted poster that contained a picture of Atkins.[5] She identified the man in the poster as her assailant. Another woman working at an adjacent store additionally identified Atkins as the perpetrator. Interestingly, during the arraignment the district attorney asked the victim, "Do you see the man who assaulted you?" At the time Atkins was handcuffed to seven white inmates and sitting in the jury box awaiting his arraignment. She immediately replied, "Yes, that's him right there" (Weinberg 2003b). All all-white jury found Atkins guilty in 1988, two years after the crime had been committed. For five years, the prosecution sought to prevent the Innocence Project from having the DNA tested. Finally, in 2000, Atkins was exonerated when DNA tests of the semen found on the victim's sweater ruled out Atkins as the perpetrator.

Anthony Porter

On August 15, 1982, two teenagers—Jerry Hillard and Marilyn Green—were killed in Washington Park on Chicago's South Side. William Taylor, who was in the vicinity at the time of the murders, was questioned by the police. He originally told the police that he didn't see the perpetrator. After seventeen hours of interrogation, however, he identified Anthony Porter, a twenty-seven-year-old gang member, as the assassin. Although the female victim's mother suggested the possibility of a different offender (Alstory Simon), the police focused their attention on Porter. Despite an absence of physical evidence, Porter was arrested and charged with the double murder. During his trial he retained Akim Gursel, a private lawyer. However, when Porter's family could not afford to pay Gursel the full agreed-upon amount, he ceased investigating the case. A transcript of the trial reveals that at least once during the proceedings Gursel feel asleep. After deliberating nine hours, the jury found Porter guilty of both murders. During the sentencing phase, in which Gursel waived his client's right to a jury trial, Judge Robert Sklodowski, who would later leave the bench due to a financial scandal, referred to Porter as "a perverse shark" and sentenced him to death. After a number of unsuccessful appeals, a volunteer attorney interested in his case had an IQ test administered to Porter. His score of 51 raised questions about his ability to understand his punishment. Just fifty hours before the execution was to be carried out, the Illinois Supreme Court granted a stay of execution while it could determine the mental fitness of Porter. The stay of execution enabled Porter's research team to obtain an affidavit from Taylor in which he recanted his testimony. And on February 3, 1999, Alstory Simon confessed to the killing of Hillard and the accidental shooting of Green. Porter was subsequently released from prison and the charges were officially dropped in March of that year. Alstory Simon was eventually found guilty of the murder of Hillard and Green and was sentenced to over thirty-seven years in prison.

Police Misconduct and the Conviction of Innocents

The conviction of innocent defendants frequently results from the coalescence of multiple contributing factors. Cases in which the impact of police misconduct resulted in a wrongful conviction are no different. The following examples provide the reader with illustrations of the complexities inherent in many of these wrongful convictions.

Clarence Lee Brandley

On August 23, 1980, Cheryl Dee Ferguson, a sixteen-year-old white Bell-ville High School volleyball player, was found murdered and raped in a loft at her high school in Conroe, Texas. Clarence Lee Brandley, the only African American custodian at the school, and Henry (Icky) Peace, who found the body, were immediately suspected by the police. At their joint interrogation, Peace notes that Texas Ranger Wesley Styles said, "One of you is going to have to hang for this." Then, looking directly at Brandley, he added, "Since you're the nigger, you're elected." Although Brandley subsequently passed a polygraph test, Styles continued to pursue Brand-ley. Three of the custodians—Gary Acreman, Sam Martinez, and John Sessum—appear to have been coached by Styles as they provided infor-mation about the crime that implicated Brandley.

An all-white grand jury from Montgomery County heard the evidence on August 28, 1980. A jury trial convened in December of that year. No physical evidence was presented to the jury that connected Brandley to the crime, as the sperm recovered from the victim's body had been destroyed without having been examined. And, contrary to the prosecution's case, a fresh blood spot from the victim's blouse was that of neither the victim nor Brandley. The trial resulted in a hung jury when one juror, William Shreck, would not convict on the basis of the evidence. When the media leaked Shreck's name, he began receiving harassing telephone calls, including one caller who threatened him with "We're going to get you, nigger lover."

Brandley's second trial began in February 1981, using a different judge. The all-white jury did not hear from one of the original witnesses, a custodian who was no longer willing to corroborate the other custo-dian's stories about the night of the crime. Instead, the prosecution brought in a new witness, Danny Taylor, a former custodian. Taylor tes-tified that Brandley, after seeing some white female students walk past him, once said, "If I got one of them alone, ain't no tellin' what I might do." During the second trial, a medical examiner testified that the cause of death was strangulation and that a belt belonging to Brandley matched the weapon used to induce strangulation. This time the jury found Bran-dley guilty and sentenced him to death.

When his appellate lawyers began their appeal of this decision, they discovered that the prosecution had lost some of the exculpatory evidence, including a Caucasian pubic hair and other hairs that were found on the victim's body that belonged neither to her nor to Brandley, and photo-graphs taken at the scene of the crime that revealed that Brandley was not wearing the belt that had been identified as the murder weapon. Combined with the destroyed semen, the missing evidence cast even more doubt over the fairness of the trial. Despite these unexplained occurrences, the Texas Court of Criminal Appeals in 1985 affirmed the conviction and capital sentence. (For more information, see *Brandley v. Texas* 1985.)

At the first evidentiary hearing it was disclosed that John Sessum, the custodian who refused to corroborate the stories of the other custodians implicating Brandley in the murder and rape during the second trial, admitted that he had seen another custodian, Gary Acreman, following Cheryl Ferguson earlier that day. He further noted that he heard the victim scream "No" and "Don't." When he informed the Texas Ranger, Wesley Styles, of this encounter, he was threatened with arrest if he didn't go along with the story line of the other custodians. Moreover, Brenda Medina, a woman from a nearby town who had heard about the Brandley case, came forward with new information. Her former lover, James Dexter Robinson, had informed her in 1980 that he had been involved in a crime that resembled the case in question. Despite the new evidence, Brandley was denied a new trial. A video of Acreman admitting that Robinson killed the victim was presented during the second evidentiary hearing. Although Acreman later recanted his story, two witnesses testified that Acreman had confessed to knowing who the murderer was and that it wasn't Brandley. Based on this new evidence, a stay of execution was granted only six days prior to Brandley's scheduled execution. A third evidentiary hearing culminated in a new trial being granted to Brandley. Finally, on October 1, 1990, the prosecution dropped all charges against Brandley. Neither the prosecution nor the Texas Ranger was ever disciplined for their behavior during the case.

Charles Harris and the Rampart Scandal

In the late 1990s the Los Angeles Police Department's Community Resources Against Street Hoodlums (CRASH) program came under close scrutiny when evidence of police corruption and brutality surfaced in the Rampart division of CRASH. As part of a plea bargain, Rafael Perez, then a member of the LAPD, provided investigators with details outlining police misconduct in the CRASH program ("6 More Convictions Overturned in LAPD Corruption Scandal" 2000). A review of the Rampart division disclosed that the police regularly planted evidence and perjured themselves to obtain convictions. Officers were also responsible for stealing and selling drugs, taking money from suspects, as well as police brutality. Almost thirty officers were implicated in these activities (Rampart Independent Review Panel 2002).

Charles Harris was wrongfully convicted in 1998 when he was framed by Perez and another police officer for the distribution and possession of cocaine. Perez later confessed that the officers illegally searched Harris's vehicle, neglected to advise Harris of his rights, and perjured themselves in their police report of the incident. Court documents also disclose that Perez stole $500 from Harris. In March 2000 a judge overturned Harris's conviction after he had served nineteen months of his sentence.

Madison Hobley

The case of Madison Hobley is extremely complex, involving numerous factors that culminated in his wrongful conviction. Accused of an arson that took the lives of his wife, his infant son, and five other tenants of an apartment complex in Chicago, Hobley is one of fourteen black men who were victims of systematic torture by members of the Chicago Police Department. When police detectives Robert Dwyer and James Lotito questioned Hobley the day after the fire, Hobley contended that he was forced to go with them to the police station and, when he refused to confess, was tortured. The officers subsequently fabricated a confession, according to Hobley.

Testimony at the 1990 jury trial in Cook County Circuit Court included the testimony of four police officers and two witnesses who identified Hobley as the individual who purchased gas from an Amoco service station prior to the fire. The physical evidence used to convict Hobley included a two-gallon gasoline can that was alleged to have been found at the fire scene by another police officer. To corroborate the arguments posed by the prosecutors, Virgil Mikus, a Chicago police detective and arson expert, testified that the burn pattern outside Hobley's apartment suggested that gasoline was present there, although no traces of gasoline were actually found. The jury found Hobley guilty of seven counts of felony murder, one count of arson, and seven counts of aggravated arson. He was sentenced to death by Judge Christy Berkos. In 1994 the Illinois Supreme Court upheld the conviction and sentence.

In 1995 a petition for postconviction relief was filed in the Circuit Court. The petition argued that the prosecution had withheld a forensic report that failed to detect fingerprints from the defendant on the gasoline can admitted into evidence. Further, the defense was not allowed access to reports that revealed the presence of a second gasoline can, which was later destroyed. Circuit Court Judge Dennis J. Porter was unimpressed, nevertheless, and denied the petition. Three years later the Illinois Supreme Court reversed Porter's decision and ordered an evidentiary hearing. An evidentiary hearing was finally convened on May 31, 2002, with Judge Porter presiding. During that hearing more exculpatory information was presented by Hobley's attorneys. One of the two witnesses who testified to seeing Hobley getting gasoline from a service station just before the fire was now himself a suspect in an arson case. There was also evidence that the jury had been intimidated during the original trial. While sequestered, jurors complained of being taunted while eating at a restaurant with chants of "Give him the death penalty" and "Hang the motherfucker." Additionally, the jury foreman, a police officer from a suburb of Chicago, was alleged to have placed a gun on the jury table during deliberations and stated, "We'll reach a verdict." Finally, testimony from a different arson expert raised doubts regarding the alleged burn patterns outside Hobley's apartment. Despite this new wealth of information, on July 8, 2002, Judge Porter again denied Hobley a new trial. At this juncture, Hobley's counsel filed a petition requesting a full pardon based on innocence. The Illinois Prisoner Review Board heard the petition on October 18, 2002. Hobley received a gubernatorial pardon on January 9, 2003, and on January 10, 2003, he was released from prison after serving 204 months for a wrongful conviction.

Eddie Joe Lloyd

On August 26, 2002, Eddie Joe Lloyd was finally exonerated of murder and rape, a miscarriage of justice that resulted in his being wrongfully incarcerated for over seventeen years of his life. Lloyd, who suffered from mental illness, was convicted of the brutal murder and rape of sixteen-year-old Michelle Jackson in Detroit, Michigan. His story begins on January 24, 1984, when, while a patient in a mental health hospital, Lloyd sent the police some suggestions for solving recent murders, including the one involving Jackson. Lloyd, who was interrogated several times while in the hospital, was convinced that if he confessed to the rape and murder of Jackson this would help the police flesh out the actual offender. His six-page statement and audiotape was graphic and accurate. He precisely described the clothing and jewelry that Jackson was wearing during the crime, the knife used to intimidate her, the long johns that were used to strangle her, and the green bottle inserted into her rectum. It was later revealed that police officers provided Lloyd with the details of the crime that he included in his confession. During the trial in May 1985, the jury deliberated for less than an hour before pronouncing him guilty. Because the state of Michigan did not have capital punishment, Lloyd was given a life sentence without parole.

After exhausting his appeals, Lloyd came to the attention of the Innocence Project in 1995. Barry Scheck, the codirector of the Innocence Project, agreed to represent Lloyd. After investigating the case, Scheck concluded the police officer who conducted the interrogation "had to know that he was feeding a paranoid schizophrenic guy, a guy with a mental disorder, in a mental institution, facts in order to clear a major homicide so everybody could look good" (Wilgoren 2002a). DNA tests of the long johns and the bottle eventually ruled out Lloyd as the perpetrator, and on August 26, 2002, he was exonerated and released from prison (Wilgoren 2002b). Two years later, at the age of fifty-six, Lloyd died. In 2006 the state and city offered to pay almost $4 million to the family of Eddie Joe Lloyd and his attorneys for the wrongful conviction ("State, City to Pay $4M for Wrongful Murder Conviction" 2006).

Prosecutorial Misconduct and the Conviction of Innocents

Misconduct by prosecutors may go largely unnoticed in many trials because many prosecutorial decisions are not transparent. Moreover, as observed in the earlier case of Clarence Brandley, prosecutorial misconduct may be only one of multiple factors leading to the conviction of innocents. The following cases represent a sample of some of the activities involving prosecutors that resulted in miscarriages of justice.

James "Bo" Cochran

Some defendants just appear guilty. Attorney Richard Jaffe, James "Bo" Cochran's legal counsel for his fourth trial, commented, "Bo clearly looked guilty." Having previously been incarcerated for manslaughter, Cochran was charged with the robbery of an A&P grocery store in Birmingham, Alabama, and murder of Stephen Ganey, the white assistant manager. When approached by the police near the A&P where the murder had occurred, Cochran began running. Asked why he tried to escape the police, Cochran said, "When I was fourteen, I was beaten up by cops. I had been running from them since." The police also found an A&P band containing money when Cochran was apprehended.

After one mistrial, Cochran was found guilty and sentenced to death. That verdict was eventually overturned because of a 1980 US Supreme Court ruling. The ruling struck down Alabama's capital statutes because the statutes did not permit juries the option to find defendants guilty of lesser charges. In 1982, in Cochran's third trial, he was again convicted and sentenced to death. The US Court of Appeals for the Eleventh Circuit upheld a district court's decision to overturn the conviction because race was a determining factor in the prosecutor's exercise of its peremptory challenges, which is unconstitutional according to *Batson v. Kentucky* (1986). In each of the earlier trials, the racial composition of the jury had been eleven whites and one black. Finally, in 1997, a jury of seven blacks and five whites found Cochran not guilty of the accusations. During the trial, defense attorney Jaffe cogently argued that there were no eyewitnesses and that the murder victim's body, which was found under a trailer in a mobile home park, could not have been moved there by Cochran because he was being chased by the police at the time (Bright 2001a; Equal Justice Initiative 2009, nd).

Walter McMillian

A second wrongful conviction from Alabama illustrates the problem of prosecutorial misconduct within the context of multiple contributing factors. The crime occurred on November 1, 1986, in Monroeville, a city that served as a model for the fictional setting of Maycomb in Harper Lee's book *To Kill a Mockingbird,* a novel about a wrongfully accused black man charged with the rape of a white woman. McMillian was charged with the rape and murder of Ronda Morrison, an eighteen-year-old white female with whom he had a romantic liaison. The young woman's body was found behind a rack of clothes in the dry cleaners where she was a part-time employee. Morrison had been shot three times and her pants and shirt had been unbuttoned. With a prior criminal record for distributing marijuana and for assault, and given the relationship between McMillian and Morrison, McMillian was suspected of the crime. While awaiting trial, McMillian was transported to Holman Correctional Facility in Atmore, Alabama, a prison where most of Alabama's death row inmates are incarcerated.

With no physical evidence linking McMillian to the offense, the prosecutors relied extensively on the testimony of Ralph Myers, a white man, who testified that he had accompanied McMillian to the cleaners, where he observed him shoot Morrison and then take money from the cleaners. He further alleged that McMillian had sodomized him several months earlier. Myers, a career criminal, later recanted his story and said that he felt pressured by the police to make his statement. Two other witnesses also testified that they saw McMillian in the vicinity of the crime that day. They, too, later recanted their testimony. The defense also called several witnesses, all of whom were black, to testify that during the time of the crime McMillian was at a church fish fry. During the trial, exculpatory evidence was withheld from the defense, including testimony that contradicted the timelines established for the crime by the prosecutors and a tape recording that raised questions about Myers's testimony. Judge John Patterson, in overturning the case on appeal, later wrote, "We conclude that there is a reasonable probability that had Myers's prior inconsistent statement been disclosed to the defense prior to trial, the results of the proceedings would have been different." Finally, on March 3, 1993, McMillian became a free man (Bright 2001b; Equal Justice Initiative, nd; see also Earley 1996).

Harold Wilson

On April 10, 1988, three persons—Dorothy Sewell, Tyrone Mason, and Cynthia Goines Mills—were brutally killed with a carpenter's axe in a home in South Philadelphia. The next day the police arrested Harold Wilson, after discovering a jacket in his basement that appeared to have blood stains from the victims. Wilson, the youngest of seven children, had dropped out of school by junior high and was involved in an active street life. Former Philadelphia Assistant District Attorney Jack McMahon was the prosecutor in Wilson's 1989 trial. As would be revealed later, McMahon was responsible for developing a training video for new prosecutors that recommended the dismissal of blacks during *voir dire*.[6] Wilson was convicted on all three counts of murder and sentenced to three death penalties. In a 1999 postconviction review his capital sentence was vacated, because it was determined that his court-appointed attorney, Willis W. Berry, Jr., who had never tried a capital case, failed to provide him with effective counsel. More specifically, Berry did not adequately investigate and present mitigating evidence during Wilson's original trial.[7] Nonetheless, the conviction was left standing and Wilson remained incarcerated.

While in prison Wilson frequently resisted unfair prison rules and often spent long periods in solitary confinement.[8] In a 2005 interview by *Democracy Now!,* Wilson recounts his ordeal on death row: "I was never taken off of death row. I remained on death row even though the courts, Pennsylvania courts, Court of Common Pleas on a postconviction relief petition, found counsel ineffective for failing to investigate. I still remained on death row, because this is the practice of Pennsylvania."

A 2003 appeal concluded that the use of peremptory strikes by McMahon in the original trial to excuse potential African American jurors was conducted in a discriminatory manner and was consequently in violation of the 1986 *Batson* decision. Further, the court ruled, when a new trial was held the case could not be tried as a capital offense. Although a subsequent trial was declared a mistrial, Wilson's third trial in 2005 finally cleared Wilson of any wrongdoing when DNA evidence excluded him as a possible assailant in the triple murder. After sixteen years on death row, Wilson was finally released from prison on November 15, 2005, with sixty-five cents in change and a bus token. Today Wilson is actively involved in helping others who have faced injustices within the criminal justice system. In addition to participating in the National Black Caucus of States Institute, the Pennsylvania Prison Society, and the Witness to Innocence Project, Wilson founded the Harold C. Wilson Foundation, which facilitates the transition from prison to society for former inmates (Campaign to End the Death Penalty 2009; Goodman 2005; Pirro 2006; Wilson 2000).

Ernest (Shujaa) Graham and Eugene Allen

Ernest (Shujaa) Graham grew up on a plantation in Louisiana where his family worked as sharecroppers. In 1961 Graham and his family moved to South Central Los Angeles. He had a troubled childhood, spending much of his time in juvenile institutions. At the age of eighteen Graham was sent to Soledad Prison in California. As a result of increasing racial pride and the black prison movement, he began to reassess his life and began teaching himself to read and write. While in prison he additionally studied history and world affairs. Graham eventually became a leader within the black prison movement. But in 1973, while incarcerated, he and Eugene Allen, another black inmate, were charged with the murder of a white correctional officer at the Deuel Vocational Institute in Stockton, California. Although the first trial ended in a hung jury, Graham and Allen were found guilty and sentenced to death in a second trial in 1976. Upon appeal the California Supreme Court reversed the conviction and granted a new trial, after noting the racial composition of the jury and questioning the prosecutors' use of peremptory challenges to dismiss African American prospective jurors (see *People v. Allen* 1979). While the third trial resulted in a hung jury again, the fourth trial led to the acquittal of Graham and Allen in March 1981. After leaving California, Graham moved to Maryland, where he learned the landscaping business. He continues to speak out against injustices within the criminal justice system and the use of capital punishment (Journey of Hope 2004).

False Confessions and the Conviction of Innocents

High-profile cases of false confessions have surfaced periodically in the United States. When the baby of Charles Lindbergh was kidnapped and murdered in 1932, for instance, more than two hundred persons falsely confessed to the crime (Macdonald and Michaud 1987; Rogge 1959). Although the history of criminal justice in the United States is replete with examples of false confessions, only recently has this issue become a matter of national concern as wrongful convictions have come to light.[9]

Some psychologists have suggested that false confessions fall into one of two categories—voluntary or involuntary (coerced). According to this typology, voluntary false confessions refer to false self-incriminating statements that are given sans police pressure. Relatively uncommon in recorded instances involving wrongful convictions, voluntary false confessions may result from a pathological need for fame and recognition, a desire to protect an acquaintance or relative, or an unconscious desire to punish oneself for previous transgressions (real or imagined). In some instances guilty persons may falsely confess to a lesser offense to diminish the severity of the sentence to be imposed by the court (Conti 1999). Psychologists have further dichotomized involuntary false confessions into coerced-compliant false confessions or coerced-internalized false confessions (Conti 1999; Kassin and Wrightsman 1985). Torture, threats, and promises made by criminal justice officials may produce coerced-compliant false confessions. In contrast, coerced-internalized false confessions occur when a highly suggestive police interrogation culminates in a false confession. This is most likely to occur in interrogations in which potentially vulnerable individuals are presented with false or misleading evidence intimating their involvement in the crime. Thus, suspects who are young, naïve, of low intelligence, fatigued, or impaired due to consumption of alcohol or other drugs are more susceptible to this type of police influence (Conti 1999).

Yet the voluntary/involuntary distinction suggested above has proved to be unsatisfactory, as this categorization of false confessions oversimplifies some important aspects of the process itself. Because confessions are typically obtained through police interrogation of suspects, an understanding of this process is warranted. Numerous manipulative interrogation practices have been deemed to be legal, making a distinction between voluntary and involuntary somewhat arbitrary. Cathleen Burnett (2010, 54–55) observes that

> police are permitted to trick the suspect . . . or bluff and deceive the suspect . . . including not telling the suspect why he or she is being questioned or even that the person asking the questions is a police officer. . . . Police are permitted to lie about incriminating evidence . . . and to state that there is an eyewitness or DNA evidence that ties the suspect to the crime when there is not. . . . Fabricating evidence, a technique designed to undermine the suspect's confidence . . . is upheld by the courts.

Given these psychological advantages by the police, it should be no surprise that research has found that the longer the interrogation, the more likely it will conclude with a confession (Westling 2001).

Because all interrogation-based confessions contain an element of psychological coercion, the authors have abandoned the voluntary/involuntary typologies. Instead, cases were coded as involving false confessions when the wrongful conviction data revealed that the defendant did not commit the crime even though he had confessed.[10] Although no further distinction was made between the various false confession cases, further review of the data sometimes revealed police coercion that exceeded the reach of that legally tolerated. Where that information was available, it is included in the narratives presented in this book.

John Duval

One of the more interesting cases of wrongful conviction involves John Duval, a transvestite prostitute from Rochester, New York, who was accused in 1973, along with fellow prostitute Betty Tyson, of bludgeoning and strangling a white, middle-aged businessman from Philadelphia who apparently was seeking the services of a prostitute. Although there was no physical evidence linking him to the crime, police believed that robbery was the motive for the murder. Duval contends that he confessed to the crime only after detective William Mahoney beat him.[11] During the trial, two teenage runaways—Jon Jackson and Wayne Wright—testified that they saw Duval and Tyson with the victim. In February 1974, Duval was found guilty and sentenced to twenty-five years to life.

In 1997 Wright acknowledged that he had lied during the trial about seeing Duval, Tyson, and the victim together. Wright contended that Mahoney had threatened him if he did not testify. It was also discovered in a police interview with Jackson that he, too, denied having seen either Duval or Tyson with Timothy Hayworth, the victim, the night of the murder. Consequently, Tyson was released in 1998 and Duval was released in 1999. Although Tyson received $1.2 million from the city of Rochester for her wrongful conviction, Duval was retried for the crime because he had on two separate occasions admitted his guilt during parole hearings. When questioned why he had falsely confessed again, Duval commented, "If you don't show remorse, they're not going to let you go. I was very upset about it . . . but I didn't have outside support, anybody saying, 'We're trying to get you out, Johnny, just hold on.'"

In 2000 Duval was presented with a plea bargain from the prosecutors. If he would plead guilty, thereby making himself ineligible for any financial remuneration, he would be allowed to remain free. Duval immediately rejected the offer. During the second trial, which began on January 20, 2000, Wright reiterated that his original testimony had been coerced, as Mahoney had threatened to charge him with the murder if he didn't testify seeing Duval with the victim. The other witness did not testify at the second trial. Duval was acquitted in April 2000, after spending twenty-five years in prison for a crime he didn't commit (Dobbin 2000; Swanson 2000).

Benjamin J. Harris III

The 1984 case of Benjamin J. Harris III from Tacoma, Washington, illustrates the role that ineffective assistance of counsel can play in false confessions. At the time of the incident "Harris was a well-known local character who sauntered the streets in a snazzy suit and hat" (O'Hagan 2003). He frequented a local coffee shop that catered to a clientele that included attorneys and legislators. While there, "He would shake hands and walk through as if he was running for president," according to Neil Hoff, a former state senator and Tacoma attorney (O'Hagan 2003). Harris fancied himself a police informant who had connections. On June 14, 1984, after Jimmie Lee Turner, a local automobile mechanic, was found shot to death, Harris contacted a detective to declare his innocence. He then offered his services to help the police locate the killer. In July 1984 Gregory "Gay Gay" Bonds was arrested and charged with the crime, based partially on information obtained from Harris. Before long, however, police began to suspect Harris, and on August 10, 1984, he was officially charged with having paid Bonds to murder Turner.

During the trial the prosecution alleged that Harris and Bonds were both responsible for firing the shots that killed Turner. Yet police department forensic records, not introduced into evidence at the trial, disclosed that a single person was responsible for firing both shots. Murray Anderson, who represented Harris at the trial, devoted little time to the preparation of a defense. He never challenged the prosecutorial decision to try the case as a capital crime, a routine procedure in death penalty cases. Anderson's total time with his client was less than two hours in duration, and he interviewed only three of thirty-two persons whose testimony could have conceivably turned the tide in favor of Harris. Most questionable was Anderson's strategy to have Harris testify that he was involved in the shooting to convince the jury that it was not a murder-for-hire case. This approach, Anderson believed, would make the crime appear to be a more routine murder and thereby reduce the likelihood that it would result in the death penalty. Throughout the trial Anderson referred to his client in derogatory terms. During the closing remarks Anderson characterized his client as someone who "doesn't have the same moral code as we expect." He further remarked that Harris was part of "a class of men who don't work, [and who] carry guns" and "kill people" (O'Hagan 2003). The jury promptly responded by finding him guilty and sentencing him to death. His co-defendant, Bonds, who was represented by different counsel, was acquitted.

After his conviction on October 31, 1984, he awaited his execution at the Washington State Penitentiary near Walla Walla. Twice he came within weeks of being executed before receiving a stay of execution. In US District Court in 1994, Judge Robert Bryan overturned the conviction and required Harris to be retried or released. With key witnesses dead, incarcerated, or unwilling to testify again, a retrial was unlikely. So the state tried a different tactic: to contend that incarceration had made Harris progressively more mentally ill and dangerous. This strategy proved unsuccessful, nonetheless, when a jury on July 16, 1997, ruled that Harris should not be incarcerated at Western State Hospital, a psychiatric facility in Lakewood, Washington. Despite this decision, the state persevered and later that year obtained a court order to have Harris admitted into a ninety-day transition program at Western State Hospital. Harris remained at that facility as recently as 2003 (O'Hagan 2003). Eventually Harris was released from the mental health facility, only to die about six months thereafter (O'Hagan 2009).

Earl Washington, Jr.

Earl Washington, Jr., was one of five children raised in a poor family in rural Virginia. He was mentally retarded and had an IQ of less than 70, which places him in the bottom 2 percent of the population. Functioning at approximately the level of a ten-year-old child, Washington was enrolled in special education classes. After experiencing failure in the classroom, he left school at the age of fifteen and worked on a farm.

Washington's saga begins at the age of twenty-two when the Virginia State Police arrested him for an alleged burglary and assault.[12] During two days of interrogation and after waiving his Miranda rights, he confessed to five unsolved crimes, most notably the murder and rape of Rebecca Lynn Williams, a nineteen-year-old white woman from Culpepper, Virginia, who had three children. His "confessions" for the four other crimes were so flawed that they were summarily dismissed as not credible. Washington was not so lucky about his confession of the Williams case. Even that confession, however, was rife with inconsistencies. For instance, he said the victim was black (she was white), he didn't know the victim's address, he didn't know that the victim had been raped, he described the victim as short (she was 5' 8" tall), he said he stabbed her two to three times (she was stabbed thirty-eight times), he told the police he kicked in the door to her apartment to enter (the door was undamaged), and he claimed that she was alone when the offense occurred (two of her young children were present in the apartment at the time). It was not until four attempts at securing a viable confession that the police finally had a confession that appeared to be congruent with the facts of the case.

When the three-day trial began, Washington's attorney, John Scott, did not mention that his client had wrongly confessed to four other crimes, nor did he mention Washington's mental limitations and low IQ. Moreover, he neglected to note the large gaps in the police notes of the interrogation that lent credence to the possibility of police coercion. And during the penalty phase of the trial, there was no attempt to counter the prosecution's argument for the death penalty. A largely white jury convicted and sentenced Washington to death on January 20, 1984.

Washington was scheduled to die on September 5, 1985. Nine days prior to the scheduled execution, he received a stay of execution when his attorneys filed a state habeas corpus petition. In 1993 the US Court of Appeals for the Fourth Circuit heard Washington's case. The court acknowledged that Washington had been denied effective assistance of counsel. Nevertheless, it concluded that given the strength of the other evidence (primarily the "confession"), the failure to introduce exculpatory evidence by his defense counsel constituted a "harmless error." It was at this juncture that a decision was made to conduct DNA testing on the biological evidence. When in October 1993 DNA tests excluded Washington as the contributor of the semen, he had already exhausted his twenty-one-day period after final sentencing to present new evidence on his behalf. At this point prosecutors speculated that Washington's DNA did not match because he had an accomplice (despite the dying words of the victim that she had been attacked by a single individual). Virginia Governor L. Douglas Wilder consequently commuted his sentence to life. When the Virginia General Assembly extended Virginia's legislation limiting new evidence to twenty-one days after final sentencing, Washington's situation looked bleak. Finally, in 2000 Virginia Governor Jim Gilmore requested more DNA testing, which again revealed that Washington could not have been the contributor. On October 2, 2000, Governor Gilmore officially pardoned Washington for the rape and murder of Williams. However, Washington remained in prison for a conviction of an unrelated crime. Then, on February 12, 2001, he was released from prison to parole supervision by the Virginia Department of Corrections.

After his release Washington married and moved to Virginia Beach, where he was employed as a maintenance man. DNA results later resulted in the identification of an inmate who was serving a life sentence for an unrelated rape as the probable perpetrator of the rape and murder of Williams. In 2007, subject to approval by the court, the state of Virginia agreed to restitution in the amount of $1.9 million for its miscarriage of justice (Glod 2007; Green 2000; National Public Radio, nd; see also Edds 2003).

Informants/Snitches and the Conviction of Innocents

The Center on Wrongful Convictions defines snitches as "witnesses with incentives to lie." In many of the known wrongful conviction cases the jury was unaware that the person testifying had an incentive to lie. A snitch (or informant), for example, may provide false testimony in return for promised leniency by the criminal justice system or for financial gain. The actual perpetrator (or acquaintance of the perpetrator) may also give false testimony to cast suspicion on someone else. In the United States the use of snitches represents the main determinant of wrongful convictions in capital cases (Center on Wrongful Convictions 2005). This section explores the cases of four African American men in which witnesses with incentives to lie played a major role in their wrongful convictions.

Levon "Bo" Jones

Convicted in 1993 of the 1987 shooting death and robbery of Leamon Grady, a local bootlegger, Levon "Bo" Jones was sentenced to death. Although Jones had a previous criminal history, much of the evidence used to convict him revolved around the damaging testimony of Lovely Lorden, Jones's lover and the prosecution's star witness. As a result of her assistance in the case, Lorden later received a $4,000 reward from the governor's office. After an appeal to the North Carolina Supreme Court in 1996 failed to overturn his conviction, Jones received a more favorable disposition in 2006, when US District Court Judge Terrence Boyle ordered that Jones be removed from death row and be awarded a new trial. The federal judge was particularly critical of the handling of the case by his defense attorneys, Graham Phillips, Jr., and Charles Henderson, citing their "constitutionally deficient" performance and their inability to examine the credibility of the state's primary witness. According to the order, "Jones received two appointed attorneys that spent virtually no time or effort investigating the offense or his background." Further, Judge Boyle argued that defense counsel had not properly explored possible mitigating circumstances that could have possibly spared Jones the death penalty.[13] In removing Jones from death row, he concluded that, "Given the weakness of the prosecution's case and its heavy reliance on the testimony of Lovely Lorden, there is reasonable probability that, but for counsel's unprofessional errors, the result of the proceeding would have been different." As Jones's new defense counsel began preparation for his second trial, Lorden signed an affidavit in which she admitted that she lied and further noted that a detective had coached her on what to say. With the primary witness recanting her story, the case against Jones was weak, and all charges were dropped on May 2, 2008 (Barksdale 2008; Locke 2008).

Darby Tillis and Perry Cobb

On the morning of November 13, 1977, two white men working at a hot dog stand in Chicago were robbed and killed. Three weeks later, based on the testimony of Phyllis Santini, both Darby Tillis and Perry Cobb were arrested and charged with the crime. Santini claimed that she drove the getaway car after Tillis and Cobb had committed the armed robbery and murdered the two men. Although there was no physical evidence linking Tillis to the crime other than Santini's testimony, when apprehended Cobb possessed a watch belonging to one of the murdered men. Cobb maintained he had purchased the watch for ten dollars from Johnny Brown, Santini's boyfriend. However, in the light of Cobb's one previous conviction for aggravated battery, his story was unconvincing. Thus began the saga of Tillis and Cobb that would span five trials.

During the first three trials the prosecution relied on Santini's testimony, the watch, and statements from a bartender across from the murder site who testified that he saw two black men in the vicinity at the time of the crime. The defense was not allowed to use the testimony of Patricia Usmani and Carol Griffin, who were willing to testify that they heard Phyllis Santini admit to being involved in the murders along with her boyfriend, Johnny Brown. After two hung juries, the third trial finally resulted in conviction and the death penalty. Four years later, the Illinois Supreme Court reversed and remanded their case because Judge Thomas J. Maloney, the presiding judge for the three trials, had barred testimony that would implicate Santini and Brown in the murders. Further, the judge had committed a judicial error in his jury instructions.[14] A story appearing in *Chicago Lawyer* magazine about the Tillis and Cobb ordeal prompted Michael Falconer to come forward with information pertaining to the case. Falconer, a local lawyer, had worked with Santini in a factory earlier, and recalled her mentioning that she and Brown had once robbed a restaurant and that Brown had shot someone during the commission of the crime. Despite the new evidence, Tillis and Cobb were tried twice more. Although the fourth trial resulted in a hung jury, the fifth eventually resulted in acquittal, primarily on the basis of Falconer's testimony. Then, in 2001, Illinois Governor George Ryan officially pardoned both men. Santini and Brown have yet to be charged with the crime. Today Tillis, a strong advocate for the abolition of the death penalty, is a preacher who counsels released death row inmates as they attempt to adjust to their new freedom. A former singer, Cobb is employed as a janitor (Justice Project 2009a; Tillis 2009).

Edward Baker

On December 20, 1973, a retired bellhop named Steve Gibbons was killed at his home in South Philadelphia during a break-in to steal money. Accused of serving as a lookout while his companions committed the crime, Edward Baker, then a teenager, maintained that he was in another section of the city at a wake during the murder and robbery. Baker was sentenced to life imprisonment in 1974 for his involvement in the crime, largely on the inconsistent and frequently contradictory testimony of Donahue Wise, a schizophrenic drug addict who received a reduced sentence in exchange for his testimony. At an evidentiary hearing in 1996 before Common Pleas Court Judge C. Darnell Jones II, Wise recanted his confession and acknowledged that he was the actual killer. He further identified his accomplices in the crime. In 1997 the judge dismissed the conviction based on the grounds that Baker's original attorney, C. George Milner, had been ineffective by not challenging the inconsistent and contradictory testimony of Wise and his credibility as a witness. In December 1999 Baker was released on bail and placed under house arrest pending a new trial. District Attorney Lynne Abraham offered Baker a plea bargain in January 2002. If he would plead no contest to the murder of Gibbons, Abraham would have his ankle monitor removed and he would be a free man. In rejecting this offer, Baker replied, "I'm innocent." At this juncture the district attorney had a decision to make: either drop all charges against Baker or retry him for the crime. Because Baker had passed a polygraph examination, the star witness against him had recanted his story, and twelve people were willing to testify as alibi witnesses, it was highly unlikely that a new trial would result in a conviction. Consequently, on February 11, 2002, all charges were dismissed and Baker was finally set free after having served twenty-six years in prison for a crime that he didn't commit.

Since gaining his freedom Baker has become a certified electrician for the city of Philadelphia (a trade he learned while incarcerated). He also married Luzetta Thorne, a childhood friend who had remained in contact with him during his prison stay. Baker has additionally received a driver's license and purchased a home and an automobile. In February 2002, as a testament to his new freedom, he received a summons for jury duty, an obligation for which he is now eligible (Centurion Ministries 2007; Klein 2002; Riley 2002).

Forensic Errors and the Conviction of Innocents

Forensic errors run the gamut from fraud by lab analysts to expert witnesses who rely on inadequately validated forensic tests. Included in the latter are tests of hair, bullets, handwriting, footprints, and bite marks. Bite marks are especially problematic, because forensic dentists are infrequently employed by accredited labs and thus have minimal oversight. According to the Innocence Project, the reliability of bite mark analysis has been examined in only three studies. These studies found evidence of false identifications in 12 to 91 percent of the cases analyzed. (For more information on invalid forensic science testimony, see Garrett and Neufeld [2009].) In contrast, DNA tests provide a level of sophistication that is unavailable using the previously mentioned methods. The following cases involve forensic errors that resulted in miscarriages of justice.

Willie Jackson

Louisiana is the state with the fourth highest per-capita rate of wrongful convictions. This Louisiana case involving Willie Jackson is particularly revealing because most of the evidence pointed to his brother as the perpetrator. His story begins on December 12, 1986, when Beverly Short, after leaving a bar in Jefferson Parish, stopped at a restaurant to pick up breakfast for her son. As she left her automobile, she was accosted by an unknown assailant who demanded that she get into his car where he proceeded to bite her and engage in oral sex. After raping her, he released her in a nearby neighborhood. He then informed her not to call the police because they wouldn't believe the story of an African American woman.

Undeterred by her assailant's warning, she notified the police. Police deputies discovered a message written on a bank receipt belonging to Willie Jackson, who had moved with his wife eight months earlier to Natchez, Mississippi, approximately 185 miles from Jefferson Parish in

Louisiana. Short's description of her rapist seemingly suggested a different perpetrator. She described her assailant as having a military-style buzz cut and clean shaven. At the time Willie Jackson had long hair and a beard. When he was asked to repeat the words spoken by the rapist, Short replied, "That's him. I'll never forget that voice." Earlier, police had confiscated from his mother's house in Jefferson Parish a sweater with his brother's name on it that matched a description provided by Short. Moreover, an automobile matching the description given to the police was owned by Jackson's mother. During the trial, a bartender testified that Milton Jackson, not Willie Jackson, was in the bar that Short had been in the night of the crime. And, in Short's statement to the police, she mentioned that her assailant complained that he couldn't meet women because he was in the military. (Milton Jackson was an army veteran.) Thus, the evidence was pointing to Milton Jackson as the attacker. To buttress the case against Willie Jackson, the prosecutor brought in a forensic odontologist who testified that the bite marks on the victim identified Willie Jackson as the assailant. Within forty-five minutes the jury found Willie Jackson guilty of attempted rape and robbery and sentenced him to forty years at Washington Correctional Institution in Angie, Louisiana.

Two days after Willie Jackson was convicted, Milton Jackson confessed to the crime, although the district attorneys did not believe him. Two lawyers from Regan and Associates in New Orleans began examining Jackson's case. They located another forensic odontologist who was willing to testify that the bite marks belonged to Milton Jackson. The handwriting on the bank statement was also identified by a handwriting expert as that of Milton Jackson. Finally, in 2004 DNA tests of semen from Short's pantyhose excluded Willie Jackson as the depositor. Based on this new evidence, Willie Jackson was granted a new trial and released on bail. In April 2006, one month before all charges were dropped, DNA tests conclusively showed that Milton Jackson's semen was on the pantyhose. At the time of Willie Jackson's release his brother Milton was serving a life sentence at the Louisiana State Penitentiary at Angola, Louisiana, for an unrelated 1998 rape (Innocence Project of New Orleans 2009b; Webster 2007).

Dan Young, Jr., and Harold Hill

On October 14, 1990, Chicago firefighters were extinguishing a blaze when the body of thirty-nine-year-old Kathy Morgan, an African American woman, was discovered. She had been raped and strangled. Her body was charred from having been soaked in gasoline prior to being ignited.

With a crime this gruesome the police felt strong pressure to close the case, but it was over seventeen months before Chicago Police Detectives Kenneth Boudreau and John Halloran obtained a confession. Harold Hill confessed that he, along with Dan Young, Jr., and Peter Williams, were responsible for the rape and murder of Morgan. Later Young and Williams confessed to having committed the crime. Of the three confessions, nineteen-year-old Williams gave the most detailed account after allegedly being handcuffed to a radiator for hours and being denied restroom privileges. Williams was also allegedly "beaten with a blackjack and subjected to a mock execution where an officer put a pistol in his mouth and pulled the trigger" (Lydersen, nd).[15] However, Williams's confession was problematic, as he was in jail on a narcotics violation when the crime took place. With a built-in alibi, his case was dismissed. Prosecutors nevertheless still had confessions from Young and Hill, so they proceeded to trial.

The two confessions were questionable at best. Young, thirty-one years of age, had an IQ of 56, which meant that he was severely retarded. He was illiterate and incapable of understanding a Miranda warning. Unable to count backward or tell time, Young did not even know what a ship was. Hill was sixteen years old when the crime occurred but was tried as an adult. Already in trouble with the law for a 1992 armed robbery, Hill knew about the highly publicized Morgan case and so confessed without benefit of an attorney. Because in their confessions they implicated each other, Young and Hill were tried separately. The defense attorneys were unsuccessful in having the judge suppress the confessions, even though they contained some obviously false information, because one of the co-conspirators was in jail during the commission of the crime. The prosecutors presented evidence from Dr. John Kenney, a forensic odontologist, that a bite mark and a hickey on Morgan's body belonged to Young and Hill. Both men were found guilty and sentenced to life in prison without possibility of parole in 1994.

Incarceration proved to be particularly difficult for Hill. According to Russell Ainsworth, an attorney who eventually represented Hill in a civil lawsuit against the city of Chicago after his release, "Doing prison time as a rapist/murderer is a much different story than doing time as an armed robber. . . . You're in maximum instead of medium security, and other inmates target rapists. Plus all this time he knows his family is wondering if he really could be a rapist and murderer." During his stay in prison, Hill contemplated suicide. He was also placed in protective custody when he refused to join a gang in prison and attack a correctional officer as part of his initiation rite.

After appeals had been exhausted in 2004, DNA tests were conducted on hairs found at the murder scene along with cellular material from under Morgan's fingernails. The tests indicated that neither Young nor Hill matched the genetic profile and that the hairs and cellular material belonged to two unidentified assailants. Further, an internationally known forensic odontologist, Dr. David Sweet, reported that due to the condition of the victim's body, the bite mark was unsuitable for comparison. Questions were additionally raised regarding the methods used to obtain confessions from Young and Hill, who were allegedly beaten, kicked, and threatened by the police while they were given information pertaining to the crime to use in their confession. Hill additionally alleges that he was interrogated all night without being allowed to sleep. On January 31, 2005, Cook County prosecutors dropped the charges against Young and Hill. Although Young was immediately released, Hill remained imprisoned for another year to complete his armed robbery sentence.[16] Fourteen months after receiving his freedom, Young died of wounds received from a hit-and-run driver (Lydersen, nd; Mills and Coen 2005; see also the December 2001 series "Cops and Confessions" and the October 2004 series "Forensics Under the Microscope" in the *Chicago Tribune*).

Calvin E. Washington and Joe Sidney Williams

In Waco, Texas, on the night of March 1, 1986, fifty-four-year-old Juanita White returned home from work around 10:00 p.m. That was the last time she was seen alive. The next morning, when White was found, she had been battered, raped, and murdered. Calvin E. Washington and Joe Sidney Williams were charged with the crime on the basis of the testimony from Booker Sterling, a jailhouse informant, and on questionable forensic testimony. Sterling testified that he overheard Washington and Williams at the C&E Motel on the night of March 1, 1986, talking about battering a woman and biting her so that she couldn't identify them. During the trial, defense counsel impeached Sterling's testimony by presenting over a dozen Waco police officers familiar with the informant who testified as to the unreliability of the witness. The prosecution, however, brought forth witnesses from the county jail who testified that they saw Washington and Williams in the victim's automobile after the crime and that they had sold some of the victim's personal property. Additionally, the prosecution called Homer Campbell, a forensic odontologist, to testify that the bite marks on White were "consistent" with the teeth of Williams. (Because most of Washington's teeth were missing, it wasn't plausible that he was responsible for the marks.) In separate trials in 1987, both men were found guilty and sentenced to life.

In 1993 Williams had his conviction overturned when the appeals court decided that the judge had allowed improper testimony to be presented at the original trial. The prosecution subsequently dismissed the charges against Williams rather than retry him. Washington, however, remained incarcerated until DNA tests of semen on the victim disclosed that the semen did not match that of Washington or Williams and DNA tests of blood found on a shirt in Washington's home revealed that it was not that of the victim, as the prosecutor had alleged. On July 5, 2001, Washington was released from prison, having spent fourteen years in wrongful confinement. Although Washington eventually received $374,999 for his wrongful conviction, he squandered it, and in 2008 his house was seized by the City of Waco and placed for sale due to delinquent property taxes. Since obtaining his freedom in 2001, Washington has been unable to be steadily employed (Associated Press 2001; CBS News 2001; Dunn 1987; Garrett and Neufeld 2009; Hall 2008).

Perjury by Criminal Justice Officials, Insufficient Evidence, and the Conviction of Innocents

The last two factors associated with false convictions examined in this study include perjury by police and/or prosecutors and insufficient evidence to support a conviction. Examples of the former are apparent in the previously discussed cases of Charles Harris, Madison Hobley, and John Duval. The following illustrations highlight some of the issues surrounding the conviction of innocents when perjury by criminal justice personnel and/or insufficient evidence are allowed to interfere with the administration of justice.

Mandis and Landis Barrow

Mandis and Landis Barrow, from the small Texas Panhandle town of Tulia, were identical twins who looked so much alike that even their mother couldn't tell them apart. In 1996 they were charged with a robbery in Amarillo that they swore they didn't commit. Nevertheless, when the prosecutor offered them ten-year probated sentences and their freedom, they chose not to contest the charge, a decision they would soon regret. Two years later they had their probation revoked when they were charged with delivering marijuana and cocaine to Tom Coleman, an undercover sheriff's deputy who was involved in a sting operation. The decision to revoke their probation was reached despite inconsistent and undocumented testimony by Coleman, who received the Texas Law Officer of the Year award after his Tulia, Texas, drug bust, which led to the arrest of 15 percent of the city's black population. The Texas Court of Criminal Appeals in 2000 upheld the decision, which resulted in the Barrow brothers being sentenced to twenty years in prison. In 2003 Dallas Judge Ron Chapman, hearing virtually the same testimony that Coleman had delivered at the probation revocation hearing, labeled the testimony perjury. Stating that Coleman was "the most devious, nonresponsive law enforcement witness" he had observed during his twenty-five years as a judge, Chapman further noted that Coleman's testimony at Mandis Barrow's hearing was replete with "perjured and misleading statements." When Texas Governor Rick Perry pardoned thirty-five of the individuals involved in the Tulia drug scandal on August 22, 2003, Mandis and Landis Barrow were ineligible because they were incarcerated for their 1996 robbery conviction. In 2009 the Texas Court of Criminal Appeals agreed to again review the cases of Mandis and Landis Barrow, nearly five years after their only witness, Coleman, had been found guilty of aggravated perjury (Bean 2004, 2009; Reynolds 2003; Sting Docket 2001).

Warren Douglas Manning

On October 29, 1988, George Tillman Radford, a white South Carolina state trooper and sixteen-year veteran, was shot to death at close range by his own gun while making a routine traffic stop. Warren Douglas Manning was charged with the crime. In his first trial, Manning contended that although he had been arrested by Radford for driving with a suspended license, he fled when Radford stopped another vehicle. Witnesses who saw Manning shortly after the incident reported that his clothing did not show evidence of blood stains. Yet, if Manning had shot the state trooper at close range as suggested by the prosecution, one would expect his clothing to be drenched in blood. Unconvinced of his innocence, the jury in 1989 convicted Manning of the murder of Radford, and he was sentenced to death. In 1991, however, the conviction was reversed and Manning was awarded a new trial in 1993. After one mistrial, Manning was found guilty again, only to have this decision subsequently overturned in 1997. His fourth trial resulted in another mistrial. Not to be deterred, prosecutors sought a fifth trial. This time, however, an expert death penalty attorney, David Bruck, was Manning's defense counsel. After he successfully argued that the case against Manning was entirely circumstantial, the jury deliberated for less than three hours and found Manning not guilty.

Dan L. Bright

The last case involves a wrongful conviction in Orleans Parish, Louisiana, resulting from multiple factors, including insufficient evidence to support the conviction of first-degree murder, prosecutorial misconduct, and the use of an informant or snitch.[17] Twenty-six-year-old Dan Bright was arrested on January 29, 1995, and charged with the robbery and murder of Murray Barnes, who had won $1,000 from a Super Bowl football pool. The district attorney's case against Bright relied heavily on the testimony of Freddie Thompson, a convicted felon in violation of his parole who was drunk at the time of the crime, information that was not disclosed to the jury. Bright was convicted in 1996 and sentenced to death. In 2000 Bright had his conviction for first-degree murder changed to second-degree murder by the Supreme Court of Louisiana due to insufficient evidence to support a first-degree murder conviction. After a subsequent trial resulted in Bright being sentenced to life without parole, the Louisiana Supreme Court on May 25, 2004, overturned his conviction after noting that there was no physical evidence linking him to the crime and questioning the veracity of the testimony provided by the state's witness, Thompson. In vacating the sentence, the court observed that "This conviction, based on the facts of this case which include a failure to disclose what the State now admits is significant impeachment evidence, is not worthy of confidence and thus must be reversed." Without their main witness, the case appeared unwinnable and the prosecution dismissed all charges. On June 14, 2004, Bright was released, after wrongfully serving four years on death row and five additional years in prison. Bright is now participating in the Innocence Project of New Orleans' Exoneree Advocacy Program and is a mentor for at-risk youth (Innocence Project of New Orleans 2009a; Victims of the State 2009).

Conclusion

This chapter has examined some of the 343 wrongful conviction cases involving African American men. The cases were selected to provide the reader with a deeper appreciation and understanding of many of the factors that contribute to wrongful convictions. Although the cases depict a sample of the diversity that exists in the conviction of innocents in the United States, the reader should be cautioned that the cases of wrongful conviction discussed in this book probably reflect only a small fraction of all wrongful convictions. As noted earlier, wrongfully convicted defendants who receive short sentences, innocent defendants who plead guilty to avoid long sentences, and those who are found guilty of crimes that they didn't commit because of the malfeasance and/or nonfeasance of their defense attorneys are typically underrepresented in the literature.

Particularly problematic is the quality of defense counsel because, typically, wrongfully convicted individuals have limited financial resources. Inadequate defense counsel is especially dramatic in capital cases. For example, a study of death-row inmates in Kentucky disclosed that one-fourth of the inmates had been represented by attorneys who were later disbarred, suspended, or incarcerated (Kroll 1991). Anecdotal evidence also suggests the heightened possibility of wrongful conviction if the defendant is poor. In Alabama, for instance, a trial had to be postponed because the defense counsel arrived in court inebriated. The next day, when court resumed, his client was promptly found guilty and sentenced to death. African American defendants in four separate trials in Georgia were represented by attorneys who repeatedly referred to their clients as "niggers." In each case, the defendant was found guilty and sentenced to death. And in Texas, the closing remarks of the defense attorney in a capital case were, "You are an extremely intelligent jury. You've got that man's life in your hands. You can take it or not. That's all I have to say" (cited in Berger, Free, and Searles 2009). His client was eventually executed.

While these anecdotal accounts do not directly address the scope of the problem, they do suggest that wrongful convictions are potentially more commonplace than available data indicate. Chapter 3 examines wrongful convictions involving murder and attempted murder. Because of the seriousness of these offenses, extended sentences and even the death penalty may await the defendant who is falsely convicted.

Notes

1. The Office of the District Attorney of Dallas, Texas, has long been known for its overzealous prosecution of individuals charged with criminal offenses. Since passage of a 2001 Texas law permitting postconviction DNA testing, 464 inmates have requested DNA tests through the Dallas County felony courts (McGonigle 2007). As of 2008, 19 of the more than 40 individuals tested have been exonerated through this process (Lohr 2009). Nearly 70 percent (13 out of 19 cases) of those who were exonerated are African American (McGonigle and Emily 2008).

2. Investigations of the importance of victim race in murder and rape or sexual assault cases suggest that offenders who victimize whites are more likely to receive harsh penalties than those who victimize African Americans (LaFree 1989; Paternoster 1991; Spohn and Spears 1996; Walsh 1987). Furthermore, in capital

cases "the race of the victim is often more significant than the race of the offender, and may reflect not only the devalued status of black victims" but also greater societal outrage over the victimization of a member of the dominant white group (Myers 2000, 460).

3. The terms "black" and "African American" are used interchangeably in this book. Because the Federal Bureau of Investigation and the US Census Bureau employ the category black to describe African Americans, black is used when analyzing data from these sources.

4. This phenomenon is known as "own-race effect" or "own-race bias," although it has not been empirically established that all races are affected by it. In fact, several studies reported by Rutledge (2001) disclosed that African American witnesses do *not* experience difficulty making cross-racial identifications.

5. The wanted poster with Herman Atkins's photograph represents an interesting case as well. In 1986 Atkins was, according to his own account, pursuing a robbery suspect when he fired two shots into the air. After being observed by the police, he panicked and fled, first to Texas and then to Arizona. Arrested during a police sweep, Atkins was informed that he was wanted on nine counts of attempted murder, three of which involved police officers. Apparently, the police felt that what they had witnessed was a drug deal gone sour. Whether the incident was an attempt to foil a robbery or a mishandled drug transaction, it was this incident that led to the poster that resulted in his being identified by the rape victim as the perpetrator of the crime in Lake Elsinore, California.

6. In the video prepared for new prosecutors in Philadelphia, McMahon comments: "The case law says that the object of getting a jury is to get—I wrote it down. I looked in the cases. I had to look this up because I didn't know this was the purpose of a jury: '*Voir dire* is to get a competent, fair, and impartial jury.' Well, that's ridiculous, you're not trying to get that. And the only way you're going to do your best is to get jurors that are as unfair and more likely to convict than anybody else in that room." McMahon further states, "Blacks from the low-income areas are less likely to convict. . . . There's a resentment for law enforcement, there's a resentment for authority, and as a result, you don't want those people on your jury." Additionally, McMahon notes, "People from Mayfair [a white neighborhood] are good and people from 33rd and Diamond [a low-income black neighborhood] stink. . . . You don't want any jurors from 33rd and Diamond" (Goodman 2005; Wilson 2000).

7. Wilson's incompetent defense counsel, Berry, later became a Pennsylvania trial judge in Philadelphia.

8. The rule infractions that resulted in Wilson being sent to solitary confinement were often minor. For example, when being interviewed for *Democracy Now!*, Wilson mentions serving thirty days in solitary confinement for having covered his air vent during the winter to restrict the flow of cold air to his prison cell. While this act would probably be considered by many to be rather inconsequential, it was construed as an act of disobedience by the prison authorities.

9. Two recent books published on this subject are particularly noteworthy. Editors Rob Warren and Steven Drizin (2009) discuss forty-nine false confessions in *True Stories of False Confessions*. An in-depth analysis of four Navy men who falsely confessed to a rape-murder (aka the Norfolk Four) appears in *The Wrong Guys* (Wells and Leo 2009).

10. Given the volume and age of many of the cases contained in this investigation, complete and undisputed information on the events leading to the false confession was often unobtainable. Recognition of these limitations necessitated the use of a single category for all false confessions.

11. William Mahoney was well-known for his unconventional tactics while interrogating suspects. He was investigated for abusing suspects on at least ten occasions and resigned in 1980 when it appeared that he had fabricated evidence against members of organized crime.

12. Earl Washington, Jr., was also convicted in May 1984 of statutory burglary and assault of a seventy-three-year-old woman whose home in Fauquier County, Virginia, was broken into, a gun and money were taken, and the woman was beaten with a chair. He received two consecutive fifteen-year sentences (Green 2000).

13. The federal judge contended that Jones's history of mental health problems and his troubled childhood could have been more effectively researched by defense counsel and used in their arguments for a noncapital sentence.

14. Judge Maloney was subsequently brought to justice himself when a federal court found him guilty of taking bribes in criminal cases. He was further accused of being particularly hard on defendants who did not provide him with financial compensation for his "services."

15. The police detectives who questioned Young, Hill, and Williams had served under Jon Burge, a white Chicago police commander who was fired after Internal Affairs in 1991 found evidence that sixty or more African American men had been tortured while under his supervision. In 2011 Burge was sentenced to four and a half years in federal prison for lying about police torture. He is currently an inmate at Butner Federal Correctional Complex in North Carolina. Approximately twenty men who claimed to have been tortured by the Chicago Police Department's so-called Midnight Crew remain incarcerated as of March 2011 (Harris 2011; "Jon Burge to Begin Prison Term" 2011).

16. It is questionable whether Harold Hill should have been required to stay an additional year in prison, because his prison sentence for armed robbery had been "enhanced" due to his involvement in the Morgan rape and murder.

17. After the conviction, it was learned that the Federal Bureau of Investigation knew the identity of the actual killer but refused to release this information, citing the killer's right to privacy. It was only after assistance from the Innocence Project of New Orleans that a federal district court judge finally ruled that Bright had a constitutional right to be told the identity of the actual killer.

3

Murder and Attempted Murder

To convict someone of murder you really should have evidence
that a killing took place—even in Alabama.
—New York Times *(referring to the Choctaw Three)*

The most common offense for which African American men were wrongfully convicted in the sample is murder/attempted murder.[1] Of the 174
cases included in this offense category, two-thirds contained only murder
charges. More specifically, 93 cases (53.4 percent) included only a single
charge for murder, whereas an additional 23 cases (13.2 percent) included
multiple counts of murder but no other offenses. Among those cases involving additional offenses, the offenses most frequently appearing in the
charges were rape/sexual assault and/or robbery.

Table 3.1 provides the reader with information pertaining to any additional charges as well as the contributing factors in the wrongful conviction for each of the murder cases. In two of the cases (Robert Wallace of
Georgia and Cornell Avery Estes of Maryland) repeated attempts to secure
information that would permit the determination of the contributing factors
to the wrongful convictions were unsuccessful. Information from Table 3.1
suggests that the more common scenario in wrongful murder convictions
involves a situation in which multiple factors coalesce to produce a failure
of justice rather than a single contributing factor (although obviously some
factors are potentially more damaging than others). An analysis of the frequency of the various factors contributing to wrongful convictions discloses that the most common factor is witness error, which is present in
42.5 percent of the murder cases. The second most common factor is police misconduct. This problem occurs in 38.5 percent of the murder cases.
Prosecutorial misconduct is a factor in 36.2 percent of the wrongful mur-

der convictions, placing it in third place. In fourth place is the use of snitches or informants. This factor is found in 33.3 percent of the murder cases. Fifth place belongs to false confessions (18.4 percent). Ineffective assistance of counsel (incompetent defense attorney) is present in 11.5 percent of the cases, making it the sixth most common factor in wrongful murder convictions. Forensic errors, the seventh most common factor, account for 10.3 percent of the murder cases. Each of the remaining factors listed in Table 3.1 is present in less than 7 percent of the wrongful convictions involving murder.

Caution should be exercised in interpreting the above statistics; the actual number of African American men wrongfully convicted for murder is undoubtedly greater than the number of cases identified in this investigation because many miscarriages of justice may go undetected. Nonetheless, the strong presence of witness error, police misconduct, and prosecutorial misconduct suggests the need to examine these factors in greater depth, as they may be related to one another. For example, questionable interrogation practices by the police can contribute to the misidentification of suspects by witnesses. The desire for prosecutors to win a case can encourage the use of unreliable witnesses or the failure to disclose to defense counsel that some witnesses failed to identify the defendant as the perpetrator. The following two sections examine cases in which these factors played a prominent role in wrongful murder convictions.

Witness Error in Wrongful Murder Convictions

As previously observed, witness error is present in slightly over four of every ten murder cases. Trials involving Clarence Brandley, Anthony Porter, Walter McMillian, Madison Mobley, John Duval, Darby Tillis, and Perry Cobb—all cases in which witness error contributed to wrongful conviction—were discussed in Chapter 2. This section analyzes six additional instances in which witness error led to a miscarriage of justice.

Ryan Matthews and Travis Hayes

A botched robbery in Louisiana on April 5, 1997, eventually led to the wrongful conviction of two borderline mentally retarded seventeen-year-olds—Ryan Matthews and Travis Hayes. During the attempted robbery of Comeaux's grocery store in Bridge City, the perpetrator, wearing a ski mask, shot the store's owner, Tommy Vanhoose, four times when he refused to hand over the money. The perpetrator then ran away, removing his ski

Table 3.1 Factors in Wrongful Convictions in Murder and Attempted Murder Cases (N=174)

Name	State	Additional Charge(s)	Contributing Factors
Medell Banks, Jr.	AL	None	Police misconduct, false confession, insufficient evidence
Melvin Todd Beamon	AL	None	Police misconduct, perjury by criminal justice officials, witness error, false confession
James "Bo" Cochran	AL	Robbery	Prosecutorial misconduct
Freddie Lee Gaines	AL	Double murder	Witness error
Walter McMillian	AL	Rape	Prosecutorial misconduct, police misconduct, witness error
Freddie Lee Wright	AL	Double murder, robbery	Snitch/informant, prosecutorial misconduct, police misconduct, ineffective assistance of counsel
Christopher McCrimmon	AZ	Triple murder, robbery, aggravated robbery, burglary	Snitch/informant, prosecutorial misconduct, police misconduct, perjury by criminal justice officials, judicial misconduct
Andre Minnitt	AZ	Triple murder, robbery, aggravated robbery, burglary	Snitch/informant, prosecutorial misconduct, police misconduct, perjury by criminal justice officials, judicial misconduct
Eugene Allen	CA	None	Prosecutorial misconduct
Timothy Atkins	CA	Robbery	Snitch/informant, witness error
Clarence Chance	CA	None	Snitch/informant, police misconduct, witness error
Tony Cooks	CA	None	Snitch/informant, police misconduct, witness error
Antoine Goff	CA	None	Prosecutorial misconduct
Ernest (Shuhaa) Graham	CA	None	Prosecutorial misconduct
Willie Earl Green	CA	None	Police misconduct, witness error
Harold Hall	CA	Double murder, rape	Snitch/informant, police misconduct, false confession, insufficient evidence
Troy Lee Jones	CA	None	Ineffective assistance of counsel
Dwayne McKinney	CA	Robbery	Prosecutorial misconduct, police misconduct, witness error
Oscar Lee Morris	CA	Robbery	Snitch/informant, prosecutorial misconduct

continues

63

Table 3.1 *continued*

Name	State	Additional Charge(s)	Contributing Factors
Aaron Lee Owens	CA	Double murder	Witness error
Benny Powell	CA	None	Snitch/informant, police misconduct, witness error
Elmer "Geronimo" Pratt	CA	None	Snitch/informant, police misconduct
John Tennison	CA	None	Prosecutorial misconduct, police misconduct, witness error
Bradford Brown	DC	None	Witness error
James Adams	FL	None	Witness error
Anthony Brown	FL	None	Snitch/informant
Joseph Green (Shabaka) Brown	FL	Rape, robbery	Snitch/informant, prosecutorial misconduct, forensic errors
Timothy Brown	FL	None	False confession
Willie Brown	FL	None	Snitch/informant
Kevin Coleman	FL	None	Prosecutorial misconduct, witness error
Johnny Frederick	FL	None	Witness error, false confession
Joseph Nahume Green	FL	None	Witness error
Robert Earl Hayes	FL	Rape	Prosecutorial misconduct, forensic errors
Rudolph Holton	FL	Rape	Prosecutorial misconduct, forensic errors
David Keaton	FL	Robbery	Witness error, false confession
Anthony Ray Peek	FL	None	Forensic errors
Derrick Robinson	FL	None	Witness error, false confession
Frank Lee Smith	FL	Rape	Witness error
Gilbert Stokes	FL	None	Snitch/informant, judicial misconduct
Delbert Lee Tibbs	FL	Rape	Snitch/informant, witness error
Jerry Frank Townsend	FL	Six murders, rape	False confession
Larry Troy	FL	None	Snitch/informant
Jerry Banks	GA	Double murder	Prosecutorial misconduct
Earl Patrick Charles	GA	Double murder, robbery	Snitch/informant, police misconduct, witness error

64

Table 3.1 *continued*

Name	State	Additional Charge(s)	Contributing Factors
Walter McIntosh	GA	Double murder	False confession
Gary Nelson	GA	Rape	Prosecutorial misconduct, witness error, forensic errors
Robert Wallace	GA	None	n/a
Kenneth Adams	IL	Double murder, rape	Prosecutorial misconduct, police misconduct, witness error, forensic errors
Randy Boss	IL	None	Prosecutorial misconduct
Revell Boss	IL	None	Prosecutorial misconduct
Marcellius Bradford	IL	Rape, robbery, aggravated kidnapping	False confession, forensic errors
Robert Brown	IL	None	Prosecutorial misconduct, witness error
LaVale Burt	IL	None	Police misconduct, false confession
Perry Cobb	IL	Double murder, robbery	Snitch/informant, witness error, judicial misconduct
Michael Evans	IL	Rape, kidnapping	Snitch/informant
Sammie Garrett	IL	None	Ineffective assistance of counsel
Hubert Geralds	IL	None	False confession
Harold Hill	IL	Rape	Police misconduct, false confession, forensic errors
Madison Hobley	IL	7 counts each: felony murder, aggravated arson; 1 count: arson	Prosecutorial misconduct, police misconduct, perjury by criminal justice officials, witness error, false confession, juror intimidation
Dana Holland	IL	Robbery, sexual assault	Perjury by criminal justice officials, witness error
Elton Houston	IL	None	Prosecutorial misconduct, witness error
Stanley Howard	IL	Attempted armed robbery	Prosecutorial misconduct, police misconduct, witness error, false confession
Verneal Jimerson	IL	Robbery, kidnapping	Prosecutorial misconduct, police misconduct, witness error, ineffective assistance of counsel
Henry Johnson	IL	None	Police misconduct, witness error
Juan Johnson	IL	None	Police misconduct, witness error
Ronald Jones	IL	Rape	Police misconduct, false confession

continues

Table 3.1 *continued*

Name	State	Additional Charge(s)	Contributing Factors
Carl Lawson	IL	None	Police misconduct
Lloyd Lindsey	IL	Murder (4 counts)	Witness error, false confession
Alton Logan	IL	None	Witness error
James Newsome	IL	Robbery, armed violence	Police misconduct, witness error
Calvin Ollins	IL	Robbery, kidnapping, sexual assault	False confession, expert witness misconduct
Larry Ollins	IL	Robbery, sexual assault	Witness error, expert witness misconduct
Leroy Orange	IL	Murder (4 counts), concealment of a homicidal death (4 counts), robbery, aggravated arson	Police misconduct, false confession, ineffective assistance of counsel
Aaron Patterson	IL	Double murder	Snitch/informant, police misconduct, false confession
Anthony Porter	IL	Double murder, robbery, unlawful restraint, unlawful use of weapons (2 counts)	Police misconduct, witness error, ineffective assistance of counsel
Willie Rainge	IL	Double murder, rape	Police misconduct, witness error
Omar Saunders	IL	Robbery, kidnapping, sexual assault	Snitch/informant, police misconduct, expert witness misconduct
Steven Smith	IL	None	Snitch/informant
Paul Terry	IL	Rape, aggravated kidnapping, deviate sexual assault, indecent liberties with a child	Snitch/informant
Franklin Thompson	IL	None	False confession
Darby Tillis	IL	Double murder, robbery	Snitch/informant, witness error, judicial misconduct
Dennis Williams	IL	Double murder, rape	Snitch/informant, prosecutorial misconduct, police misconduct, witness error, forensic errors, ineffective assistance of counsel

Table 3.1 *continued*

Name	State	Additional Charge(s)	Contributing Factors
Dan Young, Jr.	IL	Rape	Police misconduct, false confession, forensic errors
Larry Hicks	IN	Double murder	Witness error, ineffective assistance of counsel
Charles Smith	IN	Robbery	Snitch/informant, witness error, ineffective assistance of counsel
James Hall	IA	None	Prosecutorial misconduct
Terry Harrington	IA	None	Prosecutorial misconduct, police misconduct, witness error
Curtis McGhee, Jr.	IA	None	Prosecutorial misconduct, police misconduct
David Alexander	LA	Robbery	Snitch/informant, police misconduct, perjury by criminal justice officials
Dan L. Bright	LA	Robbery	Snitch/informant, prosecutorial misconduct, insufficient evidence
Shareef Cousin	LA	None	Prosecutorial misconduct
Harry Granger	LA	Robbery	Snitch/informant, police misconduct, perjury by criminal justice officials
Travis Hayes	LA	None	Police misconduct, witness error, false confession
Curtis Kyles	LA	None	Snitch/informant, prosecutorial misconduct, witness error
Dwight Labran	LA	None	Snitch/informant, prosecutorial misconduct
Ryan Matthews	LA	None	Prosecutorial misconduct, witness error, ineffective assistance of counsel, judicial misconduct
John Thompson	LA	None	Prosecutorial misconduct
Calvin Williams	LA	None	Prosecutorial misconduct
Ronald Addison	MD	Gun possession	Prosecutorial misconduct, witness error
Michael Austin	MD	Robbery	Prosecutorial misconduct, police misconduct, witness error, ineffective assistance of counsel
Cornell Avery Estes	MD	None	n/a
Anthony Gray, Jr.	MD	Rape	Snitch/informant, false confession, ineffective assistance of counsel
Eric D. Lynn	MD	None	Snitch/informant, prosecutorial misconduct

continues

67

Table 3.1 *continued*

Name	State	Additional Charge(s)	Contributing Factors
Laurence Adams	MA	Robbery	Snitch/informant, police misconduct
Christian Amado	MA	None	Witness error, insufficient evidence
Stephan Cowans	MA	Home invasion, assault & battery by means of a dangerous weapon, robbery, assault & battery on a police officer, assault by means of a dangerous weapon, unlicensed possession of a firearm	Police misconduct, perjury by criminal justice officials, witness error, forensic errors
Shawn Drumgold	MA	None	Police misconduct, witness error
Frank Grace	MA	None	Police misconduct, insufficient evidence
Donnell Johnson	MA	None	Police misconduct, perjury by criminal justice officials, witness error
Lawyer Johnson	MA	None	Snitch/informant
Bobby Joe Leaster	MA	None	Witness error, ineffective assistance of counsel
Marlon Passley	MA	None	Witness error
Louis Santos	MA	None	Police misconduct, witness error
Eddie Joe Lloyd	MI	Rape	Police misconduct, false confession
Dwight Love	MI	None	Police misconduct
Claude McCollum	MI	Rape	Prosecutorial misconduct, police misconduct, false confession
Vidale McDowell	MI	None	Snitch/informant, police misconduct
Kennedy Brewer	MS	Rape	Forensic errors
Levon Brooks	MS	Rape	Forensic errors
Cedric Willis	MS	Robbery, rape, aggravated assault	Witness error, prosecutorial misconduct

Table 3.1 *continued*

Name	State	Additional Charge(s)	Contributing Factors
Joseph Amrine	MO	None	Snitch/informant, ineffective assistance of counsel
Darryl Burton	MO	None	Snitch/informant, prosecutorial misconduct
Eric Clemmons	MO	None	Perjury by criminal justice officials
Byron Halsey	NJ	2 counts each: felony murder, aggravated manslaughter, aggravated sexual assault, child abuse; 1 count: possession of weapon	Snitch/informant, police misconduct, false confession
Larry Peterson	NJ	Aggravated sexual assault	Snitch/informant, police misconduct, witness error, forensic errors
Damaso Vega	NJ	None	Witness error
Van Bering Robinson	NM	None	Police misconduct
Terry Seaton	NM	None	Snitch informant, prosecutorial misconduct
Kareem Bellamy	NY	None	Witness error
Lamont Branch	NY	None	Snitch/informant, police misconduct
Lazaro Burt	NY	None	Witness error
Nathaniel Carter	NY	None	Snitch/informant
John Duval	NY	None	Prosecutorial misconduct, police misconduct, perjury by criminal justice officials, witness error, false confession
Anthony Faison	NY	None	Snitch/informant
Edmond Jackson	NY	None	Prosecutorial misconduct, witness error, insufficient evidence
William Maynard	NY	None	Prosecutorial misconduct, witness error
Kevin Richardson	NY	Rape, sodomy, robbery	Police misconduct, false confession, forensic errors

continues

Table 3.1 *continued*

Name	State	Additional Charge(s)	Contributing Factors
Charles Shepard Dhoruba al-Mujahid bin Wahad (aka Richard Moore)	NY	None	Snitch/informant
	NY	None	Snitch/informant, prosecutorial misconduct
Glen Chapman	NC	Double murder	Prosecutorial misconduct, police misconduct, perjury by criminal justice officials, ineffective assistance of counsel
Jonathon Hoffman	NC	None	Snitch/informant, prosecutorial misconduct
Darryl Hunt	NC	Rape	Prosecutorial misconduct, police misconduct, witness error
Levon "Bo" Jones	NC	Robbery, conspiracy	Snitch/informant, police misconduct
Charles Munsey	NC	None	Snitch/informant, prosecutorial misconduct
Samuel A. Poole	NC	None	Insufficient evidence
Christopher Spicer	NC	None	Snitch/informant, judicial misconduct
Daniel Brown	OH	Rape	Witness error
Timothy Howard	OH	Robbery	Prosecutorial misconduct, police misconduct, witness error
Gary Lamar James	OH	Robbery	Prosecutorial misconduct, police misconduct, witness error
Derrick Jamison	OH	Robbery	Snitch/informant, prosecutorial misconduct
Harllel Jones	OH	Kidnapping	Snitch/informant
Rasheem Matthew	OH	None	Prosecutorial misconduct
Allan Thrower	OH	None	Police misconduct
Charles Ray Giddens	OK	None	Snitch/informant, prosecutorial misconduct, insufficient evidence
Robert Lee Miller, Jr.	OK	2 counts each: murder, rape, burglary; 1 count: attempted burglary	Police misconduct, false confession, insufficient evidence
Adolph Munson	OK	Kidnapping	Prosecutorial misconduct, forensic errors

Table 3.1 *continued*

Name	State	Additional Charge(s)	Contributing Factors
Edward Baker	PA	Robbery	Snitch/informant, ineffective assistance of counsel
Matthew Connor	PA	Rape	Prosecutorial misconduct, police misconduct, witness error
Riky Jackson	PA	None	Forensic errors
Edward Ryder	PA	None	Prosecutorial misconduct
Drew Whitley	PA	None	Snitch/informant, prosecutorial misconduct, witness error
Harold Wilson	PA	Triple murder	Prosecutorial misconduct, ineffective assistance of counsel
Tyrone James	SC	None	Police misconduct
Warren Douglas Manning	SC	None	Insufficient evidence
Winfred Peterson	SC	None	Police misconduct
Clarence Lee Brandley	TX	Rape	Prosecutorial misconduct, police misconduct, witness error
Ben Spencer	TX	Aggravated robbery	Snitch/informant, witness error
Calvin Washington	TX	Rape	Snitch/informant
Joe Sidney Williams	TX	Rape	Snitch/informant, forensic errors
James Lee Woodard	TX	Rape	Prosecutorial misconduct, police misconduct, witness error
Russell Leon Gray	VA	None	Witness error
Troy D. Hopkins	VA	None	Witness error
Earl Washington, Jr.	VA	Rape	Police misconduct, false confession, ineffective assistance of counsel
Benjamin J. Harris III	WA	None	False confession, ineffective assistance of counsel

Note: n/a = not available.

71

mask, gloves, and shirt after jumping through an open window of a getaway vehicle. Several eyewitnesses were present at the scene when the crime was committed. Subsequently, two eyewitnesses who were outside the store during the shooting identified Ryan Matthews as the assailant. Matthews and Hayes were stopped by the police approximately four hours later because their 1981 Grand Prix, which belonged to Hayes's sister, resembled the description of the getaway vehicle. After six hours of intensive questioning by the police in which Hayes was denied food, sleep, or bathroom breaks, he finally succumbed to the questioning and confessed that he was the driver of the getaway car and Matthews was the assailant. During the trial, defense counsel provided evidence that forensic examinations of the assailant's discarded ski mask excluded Matthews and Hayes as the perpetrators. The defense counsel additionally noted that the window the assailant allegedly used to enter the vehicle was inoperative and would not roll down in the automobile the two defendants were driving when the police arrested them. Nevertheless, in 1998 Matthews was convicted of murder and sentenced to death primarily on the basis of eyewitness testimony. Hayes was convicted of second-degree murder and sentenced to life.

Matthews's innocence came to light only as a result of another murder in the same vicinity. Rondell Love, who later pleaded guilty to another murder, bragged to other inmates that he was also responsible for the death of Vanhoose. Moreover, Love (5'7") matched the description of the assailant provided by witnesses who were inside the store when the incident occurred. (Witnesses inside the store had described the assailant as between 5'4" and 5'7"; Matthews is 6'1".) Given the new evidence, Matthews was granted a new trial. In June 2004 Matthews was released on bond while awaiting trial. In August of the same year prosecutors vacated the conviction. Finally, on December 20, 2006, Hayes was released from prison and all charges against him were dropped on January 17, 2007 (Innocence Project of New Orleans 2010; Perlstein 2004).

Kenneth Adams

In 1978 in Cook County, Illinois, a white woman, Carol Schmal, and her white fiancé, Lawrence Lionberg, were abducted from a gasoline station and driven to an abandoned townhouse in the Ford Heights area. Schmal was raped repeatedly before both victims were killed. Kenneth Adams became a police suspect when Charles McCraney, who lived in proximity to the crime, identified him as one of the four men he saw in that vicinity at about the same time as the murders. Police also questioned seventeen-year-old Paula Gray, a borderline mentally retarded woman. After undergoing questioning for two nights, Gray testified before a grand jury that she was present when Adams and three other men (who would later be known as the Ford Heights Four) engaged in rape and murder. When Gray later recanted her story, claiming that she fabricated it because she felt threatened by the police, she was charged with the murders and perjury. Without Gray's statement, Adams's conviction relied heavily on Mc-Craney's testimony and forensic evidence, which was later found to be both unreliable and false. After being sentenced to seventy-five years in prison for his involvement in the crime, Adams's request for a new trial was denied. Eventually the Center on Wrongful Convictions at Northwestern University became interested in his case. During the investigation, journalism students from Northwestern University found a police report containing exculpatory evidence. The report revealed that within a week of the crime a witness had come forward who had seen four men fleeing the crime scene and the next day saw them selling personal items taken from the victims. None of the Ford Heights Four defendants was identified by the witness. Despite the potential significance of this revelation, the police failed to pursue the lead. Moreover, neither the police nor the prosecutor provided the defense with this information, contrary to *Brady v. Maryland* (1963).[2] DNA testing eventually exonerated all four men, and three of the actual perpetrators later confessed to the crime.[3] All members of the Ford Heights Four were released from prison in 1996 and received pardons from Illinois Governor Jim Edgar.

Dwayne McKinney

Many wrongfully convicted defendants have checkered histories that make it easy for prosecutors to depict them as guilty. The story of Dwayne McKinney of California is no exception. His mother, a single parent who suffered from a heart condition, died when McKinney was twelve years of age. Her death led to a series of moves in which he lived with various relatives. By age fifteen, however, McKinney had become familiar with the street life and joined the 52nd Street Crips. While a teenager he was arrested for the theft of an automobile and spent time in jail for an attempted robbery. Just a month before he was arrested and charged with the murder of a night manager at a Burger King in Orange, California, he was shot in the leg by a rival gang, which impeded his ability to walk.

His arrest, six days after the murder, resulted from the photo identification of him by four white restaurant employees who were present during the crime. With no physical evidence linking McKinney to the crime, Orange County District Attorney Tony Rackauckas focused on the testimony of the four eyewitnesses. Although McKinney had his own witnesses who testified that he was with them at his home in Ontario, California, some thirty miles away at the time when the crime occurred, Rackauckas "used thinly veiled racist comments to denigrate the credibility of these witnesses, who were all low-income African Americans" (Sherrer 2000). Moreover, some of the information obtained from the eyewitnesses contradicted the available evidence. Two of the witnesses, for instance, initially described the perpetrator as a cleanly shaven African American man who walked fast. Yet McKinney had a beard and walked with a distinct limp, a result of the drive-by shooting a month earlier. Unable to agree on the death penalty, which the district attorney had recommended, the jury settled on life without parole.

Life in prison was unkind to McKinney, who had decided to sever his ties with the Crips prior to incarceration. With no gang affiliation to afford him protection, he was stabbed multiple times during the nearly twenty years that he spent in prison. Then, in 1997, he received a break. Willie Charles Walker, a convicted felon, confessed that he drove the getaway vehicle and implicated his partner, Raymond Herman Jacquet, as the shooter. As a result of this new information McKinney's case was revisited. In 2000 a Superior Court judge ordered that McKinney be released. McKinney was released with $200 in cash and new street clothes.

After he was freed, an investigator who had assisted in his exoneration helped him get adjusted to life outside of prison. The investigator purchased clothes, helped him secure a driver's license, and got him a job at the University of California–Irvine. Two years later, a successful lawsuit against those responsible for his wrongful conviction netted McKinney $1 million. Careful not to squander this newfound fortune, he made a prudent decision to invest in the growing ATM business in South Central Los Angeles. While on vacation in Hawaii, he decided that given the tourist industry in that state, it was a fertile ground for his ATM business. He eventually owned thirty-eight machines, making him the second largest ATM operator in Hawaii. Unfortunately, McKinney's story ends on a sad note. In October 2008, while riding his motor scooter, he was killed when he lost control and hit a wooden light pole in Honolulu. McKinney died at the age of forty-seven (Associated Press News 1999; Fulginiti, Redmond, and Johnson 2008; Morales 2005; Pfeifer 2008; Sherrer 2000).

Donnell Johnson

Although the probability of offender misidentification by a witness is greater in a cross-racial encounter, it would be a mistake to assume that witness error does not occur when the offender and the witness are from the same racial group. The case involving Donnell Johnson from Massachusetts illustrates the latter.

Jermaine Goffigan was innocently sitting outside his grandmother's apartment building at the Academy Homes housing project counting his Halloween candy when shots rang out. The victim of gang cross fire, Goffigan was dead at the young age of nine. Sixteen-year-old Donnell Johnson was arrested the next day after the victim's mother, brother, and an unrelated witness identified him as one of two gunmen who fled after firing shots. The shooting supposedly was in retaliation for an earlier incident in which members of the Heath Street gang were injured. Johnson was convicted of the murder of Goffigan twice—once by a judge in March 1996 and again by a jury in November 1996—primarily on the eyewitness testimony of the victim's family. However, during the first trial the police did not disclose to Johnson's lawyer an interview they had with Johnson suggesting that during the crime he was home watching *Monday Night Football* on television. The interview was not acknowledged by the police until midway through the second trial. Moreover, Boston Police Sergeant Detective William Mahoney had previously testified that Johnson was uncooperative and refused an interview. Johnson's freedom came unexpectedly in 2000 when a federal drug investigation at the Bromley-Heath project resulted in testimony that exonerated Johnson. Despite that testimony, Goffigan's grandmother remains convinced that Johnson was her grandson's assassin. After being informed that Johnson was to be released because criminal justice officials now believed that Johnson had been wrongfully convicted due to the "mistaken" testimony of eyewitnesses, she told reporters, "All I have to say is the criminal justice (system) here in Boston, Massachusetts, killed my grandson again. They put a bullet in him again" (Murphy and Ellement 2000).

Darryl Hunt

Deborah Sykes was an attractive twenty-five-year-old brunette who moved with her husband from Tennessee to North Carolina during the summer of 1984. Sykes went to work at the *Sentinel,* a newspaper in Winston-Salem, where she edited stories and wrote headlines. On August 10, 1984, however, she didn't show up for work. Later that day the police found her body. She had been stabbed sixteen times, raped, and sodomized. The pathologist collected semen from her vagina and anus, hairs from her thighs and mouth, as well as foreign substances from under her fingernails. The knife used to kill her was never recovered.

Witnesses who saw Sykes, a white woman, early the morning of her demise varied in their accounts of that day. Some said that she was accompanied by two black men; others recalled seeing only one black man. Initial composite drawings developed by the police did not resemble Hunt. Although witnesses described a man with medium-brown skin and short cropped hair, nineteen-year-old Hunt was dark-skinned and wore cornrows. And the state's lead witness, Johnny Gray, who spent much of his time in pool halls, initially identified a different assailant when he first talked to the police almost two weeks after the incident. Yet Hunt was convicted, twice, primarily on the basis of witness accounts that contradicted his alibi or placed him at the crime scene. The racial composition of the jury probably contributed to this verdict as well. In the first trial only one black was seated on the jury, despite the fact that the county is almost one-fourth black. In a change of venue, the second trial was moved to rural Catawba, where there were no black jurors.

As questions regarding Hunt's guilt lingered, he was offered a chance for freedom in 1990. If he would admit his guilt, he would be released after being given credit for time served. In 1993, after having refused the earlier offer, Hunt was given the possibility of having his life sentence reduced to forty years if he would admit guilt. Again, he refused the offer. His release appeared imminent in 1994 when new DNA tests excluded him as Sykes's killer. The prosecutor, however, chose not to release Hunt at this time because he still believed that Hunt could have had some involvement in the crime. After promising to find the individual whose DNA matched the semen sample, District Attorney Tom Keith never tested any new suspects. Finally, on December 22, 2003, Willard Brown confessed to the rape and murder of Sykes, and DNA tests could not exclude him as the contributor. Pending a hearing, Hunt was released on bond on Christmas Eve of 2003. His conviction was vacated on February 6, 2004, after over eighteen years of incarceration. The governor of North Carolina granted a full pardon to Hunt on April 15, 2004, and he eventually won $2.4 million in compensation for his time in prison (Zerwick 2003).

Police and Prosecutorial Misconduct in Wrongful Murder Convictions

The second and third most common factors in wrongful murder convictions are police misconduct and prosecutorial misconduct, respectively. Each is present in over one-third of the murder convictions. Police and/or prosecutorial misconduct were present in the wrongful murder convictions of Clarence Brandley, Eddie Joe Lloyd, Anthony Porter, James "Bo" Cochran, Walter McMillian, Harold Wilson, Ernest Graham, Eugene Allen, Madison

Hobley, John Duval, Earl Washington, Jr., Levon "Bo" Jones, Dan Young, Jr., Harold Hill, and Dan L. Bright, as highlighted in the preceding chapter. Additionally, all six cases discussed in the previous section exhibited signs of police and/or prosecutorial misconduct. This section commences with what is arguably the most bizarre case uncovered by this research, a fifteen-year sentence for the murder of a nonexistent infant.

Medell Banks, Jr.

The history of wrongful convictions includes cases in which defendants were convicted even though the bodies of their alleged victims were missing. In 1987, for example, on the centennial anniversary of the hanging of William Jackson Marion for the murder of a man who was discovered alive four years later, Nebraska governor Bob Kerrey posthumously pardoned the deceased victim of failed justice. More recently, in 1975 Antonio Rivera and Merla Walpole were convicted of murdering their daughter. While they were appealing their incarceration, their daughter was found alive in San Francisco.

Although cases such as these permeate the history of wrongful convictions, the story of the so-called Choctaw Three from Alabama departs from this scenario in that the victim never existed. A chronicle of the events leading up to the wrongful conviction of two women and one man begins in February 1999. Twenty-seven-year-old Victoria Banks, an impoverished African American woman with an IQ of 40, was in the Choctaw County jail in Butner, Alabama, when she concocted a story that she was pregnant, hoping to be released.[4] Although the first doctor to examine her could not substantiate her claim, the second doctor thought he heard the faint heart beat of a fetus. Neither doctor conducted a pelvic examination and no tests were run to corroborate her statement. She was subsequently released because the jail had no provisions for prenatal care. In August 1999 the Choctaw County sheriff approached Victoria Banks to inquire about her baby. After she informed him that she had miscarried the fetus, the sheriff became suspicious and had her visit the office of the second doctor who had examined her in the jail. The examination found no evidence of a pregnancy. Shortly thereafter, she was questioned by the police, as were her estranged husband, Medell Banks, Jr., and her sister, Dianne Tucker. All three admitted to the police that Victoria Banks was never pregnant and that she had had a tubal ligation in 1995, making pregnancy impossible. Medell Banks, who has an IQ of 57, was interrogated over several days without benefit of an attorney. He consistently maintained that "he knew nothing about a dead baby" until the last night when he reluctantly agreed with the police that "he heard a baby cry," after which he asked if he could go home (Sherrer 2003, February).[5] It was this "confession" that was used in his trial to convict him of killing the phantom infant. Despite an absence of physical evidence that an infant ever existed, all three were convicted of manslaughter after initially being indicted for capital murder. All members of the Choctaw Three received terms of fifteen years in prison.

Rick Hutchinson and Jim Evans, Medell Banks's court-appointed attorneys, however, were determined to have their client acquitted. Money was raised to perform a hysterosalpingogram (HSG) on Victoria Banks, which would prove that she could not have naturally conceived a child. Dr. Michael Steinkampf, a noted fertility expert and the director of Reproductive Endocrinology and Fertility at the University of Alabama's School of Medicine, concluded that it was physically impossible for Victoria Banks to have become pregnant. On July 16, 2001, Banks's attorneys filed a motion to withdraw his guilty plea and two days later requested a retrial. On September 28, 2001, Judge McPhearson denied the request and the decision was appealed. The Alabama Court of Appeals reversed the earlier ruling on August 9, 2002, and permitted Medell Banks to withdraw his guilty plea. Given the adverse publicity and the absence of any evidence to substantiate the accusations, the Choctaw County prosecutor sought to save face by offering to drop the capital murder charge being sought in the retrial and allowing Medell Banks to plead guilty to a misdemeanor charge of tampering with unspecified evidence, although the prosecutor had admitted during a 2002 interview with a *New York Times* columnist that there was no physical evidence in the case. Finally, on January 10, 2003, Medell Banks was released after serving forty-one months for a nonexistent crime. Dianne Tucker had been released on July 17, 2002, after having been resentenced to one year in jail and one day on probation. Because Victoria Banks was imprisoned for an earlier conviction, her resentencing was postponed. The convictions of Victoria Banks and Dianne Tucker for the death of an infant remained intact as of July 2008 ("Expert Testimony" 2009; Luo 2002; Sherrer 2003, February, March; Webb 2009).

Freddie Lee Wright

An earlier case from Alabama also raises questions about the fairness of the criminal justice system in that state. In Mount Vernon, a city in southern Alabama, a white couple—forty-year-old Warren Green and his thirty-seven-year-old wife, Lois—owned and managed a Western Auto store. On December 1, 1977, robbers took them to the back of their store, tied them, and shot them in the head. After learning about the crime from the news media, Mary Johnson, who was exiting the store before the incident, contacted the police; she identified a man she saw entering the store as Theodore Otis Roberts. Although the handgun used in the slayings belonged to Roberts, charges against him were eventually dropped and four other African American men, one of whom was Freddie Lee Wright, were indicted. Wright was almost acquitted in his first trial when the mixed-race jury voted 11–1 to acquit. During that trial there was no physical evidence connecting Wright to the crime. Wright's alleged accomplices—Roger McQueen, Percy Craig, and Reginald Tinsley—were offered leniency if they would testify against him, and so they initially testified that Wright was the gunman.[6] However, when McQueen and Craig considered recanting their statements, the prosecutor threatened them with the death penalty. But in a written affidavit prior to the trial, Tinsley identified another man as the assassin. Johnson was never called to testify on Wright's behalf.

After the first trial culminated in a hung jury, a second trial was scheduled. During *voir dire* no African Americans were chosen to serve as jurors. The state presented a new witness, Doris Lacey Lambert, who was Wright's former lover and the mother of his child.[7] Lambert was prone to hallucinations and used drugs, but this information was withheld from the jury. It is also believed that Lambert was offered assistance in regaining custody of her children as an incentive to testify against Wright.[8] An all-white jury in 1979 found Wright guilty of capital murder and sentenced him to die in the electric chair. Wright's attorney, who continued to represent him while appealing the verdict, was later disbarred. At 12:11 a.m. on March 3, 2000, Wright was executed when, in a 7–2 decision, the Alabama Supreme Court failed to grant a stay of execution. In a dissent, Justice Douglas Johnstone of Mobile, Alabama, wrote: "Whether Wright is electrocuted or injected seems insignificant compared to the likelihood that we are sending an innocent man to his death" (Canadian Coalition Against the Death Penalty 2001; "Freddie Lee Wright: Executed March 3, 2000 by Electric Chair in Alabama" 2009; "Freddie Lee Wright: Petition for a Writ of Certiorari" 1999; Wright 1999).

Chris McCrimmon and Andre Minnitt

Around 10:15 p.m. on June 24, 1992, Tucson, Arizona, police responded to a 911 call from a resident living near the El Grande Market, who reported hearing what sounded like firecrackers. Arriving on the scene, the officers found the bodies of three men. Fred Gee, the manager, and Zwan Wong, Gee's uncle and store employee, were dead at the scene. Raymond Arriola, also an employee of the market, died while in transit to a local hospital. Investigators at the murder scene found no evidence that the victims had struggled with their assailants or tried to escape. Although ostensibly the motive was robbery, this interpretation of the crime fails to account for the fact that the perpetrators absconded with approximately $300 while ignoring thousands of dollars in cash in cigarette cartons in the back of the store (Corella and Duarte 1992; Toobin 2005).

Later that summer, Keith Woods, a three-time felon who had recently been released from prison, was arrested on drug charges. On September 8, 1992, in return for having his drug charges dismissed, Woods implicated Chris McCrimmon, Andre Minnitt, and Martin Soto-Fong, a seventeen-year-old high school dropout, in the triple slaying. McCrimmon, Minnitt, and Soto-Fong were subsequently charged with first-degree murder, armed robbery, aggravated robbery, and burglary.[9] Woods also implicated McCrimmon and Minnitt in a robbery and shooting at Mariano's Pizza.

In 1993, in separate trials, McCrimmon and Minnitt were found guilty and sentenced to death. However, in 1996 the Arizona Supreme Court overturned their death sentences due to jury error and ordered new trials for both defendants. After a mistrial was declared in 1997, Minnitt was found guilty during a third trial and again sentenced to death in 1999. During McCrimmon's retrial, Tucson homicide detective Joseph Godoy confessed that he gave false testimony regarding information obtained on the three men charged with the crime. A jury in 1997 acquitted McCrimmon of the murder charges. In 2002 the Arizona Supreme Court vacated the conviction and death sentence of Minnitt when it found that Kenneth Peasley, the lead prosecutor, had solicited false testimony from Godoy during the first two trials of Minnitt and McCrimmon.[10] Additionally, the third trial of Minnitt constituted a violation of the double-jeopardy law. McCrimmon and Minnitt, who were found guilty in the Mariano's Pizza trial on the basis of Woods's questionable testimony,[11] remain incarcerated for the shooting and robbery of that establishment on August 26, 1992, and are not eligible for release until 2023 (Arizona Supreme Court oral argument case summary 2002; "El Grande Murder Conviction Tossed Out" 2002; Toobin 2005).

Use of Informants/Snitches in Wrongful Murder Convictions

The fourth most common contributing factor to the conviction of innocents in murder cases is the testimony of snitches or informants, which is defined by the Center on Wrongful Convictions as witnesses who have an incentive to lie. As discussed in Chapter 2, testimony from snitches contributed to the wrongful convictions of Edward Baker, Levon "Bo" Jones, Darby Tillis, Percy Cobb, Calvin Washington, Joe Sidney Williams, and Dan L. Bright. In this chapter, false testimony by snitches was one of several factors in the wrongful convictions of Freddie Lee Wright, Chris Mc-Crimmon, and Andre Minnitt. This section examines four additional cases in which the false testimony of snitches was primarily responsible for the miscarriage of justice.

Joseph Amrine

While incarcerated in a Missouri supermax prison for robbery, burglary, and forgery, Joseph Amrine of St. Louis was convicted of the murder of Gary "Fox" Barber, a fellow inmate, on October 30, 1986. With no physical evidence linking him to the murder, the state relied on the testimony of three inmates. Terry Russell, one the three informants, was himself a suspect in the murder. Six other inmates, however, stated that Amrine was playing cards during the time the crime was committed. Despite inconsistent statements by the informants, his court-appointed attorney failed to convince the jury of his client's innocence, and Amrine was sentenced to death.

In 1989, during a postconviction hearing, Russell and another informant, Randall Ferguson, recanted their testimony, admitting that they lied in exchange for protection.[12] And in 1997 the third informant, Jerry Poe, recanted his testimony. Prior to 1997, appeals on behalf of Amrine were denied because Poe's testimony still implicated him. Subsequent appeals were denied on the basis of Poe's unreliable retraction. After four unsuccessful appeals and an unsuccessful request for a gubernatorial pardon, Amrine's attorneys, Sean O'Brien and Kent Gipson, finally appealed his case to the Missouri Supreme Court. Arguing that the Supreme Court did not have jurisdiction over the case because no constitutional errors were committed during the initial trial, Assistant Attorney General Frank Jung went so far as to advocate that Amrine should be executed even if he was innocent. In a 4–3 decision in April 2003 the justices determined that the Missouri Supreme Court has the right to intervene in capital cases if "actual innocence" can be ascertained, regardless of whether or not constitutional errors are present. Writing for the majority, Justice Richard B. Teitelman stated, "It is difficult to imagine a more manifestly unjust and unconstitutional result than permitting the execution of an innocent person." Having the conviction overturned, prosecutor Bill Tacket in June 2003 again filed murder charges against Amrine for the death of Barber.

But with no evidence to connect him to the murder and with a statement from a correctional officer who saw the exonerating incident, Amrine was released on July 28, 2003, when Tacket decided against retrying him. Rather than admitting that a miscarriage of justice had occurred, however, Tacket announced that he was not going to retry Amrine because the DNA evidence had deteriorated to the point that it was unusable. In reality, however, tests of the sample had revealed that the blood did not match that of the murder victim. And although there was another suspect in this case, the prosecutor acknowledged that he was not going to prosecute anyone else for the murder of Barber, thereby leaving the public impression that he felt that Amrine had indeed committed the crime. Not unexpectedly, Tacket never apologized for the false conviction. If Amrine had not been wrongfully convicted of Barber's murder, he would have been released from prison in 1992 for his earlier crimes (Burnett 2010; Hollingsworth 2004; "Joseph Amrine" 2005).

Anthony Brown

Anthony Brown was a high school dropout with a fourteen-page rap sheet. So when James Dasinger, a delivery man, was shot to death in Escambia County, Florida, in 1982, Brown was one of the "usual suspects." His alleged accomplice, Wydell Rogers, was offered a reduced charge (second-degree murder) if he would implicate Brown. When the jury found Brown guilty in 1983 and recommended a life sentence, Circuit Judge Joseph Tarbuck overrode the jury's recommendation and imposed the death penalty. After the Florida Supreme Court vacated Brown's conviction in 1985, Brown was awarded a new trial. During the second trial Rogers confessed that he lied about Brown in order to receive a lighter sentence, and Brown was acquitted in 1986.

One year after receiving his freedom, however, Brown was arrested on robbery charges that were later dropped. Trying to move on with his life, he briefly lived in Detroit, where he was employed by a nursing home. He returned to Florida and in February 1990 found himself charged with aggravated assault after "he squared off with a man wielding a bottle in a bar and stabbed him with a pocketknife." In a bit of irony, after pleading guilty to the charge, Brown was sentenced to thirty years at Union Correctional Institution by the same judge who had previously sentenced him to death. When interviewed in 1999, Brown, being somewhat philosophical about this situation, commented, "I feel safe here, safer than the street. I could have been killed in a drive-by. If I hadn't have been on death row, who knows if I'd be dead or alive?" (Freedberg 1999).

Willie Brown and Larry Troy

In 1981 Willie Brown was in Florida's Union Correctional Institution serving twenty years for a Pinellas County robbery. Concomitantly, Larry Troy was serving a twenty-five-year sentence for murder. When Earl Owens, a white inmate, was stabbed to death that year, Brown and Troy became suspects. For seventeen months prior to their arrests, Brown and Troy were in solitary confinement. They were convicted and sentenced to death primarily on the basis of the prosecution's key witness, Frank Wise, an inmate who testified to seeing the two men exiting the area where Owens had been murdered. While on death row, Esther Lichtenfels, an anti-death penalty activist, became romantically interested in Brown and agreed to engage in a sting operation. Wearing a legally hidden microphone, Lichtenfels got a confession from Wise that he had lied during the trial and would be willing to recant this statement for $2,000. After the Florida Supreme Court overturned the convictions of Brown and Troy in 1987 on an unrelated issue, prosecutors decided not to retry the two men and the murder charge was dropped. Brown was released from prison in 1988; Troy was released from prison in 1990.

Unfortunately, both men have had run-ins with the law since their release from Union Correctional Institution. Immediately after his release, Brown married his prison sweetheart, Lichtenfels. However, he subsequently served time in prison for a bank robbery in Springfield, Massachusetts, and in 1999 he was arrested in Florida "after he allegedly robbed a bank in Dunedin with a broken broomstick, stole a car, and led police on a high-speed chase." Drugs and robberies have characterized his life since his wrongful conviction. Within seven months of Troy's release, he was arrested for selling cocaine and sentenced to Charlotte Correctional Institution in Florida (Freedberg 1999).

False Confessions in Wrongful Murder Convictions

False confessions, the fifth most commonly occurring factor in wrongful murder convictions, rarely occur in isolation. Typically, they are the result of overzealous police attempting to extract a confession from a suspect. This was apparent in the wrongful convictions of Travis Hayes and Medell Banks, Jr., examined earlier in this chapter. It was also noted in the false confessions of Eddie Joe Lloyd, Madison Hobley, John Duval, Earl Washington, Jr., Dan Young, Jr., and Harold Hill discussed in Chapter 2. The following cases continue to reveal a strong police presence behind false confessions.

Byron Halsey

Byron Halsey lived in a rooming house in Plainfield, New Jersey, with Margaret Urquhart and her two young children, ages seven and eight. A factory worker, Halsey was helping Urquhart raise her son and daughter. On the night of November 14, 1985, Halsey was visiting friends after having a neighbor, Clifton Hall, drive him there. When he returned home he was unable to find the children. Concerned by their absence, Halsey called their mother who was at work as well as other relatives in an attempt to locate them. A repairman found the children the next morning in the basement. The girl, Tina Urquhart, had been strangled and sexually attacked, and her skull had been fractured from the impact of a brick. Her brother, Tyrone Urquhart, had also been sexually assaulted; he had also been stabbed with scissors and had four nails impaled in his skull.

Suspicion immediately fell upon Halsey and Hall. Halsey, who has a sixth-grade education and learning disabilities, had been questioned by police for thirty hours during a forty-hour period when he confessed to the heinous crimes. His confession, however, did not always coincide with the evidence that the police had obtained. Halsey was initially wrong in his identification of the location of the bodies and his description of how they were killed. A detective involved in interrogation later confessed that frequently Halsey's answers were "gibberish" and Halsey appeared to be in a trance during the questioning, none of which was mentioned during the trial.

The trial began in early March of 1988, with the prosecutors seeking the death penalty. Clifton Hall, the state's key witness and one-time suspect in the case, offered testimony implicating Halsey. And although Halsey had witnesses who could corroborate his activities on the night of November 14, his confession ultimately made his alibi seem less likely. When the jury acquitted Halsey of some of the charges after five days of deliberation, he was no longer eligible for the death penalty.[13] Consequently, Halsey received two life sentences plus twenty years.

After exhausting his appeals, Halsey wrote to the Innocence Project in New York in 2004. During the 1988 trial DNA tests on the underwear found in the mouth of the female victim had been inconclusive and tests on the semen revealed Halsey's blood type (it was also Hall's blood type). Advances in DNA testing subsequent to 1988 made it possible to refine the analysis, which later exonerated Halsey and implicated Hall. In 2007 Superior Court Judge Stuart L. Peim vacated the verdict, saying that the new DNA evidence "would probably change the verdict." While awaiting a decision by prosecutors in Union County to either retry the case or drop the charges, Halsey was released after posting a $55,000 bail. He was also required to wear an electronic monitoring ankle bracelet. Finally, on July 9, 2007, prosecutors agreed to drop all charges against Halsey.

Today Halsey lives in Newark, where he is employed by a sign company. Since leaving prison he has gained twenty pounds and reports that he especially enjoys taking baths, something that he was unable to do during the twenty-two years he spent in prison. Clifton Hall, implicated by the new DNA evidence, was subsequently charged with the crimes. While awaiting his trial, incarcerated for three unrelated sex offenses committed in the early 1990s, he died of kidney failure at age fifty-two (Associated Press 2007; CBS News 2009; Gold 2007; Kelley 2007; Ryan 2007).

Kevin Richardson

Kevin Richardson was fourteen years old when a young white woman was jogging in New York's Central Park the night of April 19, 1989. The victim, who was brutally attacked and sexually assaulted, was an investment banker. When found, she was almost dead. With a body temperature of only 84 degrees, a fractured skull, and the loss of 75 percent of her blood, the victim was in a coma. When she finally regained consciousness almost two weeks later, she had no recollection of the event. With the media hyping the story,[14] the police hurriedly began looking for possible suspects. Richardson was one of five black Harlem teenagers who were wrongfully convicted after prolonged interrogations by the police.[15] During two separate trials in 1990 and 1991, all five juveniles were convicted. Because of his age, Richardson was tried as a juvenile and received a sentence of five to ten years for attempted murder, rape, sodomy, and robbery. The state's primary evidence used in the convictions revolved around the confessions elicited by the police after interrogations ranging from fourteen to twenty-eight hours in duration. Yet the confessions were often at odds with the actual facts of the case, differing in such aspects as the time, location, and participants involved in the incident. Three hairs found on Richardson were also identified by the prosecution as being "consistent with" that of the victim.

Although some members of the news media had for some time suspected that the five teens convicted of the assault were innocent, proof of their innocence did not emerge until January 2002 when Matias Reyes, who was serving a thirty-three-year sentence for murdering one woman and raping three others, confessed that he was the lone assailant in the Central Park jogger case. Later that year DNA testing provided biological evidence to support Reyes's claim. According to an article in the *New York Times:* "DNA tests established—'to a factor of one in 6,000,000,000'—that Mr.

Reyes was the source of the DNA found on the jogger's sock and in her cervix. It was the only DNA found. In addition, DNA tests established that Mr. Reyes was the source of a pubic hair found on the sock" (McFadden and Saulny 2002). Moreover, DNA tests unavailable at the time of the trial disclosed that none of the hairs found on Richardson matched those of the jogger. Richardson, who had been released in October 1995 after being incarcerated for six and a half years, was exonerated on December 19, 2002, when the convictions of all of the young men were vacated.

Ineffective Assistance of Counsel in Wrongful Murder Convictions

Inadequate legal counsel represents the sixth most common factor in wrongful murder convictions. The earlier cases of Harold Wilson, Benjamin Harris III, Earl Washington, Jr., and Edward Baker found in Chapter 2, as well as the cases of Ryan Matthews and Joseph Amrine from this chapter, disclose the impact of ineffective assistance of counsel on those outcomes. Two additional murder cases in which incompetence on the part of defense counsel contributed to the wrongful conviction are explored in this section.

Sammie Garrett

This is a story about a twenty-one-year-old African American man from Illinois and his twenty-eight-year-old white female companion, Karen Thompson. Sammie Garrett and Thompson were both married to others and had children. They began seeing each other romantically in August 1969, having met at Prairie State College in Chicago Heights. On November 8, 1969, the two were sleeping at the Ford City Motel after a night of alcohol consumption and marijuana use. According to Garrett, he woke up the following morning to find Thompson dead and a shotgun beside her, although he claimed that he did not hear any gunshots during the night. Panicked, Garrett quickly hid the weapon. When the Cook County sheriff's police arrived, Garrett took the officers to the hidden shotgun. When the officers inquired about why the shotgun was in the victim's possession, Garrett explained that he had found it in an alley shortly before his arrival at the motel. Although this explanation seemed incredible, several witnesses corroborated Garrett's statement. Also at the crime scene they found a suicide note, apparently written by the victim, that curtly stated, "I killed myself, Karen."

An autopsy was performed on Thompson's body on November 10 by Edward Shalgos, a Cook County pathologist. His report concluded that the victim had died of trauma to the head caused by the shotgun blast. He further concluded that, absent powder burns on the body, the fatal shot would have had to have been fired from four or more feet from the victim. Because the autopsy effectively ruled out the possibility of a suicide, Garrett was charged with the murder of Thompson.

Judge Philip Romiti presided over the bench trial in April 1970. Although the prosecution never questioned the handwriting on the suicide note, it attributed Thompson's death to a shotgun blast fired by Garrett. Shalgos reiterated what he had uncovered in his autopsy, which suggested that the instrument used to kill the victim could not have been fired from the victim because there were no powder burns. Moreover, the pathologist acknowledged that he had removed Thompson's palate and tongue and sent them to Frank Florese, a state toxicologist, for further analysis.

Garrett hired a private attorney, Seymour Vishny, to defend him. Yet his defense counsel did not attempt to question Shalgos's conclusion by bringing in his own independent expert witness. Additionally, either Vishny did not read or did not comprehend Florese's report, because the toxicologist's report concluded that the bullet had entered the roof of the victim's mouth and exited through her skull, a trajectory suggestive of suicide. Nor did Vishny attempt to call the state toxicologist to testify. By the trial's end, Vishny had called no witnesses to testify on his client's behalf. As a result Judge Romiti found Garrett guilty and sentenced him to twenty to forty years for the murder of Thompson.

In 1972, Cook County Public Defender James Doherty and his assistant, Matthew Beemsterboer, filed a petition requesting that the conviction be vacated due to ineffective assistance of counsel. After several unsuccessful appeals, the Illinois Supreme Court in 1975 ordered that Garrett be released on bond pending an evidentiary hearing. Given the disparity between the conclusions of the pathologist and the toxicologist, prosecutors dropped all charges against Garrett in 1976.

Troy Lee Jones

In December 1981 the body of Carolyn Grayson was found in a field near Los Banos, California. Grayson had been shot six times. Grayson's boyfriend, Troy Lee Jones, was charged with her death, despite the absence of physical evidence tying him to the crime. Prosecutors contended that he killed Jones to keep her from identifying him as the perpetrator of another murder almost one year before, a murder for which he was never charged.[16] In 1982 Jones was convicted of murder and sentenced to death.

After he had survived fourteen years on death row, Jones's case reached a pro–death penalty California Supreme Court. In a rare moment, the California Supreme Court ruled unanimously to overturn his conviction and death sentence, given the gross nonfeasance of his legal representation. Noting that Jones's trial lawyer, Hugh Wesley Goodwin, did not request pretrial investigative funds, conduct an adequate pretrial investigation, interview potential exculpatory witnesses, or even request a police report, the court ruled that Jones had been denied effective assistance of counsel. Chief Justice Ronald George wrote, "We conclude that defense counsel's performance before and during the guilt phase of the trial was marked by numerous deficiencies and that the cumulative impact of counsel's shortcomings at that phase of the proceedings was prejudicial with regard to the judgment of guilt." In November 1996 the Fresno County district attorney's office dismissed all charges against Jones (Death Penalty Focus 2008; Goodin 1996).

Forensic Errors in Wrongful Murder Convictions

The last contributor to wrongful conviction in murder trials involves forensic errors. Murder cases involving forensic errors previously discussed in the book include Dan Young, Jr., Harold Hill, Joe Sidney Williams, Kenneth Adams, and Kevin Richardson. This section analyzes three additional cases in which forensic errors contributed to a miscarriage of justice.

Larry Peterson

Larry Peterson was a thirty-six-year-old divorced father of three who lived at home with his mother in Pemberton, New Jersey, when Jacqueline Harrison, a young, attractive black woman, was found dead in a field on August 24, 1987. A mother of two, Harrison had been sexually assaulted and murdered after what appeared to be a night of partying.[17] A woman walking her dog discovered Harrison's body, which was partially nude. She had sticks protruding from her mouth and vagina. Peterson, who lived near the crime scene, had a history of alcohol and drug abuse and a prior criminal record involving petty crimes. After the crime became known to the public, a neighbor, noticing that Peterson had recent scratch marks, came forth. When questioned, Peterson denied any wrongdoing. Three weeks later, however, Peterson was charged with murder and aggravated sexual assault. In February 1989, after he had spent seventeen months in jail, his trial began.

Gail Tighe, a forensic scientist from the New Jersey State Police crime laboratory, provided biological evidence of Peterson's guilt. She testified that the hairs found on Harrison's body and on the stick used in the assault "compared" to those of Peterson. The prosecution also included testimony from Robert Elder and two other men that implicated Peterson as the perpetrator. Even Peterson admitted during a 2007 interview for National Public Radio, "If I was sitting on the jury, I would be inclined to convict the person also." Convicted of felony murder and aggravated sexual assault, Peterson was sentenced to forty years at Trenton State Prison.

In 2005 the Innocence Project agreed to examine his case. When the hairs from Peterson's trial were reexamined, DNA tests revealed that the hairs belonged to the victim and not to Peterson. And although the New Jersey State Police crime laboratory had erroneously reported at the trial that there was no semen in the victim's rape kit, DNA tests disclosed the tissue and semen of an unidentified man. Furthermore, an analysis was performed on hair collected from the crime scene that had not been used in the trial. DNA tests excluded Peterson as the donor. Consequently, Judge Thomas Smith vacated Peterson's conviction in July 2005. Prosecutor Robert Bernardi, however, was not finished with the case. Intent on retrying Peterson, he had him rearrested and transferred from Trenton State Prison to the Burlington County jail. Unable to raise the required $20,000 bail for a month, Peterson remained in jail until August 27, 2005.

Before the new trial could begin, the prosecution learned that the state's key witness, Elder, had recanted his testimony. Elder, an abuser of alcohol and other drugs, had been in trouble with the law himself, having spent some time in the county jail. In recanting his statement that Peterson had confessed to the crime, Elder admitted that he fabricated the story in order to avoid an interrogation that had been ongoing for three days. He acknowledged that he had overheard the police discussing the incident and used that information in his testimony.[18] With the state's key witness recanting his testimony, Bernardi announced in June 2006 that he would not retry Peterson for the sexual assault and murder of Harrison (Buckley 2007, June 12 and June 13).

Levon Brooks and Kennedy Brewer

Perhaps nowhere is the problem associated with forensic mistakes more apparent than in these two Mississippi cases involving child molestation and murder. Although the crimes were committed eighteen months apart, the actual perpetrator of both crimes was the same individual. A review of the background of each of the cases discloses striking similarities.

In 1990 three-year-old Courtney Smith, from Noxubee County, Mississippi, was abducted from her home during the middle of the night and raped and murdered. Her body was later discovered in a nearby pond. The mother of the deceased girl, Sonya Smith, was a former girlfriend of Levon Brooks, who was subsequently arrested and charged with the crime. After spending two years in jail awaiting trial, Brooks was found guilty and sentenced to life after testimony suggested that the "bite marks" on the victim's wrists came from Brooks.

A year and a half later, an almost identical crime occurred in the same county. Three-year-old Christine Jackson was the daughter of Kennedy Brewer's girlfriend, Gloria Jackson. In May 1992 Brewer was babysitting Christine and two other children for Jackson. When Jackson returned home shortly after midnight, Brewer remained in the house. According to Jackson, Brewer got up twice during the night in which the little girl was taken from her house and raped and strangled: once to change a baby diaper and later to heat up a baby bottle. It wasn't until the next morning that Christine's absence was detected. Her abandoned body was found in a nearby creek two days later. Although both Brewer and Jackson were initially arrested, Jackson's charges were eventually dropped. Brewer, a mildly retarded laborer who had dropped out of school when his father became disabled because of diabetes, was found guilty and sentenced to death in 1995, predominantly on the strength of forensic evidence provided by the same forensics expert who testified in the trial of Brooks. And, as in the preceding case, "bite marks" found on the victim were identified as matching the teeth of the defendant.[19]

In both cases the same officer investigated the crime and Mississippi District Attorney Forrest Allgood prosecuted the case. And in each case the medical examiner was Steven Hayne, and the dentist who testified that marks on the victim matched the teeth of the defendant was Michael West.[20] West, who frequently collaborated with Hayne, is a very colorful individual. According to Radley Balko (2008),

> [West] once claimed he could definitively trace the bite marks in a half-eaten bologna sandwich left at the crime scene back to the defendant. He has compared his bite-mark virtuosity to Jesus Christ and Itzhak Perlman. And he claims to have invented a revolutionary system of identifying bite marks using yellow goggles and iridescent light that, conveniently, he says can't be photographed or duplicated.[21]

In 2001 the Innocence Project became interested in Brewer's case. Semen from the victim's body was analyzed using DNA testing. Results excluded Brewer as a possible donor. Although the conviction was vacated, Allgood refused to accept the DNA test results as proof of Brewer's innocence, and so Brewer was relocated to the county jail. Five years later Brewer remained in jail as Allgood failed to bring the case to trial. In the summer of 2007 the Innocence Project requested the assistance of Andre de Gruy from Mississippi's Office of Capital Defense Counsel to secure the release of Brewer. It was at this juncture that the Innocence Project noticed the similarities between the cases of Brewer and Brooks. Unfortunately, the biological evidence in Brooks's case had deteriorated and wasn't suitable for DNA tests. While investigating the cases, the Innocence Project discovered that Justin Albert Johnson had been a suspect in both cases before the police settled on Brooks and Brewer. Johnson, moreover, had a history of sexual assaults involving women and young girls and was the only suspect with that background. A DNA test of biological evidence from the Brewer case disclosed a match with Johnson. When the attorney general's office arrested Johnson, he confessed to the rape and murder of both young girls, thus exonerating Brooks and Brewer. On February 15, 2008, all charges against Brewer were dismissed. Brooks was cleared of all charges on March 13, 2008. In August 2008 the state of Mississippi terminated its contract with Steven Hayne, the state pathologist involved in the two cases (Associated Press 2008; Balko 2007, 2008; Byrd 2008, February 5 and 12; Coffey 2010; Dewan 2007, 2008; Farish 2008; Mississippi Innocence Project 2010a,b; Mott 2008).

Victim Characteristics and Wrongful Murder Convictions

Table 3.2 provides additional information on each of the 174 wrongful murder convictions. Of particular interest are the characteristics of the victims. Where possible, data on the age, gender, and race of each of the victims were collected. The number of victims is also noted in the table. When victim characteristics in wrongful murder convictions in this study are compared with victim characteristics in offenses involving murder as reported in the Federal Bureau of Investigation's 2008 Uniform Crime Reports (UCR), some interesting differences emerge.

An examination of the murder cases for which data on victim age were available reveals that the vast majority of victims were eighteen years of age or over. Slightly less than 20 percent of the victims in the study were under the age of eighteen. In comparison, according to the UCR, 10.5 percent of all murder victims in 2008 were under eighteen years of age (Federal Bureau of Investigation 2009, Table 2). The UCR further divides the data on homicide according to the race and gender of the victim by race of

Table 3.2 Victim and Case Characteristics in Murder and Attempted Murder Cases (N=174)

Name	#	Age	Gender	Race	Sentence	Convicted	Released	Cleared
			Victim Characteristics					
AL								
Medell Banks, Jr. (accused of murdering nonexistent infant)	1	n/a	n/a	n/a	15 years	2001	2003	2003
Melvin Todd Beamon	1	n/a	Male	White	25 years	1989	1990	1990
James "Bo" Cochran	1	n/a	Female	Black	Death	1976	1997	1997
Freddie Lee Gaines	1	n/a	Female	White	30 years	1974	1985	1991
Walter McMillian	1	18	Female	White	Death	1988	1993	1993
Freddie Lee Wright	2	37	Female	White	Death	1979	Executed in 2000	
		40	Male	White				
AZ								
Christopher McCrimmon	3	32	Male	Latino	Death	1993	—	1997
		45	Male	Chinese				
		75	Male	Chinese				
Andre Minnitt	3	32	Male	Latino	Death	1993	—	2002
		45	Male	Chinese				
		75	Male	Chinese				
CA								
Eugene Allen	1	n/a	Male	White	Death	1976	n/a	1981
Timothy Atkins	1	n/a	Male	Latino	32 years	1987	2007	2007
Clarence Chance	1	23	Male	Black	Life	1975	1992	1992
Tony Cooks	1	42	Male	White	15 years to life	1981	1986	1986
Antoine Goff	1	18	Male	Black	27 years to life	1990	2003	2003
Ernest (Shuhaa) Graham	1	n/a	Male	White	Death	1976	1981	1981
Willie Earl Green	1	25	Female	Black	33 years to life	1984	2008	2008

92

Table 3.2 *continued*

Name	#	Victim Characteristics Age	Gender	Race	Sentence	Convicted	Released	Cleared
Harold Hall	2	35	Female	n/a	Life	1990	2004	2004
		26	Male	n/a				
Troy Lee Jones	1	32	Female	n/a	Death	1982	1996	1996
Dwayne McKinney	1	19	Male	n/a	Life	1981	2000	2000
Oscar Lee Morris	1	n/a	Male	White	Death	1983	2000	2000
Aaron Lee Owens	2	n/a	Male	n/a	Life	1973	1982	1982
		n/a	Female	n/a				
Benny Powell	1	23	Male	Black	Life	1975	1992	1992
Elmer "Geronimo" Pratt	1	27	Female	White	Life	1970	1997	1997
John Tennison	1	18	Male	Black	25 years to life	1990	2003	2003
DC								
Bradford Brown	1	n/a	Male	n/a	18 years to life	1975	1979	1979
FL								
James Adams	1	61	Male	White	Death	1974	Executed in 1984	
Anthony Brown	1	n/a	Male	n/a	Death	1983	1986	1986
Joseph Green Brown	1	n/a	Female	White	Death	1974	1987	1987
Timothy Brown	1	29	Male	White	Life	1991	2003	2003
Willie Brown	1	n/a	Male	White	Death	1983	1988	1988
Kevin Coleman	1	19	Male	Black	Life	1992	2004	—
Johnny Frederick	1	n/a	Male	n/a	Life	1971	1973	1973
Joseph Nahume Green	1	n/a	Female	White	Death	1993	2000	2000
Robert Earl Hayes	1	32	Female	White	Death	1991	1997	1997
Rudolph Holton	1	17	Female	Black	Death	1986	2003	2003

continues

Table 3.2 *continued*

		Victim Characteristics						
Name	#	Age	Gender	Race	Sentence	Convicted	Released	Cleared
David Keaton	1	n/a	Male	n/a	Death	1971	1979	1973
Anthony Ray Peek	1	65	Female	n/a	Death	1978	—	1987
Derrick Robinson	1	n/a	n/a	n/a	7 years	1989	1992	1992
Frank Lee Smith	1	8	Female	Black	Death	1986	Died in prison	2000
Gilbert Stokes	1	18	Male	Black	Life	2002	—	2005
Delbert Lee Tibbs	2	17	Female	White	Life (rape)	1974	1977	1982
		27	Male	White	Death (murder)			
Jerry Frank Townsend	6	13	Female	n/a	7 life sentences	1980/1982	2001	2001
		n/a	Female	n/a	(6 for murder &			
		n/a	Female	n/a	1 for rape)			
		n/a	n/a	n/a				
		n/a	n/a	n/a				
		n/a	n/a	n/a				
Larry Troy	1	n/a	Male	White	Death	1983	1990	1988
GA								
Jerry Banks	2	n/a	Male	White	Death	1975	1980	1980
		n/a	Female	White				
Earl Patrick Charles	2	42	Male	White	Death	1975	1978	1978
		76	Male	White				
Walter McIntosh	2	n/a	Male	Black	Life	1980	Died in prison	
		n/a	Female	Black				
Gary Nelson	1	6	Female	n/a	Death	1980	1991	1991
Robert Wallace	1	27	Male	Black	Death	1980	1987	1987
IL								
Kenneth Adams	2	23	Female	White	75 years	1979	1996	1996
		29	Male	White				

Table 3.2 *continued*

Name	#	Age	Gender	Race	Sentence	Convicted	Released	Cleared
			Victim Characteristics					
Randy Boss	1	52	Male	n/a	50 years	1994	—	2001
Revell Boss	1	52	Male	n/a	40 years	1994	—	2001
Marcellius Bradford	1	23	Female	White	12 years	1988	2002[a]	2001
Robert Brown	1	n/a	Male	Black	35 years	1984	1989	1989
LaVale Burt	1	2	Male	Black	Not sentenced	1986	1986	1986
Perry Cobb	2	n/a	Male	White	Death	1979	1987	1987
		n/a	Male	White				
Michael Evans	1	9	Female	White	Life+	1976	2003	2003
Sammie Garrett	1	28	Female	White	20–40 years	1970	1976	1976
Hubert Geralds	1	24	Female	Black	Life	1997	—	2000
Harold Hill	1	39	Female	Black	Life	1994	2006	2005
Madison Hobley	7	7	Female	Black	Death	1990	2003	2003
		21	Female	Black				
		23	Female	Black				
		34	Female	Black				
		1	Male	Black				
		36	Male	Black				
		40	Male	Black				
Dana Holland	2	22	Female	Black	118 years	1993	2003	2003
		38	Female	Black				
Elton Houston	1	n/a	Male	Black	35 years	1984	1989	1989
Stanley Howard	1	41	Male	Black	Death	1984	—	2003
Verneal Jimerson	2	23	Female	White	Death	1985	1996	1996
		29	Male	White				
Henry Johnson	1	n/a	Male	n/a	Life	1991	2002	—

continues

Table 3.2 *continued*

Name	#	Age	Gender	Race	Sentence	Convicted	Released	Cleared
				Victim Characteristics				
Juan Johnson	1	n/a	Male	n/a	Life	1991	2002	2004
Ronald Jones	1	28	Female	Black	Death	1989	1999	1999
Carl Lawson	1	8	Male	Black	Death	1990	1996	1996
Lloyd Lindsey	4	7–17	Male	Black	40–80 years	1975	1979	1979
			Female	Black				
			Female	Black				
			Female	Black				
Alton Logan	1	n/a	Male	Black	Life	1982	2008	2008
James Newsome	1	72	Male	White	Life	1979	1994	1994
Calvin Ollins	1	23	Female	White	Life	1988	2001	2001
Larry Ollins	1	23	Female	White	Life	1988	2001	2001
Leroy Orange	4	27	Female	Black	Death	1984	2003	2003
		30	Female	Black				
		10	Male	Black				
		25	Male	Black				
Aaron Patterson	2	62	Female	Latina	Death	1986	2003	2003
		73	Male	Latino				
Anthony Porter	2	19	Female	White	Death	1983	1999	1999
		18	Male	White				
Willie Rainge	2	23	Female	White	Life	1979	1996	1996
		29	Male	White				
Omar Saunders	1	23	Female	White	Life	1988	2001	2001
Steven Smith	1	n/a	Male	Black	Death	1985	1999	1999
Paul Terry	1	9	Female	Latina	200–400 years	1977	2003	2003
Franklin Thompson	1	41	Female	Black	24 years	1997	2003	2003
Darby Tillis	2	n/a	Male	White	Death	1977	1987	1987
		n/a	Male	White				

Table 3.2 *continued*

Name	#	Victim Characteristics			Sentence	Convicted	Released	Cleared
		Age	Gender	Race				
Dennis Williams	2	23	Female	White	Death	1979	1996	1996
		29	Male	White				
Dan Young, Jr.	1	39	Female	Black	Life	1994	2005	2005
IN								
Larry Hicks	2	n/a	Male	Black	Death	1978	1980	1980
		n/a	Male	Black				
Charles Smith	1	20	Female	White	Death	1983	1991	1991
IA								
James Hall	1	n/a	n/a	n/a	50 years	1974	1984	1984
Terry Harrington	1	n/a	Male	White	Life	1978	2003	2003
Curtis McGhee, Jr.	1	n/a	Male	White	Life	1978	2003	2003
LA								
David Alexander	1	elderly	Male	n/a	Life	1976	2006	2006
Dan L. Bright	1	n/a	Male	n/a	Death (commuted to life)	1996	2004	2004
Shareef Cousin	1	25	Male	White	Death	1996	—	1999
Harry Granger	1	elderly	Male	n/a	Life	1976	2006	2006
Travis Hayes	1	n/a	Male	White	Life	1998	2006	2007
Curtis Kyles	1	60	Female	White	Death	1984	1998	1998
Dwight Labran	1	n/a	Male	n/a	Life	1997	2001	2003
Ryan Matthews	1	n/a	Male	White	Death	1999	2004	2004
John Thompson	1	34	Male	White	Death (commuted to life)	1985	2003	2003

continues

Table 3.2 *continued*

Name	#	Age	Gender	Race	Sentence	Convicted	Released	Cleared
		Victim Characteristics						
Calvin Williams	1	n/a	Male	Black	Life	1977	1992	1996
MD								
Ronald Addison	1	34	Male	n/a	30 years	1996	2005	2005
Michael Austin	1	n/a	Male	Black	Life	1975	2001	2002
Cornell Avery Estes	1	n/a	Female	n/a	20 years	1979	1980	1980
Anthony Gray, Jr.	1	38	Female	White	2 life sentences	1991	2000	1999
Eric D. Lynn	1	n/a	Male	Black	Life	1994	2007	2007
MA								
Laurence Adams	1	n/a	Male	n/a	Death (commuted to life)	1974	2004	2004
Christian Amado	1	28	Male	Black	Life	1980	1982	1982
Stephan Cowans	1	n/a	Male	White	30–45 years	1998	2004	2004
Shawn Drumgold	1	12	Female	Black	Life	1989	2003	2003
Frank Grace	1	19	Male	Black	Life	1974	1985	1985
Donnell Johnson	1	9	Male	Black	Life	1996	2000	2000
Lawyer Johnson	1	30	Male	White	Death	1971	1982	1982
Bobby Joe Leaster	1	n/a	Male	n/a	Life	1971	1986	1986
Marlon Passley	1	18	Male	Black	Life	1996	1999	1999
Louis Santos	1	32	Female	White	Life	1985	1988	1990
MI								
Eddie Joe Lloyd	1	16	Female	n/a	Life	1985	2002	2002
Dwight Love	1	n/a	Male	n/a	4 life terms	1981	1998	2001

Table 3.2 *continued*

Name	#	Age	Gender	Race	Sentence	Convicted	Released	Cleared
			Victim Characteristics					
Claude McCollum	1	60	Female	White	Life	2005	2007	2007
Vidale McDowell	1	37	Female	Black	Life	2002	2004	2004
MS								
Kennedy Brewer	1	3	Female	Black	Death	1995	2007	2008
Levon Brooks	1	3	Female	Black	Life	1992	2008	2008
Cedric Willis	3	n/a	Male	n/a	Life + 90 years	1997	2006	2006
		n/a	Female	n/a				
		n/a	Female	n/a				
MO								
Joseph Amrine	1	n/a	Male	Black	Death	1986	2003	2003
Darryl Burton	1	26	Male	Black	Life	1985	2008	2008
Eric Clemmons	1	n/a	Male	Black	Death	1987	—	2000
NJ								
Byron Halsey	2	7	Female	Black	2 life terms + 20 years	1988	2007	2007
		8	Male	Black				
Larry Peterson	1	25	Female	Black	40 years	1989	2005	2006
Damaso Vega	1	16	Female	Black	Life	1982	1989	1989
NM								
Van Bering Robinson	1	36	Male	Latino	Life	1981	1983	1983

continues

Table 3.2 *continued*

Name	#	Age	Gender	Race	Sentence	Convicted	Released	Cleared
				Victim Characteristics				
Terry Seaton	1	n/a	Male	n/a	Life	1973	1979	1979
NY								
Kareem Bellamy	1	n/a	Male	Black	25 years to life	1994	2008	—
Lamont Branch	1	37	Male	Black	Life	1990	2002	2002
Lazaro Burt	1	28	Male	n/a	25 years to life	1994	2002	2002
Nathaniel Carter	1	60	Female	Black	25 years to life	1982	1984	1984
John Duval	1	52	Male	White	25 years to life	1973	1998	2000
Anthony Faison	1	46	Male	Black	Life	1988	2001	2001
Edmond Jackson	1	n/a	Male	n/a	20 years to life	1971	1978	1978
William Maynard	1	n/a	n/a	n/a	10–20 years	1971	1978	1978
Kevin Richardson	1	28	Female	White	5–10 years	1990	1995	2002
Charles Shepard	1	46	Male	Black	Life	1988	2001	2001
Dhoruba al-Mujahid bin Wahad (aka Richard Moore)	2	n/a	Male	White	25 years to life	1973	1990	1995
		n/a	Male	White				
NC								
Glen Chapman	2	n/a	Female	Black	Death	1994	2008	2008
		n/a	Female	White				
Jonathon Hoffman	1	n/a	Male	White	Death	1995	2007	2007
Darryl Hunt	1	25	Female	White	Life	1985/1990	2004	2004
Levon "Bo" Jones	1	67	Male	White	Death	1993	2008	2008
Charles Munsey	1	66	Female	n/a	Death	1996	Died in prison	1999
Samuel A. Poole	1	n/a	n/a	n/a	Death	1973	1974	1974
Christopher Spicer	1	n/a	Male	n/a	Death	1973	1975	1975

Table 3.2 *continued*

Name	#	Age	Gender	Race	Sentence	Convicted	Released	Cleared
OH								
Daniel Brown	1	n/a	Female	n/a	Life	1982	2001	2001
Timothy Howard	1	74	Male	n/a	Death/Life	1976/1978	2003	2003
Gary Lamar James	1	74	Male	n/a	Death/Life	1976/1978	2003	2003
Derrick Jamison	1	n/a	Male	n/a	Death	1985	—	2005
Harllel Jones	1	n/a	Male	Black	Life	1972	1977	1977
Rasheem Matthew	1	n/a	Male	Black	45 years to life	1990	—	2006
Allan Thrower	1	n/a	Male	White	Life	1973	1979	1979
OK								
Charles Ray Giddens	1	n/a	Female	n/a	Death	1978	1981	1981
Robert Lee Miller, Jr.	2	83	Female	White	Death	1988	1998	1998
		92	Female	White				
Adolph Munson	1	n/a	Female	n/a	Death	1985	1995	1995
PA								
Edward Baker	1	75	Male	Black	Life	1974	1999	2002
Matthew Connor	1	11	Female	Black	Life	1978	1990	1990
Riky Jackson	1	n/a	Male	Black	Life	1997	1999	1999
Edward Ryder	1	n/a	Male	n/a	Life	1974	1993	1993
Drew Whitley	1	22	Female	White	Life	1989	2006	2006
Harold Wilson	3	64	Female	n/a	3 death sentences	1989	2005	2005
		40	Female	n/a				
		33	Male	n/a				

continues

101

Table 3.2 *continued*

| Name | # | Victim Characteristics | | | Sentence | Convicted | Released | Cleared |
		Age	Gender	Race				
SC								
Tyrone James	1	n/a	n/a	n/a	Life	1982	1983	1983
Warren Douglas Manning	1	n/a	Male	White	Death	1989	1999	1999
Winfred Peterson	1	n/a	n/a	n/a	Life	1982	1983	1983
TX								
Clarence Lee Brandley	1	16	Female	White	Death	1981	1990	1990
Ben Spencer	1	33	Male	White	Life	1988	—	—
Calvin Washington	1	54	Female	n/a	Life	1987	2001	2001
Joe Sidney Williams	1	54	Female	n/a	Life	1987	1993	1993
James Lee Woodard	1	21	Female	Black	Life	1981	2008	2008
VA								
Russell Leon Gray	1	n/a	n/a	n/a	52 years	1987	1990	1990
Troy D. Hopkins	1	37	Male	Black	28 years	1990	2001	2005
Earl Washington, Jr.	1	19	Female	White	Death	1984	2001	2000
WA								
Benjamin J. Harris III	1	n/a	Male	n/a	Death	1985	Released to a mental hospital	1997

Notes: n/a = not available.
a. Was released after 6.5 years but was reincarcerated later for burglary conviction.

the offender. This information makes it possible to draw a finer distinction between the data in Table 3.2 and the homicide data for 2008. Whereas data from the investigation disclose that males comprised less than 60 percent of the victims in wrongful murder convictions, 78 percent of the murder victims in black-perpetrated homicides in 2008 were male. And although approximately 15 percent of black-perpetrated homicides in 2008 involved white victims (Federal Bureau of Investigation 2009, Table 6), 46.5 percent of the victims in wrongful murder convictions in the sample were white. While caution should be exercised in interpreting these findings due to missing data, this analysis suggests that wrongful conviction murder cases involving black males are atypical in that they are more likely than comparable data from the UCR to include younger victims, female victims, and white victims.

Finally, when analysis of the data from this research is confined to wrongful convictions in which both the race and gender of the victim can be ascertained for blacks and whites, we find that black males are only slightly more likely than their white counterparts to be murder victims (46.7 percent versus 44.4 percent). In contrast, white females are slightly more likely than black females to be murdered (50 percent versus 46.9 percent).[22] Again, because victim data were unavailable in a number of wrongful murder conviction cases, caution should be exercised in the interpretation of these statistics.

Other Case Characteristics

Table 3.2 additionally includes information on the sentence as well as the year of conviction, release, and exoneration. Initial verdicts of death accompanied almost 38 percent of the wrongful murder convictions. When the conviction/release/exoneration data are collapsed into categories according to decade, we discover that the largest number of convictions occurred during the 1980s (almost 40 percent) and the second largest number of convictions occurred during the 1970s (32 percent). Just over a fourth of the convictions were from the 1990s. In contrast, the largest number of cases in which the wrongfully convicted individual was released occurred between 2000 and 2008. Nearly one-half of the releases happened during this period. An additional quarter of the releases took place during the 1990s. Similarly, the number of cleared cases has steadily risen over time. Although only about 8 percent of the exonerations transpired during the 1970s, this figure swelled to 18 percent by the 1980s. This figure continued to grow during the 1990s, accounting for almost one-fourth of the wrongful murder convictions. Even more dramatic, however, was the fact that slightly over half of the exonerations in the sample took place between 2000 and 2008.

Conclusion

This chapter focuses on 174 wrongful conviction cases in which the most serious offense is murder or attempted murder. As much wrongful conviction research reveals, these miscarriages of justice are typically the result of the coalescence of multiple factors rather than the result of a single factor. Witness error was the most frequently occurring factor in the murder cases examined here. Slightly over four of every ten wrongful convictions revealed evidence of witness misidentification. Unfortunately, attempts to ascertain witness race proved largely futile, so it was impossible to determine the extent to which cross-racial misidentifications contributed to witness error. In addition to witness error, the most common contributing factors to false conviction were police misconduct (38.5 percent), prosecutorial misconduct (36.2 percent), and use of snitches or informants (33.3 percent). Other important factors in descending order of frequency were false confessions, ineffective assistance of counsel, and forensic errors.

False confessions, which were found in over 18 percent of the wrongful murder convictions (N=32), represent a very interesting area for additional analysis. A majority of cases involved adult defendants rather than juvenile defendants. Of the twenty-seven false convictions where it was possible to identify the age of the defendant, nineteen were adults. In the vast majority of all false confessions police misconduct in some form contributed to the false admission of guilt. Physical and/or psychological coercion were present in many of these cases. Prolonged interrogations also probably contributed to some of the false admissions of guilt. Further, in at least nine false confessions the defendant was characterized as having a low IQ. Perhaps the most intriguing case, however, involved Benjamin Harris III of Washington State. Harris, who suffered from a mental disorder, falsely confessed to a murder he did not commit on instructions from his incompetent legal counsel, who believed that the court would be more willing to show mercy on his client if he admitted his involvement in the crime.

A comparison of the sample with known homicide cases in 2008 discloses some interesting findings as well. The victims in the sample were somewhat younger and more likely to be female than the UCR data on murder would seem to indicate. The most pronounced differences, however, were disclosed when the race of the victim was analyzed. In 2008 approximately 15 percent of black-perpetrated homicides involved white victims. In contrast, 46.5 percent of the murder victims in this investigation were white, a figure three times greater than recent statistics on murder would suggest. This finding reiterates a theme found in much of the race-based research: that victim race is an important variable in discussions of sentencing.

Notes

1. There were only three cases in which the charge was *attempted* murder. The three defendants were Dana Holland of Illinois and Kevin Richardson and Dhoruba al-Mujahid bin Wahad (aka Richard Moore) of New York. Additionally, there was a single case (Stephan Cowans, Massachusetts) in which the official charge was armed assault with intent to murder.

2. According to the 1963 Supreme Court case *Brady v. Maryland,* a violation of due process occurs if the prosecution withholds from the defense exculpatory evidence that is "material" to the determination of the guilt or innocence of the defendant or to the appropriate punishment. Generally speaking, exculpatory evidence is deemed to be "material" if there is reasonable probability that a different verdict or sentence would have been forthcoming had the missing evidence been available during the trial.

3. The fourth perpetrator was dead.

4. Victoria Banks was arrested in October 1998, when teachers reported her to the authorities after her eleven-year-old daughter showed up for school with bruises. Although George Bonner, the mother's new boyfriend, had raped her daughter, the police surmised that when Banks was unable to sexually satisfy Bonner, she had allowed him sexual access to her daughter (Luo 2002).

5. Besides instilling the notion that he had heard an infant crying, the police during the interrogation told Medell Banks that they had DNA evidence to prove the existence of a baby, even though no such evidence existed.

6. Interestingly, under oath McQueen stated that he met Wright for the first time in February 1978, which was three months after the robbery and murder.

7. Lambert was originally scheduled to testify in the first trial on behalf of the defense.

8. Lambert testified that, during confession at her Catholic church in June 1977, she informed her priest that Wright had admitted committing the crime. However, the crime occurred on December 1, 1977, almost six months after the alleged confession.

9. Martin Soto-Fong, whose father was Mexican and whose mother was Chinese, was convicted primarily on the basis of evidence linking him to the crime scene. Tucson police found his fingerprints on plastic bags and a food stamp at the El Grande Market. However, there were questions regarding the police collection of the evidence, and Timothy O'Sullivan, the expert who examined the prints, was dying of cancer and heavily medicated at the time. Moreover, because Soto-Fong had previously worked at the El Grande Market, the presence of his fingerprints

on the bags and food stamp does not necessarily place him at the crime scene at the time of the crime.

10. On May 28, 2004, Kenneth Peasley, two-time Arizona Prosecutor of the Year and the individual responsible for sending one-tenth of that state's death row population to prison, was disbarred as a result of his prosecutorial misbehavior during the Minnitt trial.

11. Keith Woods was later convicted in Nevada on federal cocaine charges and given a thirteen-year sentence. He received an additional sentence of twenty-seven months for possession of marijuana and heroin while incarcerated.

12. Russell later admitted he lied to avoid being suspected of killing Barber.

13. On December 17, 2007, New Jersey officially abolished the death penalty.

14. The term "wilding" was used by the media to describe the brutal attack. According to the *New York Post,* wilding refers to "packs of bloodthirsty teens from the tenements, bursting with boredom and rage, [who] roam the streets getting kicks from an evening of ultra-violence" (cited in Hancock 2003).

15. The other black teenagers wrongfully convicted of the brutal beating and raping of the Central Park jogger were Yusef Salaam, Antron McCray, Raymond Santana, and Kharey Wise. All of the teenagers at the time were between fourteen and sixteen years of age.

16. In support of the prosecution's argument, a neighbor testified that Jones had assaulted Grayson with a tire iron a few weeks before her death and claimed that Grayson said that she wouldn't tell anybody what she knew. It is unclear if those remarks referred to the earlier murder with which Jones was never charged.

17. The victim had used crack cocaine and had engaged in sexual activity with multiple partners prior to her death.

18. It was also revealed that the police had used multiple interrogations of the same persons to get the witnesses to testify that the defendant had confessed to the crime.

19. The "bite marks" were actually the result of insect and animal bites that occurred while the victim's body was in the creek.

20. Hayne, who conducted almost all of the autopsies for prosecutors in Mississippi at the time, was not board certified, yet he was making almost $1 million annually for his services.

21. He modestly refers to this procedure as the West Phenomenon and has used his invention to discover bite marks on a decomposed woman's breast (Balko 2007).

22. The UCR does not provide comparable data.

4

Rape and Sexual Assault

These sons of bitches are guilty as sin. There's no question in my mind.
This is not a case of innocence. . . . These two bastards are guilty.
I just can't prove it.

—*Comments from Jefferson County (Alabama) Assistant District Attorney*
Arthur Green, Jr., after DNA tests of semen and hair excluded the
Mahan brothers as the perpetrators of the rape and matched the
DNA profile of the victim's boyfriend.

This study identified 109 cases in which the most serious offense was rape or sexual assault, making this the second most common offense category involving the wrongful conviction of African American men. A list of the individuals who were wrongfully convicted of rape or sexual assault appears in Table 4.1. The table further includes the state in which the wrongful conviction occurred, any additional offenses with which the defendant was charged, and factors associated with the wrongful conviction. An examination of that table follows.

Almost 70 percent of the cases initially included one or more additional charges, the most common of which was robbery. Kidnapping was the second most common additional charge. Sodomy and burglary tied for third place, and assault (other than sexual assault) was the fifth most common additional charge. An examination of the factors related to the wrongful conviction reveals that in almost 93 percent of the cases involving rape and sexual assault, witness error was a contributing factor. Forensic errors were present in over 30 percent of the cases, and police misconduct accounted for wrongful convictions almost 23 percent of the time. Prosecutorial misconduct was found in almost 15 percent of the cases. Ineffective assistance of counsel and false confessions contributed to 11 and 10 percent of the wrongful convictions, respectively. Insufficient evidence and the use of a snitch or informant were present in one case each.

107

Table 4.1 Factors in Wrongful Convictions in Rape and Sexual Assault Cases (N=109)

Name	State	Additional Charge(s)	Contributing Factors
Dale Mahan	AL	Kidnapping	Witness error
Ronnie Mahan	AL	Kidnapping	Witness error
Herman Atkins	CA	2 counts: rape, forcible oral copulation; 1 count: robbery	Witness error
Damon Auguste	CA	Sodomy	Prosecutorial misconduct, witness error, forensic errors
Frederick Daye	CA	Rape (2 counts), kidnapping, robbery, motor vehicle theft	Prosecutorial misconduct, police misconduct, witness error, forensic errors
Albert Johnson	CA	Sexual assault (2 counts)	Police misconduct, witness error, ineffective assistance of counsel
Mark Reid	CT	Kidnapping	Witness error, forensic errors
James Tillman	CT	Kidnapping, robbery, assault, larceny	Witness error
Larry Bostic	FL	Robbery	Witness error, false confession
Alan Crotzer	FL	Kidnapping, burglary, aggravated assault, robbery, attempted robbery	Witness error
Robert Clark	GA	Kidnapping, robbery	Police misconduct, witness error
Douglas Echols	GA	Kidnapping, robbery	Witness error
Clarence Harrison	GA	Kidnapping, robbery	Witness error
Calvin Johnson, Jr.	GA	Rape (2 counts), sodomy, burglary	Witness error
Samuel Scott	GA	Kidnapping, robbery	Witness error
John Jerome White	GA	Aggravated assault, burglary, robbery	Witness error, forensic errors

Table 4.1 *continued*

Name	State	Additional Charge(s)	Contributing Factors
Willie "Pete" Williams	GA	Kidnapping, sodomy	Witness error
Ronnie Bullock	IL	Aggravated kidnapping	Witness error
Dean Cage	IL	None	Witness error, forensic errors
Richard Johnson	IL	Robbery	Witness error
Marcus Lyons	IL	Criminal sexual assault (2 counts), unlawful restraint	Witness error
Jerry Miller	IL	Kidnapping, robbery	Witness error
Marlon Pendleton	IL	Robbery	Witness error, forensic errors
Donald Reynolds	IL	Attempted criminal sexual assault, robbery, attempted robbery	Witness error, forensic errors
Lafonso Rollins	IL	Rape (4 counts), robbery	Police misconduct, false confession, ineffective assistance of counsel
Billy Wardell	IL	Attempted criminal sexual assault, robbery, attempted robbery	Witness error, forensic errors
John Willis	IL	Sexual assault (2 counts), robbery (5 counts)	Prosecutorial misconduct, police misconduct, witness error
Harold Buntin	IN	Robbery	Witness error
Larry Mayes	IN	Robbery, unlawful deviate conduct	Police misconduct, witness error
William Gregory	KY	Attempted rape, burglary	Witness error, forensic errors

continues

Table 4.1 *continued*

Name	State	Additional Charge(s)	Contributing Factors
Gene Bibbins	LA	Burglary	Police misconduct, witness error, forensic errors
Dennis Brown	LA	Burglary, crimes against nature	Witness error, false confession, forensic errors
Clyde Charles	LA	None	Witness error
Allen Coco	LA	Burglary	Witness error
Willie Jackson	LA	Robbery	Witness error, forensic errors
Rickey Johnson	LA	None	Witness error, forensic errors
Johnny Ross	LA	None	Police misconduct, witness error, false confession
Michael Williams	LA	None	Witness error
Calvin Willis	LA	None	Witness error, forensic errors
Bernard Webster	MD	Daytime housebreaking	Witness error, forensic errors
Ulysses Rodriguez Charles	MA	Robbery, unlawful confinement, entering a dwelling armed with intent to commit a felony	Prosecutorial misconduct, police misconduct, witness error
Neil Miller	MA	Robbery	Police misconduct, witness error
Marvin Mitchell	MA	2 counts each: forcible sexual intercourse of a minor, unnatural sexual intercourse of a minor	Witness error, forensic errors
Guy Randolph	MA	None	Prosecutorial misconduct, witness error, ineffective assistance of counsel, insufficient evidence
Nathaniel Hatchett	MI	Kidnapping, carjacking, robbery	Prosecutorial misconduct, police misconduct, witness error, false confession, forensic errors
Walter Swift	MI	Robbery	Prosecutorial misconduct, police misconduct, witness error, ineffective assistance of counsel

Table 4.1 *continued*

Name	State	Additional Charge(s)	Contributing Factors
David Brian Sutherlin	MN	None	Witness error
Arthur Johnson	MS	Burglary	Witness error
Johnny Briscoe	MO	Sodomy, burglary, robbery, stealing, armed criminal action	Witness error, forensic errors
Lonnie Erby	MO	Kidnapping, armed criminal action, sodomy, robbery, sexual abuse, attempted rape, attempted robbery, felonious restraint, stealing	Witness error
Larry Johnson	MO	Kidnapping, sodomy, robbery	Witness error
Steven Toney	MO	Sodomy	Prosecutorial misconduct, witness error
Earl Berryman	NJ	Kidnapping	Witness error, ineffective assistance of counsel
Michael Bunch	NJ	Kidnapping	Witness error, ineffective assistance of counsel
McKinley Cromedy	NJ	Robbery, burglary, criminal sexual contact, terrorist threats	Witness error, ineffective assistance of counsel
Clarence Moore	NJ	None	Prosecutorial misconduct, witness error
David Shepard	NJ	Robbery, weapons violations, terrorist threats	Witness error
Nathaniel Walker	NJ	Kidnapping, sodomy	Witness error
Marion Coakley	NY	Robbery	Witness error
Charles Dabbs	NY	None	Witness error, forensic errors

continues

111

Table 4.1 *continued*

Name	State	Additional Charge(s)	Contributing Factors
Vincent Jenkins (aka Habib Wahir Abdal)	NY	None	Witness error
Lee Long	NY	Robbery	Prosecutorial misconduct, witness error
Antron McCray	NY	Assault	Police misconduct, false confession, forensic errors
Alan Newton	NY	Robbery, assault	Witness error
Yuself Salaam	NY	Assault	Police misconduct, false confession, forensic errors
Raymond Santana	NY	Assault	Police misconduct, false confession, forensic errors
Kharey Wise	NY	Assault, riot	Police misconduct, false confession, forensic errors
Ronald Cotton	NC	2 counts each: rape, burglary	Witness error, forensic errors
Sylvester Smith	NC	Double rape	Witness error
Donte Booker	OH	Kidnapping, robbery, gross sexual imposition	Witness error
Anthony Michael Green	OH	Aggravated robbery	Witness error, forensic errors
Robert McClendon	OH	Kidnapping	Witness error
Walter D. Smith	OH	Triple rape, kidnapping, robbery	Witness error
Arvin McGee	OK	Kidnapping, robbery, forcible sodomy	Witness error
Calvin Lee Scott	OK	None	Forensic errors
Thomas Doswell	PA	Criminal attempt, assault, terrorist threats, unlawful restraint	Witness error

Table 4.1 *continued*

Name	State	Additional Charge(s)	Contributing Factors
Vincent Moto	PA	Involuntary deviate sexual intercourse, criminal conspiracy, robbery	Witness error
Perry Mitchell	SC	None	Witness error, forensic errors
Clark McMillan	TN	Robbery	Witness error
A. B. Butler	TX	Kidnapping	Witness error
Kevin Byrd	TX	None	Police misconduct, witness error
Charles Allen Chatman	TX	None	Witness error, forensic errors
Tim Cole	TX	None	Police misconduct, witness error
Wiley Fountain	TX	None	Witness error
Larry Fuller	TX	None	Police misconduct, witness error
James Curtis Giles	TX	None	Prosecutorial misconduct, witness error
Eugene Henton	TX	None	Witness error, false confession
Antrone Lynelle Johnson	TX	None	Prosecutorial misconduct
Johnnie Earl Lindsey	TX	None	Witness error
Thomas Clifford McGowan	TX	Burglary	Police misconduct, witness error
Billy Wayne Miller	TX	None	Police misconduct, witness error
Arthur Mumphrey	TX	None	Snitch/informant, police misconduct
Ricardo Rachell	TX	None	Prosecutorial misconduct, police misconduct, witness error, ineffective assistance of counsel
Anthony Robinson	TX	None	Witness error

continues

113

Table 4.1 *continued*

Name	State	Additional Charge(s)	Contributing Factors
Billy James Smith	TX	None	Police misconduct, witness error, ineffective assistance of counsel
Josiah Sutton	TX	Carjacking	Witness error, forensic errors
Ronald Gene Taylor	TX	None	Witness error, forensic errors
Keith Turner	TX	None	Witness error
James Waller	TX	None	Witness error, forensic errors
Patrick Waller	TX	Aggravated robbery, aggravated kidnapping	Witness error
Marvin Anderson	VA	Abduction, sodomy, robbery	Police misconduct, witness error, ineffective assistance of counsel
Julius Earl Ruffin	VA	Sodomy	Witness error
Lindsey Scott	VA	None	Prosecutorial misconduct, witness error
Phillip Leon Thurman	VA	Abduction, assault	Witness error, forensic errors
Troy Webb	VA	Kidnapping, robbery	Witness error
Arthur Lee Whitfield	VA	Rape (2 counts), sodomy, robbery	Witness error, false confession
Jarrett Adams	WI	None	Prosecutorial misconduct, witness error, ineffective assistance of counsel
Dimitri Henley	WI	None	Prosecutorial misconduct, witness error, ineffective assistance of counsel
Anthony Hicks	WI	Robbery	Witness error, forensic errors

The next few sections examine in greater detail some of the rape and sexual assault cases that resulted in wrongful convictions. Because witness error was so prominent in the failure of justice for these offenses, the first section focuses on cases in which witness error played a prominent role in the outcome.

Cases in Which Witness Error Was the Primary Cause of the Wrongful Conviction

A recurring theme in many of the rape/sexual assault cases is the misidentification of the perpetrator by the victim. Typically, the error was not malicious but rather a case of mistaken identity. In some cases, however, the victim was deliberately misidentifying the perpetrator to cast suspicion on someone other than the actual perpetrator. In the first case in this section, two brothers from Alabama were identified as the perpetrators of an abduction and rape. Although the victim remained adamant that she had been raped by the two men, DNA tests later raised questions regarding her assertions.

Ronnie and Dale Mahan

On November 30, 1983, eighteen-year-old Pamela Pope informed the police that she had been abducted from a shopping mall in Bessemer, Alabama, by two men who were wearing stocking masks, and that they had driven her to a wooded area where she was repeatedly raped by one of the men while the other held her down. Six weeks subsequent to her attack, Pope identified Ronnie and Dale Mahan as her assailants from a photographic lineup. She also noted that one of her assailants stuttered, a speech impediment suffered by Dale Mahan. During the 1984 trial she further testified that she was beaten, burned on her arm with cigarettes, and forced to consume beer and smoke marijuana. Medical reports revealed the presence of burns on her arm, abrasions on her chest, neck, and face, and a chipped tooth, but no vaginal tears or bruising. Although DNA testing was unavailable in 1984, the blood type of the brothers was the same as that from the semen found on the victim. Defense counsel argued that at the time of the assault the two men were at a tavern celebrating their sister's birthday, an account that was corroborated by both family and nonfamily witnesses. After deliberating for two days, the jury found Ronnie and Dale Mahan guilty. Because Ronnie had prior burglary convictions, he received a life sentence for being a habitual criminal. Dale received a thirty-five-year sentence for his alleged role in the crime.

In November 1997 DNA tests on the semen taken from the rape kit disclosed that the Mahan brothers' DNA did not match that of the semen specimen. It was at this juncture that Pope confessed to having had sex with her now ex-husband the day of the rape. When it was further revealed that the DNA did not match that of her estranged husband, she amended her sworn affidavit to include the fact that she had also been involved in a sexual liaison prior to the attack with Toby Tyler, a former boyfriend who was later killed by police in Mississippi. Although the DNA tests disclosed a match between the semen and Tyler's DNA, Assistant District Attorney Arthur Green, Jr., remained unconvinced of the innocence of the Mahans and so decided to pursue the case again. Green now amended his account of the rape to suggest that the actual rapist did not ejaculate at any time during the four times that Pope was raped. A pubic hair recovered from the victim's clothing was then submitted for DNA testing by the prosecutor. Tests on the hair disclosed a genetic profile that did not match Pope's estranged husband, ex-boyfriend, or either of the Mahan brothers. Moreover, the victim's credibility had been severely compromised by her lack of complete disclosure of the sexual encounters that preceded the criminal incident as well as her psychiatric history since the event. With defense counsel now contending that the pubic hair must have come from the actual rapist, the prosecution decided to drop the case. By the time of their release, the Mahan brothers had served over eleven years of their sentences in prison for a crime that they had not committed. On December 3, 2002, Dale Mahan died in an automobile crash at the age of forty-one (Possley and Mills 2003; Sack 1997).

Marcus Lyons

In 1987 Marcus Lyons seemingly had everything going his way. The Navy Reserve officer was engaged to be married, enrolled at the College of DuPage in Illinois, and employed at AT&T as a computer operator. During the weekend he enjoyed the company of his four brothers, roller skated with his friends, and rode his motorcycle. He eagerly anticipated his return to active duty and a possible assignment in Hawaii. But at approximately 8:30 p.m. on November 30, 1987, everything changed. It was then that a twenty-nine-year-old white woman who lived in his apartment complex was orally and vaginally raped after she allowed a black stranger who asked to use her bathroom to enter her apartment. A composite sketch based on the victim's description was shown to others living in the apartments.[1] Two other women living there said that the drawing resembled Marcus Lyons, the apartment complex's lone black inhabitant. The victim further identified Lyons as her attacker in a photographic lineup. He was subsequently arrested and charged with the crime. An all-white jury found Lyons guilty of the accusations, and in October of 1988 he was sentenced to six years in prison.

During his incarceration Lyons obtained the services of a private attorney who was supposed to file an appeal but took no formal action during the two and a half years that Lyons was in prison. After Lyons was released on parole in March of 1991, he was required to register as a sex offender. Desperate to clear his name, two weeks after he was paroled he went to the DuPage County Courthouse with an 8'x6' crucifix constructed from railroad ties, whereupon he proceeded to drive a nail into his foot in an attempt to call attention to his plight. His protest resulted in conviction on three misdemeanor charges but no immediate interest in the circumstances of his earlier conviction. Finally, in 2006 Lyons hired an attorney from Jed Stone and Associates to file for DNA testing. The only remaining article of clothing from the case was the victim's bra, which contained semen from the rapist. Results from the DNA analysis excluded Lyons as the possible contributor of the semen. After over two years in prison and sixteen years as a registered sex offender, Lyons was exonerated in 2007 of the crime when DuPage County State's Attorney Joseph Birkett, the same prosecutor who had convicted Lyons during the first trial, dismissed the charges.

Today Lyons lives in Gary, Indiana, and infrequently visits his brothers. His fiancée, who left him after he was convicted, is only a faint memory. Although he is a certified biomedical engineer, Lyons struggles to find stable employment. He prays as a means of coping with depression and has difficulty in his relationships with women when they learn of his previous sex offender status (Smith 2007). According to the Innocence Project, Lyons is petitioning for executive clemency, which, if successful, would make him eligible for compensation for his wrongful conviction.

Clark McMillan

On the night of October 26, 1979, a sixteen-year-old white girl and her boyfriend were parked in the Overton Park area in Memphis, Tennessee, when a black man approached their car. Wielding a knife, the man forced them from the vehicle and began robbing the girl's boyfriend. He then took them into the woods and coerced them into taking off their clothes. The perpetrator then proceeded to rape the teenage girl while her boyfriend was told to lie face down. During the assault the rape victim was cut as she struggled with her assailant. After the perpetrator left, the two victims, unable to locate their keys, got the attention of a passing motorist and were taken to the home of the girl's Sunday school teacher. The police were notified and a rape kit was used to collect evidence of the sexual assault.

During police questioning, both parties gave similar descriptions of the assailant; however, neither mentioned that the assailant walked with a limp. When Clark McMillan was arrested four days later, he was sporting a leg brace and had a noticeable limp, the result of a gunshot wound two years previous. By the time that the trial started in May 1980, the limp had been added to the girl's description of her assailant. Moreover, during the initial photographic lineup, which included a picture of McMillan, neither victim selected McMillan. At the live lineup, however, the girl identified McMillan as her assailant, though her boyfriend selected another individual. Yet during the trial both identified McMillan in a lineup.

Although the rape victim's blue jeans contained semen from the rapist, no testing was performed during the original trial, other than a visual inspection of the clothing and a presumptive screening for seminal fluid. McMillan's defense was based on his assertion that he was at his sister's house with his girlfriend when the crime was committed. Both his sister and girlfriend corroborated his testimony at the trial. Despite the alibi, McMillan was found guilty of rape and robbery with a deadly weapon and sentenced to 119 years in prison.

In 1996 McMillan approached the Innocence Project with his case, as all of his appeals had been exhausted. Given the age of the case and problems with his original defense attorney, the process was delayed. Eventually, Kemper Durand, a criminal defense attorney from Memphis, became involved in his case as well. In April 2002 a DNA test of the semen-soaked crotch of the girl's blue jeans disclosed that McMillan could not have been the assailant. On May 2, 2002, his conviction was vacated and the charges against him were dismissed. Because McMillan was in prison on an unrelated gun possession charge from 1979, he wasn't released from prison until May 15, 2002, after being given credit for time served. At the time of his exoneration he had spent twenty-two years behind bars for a crime he didn't commit.

The Tennessee General Assembly awarded McMillan $832,000 in 2004, in compensation for his wrongful conviction. According to the Tennessee Code, up to $1 million can be awarded for a wrongful conviction. The actual compensation is determined by such factors as the amount of physical and mental suffering as well as the loss of earnings due to the wrongful confinement. Although McMillan was awarded over $800,000, as of January 2009 he had received only one payment of $250,000, which has largely been spent on recurring medical expenses accrued by McMillan and his wife (Kamionski 2009).

A. B. Butler

Another case in which an erroneous cross-racial identification led to a wrongful conviction occurred in Tyler, Texas, in 1983. A twenty-five-year-old white woman was abducted from a hotel parking lot. She was forced to drive to a remote area where her assailant raped her twice. The victim initially identified A. B. Butler through a mug shot and later through a live lineup. During the trial the victim without hesitation identified Butler as the perpetrator. Although Butler presented three alibi witnesses at the trial, he was found guilty and sentenced to ninety-nine years in prison. Repeated attempts to have the semen and hair samples from the scene tested for DNA proved futile. Finally, in 1999 Butler's lawyer secured a court order requiring that the evidence be tested. DNA tests of the semen and three hairs concluded that Butler could not have been the assailant. As a result of the test results, after posting $100,000 bail, Butler was released in January 2000. He was officially pardoned by Governor George W. Bush in May 2000 (Stern 2000).

Today Butler drives a dirt truck in Tyler, Texas. Presently in his fifties, he was twenty-eight years old when he was wrongfully convicted. In a November 2008 interview by *Texas Monthly* magazine, Butler commented:

> There are a lot of people my age already set for life, friends who I grew up with. They are pretty much settled in, and I'm out here working. . . . [Y]ou make up your mind on what you're going to do with your life in your thirties, and you're still able to get out there and do it, whereas I'm in my fifties now. I can't really work as hard as I could back when I was in my twenties and thirties. I just try to do the best I can.

Tim Cole

In the mid-1980s there had been a series of high-profile rapes near the Texas Tech University campus in Lubbock, Texas. One of those rapes resulted in the wrongful conviction of Tim Cole, a Texas Tech business student. In March 1985 Michelle Mallin, a twenty-year-old white student at Texas Tech University, was walking to her parked car when she was confronted by a black man asking for jumper cables. The assailant then stuck a knife to her neck and forced her inside her car. After driving her to a remote area, he assaulted her sexually. The following day, the victim identified Cole as her attacker from a picture lineup and later from a live lineup. She also informed the police that her assailant was a heavy smoker, although Cole suffered from asthma and didn't smoke. Cole, who had recently returned from a stint in the army, was offered a plea bargain: if he would confess his guilt, he would be given probation. After he rejected the offer, he was found guilty in September 1985 and given a twenty-five-year sentence. During his incarceration, Cole was offered parole if he would admit his role in the rape, and again Cole refused to confess to a crime he didn't commit. His refusal came at a cost, however. Cole, who made frequent trips to the prison infirmary and the Galveston hospital as prison conditions worsened his asthma, was eventually overcome by his childhood affliction and died in prison on December 2, 1999.

Unbeknownst to Cole, the actual rapist, Jerry Johnson, who had been convicted of other rapes, had been trying to get the attention of the Lubbock District Court clerk since 1995. In a letter to the court Johnson confessed to raping Mallin in 1985. The confession, however, fell on deaf ears. It wasn't until 2007 that Cole's family found out that Johnson had confessed to the crime, when a letter addressed to Tim Cole arrived at his family's home. Johnson, who had not yet learned of Cole's death, wrote in his letter dated May 11, 2007:

> I have been trying to locate you since 1995 to tell you I wish to confess I did in fact commit the rape Lubbock wrongly convicted you of. It is very possible that through a written confession from me and DNA testing, you can finally have your name cleared of the rape . . . if this letter reaches you, please contact me by writing so that we can arrange to take the steps to get the process started. Whatever it takes, I will do it. ("Texan Who Died in Prison Cleared of Rape Conviction" 2009)

After learning of the letter, the Innocence Project began to investigate the circumstances of the case. In May 2008 DNA tests confirmed that Johnson was the perpetrator. One month later, after DNA results were released to the general public, a three-part series about Cole's ordeal was published in the *Lubbock Avalanche-Journal*. Finally, on April 7, 2009, Judge Charlie Baird made headlines when he conferred the state's first posthumous exoneration on Cole. Judge Baird was especially critical of the Lubbock Police Department for its "snap judgment" and the fact that it "downplayed or deliberately ignored" possible exculpatory evidence. In issuing the exoneration, Judge Baird said,

> I want to say this with absolute clarity, that I have reviewed everything possible to review in this case. The evidence is crystal clear that Timothy Cole died in prison an innocent man, and I find to a 100 percent moral, legal, and factual certainty that he did not commit the crime of which he was convicted. (Blackburn 2009)

Influenced by the circumstances of this case, Governor Rick Perry in 2009 signed into law a bill that increased to $80,000 per year of incarceration the amount of compensation wrongfully convicted individuals may receive (Blackburn 2008; Castano 2009; "Governor Signs Tim Cole Act After Wrongful Lubbock Conviction" 2009).

Neil Miller

In late summer of 1989 another case involving cross-racial witness error unfolded in Boston, Massachusetts. A nineteen-year-old white coed from Emerson College was sleeping in her apartment when she heard the sound of an intruder. An African American man brandishing a screwdriver broke into her apartment, where he proceeded to rob, rape, and sodomize her. After reporting the incident to the Boston Police Department, the victim was shown pictures of possible suspects. She was unable to identify her assailant at this time. After viewing more photographs a few weeks after the incident, the victim was still unable to pick out her attacker. At this point a composite sketch was developed by the police based on her description of the rapist. Some of the police officers commented that the sketch resembled Neil Miller, who had been arrested several years earlier for receiving stolen goods, although he never served any time in prison. Several weeks later when Miller's mug shot from the earlier arrest was included in a new photographic lineup, the victim identified him and another suspect as the possible perpetrator. After arresting Miller on an unrelated disorderly conduct charge, the police took his picture and presented the victim with yet another photographic lineup. At this juncture the victim identified only Miller as the assailant. During the pretrial hearing, she testified that Miller was the man in her apartment the night of the rape. Because tests on the physical evidence obtained from the victim's apartment were inconclusive, the prosecution's case relied primarily on the victim's eyewitness testimony that Miller was responsible for the crime. Miller was found guilty and sentenced to twenty-six to forty-five years in prison on December 19, 1990.

In 1998 the Innocence Project became interested in Miller's case. The Innocence Project was able to get approval for DNA testing of the semen stain found on the bedsheets at the victim's apartment. The results of that test excluded Miller as the contributor. The semen stain had not been examined earlier because the lead detective, Margot Hill, who has since been promoted to deputy superintendent, had stated that the stain had originated from the victim's live-in boyfriend. Even more curious is the fact that none of the fingerprints found in the victim's apartment matched that of Miller, even though the victim said that her assailant had touched many of the items in her apartment. It is also alleged that Hill lied to the victim, telling her that Miller had previously been responsible for the rape of a ninety-year-old woman. After serving ten years in prison for a crime he did not commit, Miller was released in 2000. In 2005 Larry Taylor pleaded guilty to the rape of the Emerson College coed as well as the rape of two other women, after the state's DNA database identified him as the source of the semen.

Miller experienced difficulty adjusting to his freedom. Upon his release he spent a year with his sister, Demaris, and her husband, Dana Smith. During this time he encountered little success in locating employment. Today he plays video games and drinks to escape his situation. In an interview with *Frontline,* Miller said, "I drink more than I eat, at times. I drink more than I laugh. The only bit of solace and peace that I have is drinking." And his drinking comes at a cost. In 2003 he was placed on probation after being charged with two counts of assault and battery stemming from two separate drinking episodes. In March 2006 Miller won a $3.2 million settlement for his wrongful conviction from the city of Boston. When asked by the *Boston Globe* what he intends to do with the money, Miller responded, "I'm going to give it away. I don't know to who, maybe some other righteous person who could use it. It'll do some good for a while" (Abel 2005; Public Broadcasting System 2003; Richardson and Mulvihill 2004).

Sylvester Smith

In 1984 four-year-old Gloria Ogundeji told her mom, Ann Ogundeji, that her stomach hurt and she didn't feel like going to school. Because the little girl had been complaining earlier about not feeling well, her mother decided to take her to the emergency room at New Hanover Memorial Hospital. After the child had been examined, the mother was escorted to another room where she was informed that her daughter had been sexually assaulted. The mother became concerned when she was questioned by a police detective and a social worker. Fearful that she could lose custody of her daughter, she responded truthfully to all of their queries. When asked if her daughter had been alone with anyone else, she replied that Sylvester Smith, her live-in boyfriend, had spent time with her daughter.

A long trial ensued. Mike Easley, who later became the governor of North Carolina, and Wanda Bryant, who later became a state appeals court judge, served as prosecutors during the case. Leantha Smith, a six-year-old cousin of the victim, also testified that she had been sexually abused about the same time. During the trial it was reported that both girls had sexually transmitted diseases. Sylvester Smith refused to be tested for a sexually transmitted disease or to allow the court to obtain his medical records. Convicted in 1984, he was sentenced to two life terms for his alleged involvement in the sexual assaults.

In late 2004 District Attorney Rex Gore of Brunswick County, North Carolina, announced his intention to reopen the twenty-year-old case given the availability of some recent evidence suggesting that Smith was not guilty. Gloria Ogundeji, now twenty-four years old and the mother of two, recanted her original testimony implicating Smith. Instead, she said, her nine-year-old cousin, Benjamin Peterson, had been the actual perpetrator of the two sexual assaults.[2] The victim further indicated that her grandmother had encouraged her to accuse Smith of the crime to protect her young cousin. The other victim, Leantha Smith, now twenty-six years old, reluctantly testified that Smith had not molested her, either. However, she denied any sexual involvement with Peterson and eventually claimed that she was never sexually assaulted when she was six years old.

At the November 5, 2004, hearing both victims testified that Smith was innocent of the charges. During the hearing Rex Gore presented testimony from the original trial in which the four-year-old victim was asked by Smith's defense attorney, "Has anyone told you to say that Sylvester put his 'worm' in you?" to which the young girl replied, "My grandma." When he asked her, "Sylvester never really did this to you, did he sweetheart?" the girl replied, "No." The prosecutor then asked Gloria Ogundeji, "Did anyone tell you what to say when you got to court?" The girl responded that she was told to tell the truth, which she had done. Superior Court Judge William Gore (no relation to Rex Gore) also heard from Ann Ogundeji, who was upset that her deceased mother had been incorrectly portrayed as a criminal. In addition, she raised questions about the accuracy of her daughter's recollections. After a careful review of the facts of the case, Judge Gore found in a favor of a new trial for Smith. Immediately, the Brunswick County DA dismissed the charges against Smith, citing an absence of evidence. At that point the judge released Smith, twenty years after his wrongful conviction (Associated Press 2004; Barrett 2004; Blueline Radio, nd; United Press International 2004).

Earl Berryman and Michael Bunch

In 1983 a Brazilian woman from Irvington, New Jersey, was abducted by three African American men, who took her to an abandoned warehouse where they raped her. One and a half years after she was attacked, the victim identified Earl Berryman and Michael Bunch as two of her assailants while looking at photographs in mug books.[3] When Berryman was arrested he was given the opportunity to have his charges dropped if he would testify against Bunch, who had an extensive criminal arrest record. When he refused, both Berryman and Bunch were tried for sexual assault and kidnapping. Neither defendant had an opportunity to discuss their case with their court-appointed attorneys prior to the trial. Berryman's attorney, Nicholas DePalma, was eventually disbarred.

The state's case rested primarily on the victim's uncorroborated identification of Berryman and Bunch. Yet "the record shows that she gave vastly different physical descriptions of her attackers on three separate occasions, all of which varied substantially from Bunch and Berryman's actual physical features. The victim also contradicted herself at both trials by denying that she had initially given the police various physical descriptions of her assailants" (National Association of Criminal Defense Lawyers 2010). Upon being found guilty in 1985, both men received twenty-five- to fifty-year prison sentences at Trenton State Prison, a maximum security facility.

At the age of thirty, Bunch died of AIDS while still incarcerated, despite futile attempts by his attorney, Paul Casteleiro, to have his conviction overturned. Berryman was more fortunate. He was released in July 1995 when Federal District Judge Dickinson Debevoise noted that he had "very substantial doubt" that Berryman had committed the crime. Judge Debevoise additionally commented, "If there ever was an ineffective assistance of counsel situation, this was it" (Hester 1995, 6). Berryman's release was the culmination of five years' work by Centurion Ministries.

David Brian Sutherlin

Before describing the incidents that led to this wrongful conviction, it should be noted that this case is atypical in that the defendant was wrongly convicted of rape but was probably correctly convicted of two unrelated homicides. It is also atypical in that the DNA tests that exonerated David Brian Sutherlin (now known as Delegance Deangelo Sutherlin) were requested by the prosecutor's office as a result of a $859,000 grant from the Department of Justice to review pre-1995 criminal convictions involving DNA evidence.

Early on the morning of March 2, 1985, a woman was walking near her home in the Summit Hill area of St. Paul, Minnesota. She was accosted by a black man who hit her several times on the head with a metal object before taking her to a wooded area to rape her. At the police station she identified David Brian Sutherlin in a photographic lineup. On March 10, 1985, Sutherlin was arrested and charged with the rape. He was released from jail on March 12, 1985, after posting bail. While awaiting trial for rape, Sutherlin was involved in an altercation at a St. Paul bar in which two men were killed. During his rape trial, the victim became less certain of her identification, saying only that he resembled her assailant. Circumstantial evidence also implicated Sutherlin as the probable attacker because he lived in proximity to the rape scene and possessed an automobile similar to the one that had been seen in that area that night. In June 1985 a jury found Sutherlin guilty of rape. The following month he was convicted of the two unrelated homicides. Sutherlin received a sentence of forty-three months for the rape and a life sentence for the double homicide. In 2002 DNA from the semen found on the rape victim's clothing was tested. The results of the test excluded Sutherlin as the attacker. Further, the DNA testing disclosed a match with another man who had been released from prison earlier that year after being incarcerated for four and a half years on aggravated robbery charges. Because the statute of limitations had expired, the actual rapist could not be prosecuted for the crime. Sutherlin will now be eligible for parole earlier than he would have been if the wrongful conviction had not been detected, because the forty-three-month rape sentence was to run consecutive to the life sentence (Baran 2009; Gaertner 2010).

Cases in Which Witness Error Was One of the Factors in the Wrongful Conviction

The sample disclosed numerous situations in which witness error was one of the contributing factors in the miscarriage of justice. In this section a select number of cases are examined in some detail to reveal the dynamics at play in wrongful convictions involving rape and sexual assault.

Marvin Anderson

In 1982 Marvin Anderson found himself in an unenviable position. He was accused of the sodomy, rape, abduction, and robbery of a twenty-four-year-old white woman; but his attorney had previously represented the actual perpetrator and warned him that he was a suspect in the case. The victim had identified Anderson as her attacker, and the case was to be presented to an all-white jury. As a result, there was an abbreviated trial (approximately five hours in length) in which Anderson was found guilty and sentenced to 210 years in the Virginia State Penitentiary.

The incident that preceded this wrongful conviction occurred on the evening of July 17, 1982, when a young woman decided to take a shortcut to her house while returning from a shopping trip. She observed a young black man, who had previously passed her on his bicycle, lying on his side and apparently hurt (he was holding his knee). The woman stopped to render aid when he grabbed her and dragged her into a heavily wooded area. For the next two hours he threatened her with a gun, raped her repeatedly, and forced her mouth open as he engaged in oral sex. The assailant also urinated on the woman and forced her to eat feces. After the ordeal she fled back to the shopping center and was immediately taken to a local hospital where a rape kit was prepared. Her account of the incident included a description of her attacker and a comment that he had made that she resembled his white girlfriend.[4] It was the latter comment that led to his arrest when a police officer mentioned that Anderson was the only black man he knew in the community who lived with a white woman. Because Anderson did not have a previous criminal record, the police had no photographs on file, and so they obtained a photograph from his employer. The victim was shown Anderson's color picture along with some black-and-white mug shots of other possible suspects. She identified Anderson as her attacker. Shortly thereafter police asked her to identify her assailant in a physical lineup in which Anderson was the only person whose picture had appeared in the original photographic lineup. Again, the victim picked out Anderson as the perpetrator.

During the trial the victim explicitly recounted the events of that evening and once more identified Anderson as her assailant. Forensic tests conducted at the time were inconclusive regarding the identity of the rapist. Anderson's attorney, Donald White, rested his defense entirely on three alibi witnesses who testified that his client was not in the vicinity during the commission of the crime. Requests by Anderson and his mother to call to the witness stand the actual owner of the bicycle (it had been stolen earlier that day) and John Otis Lincoln, a man who had a criminal record for sex crimes and was reportedly seen by witnesses riding a bicycle in the vicinity shortly before the sexual assault, were ignored by White. On December 14, 1982, at the age of eighteen, Anderson was convicted of the charges and sentenced to a term of 210 years in prison.

In August 1988 during a state habeas hearing, Lincoln confessed under oath that he was responsible for the crime. Soon thereafter Lincoln recanted his confession, and Judge Richard Taylor, who had presided over the original trial, denied the writ. A model prisoner, Anderson was eventually granted parole in 1997. Determined to clear his name, he persisted in his attempt to be exonerated. After being denied clemency in 1993, Anderson sought the services of the Innocence Project. It was not until May 2001, however, when the Commonwealth of Virginia adopted a new statute that allowed individuals convicted of felonies to request forensic analysis of untested scientific evidence that sperm and semen samples taken from the victim were subjected to DNA testing. On December 6, 2001, DNA tests excluded Anderson as the assailant. Further, the profile obtained from the tests matched Lincoln.[5] Governor Mark Warner in April 2002 officially pardoned Anderson, making him eligible for compensation for his wrongful conviction. The following year the Virginia General Assembly awarded him $750,000 for fifteen years of wrongful imprisonment. According to the Center on Wrongful Convictions, after obtaining his freedom Anderson got married, had a child, and worked as a truck driver.

Josiah Sutton

A forty-one-year-old woman was abducted by two African American men from the parking lot of her apartment complex in southwest Houston in 1998. She was subsequently raped in her SUV and abandoned in a field in Fort Bend County. She initially described one of her assailants as a young 5'7" black male who weighed approximately 135 pounds and was wearing a baseball cap that faced to the side. Her other assailant was initially described as a young black male who was about the same height and somewhat slimmer, who was wearing a skull cap that hid part of his face. A few days after the attack, while driving her automobile, she saw Josiah Sutton (who was six feet tall and weighed 200 pounds) and his friend walking down the street. The victim identified the two as her assailants. She would later testify that she recognized them because they were wearing the same hats as those her attackers had worn. Sutton, then sixteen years old, and his friend agreed to have saliva and blood samples taken to prove their innocence. DNA tests conducted by the Houston Police Department crime lab ruled out Sutton's friend but could not eliminate Sutton as a suspect.

During the trial the prosecution's case revolved around the victim's eyewitness testimony and forensic evidence that pointed to Sutton as the probable attacker. The forensic evidence was especially strong: the Houston crime lab employee testified that the DNA from the semen found in the SUV was an exact match with Sutton's DNA. More specifically, the report concluded that the DNA profile extracted from the backseat "can be expected to occur in 1 out of 694,000 people among the black population" in the United States. Now, instead of being the captain of his high school's football team and looking forward to a college scholarship for football after graduation, Sutton faced the possibility of being incarcerated. In 1999 he was convicted and sentenced to twenty-five years in prison. He spent four and a half years in the Clemens Unit in Brazoria, Texas, prior to his release.

The Houston Police Department crime lab, which contributed to the wrongful conviction, was audited by the state of Texas after Sutton's trial. A scathing audit resulted in a suspension of DNA testing due to the shoddy practices at that facility. Concomitantly, the Harris County district attorney's office ordered a review of hundreds of cases that utilized evidence processed at the Houston lab. When the forensic evidence from Sutton's trial was reexamined, it was determined that the semen stain found in the automobile did not match that of Sutton, as reported at the trial. More specifically, the DNA taken from the crime scene could be found in 1 out of 16 African American men, not 1 out of 694,000. On March 12, 2003, Sutton was released after a second DNA test also excluded him as the contributor of the semen. In May 2004 Sutton received a pardon from the Texas governor.

Although Sutton spent less than five years wrongfully confined, his early prison experience was especially traumatic. According to his mother, Carol Batie, during the first months of his incarceration her son was exposed to graphic violence at the prison in Brazoria: "This was a (teenager) physically defending himself against men. He witnessed another inmate getting his throat slashed. He saw the guy lying on the ground, kicking, dying before his eyes. He saw another prisoner die after he was thrown over a railing" ("Houston Crime Lab Scandal" 2003). For solace in prison Sutton turned toward religion and became a Muslim. But the harsh realities of prison life can change a person, especially one so young. By the time he was released, Sutton sported a tattoo on his left arm. The tattoo featured a globe covered in ice with the inscription, "It's a cold world."

Sutton had a difficult time adjusting to his new freedom. A teenager when he entered prison, he was now an adult, with attendant responsibilities. Unable to locate employment that would provide him with a livable wage, he struggled mightily during the first year of his release. It was during this time that he learned that he had impregnated a woman whom he had briefly dated. And in the back of his mind was a nagging fear that he was only a misstep away from being reincarcerated. Always cognizant that he needed to have an alibi, Sutton saved toll, gas, and movie theater receipts to document his whereabouts. In October 2007—four years after his release from prison—Sutton was arrested on a misdemeanor marijuana possession charge and given a ten-day sentence in the Harris County jail ("DNA Frees Another" 2003; Fergus 2004a,b; "Josiah Sutton Back in Jail" 2007; "Justice for Josiah Sutton" 2004; Khanna and McVicker 2003; Liptak 2003).

Billy James Smith

Billy James Smith was on parole for robbery on August 7, 1986, when Dallas police officers arrested him for the aggravated rape of a woman. The victim had been doing her laundry at an apartment complex when she was abducted by a black man carrying a knife. After demanding money, the perpetrator forcibly took her to a grassy field nearby, placed his hat over her head, and sexually assaulted her. When the victim described the attacker to her boyfriend, who was the manager of the building, he was convinced that the perpetrator was Smith. And although he had not actually witnessed the rape, during the trial both the victim and her boyfriend were called as witnesses. Despite the presence of semen in the rape kit, neither the defense counsel nor the police sought to have the semen tested.[6] Moreover, defense counsel refused to call to the stand one of the alibi witnesses who could corroborate Smith's contention that he was at his sister's house at the time of the crime.[7] Smith was convicted of aggravated rape on February 5, 1987, and sentenced to life imprisonment.

While in prison Smith used his time productively. During his earlier incarceration he had earned his GED. He found that his newly acquired Muslim faith provided him with the comfort and positive direction that he needed to turn his life around. Smith became interested in the law on wrongful incarceration litigation in Texas. In 2001 he requested that DNA tests be run on the semen sample from the rape kit. After several unsuccessful appeals, the Texas Court of Criminal Appeals finally granted his request. When DNA testing confirmed that Smith could not have been the contributor of the semen, he was released on July 7, 2006. In December of that year he was officially exonerated of the crime by the Texas Court of Criminal Appeals (Clements 2007; Texas Wesleyan University School of Law 2007; Wilonsky 2007).

Ricardo Rachell

In the mid-1990s pellets from a shotgun left Ricardo Rachell's face permanently disfigured. His facial deformity made him drool and look frightening to small children.[8] Perhaps the fact that he looked different made it easier for others to assume that he was guilty of molesting a young boy. For whatever reason, however, the biological evidence from the rape kit was not tested prior to his trial. Ricardo Rachell's wrongful conviction represents an interesting example of a case in which requests for DNA testing by the police, the prosecutor, or the defense could have avoided this miscarriage of justice.

On October 20, 2002, an eight-year-old boy reported that he was approached by a stranger riding a bicycle while he and a friend were playing hide-and-go-seek. The stranger, who was wearing a scarf over his face, offered to pay them ten dollars for assistance with trash removal. When the boys met him at the designated location for the job, the attacker "spirited the victim away on his bicycle" to a vacant building and "undressed him and tried to sodomize him" (Olsen, Schiller, and Khanna 2008). On October 23, 2002, Rachell was arrested after the victim identified him as his assailant. While Rachell was in jail awaiting his trial, there was another attack on an eight-year-old boy in the same South Houston neighborhood. The events were similar to those of Rachell's case. In both incidents the attacker rode a bicycle, used a knife to threaten the victim, and lured the victim with a promise of money for doing some chore (in the latter case the offer was fifteen dollars to throw some newspapers). Rachell sent his defense counsel, Ron Hayes, a copy of the story that appeared in the *Houston Chronicle* and asked him to investigate it. Although it was another six months before a jury would find Rachell guilty and wrongfully sentence him to forty years in prison, Hayes decided that the cases were sufficiently different to ignore his client's request. And despite the fact that a similar incident occurred while Rachell was incarcerated, the police, the prosecutor, and the defense all declined the opportunity to have the biological evidence examined. Instead, the eyewitness testimony of the young boy and his younger friend was used to convict Rachell on June 5, 2003. Meanwhile, attacks on young boys continued in South Houston. At least three more young boys were attacked by an adult male using a similar modus operandi during Rachell's wrongful incarceration.

His appeals were unsuccessful. On September 30, 2004, the Eleventh Court of Appeals affirmed the verdict. Knowing that he was innocent and believing that the truth would eventually prevail, Rachell continued to push on. Finally, in March 2008 the district attorney's office requested that the biological evidence be subjected to DNA testing. In November 2008 the DNA test results were revealed: Rachell was excluded as the perpetrator of the sexual assault. On December 12, 2008, Judge Susan Brown of the 185th District Court ordered the release of Rachell, thereby bringing to a close his six-plus years of wrongful confinement (Khanna 2008; Khanna, Olsen, and Schiller 2008).

Donald Reynolds and Billy Wardell

It was shortly after 10 p.m. on the night of May 3, 1986. Two white University of Chicago coeds were walking near their residence hall when they heard the sound of some men. Three African American men approached them demanding money and threatening them with a gun. While on her knees one of the victims handed the only cash she had to one of the assailants. The victims were then escorted to a nearby vacant lot, where one was raped three times by one man and once by another—but not until she had scratched one of her assailants on the face and neck. The other woman avoided getting raped after a violent struggle ensued with the remaining attacker. After the attack the women used a university security telephone to summon the police. At the hospital a rape kit was prepared for each victim. Three days later, the police arrived at their residence hall to take them to the police station to develop a composite sketch of their assailants. While en route, the police officers and the victims saw a detective questioning Donald Reynolds who had been detained because he resembled one of the rapists. One victim identified him as one of the three perpetrators. Almost a month elapsed before Billy Wardell was tentatively identified from a photographic lineup as the second assailant by the other victim. The third assailant was never identified.

Prior to the 1988 trial, codefendants Reynolds and Wardell filed a motion requesting that the rape kits be tested for DNA. Cook County Circuit Court Judge Arthur J. Cieslik denied their motion. During the trial both victims testified that Reynolds and Wardell were their attackers. Forensic work performed at the Chicago police crime lab was used to corroborate the women's accounts. Pamela Fish, whose credibility would eventually be questioned after an examination of her statements at numerous criminal trials, incorrectly informed the jury that the semen from the rape kit could only be found in 38 percent of the black male population when, in fact, it was prevalent in 80 percent of black males. Fish also neglected to mention that hairs found on Reynolds's body were not from either victim. Both Reynolds and Wardell were found guilty. Prior to sentencing, Judge Cieslik told the two defendants, "You weren't satisfied with [robbing the victims]. You were going to have some more fun with some white girls." At this juncture the judge sentenced them to sixty-nine years apiece.

In 1992 the Illinois Appellate Court affirmed the convictions but remanded the case for resentencing based on the possible prejudicial attitude of the judge, given his remarks about having "more fun with white girls." The sentences were eventually reduced to fifty-five years each. Then in 1996, Wardell obtained the services of Attorney Kathleen Zellner and Reynolds obtained the services of Attorney David Gleicher. The two attorneys were able to get the Cook County State's Attorney Office to consent to DNA testing given the precedents established by earlier cases involving Steven Linscott and the Ford Heights Four. DNA tests in August 1997 concluded that neither Reynolds nor Wardell were contributors of the semen recovered from the victim. On November 16, 1997, Assistant State's Attorney Thomas Gainer acknowledged that Reynolds and Wardell had been wrongfully convicted. Reynolds and Wardell experienced freedom for the first time in eleven years when a judge vacated their convictions.

Cases in Which Witness Error
Was Not a Contributing Factor to the Wrongful Conviction

As noted previously, witness error contributed to wrongful convictions in over nine of every ten rape and sexual assault cases. Thus, there were relatively few cases that excluded witness error as a contributing factor in the wrongful conviction. This section discusses four cases in which factors other than witness error led to the conviction of an innocent.

Lafonso Rollins

At the age of seventeen, Lafonso Rollins was accused of a series of rapes and robberies involving elderly women who lived in a public housing project in Chicago. Rollins, a ninth-grade special education student with a second-grade writing ability, was convicted of the rape of a seventy-eight-year-old woman and sentenced as an adult to seventy-five years in prison in 1993. The main evidence used to convict him was a controversial confession, which he signed but did not write. In that confession Rollins admitted to attacks on two elderly women. Although biological evidence was available, his attorney, Madison Gordon, never requested DNA testing of the sperm found at the crime scene.[9] In June 2004, when public defenders were successful in having the sperm examined, DNA tests excluded Rollins as the contributor in the assault of the seventy-eight-year-old woman. Further testing excluded Rollins as the perpetrator of the attack on a ninety-two-year-old woman, an assault to which he had confessed but for which he was never convicted. The tests additionally confirmed that the same man was responsible for both attacks. Based on the test results, the public defenders and prosecutor's office filed to vacate his conviction. Rollins was released in 1994 and received a gubernatorial pardon in 2005.

After serving over eleven years in prison, Rollins sued the Chicago Police Department for its role in the wrongful confinement. Deprived of sleep and coerced by the police, who promised to let him go home if he would sign the confession, Rollins admitted to the crimes. He also maintains that the police assured him that DNA tests would be forthcoming. However, DNA tests in rape cases were not routinely performed by the police in 1993. In 2006 the city of Chicago agreed to settle its case with Rollins and he was awarded $9 million. Later that year Rollins began a foundation called Right the Wrong Complications and donated $10,000 to the Pilgrim Baptist Church on the city's South Side. The money was used to help rebuild the church after it was destroyed by a fire in January 2006 (Crimmins 2004; Gutierrez 2006; Meincke 2006).

Calvin Lee Scott

In 1982 in Pontotoc County, Oklahoma, a young woman was asleep with her four-month-old infant. She was awakened by an intruder who held a knife to her throat and demanded that she give him her purse. When she informed the intruder that she didn't have any money, she was told to remove her underpants, whereupon he proceeded to rape her. A pillow placed over her face obstructed the victim's view of her attacker, making a positive identification of her assailant impossible. Nevertheless, she was able to make out some general characteristics of her attacker. She informed the police that the rapist was a black man with a mustache who was between 5'8" and 5'11" in height. She also characterized him as being of medium build. Four months elapsed before the police had their first lead. An anonymous telephone call caused them to suspect Calvin Lee Scott, who was in jail for larceny. The police asked Scott to provide them with samples of his hair and saliva for comparison with the biological evidence found at the crime scene. Scott acquiesced and submitted the samples. During the trial a state criminologist who had examined the hairs concluded that Scott's hair was microscopically consistent with the hairs obtained from the victim. In reaching its verdict, the jury relied extensively on the conclusions of the forensic criminologist. Scott was convicted of first-degree rape and sentenced to twenty-five years in prison in 1983. It wasn't until 2003 that the vaginal swab from the rape kit was subjected to DNA testing. When the test was concluded, the results matched another man who was serving time for an unrelated rape. Because of the statute of limitations, the actual perpetrator could not be tried for the rape. Finally, after twenty years of wrongful confinement, Scott was released from prison.[10]

Arthur Mumphrey

In Conroe, Texas, a small town approximately fifty miles from Houston, on the night of February 28, 1986, a thirteen-year-old girl was walking down the railroad tracks. Headed toward town, she heard the sound of two men behind her. As they began a conversation, one of the men seized her and took her to a wooded area, where both men raped her repeatedly while holding a knife to her throat. The two men, who had been drinking wine during the attack, threatened to kill her if she screamed. Eventually they released her, and later that night she was examined at a local hospital, where a rape kit was collected. Although the victim was never able to identify her assailants, a police investigation resulted in the questioning of a mentally retarded and illiterate man, Steve Thomas. He admitted to the rape and implicated Arthur Mumphrey as the second rapist. He agreed to testify against Mumphrey in court in exchange for leniency. During the investigation, however, Arthur Mumphrey's fifteen-year-old brother, Charles Mumphrey, confessed to the crime. When threatened with perjury, Charles recanted his testimony, stating that he lied because he knew that he would receive a lighter sentence than his twenty-two-year-old brother because he was a juvenile. At the trial Thomas testified against the older Mumphrey, and another witness told the jury that he had heard Thomas talk about the sexual assault the same night as the attack and that Arthur Mumphrey, who was standing only four feet away, made no attempt to dispute the story. The witness also noted that both men were drunk at the time. Mumphrey was convicted of aggravated sexual assault in 1986 and sentenced to thirty-five years in prison. In 2000, after serving fourteen years of his sentence, he was released on parole. His freedom was short lived, nonetheless, as he was reincarcerated for violating the conditions of his parole in 2002.[11]

Houston defense attorney Eric Davis began representing Mumphrey in 2002. After a series of unsuccessful attempts to locate the rape kit, Davis was finally successful and was granted a motion for DNA testing in fall 2005. Semen from the rape kit and on the victim's panties was analyzed. DNA tests revealed that the semen belonged to Thomas and an unknown assailant, thus exonerating Mumphrey. Released on January 27, 2006, on his own recognizance, Mumphrey was officially pardoned by Governor Rick Perry in March of the same year. After his brother's release, Charles Mumphrey again confessed to the 1986 rape while incarcerated for the unauthorized use of a motor vehicle. Because the statute of limitations had expired, Mumphrey's brother was not prosecuted. Arthur Mumphrey has not talked to his brother since his conviction.

Because he received a pardon, Mumphrey was immediately eligible for restitution from the state of Texas. In 2006 he was awarded $452,082 for his wrongful incarceration. Early indications suggest that the compensation will have little impact on his lifestyle. After he was released from prison he moved to Houston where he started working at a glass company. Shortly thereafter he began employment at a Houston steel company where he works six days a week. According to his wife, Angela Mumphrey, whom he began dating during his first release from prison, Arthur Mumphrey is a "homebody" who enjoys watching football and basketball on television and playing dominoes with her dad on Sundays.[12] He also talks regularly to his sisters (Lee 2006; Levy 2006; "Texas Awards $450,000 to Man Who Spent 18 Years in Prison on Wrongful Conviction" 2006).

Antrone Lynelle Johnson

The last case discussed in this section involves a Brady violation. According to the 1963 *Brady v. Maryland* Supreme Court case, it is a violation of a defendant's constitutional rights if a prosecutor, either intentionally or accidentally, fails to turn over potentially exculpatory evidence to the defense. In Texas, however, there are no sanctions for prosecutors that violate the terms of this decision, making it difficult for defendants to enforce this right. Attorney Robert Guest (2008) observes, "Parties in a car wreck, or a divorce case in Texas, have a much greater right to discovery than criminal defendants." For example, both police reports and grand jury testimony may be withheld from defendants in that state. It is thus possible for defendants to remain uninformed of information that could potentially exonerate them of the crimes of which they are accused.

Antrone Lynelle Johnson was a seventeen-year-old attending a Texas high school in 1995 when he was accused of having oral sex with a female student. However, a note that was not given to the defense by the prosecution suggests that there was no sexual contact between the two. The note from February 5, 1995, revealed that "Johnson did not make her give him oral sex. He took her in the bathroom and she told him she didn't want to do it, so he stayed in there and pretended and then let her out" (Emily 2008). Moreover, prosecutorial interviews of the girl's teachers raised questions regarding her credibility. Another undisclosed note from one school official claimed that the alleged victim is "a great liar and if you really didn't know her, you'd think that she is telling the truth" (Emily 2008). Still, the prosecutor continued to pursue the case. Johnson eventually agreed to plead guilty to sexual assault in return for ten years' probation.

Later that same year, Johnson found himself again involved in an illicit sexual encounter. While on probation he was charged with having sex with a thirteen-year-old girl in the boys' restroom at the Seagoville High School. The female student was only three months away from her fourteenth birthday—an important milestone in Texas, because a female is eligible to give consent to sex with a minor male when she reaches this age.

During the day of the alleged sexual assault, the girl had arrived at school with condoms intent on having sex with multiple partners. In fact, she had had sex with three other students under the basketball bleachers earlier that same day.[13] Prosecutorial records disclose that the girl gave conflicting statements about the activities of the day. She also denied having sex with Johnson in an appearance before the grand jury. Nevertheless, none of this information was passed on to the defense. Given the evidence, grand juries were initially unwilling to indict Johnson for the sexual encounter.[14] After a third grand jury finally agreed to indict Johnson for the sexual assault of a child, the late Judge Mark Tolle sentenced him to five years in prison for the second crime. The judge further revoked his probation and sentenced him to life for the first crime. No DNA tests were conducted in either case.

The withheld evidence was not discovered until 2008. After uncovering the information, Johnson's lawyer, Shirley Baccus-Lobel, filed a writ of habeas corpus on October 31 of that year. On November 17, 2008, state District Judge Robert Francis held a hearing. The following day Johnson was released on his own recognizance when the judge recommended that Johnson's conviction and life sentence be vacated. Finally, after the Texas Court of Criminal Appeals ruled on May 20, 2009, that Johnson should be awarded a new trial, Dallas County District Attorney Craig Watkins agreed to drop the case.

Victim Characteristics and Wrongful Rape/Sexual Assault Convictions

Additional information on the rape and sexual assault cases in the study can be gleaned from Table 4.2. An examination of the data on victim characteristics discloses that most cases involved a lone victim. Although data regarding the age of the victim were unobtainable for half of the victims, the case narratives frequently referred to the victim as "young." This seems to be corroborated when one analyzes the sixty-six cases in which information on victim age was available. Almost one-half of the victims were between eighteen and twenty-nine years of age. An additional one-third of the victims were under the age of eighteen. As anticipated, the victims were overwhelmingly female. Only four males were found among victims in the wrongful convictions for sexual assault. The most intriguing finding, however, involved the race of the victim. Although most violent crimes in the United States are *intra*racial, a majority of the wrongful convictions for rape/sexual assault were *inter*racial. Over 81 percent of the 74 victims for which it was possible to identify their race were white. Black victims comprised only 16.2 percent of the victims. Although it was impossible to determine the race of about 45 percent of the victims, the case narratives commonly suggested the possibility that the perpetrator and the victim were of different races. Nonetheless, absent specific information on victim race, victim race was treated as missing data.

In addition to a disproportionate number of white victims, the sentences imposed on the offenders were frequently quite severe. Referring again to Table 4.2, almost 83 percent of the cases resulted in a maximum sentence of twenty-five years or more. The table also discloses that approximately three-fourths of the wrongful convictions for rape/sexual assault occurred during the 1980s, whereas slightly more than one-fifth of the wrongful convictions occurred during the 1990s. Wrongfully convicted African American men were commonly incarcerated for lengthy periods of time as suggested by the fact that almost 60 percent of those released were not freed until the twenty-first century. An analysis of the clearance data reveals that over seven of every ten defendants were exonerated during this same time frame.

Conclusion

This investigation found 109 cases of wrongful conviction in which rape/sexual assault is the most serious offense. An analysis of these cases reveals that the charge of rape/sexual assault is frequently accompanied by one or more additional charges, the most common of which is robbery. Although the typical case involved a lone victim, a few cases involved multiple victims. Mirroring the finding involving wrongful murder convictions, most wrongful rape/sexual assault convictions resulted from multiple factors. When the miscarriage of justice resulted from a single factor, it was most commonly witness error.

Perhaps the most important finding involves the extent to which witness error contributed to these wrongful convictions. In over nine of every ten cases witness error played some role in the miscarriage of justice. (Witness error was three times more common than forensic errors, the second most common factor.) Particularly noteworthy is the extent to which many of these witness errors involved white witnesses (usually the victim), thus raising further concerns regarding the accuracy of cross-racial identifications. Another significant finding involves the larger than expected number of interracial rapes/sexual assaults. Of the 74 victims for which it was possible to identify race, over 81 percent were white. Thus, whereas most crimes of this genre are intraracial, the ones that result in wrongful convic-

Table 4.2 Victim and Case Characteristics in Rape and Sexual Assault Cases (N=109)

Name	#	Victim Characteristics			Sentence	Convicted	Released	Cleared
		Age	Gender	Race				
AL								
Dale Mahan	1	18	Female	n/a	35 years	1984	1998	1998
Ronnie Mahan	1	18	Female	n/a	Life w/o parole	1984	1998	1998
CA								
Herman Atkins	1	23	Female	White	45 years	1988	2000	2000
Damon Auguste	1	15	Female	n/a	18 years	1998	2004	2004
Frederick Daye	1	n/a	Female	White	Life+	1984	1994	1994
Albert Johnson	2	n/a	Female	White	39 years	1992	2002	2002
		n/a		n/a				
CT								
Mark Reid	1	n/a	Female	White	12 years	1997	deported	2003
James Tillman	1	26	Female	White	45 years	1989	2006	2006
FL								
Larry Bostic	1	30	Female	n/a	8 years + 5 yrs. probation	1989	2007	2007
Alan Crotzer	2	12	Female	White	130 years	1982	2006	2006
		38	Female	White				
GA								
Robert Clark	1	29	Female	n/a	Life+	1982	2005	2005
Douglas Echols	1	n/a	Female	n/a	5 years	1987	1992	2002
Clarence Harrison	1	n/a	Female	Black	Life	1987	2004	2004

138

Table 4.2 *continued*

Name	#	Victim Characteristics			Sentence	Convicted	Released	Cleared
		Age	Gender	Race				
Calvin Johnson, Jr.	1	n/a	Female	White	Life+	1983	1999	1999
Samuel Scott	1	n/a	Female	n/a	Life+	1987	2001	2002
John Jerome White	1	74	Female	n/a	Life + 40 years	1980	2007	2007
Willie "Pete" Williams	1	n/a	Female	n/a	45 years	1985	2007	2007
IL								
Ronnie Bullock	1	9	Female	Black	60 years	1984	1994	1994
Dean Cage	1	15	Female	n/a	40 years	1996	2008	2008
Richard Johnson	1	21	Female	White	36 years	1991	1995	1995
Marcus Lyons	1	29	Female	White	6 years	1988	1991	2007
Jerry Miller	1	n/a	Female	White	45 years	1982	2007	2007
Marlon Pendleton	1	n/a	Female	n/a	Life	1992	2006	2006
Donald Reynolds	2	College age	Female	White	69 years (reduced to 55)	1988	1997	1997
Lafonso Rollins	4	College age	Female	White	75 years	1994	2004	2004
		78	Female	Black				
		92	Female	Black				
		Elderly	Female	Black				
		Elderly		Black				
Billy Wardell	2	College age	Female	White	69 years (reduced to 55)	1988	1997	1997
John Willis	2	College age	Female	White	100 years	1992	1999	1999
		n/a	Female	n/a				
		n/a	Female	White				

continues

Table 4.2 *continued*

Name	#	Victim Characteristics			Sentence	Convicted	Released	Cleared
		Age	Gender	Race				
IN								
Harold Buntin	1	22	Female	n/a	50 years	1986	2007	2005
Larry Mayes	1	n/a	Female	White	80 years	1982	2001	2001
KY								
William Gregory	2	n/a	Female	White	70 years	1993	2000	2000
		n/a	Female	n/a				
LA								
Gene Bibbins	1	13	Female	Black	Life	1987	2003	2003
Dennis Brown	1	n/a	Female	White	Life	1985	2004	2005
Clyde Charles	1	n/a	Female	White	Life	1982	1999	1999
Allen Coco	1	n/a	Female	n/a	Life	1997	2006	2006
Willie Jackson	1	n/a	Female	Black	40 years	1989	2005	2006
Rickey Johnson	1	22	Female	Black	Life	1983	2008	2008
Johnny Ross	1	n/a	Female	White	Death	1975	1981	1981
Michael Williams	1	22	Female	n/a	Life	1981	2005	2005
Calvin Willis	1	10	Female	n/a	Life	1982	2003	2003
MD								
Bernard Webster	1	n/a	Female	White	30 years	1983	2002	2002
MA								
Ulysses Rodriguez Charles	3	n/a	Female	White	72–80 years	1984	2001	2001
		n/a	Female	White				
		n/a	Female	White				

Table 4.2 continued

Name	#	Victim Characteristics			Sentence	Convicted	Released	Cleared
		Age	Gender	Race				
Neil Miller	1	19	Female	White	26–45 years	1990	2000	2000
Marvin Mitchell	1	11	Female	n/a	9–25 years	1990	1997	1997
Guy Randolph	1	6	Female	n/a	10 years (suspended)	1991	1991	2008
MI								
Nathaniel Hatchett	1	23	Female	n/a	25–40 years	1998	2008	2008
Walter Swift	1	35	Female	White	20–40 years	1982	2008	2008
MN								
David Brian Sutherlin	1	n/a	Female	n/a	43 months	1985	—	2002
MS								
Arthur Johnson	1	n/a	Female	n/a	55 years	1993	2008	2008
MO								
Johnnie Briscoe	1	28	Female	White	45 years	1983	2006	2006
Lonnie Erby	5	14	Female	n/a	115 years	1986	2003	2003
		Teenager	Female	n/a				
		Teenager	Female	n/a				
		Teenager	Female	n/a				
		Teenager	Female	n/a				
Larry Johnson	1	n/a	Female	White	Life + 15 years	1984	2002	2002
Steven Toney	1	n/a	Female	White	Life (2 times)	1983	1996	1996

continues

Table 4.2 *continued*

Name	#	Age	Gender	Race	Sentence	Convicted	Released	Cleared
			Victim Characteristics					
NJ								
Earl Berryman	1	n/a	Female	Latina	25–50 years	1985	1995	1995
Michael Bunch	1	n/a	Female	Latina	25–50 years	1985	died in prison	—
McKinley Cromedy	1	n/a	Female	White	60 years	1994	1999	1999
Clarence Moore	1	n/a	Female	White	Life	1985	2001	2001
David Shepard	1	n/a	Female	White	30 years	1984	1994	1994
Nathaniel Walker	1	21	Female	n/a	Life + 50 years	1975	1986	1986
NY								
Marion Coakley	1	n/a	Female	White	15 years	1985	1987	1987
Charles Dabbs	1	n/a	Female	Black	12.5–20 years	1984	1991	1991
Vincent Jenkins (aka Habib Wahir Abdal)	1	n/a	Female	White	20 years to life	1982	1999	1999
Lee Long	1	n/a	Female	n/a	8–24 years	1995	2000	2000
Antron McCray	1	28	Female	White	5–10 years	1989	1995	2002
Alan Newton	1	25	Female	n/a	13 1/3–40 years	1985	2006	2006
Yuself Salaam	1	28	Female	White	5–10 years	1989	1995	2002
Raymond Santana	1	28	Female	White	5–10 years	1989	1997	2002
Kharey Wise	1	28	Female	White	5–15 years	1989	2002	2002
NC								
Ronald Cotton	2	22 / n/a	Female / Female	White / n/a	Life + 54 years	1985, 1987	1995	1995
Sylvester Smith	2	4 / 6	Female / Female	n/a / n/a	Life	1984	2004	2004

Table 4.2 *continued*

Name	#	Age	Gender	Race	Sentence	Convicted	Released	Cleared
		Victim Characteristics						
OH								
Donte Booker	1	n/a	Female	White	10–25 years	1987	2002	2005
Anthony Michael Green	1	n/a	Female	White	20–50 years	1988	2001	2001
Robert McClendon	1	10	Female	n/a	15 years to life	1991	2008	2008
Walter D. Smith	3	n/a	Female	n/a	78–190 years	1986	1996	1996
		n/a	Female	n/a				
		n/a	Female	n/a				
OK								
Arvin McGee	1	20	Female	n/a	365 years (reduced to 298)	1989	2002	2002
Calvin Lee Scott	1	n/a	Female	n/a	25 years	1983	2003	2003
PA								
Thomas Doswell	1	n/a	Female	White	13–26 years	1986	2005	2005
Vincent Moto	1	n/a	Female	n/a	12–24 years	1987	1996	1996
SC								
Perry Mitchell	1	17	Female	White	30 years	1984	1998	1998
TN								
Clark McMillan	1	16	Female	White	119 years	1980	2002	2002

continues

Table 4.2 *continued*

Name	#	Victim Characteristics			Sentence	Convicted	Released	Cleared
		Age	Gender	Race				
TX								
A. B. Butler	1	25	Female	White	99 years	1983	2000	2000
Kevin Byrd	1	25	Female	Black	Life	1985	1997	1997
Charles Allen Chatman	1	n/a	Female	White	99 years	1981	2008	2008
Tim Cole	1	20	Female	White	25 years	1985	died in prison	2008
Wiley Fountain	1	n/a	Female	Black	40 years	1986	2002	2002
Larry Fuller	1	n/a	Female	White	50 years	1981	2006	2006
James Curtis Giles	1	n/a	Female	White	30 years	1983	1993	2007
Eugene Henton	1	n/a	Female	n/a	4 years (plea bargain)	1984	1986[a]	2006
Antrone Lynelle Johnson	2	13	Female	n/a	Life	1995	2008	2008
		n/a	Female	n/a				
Johnnie Earl Lindsey	1	27	Female	White	Life	1983/1985	2008	2008
Thomas Clifford McGowan	1	n/a	Female	n/a	Life (2 consecutive terms)	1985/1986	2008	2008
Billy Wayne Miller	1	n/a	Female	n/a	Life	1984	2006	2006
Arthur Mumphrey	1	13	Female	n/a	35 years	1986	2000[b]	2006
Ricardo Rachell	1	8	Male	n/a	40 years	2003	2008	2008
Anthony Robinson	1	n/a	Female	n/a	27 years	1987	1997	2000
Billy James Smith	1	n/a	Female	n/a	Life	1987	2006	2006
Josiah Sutton	1	41	Female	n/a	25 years	1999	2003	2004
Ronald Gene Taylor	1	n/a	Female	n/a	60 years	1995	2007	2008
Keith Turner	1	n/a	Female	n/a	20 years	1983	1987	2005
James Waller	1	12	Male	White	30 years	1983	1993	2007
Patrick Waller	4	n/a	Female	White	Life	1992	2008	2008
		n/a	Male	White				
		n/a	Female	n/a				
		n/a	Male	n/a				

Table 4.2 *continued*

Name	#	Victim Characteristics			Sentence	Convicted	Released	Cleared
		Age	Gender	Race				
VA								
Marvin Anderson	1	24	Female	White	210 years	1982	1997	2001
Julius Earl Ruffin	1	32	Female	White	Life	1981	2003	2003
Lindsey Scott	1	35	Female	White	35 years	1983	1988	1988
Phillip Leon Thurman	1	37	Female	n/a	31 years	1985	2004	2005
Troy Webb	1	n/a	Female	n/a	47 years	1989	1996	1996
Arthur Lee Whitfield	2	n/a	Female	n/a	63 years	1982	2004	2004
		n/a	Female	n/a				
WI								
Jarrett Adams	1	College-age	Female	White	28 years	2000	2007	2007
Dimitri Henley	1	College-age	Female	White	28 years	2000	2008	n/a
Anthony Hicks	1	n/a	Female	White	20 years	1991	1996	1997

Notes: n/a = not available.
a. Returned to prison in 1995 after being convicted of two unrelated felonies. Eventually released from prison in 2007.
b. Released on parole in 2000. Returned to prison in 2002 for a violation of the conditions of parole.

tion apparently are more likely to be interracial. This is due, at least in part, to the misidentification of the perpetrator by the white victim. It may also reflect a greater concern to "bring to justice" African American assailants who single out white females as their targets. To the extent that this may lead to a rush to judgment, interracial rapes/sexual assaults may be particularly vulnerable to miscarriages of justice.

In addition to witness and forensic errors, police misconduct and prosecutorial misconduct were present in approximately 23 and 15 percent of the wrongful rape/sexual assault convictions. Ineffective assistance of counsel (11 percent) and false confession (10 percent) complete the list of contributing factors that accounted for at least 10 percent of the false convictions. When false confessions for rape and sexual assault are compared with those involving murder, at least three differences emerge. First, false confessions are less numerous in rapes and sexual assault than in murder. Second, unlike wrongful convictions involving murder, where a majority of the defendants are adults, false confessions for rape and sexual assault are more likely to involve juveniles. And finally, the data suggest the possibility that prolonged interrogations may have played a greater role in obtaining false confessions for rape and sexual assault than for murder.

It should additionally be noted that a majority of the releases and exonerations did not occur until the 2000s, which reflects the important role that forensic testing of DNA has played in clearing those who have been wrongfully incarcerated. Largely unavailable until late in the twentieth century, sophisticated DNA tests now provide an alternative to eyewitness accounts. As DNA testing continues to become an accepted part of the criminal justice system, one would surmise that the number of overturned convictions will continue to rise in the foreseeable future.

Notes

1. The victim originally described her attacker as a black man who weighed 200 pounds and who had a "large belly and hips" (Smith 2007). Lyons weighed 165 pounds and had a size 32 waist. The victim further noted that she had burned the coat of her attacker with her cigarette. Lyon's coat, however, contained no evidence of a cigarette burn.

2. After learning of these accusations Peterson immediately wrote to his mother disputing his cousins' accusations that he was the abuser. Peterson is currently serving a life sentence for killing a man when he hit him on the head with a baseball bat while robbing a fish market in 1992. He also had a prior arrest for rape, which was eventually dismissed.

3. The mug books contained photographs of suspects according to the first letter of their last name. Police informed the victim that she would need to examine

mug books for all twenty-six letters of the alphabet until she found her attackers. She had just finished the "A" mug book when she decided that all three of her assailants had their pictures in the "B" mug book (Peters 2000).

4. The victim initially described her assailant as having a medium complexion, a thin mustache, and a scratch from the struggle during the encounter. At the time Anderson had no mustache or scratches. Moreover, his complexion was dark, not medium.

5. Lincoln was convicted of the sexual assault in 2002, some twenty years after the commission of the crime.

6. Smith's first court-appointed attorney, Jerry Birdwell, did request that blood and hair samples be taken from his client for comparison purposes with the biological evidence from the crime scene. However, on the scheduled date for departure to Parkland Hospital, the lawyer informed Smith that there were no police officers available to drive him to the hospital. Consequently, no samples that could prove his innocence were available at the trial. A short time thereafter, Birdwell resigned as his counsel.

7. In fact, the second court-appointed attorney, Howard Wilson, did not meet with Smith until the day that the court convened to empanel a jury. Interestingly, a short while after Smith's conviction, Wilson was hired by the Dallas County district attorney's office.

8. According to the comments made by one blogger, children would run from him and call him "Freaky Rickey."

9. Gordon was suspended from practicing law by the Illinois Supreme Court on September 29, 1995. According to James Grogan, chief counsel for the Attorney Registration and Disciplinary Commission, the attorney was suspended because he committed "multiple acts of neglect . . . and failed to appear at his own disciplinary hearing." Gordon never applied for reinstatement.

10. While in prison for a rape that he didn't commit, Scott was involved in an assault. He would have been released for his rape conviction *prior* to the DNA exoneration if he had not been involved in the altercation.

11. More specifically, Mumphrey was sent back to prison in 2002 for failing to contact his parole officer.

12. Mumphrey's father died in 1996 while he was incarcerated. Other family members died as well during his wrongful conviction, and he was not permitted to attend their funerals.

13. One of the students received a five-year probated sentence; another received a ten-year probated sentence. The outcome of the third student, who was a juvenile at the time, is unknown.

14. The first grand jury refused to indict Johnson and the second grand jury agreed to indict him for only a misdemeanor—public lewdness.

5

Drug Offenses

A large portion of the wholesale killings in the South
during recent years have been the direct result of cocaine,
and frequently the perpetrators of these crimes have been
inoffensive, law-abiding Negroes.
—*1913 American Medical Association Report*

As previously observed, there were forty wrongful convictions involving African American men in which the most serious offense for which they were incarcerated was a drug offense. Thirty-nine of these miscarriages of justice occurred in two major drug busts in Tulia, Texas, and Mansfield, Ohio. To put these events into historical perspective, it is necessary to examine the evolution of drug prohibition as it pertains to the control of minority groups in the United States.

Opium and the Chinese:
The Beginning of Drug Prohibition

For many years there were no laws regulating the use of drugs in the United States, although drugs were readily available and freely used. Because the addictive qualities of morphine were unknown for many years, cough elixirs in the 1800s contained morphine. Morphine was also extensively used to medicate injured soldiers during the Civil War. It was so widely employed in the treatment of Civil War soldiers that morphine addiction was commonly referred to as "the soldiers' disease." Bordeaux wines, Coca-Cola, liquors, cigarettes, tablets, ointments, and sprays contained cocaine. Marijuana was used to alleviate migraine headaches, asthma, as well as other maladies. Physicians used cocaine to treat fatigue and morphine addiction. Sigmund Freud hailed cocaine as a wonder drug, and it was once endorsed as the official remedy of the Hay Fever Association. Opium was so commonly prescribed to middle-aged white women from the middle to upper classes to alleviate gynecological and nervous problems that this demographic group constituted the typical drug users of that period. Moreover, because the properties of opium were thought to accelerate an individual's physical and mental performance, employers encouraged workers to use it to increase their productivity and ultimately make their labor more profitable (Berger, Free, and Searles 2009; Breecher 1972; Kennedy 2003).

During the nineteenth century the Chinese were the primary consumers of opium, the first drug to be regulated in the United States. Unlike the first wave of Chinese immigrants, who were typically affluent, the second wave predominantly comprised laborers who were employed in mining and the construction of the transcontinental railroad from the West Coast, the latter a job declined by many white laborers because of the dangers associated with its development. Resentment against the Chinese escalated as whites saw these low-paid Chinese possessing an unfair advantage because opium was thought to enhance worker productivity. In 1875 San Francisco passed an ordinance prohibiting opium dens and smoking in the city. The following year Virginia City, Nevada, passed similar legislation. By 1887 federal legislation had been enacted that prohibited the importation of opium *by the Chinese*.[1] The Chinese Exclusion Act, which prohibited the immigration of additional Chinese into the country, was passed two years later (Helmer 1975; Musto 1987; Regoli and Hewitt 1997).

Cocaine and African Americans During the Early Twentieth Century

In December 1914 Congress passed the Harrison Act,[2] requiring producers, sellers, and distributors of narcotics to pay taxes on the drugs and to register with the Treasury Department. Although the Harrison Act singled out cocaine and opium and its derivatives, it neglected to mention marijuana among the controlled substances. (This omission was remedied in 1937 with the passage of the Marijuana Tax Act.) In 1919 the Supreme Court ruled that the Harrison Act also prohibited physicians and pharmacists from supplying addicted individuals with narcotics. By the mid-1920s approximately thirty thousand physicians had been arrested for providing their addicted patients with narcotics. An estimated 10 percent of those arrested were incarcerated for violating the Harrison Act. Consequently, physicians began to abandon their addicted patients, and the reconceptualization of drug use from a medical model to a criminal justice model was now complete (Goode 2002).

As the quote appearing at the beginning of this chapter suggests, cocaine use during the early twentieth century was associated with African Americans. Although the drug was used during this time by impoverished blacks for relief from bronchial disease and tuberculosis, there is no empirical evidence to support the view that it was disproportionately used by the black population. In fact, a case could be made that whites were more likely than blacks to use cocaine for these purposes, because whites were more likely to receive medical attention and hence receive physicians' prescriptions for drugs (Helmer 1975; Kennedy 2003). Nevertheless, the perception that cocaine was a drug used predominantly by African Americans prevailed, a theme echoed by the media at the time. An article appearing in the *New York Tribune* in 1903, for instance, asserted that "many of the horrible crimes committed in the Southern states by the colored people can be traced directly to the cocaine habit." Eleven years later the *Literary Digest,* a well-respected and influential magazine of this epoch, proclaimed that "most of the attacks upon white women of the South are a direct result of a cocaine-crazed Negro brain" (cited in Regoli and Hewitt 1997, 379–380).

This fear of cocaine and the belief that it created superhuman strength may have led to the use of more powerful pistols (from .32-caliber to .38-caliber) by police in the South during this time (Musto 1987). By the conclusion of the 1920s, African Americans comprised 23 percent of the incarcerated population despite being only 9 percent of the American population (Kennedy 2003). Yet this disproportionate representation would pale in contrast to the overrepresentation of African Americans that occurred during the crack cocaine scare of the mid-1980s.

Marijuana and Mexican Immigrants

Because marijuana was not specified among the controlled substances in the Harrison Act, it did not originally come under the control of the Federal Bureau of Narcotics (FBN), which was responsible for arresting violators of the law. Statutes prohibiting the use of marijuana, however, did exist in some jurisdictions by the mid-1920s. Like the Chinese immigrants before them, Mexican immigrants, who were thought to be the primary users of marijuana, were willing to work at substandard wages, thus exacerbating the fear of immigrants from beyond the country's southern border. Prior to the stock market crash of 1929 and the subsequent Great Depression, whites were tolerant of Mexican immigrants working in the United States, because prosperity prevailed. After these events and the disappearance of many jobs, tolerance turned to intolerance, and Mexican immigrants were seen as threats to the gainful employment of white US citizens. As the anti-Mexican campaign began to hit its stride, employers in agriculture and other industries came on board because Mexicans had been successfully organizing unions and strikes. There was also the belief that violence and sexual promiscuity accompanied marijuana use, a notion capitalized on by Harry Anslinger of the FBN as he began a successful campaign to have marijuana included among the list of controlled substances under his jurisdiction.[3] The powers of the FBN were greatly expanded in 1937 with the passage of the Marijuana Tax Act (MTA). By 1938, the first full year of enforcement of the provisions of the MTA, one of every four federal drug convictions involved a violation of this act. And, as anticipated, violations of the MTA expedited the deportation of Mexican nationals back to their country.

The Crack Cocaine Scare of the Mid-1980s and African Americans

Concern over cocaine use among African Americans resurfaced in the latter part of the twentieth century when media attention focused on crack cocaine (Chiricos 1996; Reeves and Campbell 1994). Crack, a smokeable form of cocaine, was cheaper than its powdered counterpart and consequently was more attractive to individuals with limited financial resources. By 1984 media stories describing the disturbing qualities of crack cocaine (e.g., instantly addicting, inciting homicidal tendencies in the user) began to appear in print.[4] But by spring 1986 drug coverage had become a virtual feeding frenzy, and it was difficult to walk past a newsstand without seeing one or more articles on the crack cocaine epidemic. The stories now contended that crack cocaine had permeated the middle class and was being used in suburbs, no longer being restricted to the poor denizens living in a few of the inner cities of America. Crack cocaine had now become a "national crisis." Despite the hyperbole, there was little evidence to suggest that crack use had evolved into a "coke plague." Even the federal Drug Enforcement Administration announced in 1986 that "crack was not a major problem in most areas of the country" (Brownstein 1996, 41; Orcutt and Turner 1993; Reinarman and Levine 1989).

It was in this charged environment that the federal Drug Abuse Acts of 1986 and 1988 were passed. These acts specified mandatory prison terms for federal drug offenders (the length of time depending on the quantity of the drug) and made penalties for crack cocaine one hundred times greater than for comparable amounts of powder cocaine. Under the 1988 legislation a first-time offender convicted in federal court for possession of five grams of crack cocaine (which would provide the user with fifteen to twenty "hits") would now receive a mandatory minimum sentence of five years in prison instead of probation, which was typically given to first-timers before the law was enacted. In contrast, an offender would need to possess five hundred grams of powder cocaine to receive the same sentence.[5] Moreover, the possession of five grams of powder cocaine was only a misdemeanor (Wallace 1993).

Again, this federal drug legislation and the state legislation that followed disproportionately affected people of color. In 1986 whites and African Americans were about equally likely to be incarcerated in state penal institutions for drug violations. Seven percent of all incarcerated African Americans and 8 percent of all incarcerated whites in state prisons were serving time for a drug offense. Yet five years later, after the drug scare involving crack cocaine, African Americans were much more likely than whites to be incarcerated for drugs. In 1991, 12 percent of all white state inmates were imprisoned on drug charges, while 25 percent of their African American counterparts were imprisoned on similar charges. Thus, in a five-year span, the percentage of white inmates whose most serious offense involved a violation for drugs had increased by 4 percent, whereas the percentage of African American inmates whose most serious offense involved a violation for drugs had increased 18 percent (US Department of Justice 1993, Figure 4).[6] Similarly, the proportion of drug-possession arrests spiraled for African Americans between 1980 and the early 1990s, increasing from 21 percent to about 35 percent despite rates of reported drug use similar to that of whites. And although in 1980 the drug arrest rate for white juveniles was actually higher than it was for African American juveniles, the arrest rates for drug possession for African American youths rose from 13 percent in 1980 to around 40 percent by the early 1990s (Mauer 1999).[7] It is against this backdrop that wrongful drug convictions must be evaluated.

The War on Drugs and African Americans: The Case of Tulia, Texas

Tulia is a small town of about five thousand people in the Texas panhandle. On the morning of July 23, 1999, a controversial predawn sting operation involving many of its black inhabitants will be forever linked to that city. On that summer morning forty-seven men and women were arrested,

most of whom had no idea what was going on, why they were being arrested, or even what crime they had committed. All of those arrested were
alleged to have drug ties. This assumption was based on very little evidence and the word of a rogue undercover agent, Tom Coleman.

Coleman was living in the shadow of his father, a former Texas
Ranger. His goal, it seems, was to make a huge drug bust by any means
possible, whether it was legal or not. As the accused "drug dealers" started
going to trial, they were quickly convicted by the all-white juries hearing
the cases in Tulia. In nearly all of the trials of the accused, nothing was
mentioned about Coleman's checkered career in law enforcement or his
lack of evidence in the Tulia cases. The all-white juries sent the bewildered
citizens of Tulia to prison on the basis of Coleman's testimony, a bag of
cocaine, and little else. His word alone was deemed by the juries as sufficient evidence to convict, as Coleman did not have witnesses to corroborate the charges that he made nor did he have any video of the alleged
crimes. All he had was his word—but in a Tulia courtroom, that was
enough to obtain a conviction.

The juries who convicted the Tulia defendants apparently thought that
they were convicting actual drug dealers. In fact, after the arrests were made,
it was widely believed that law enforcement personnel had cleaned up Tulia
and had virtually eliminated the city's drug problem. As the deputies proceeded from one house to the next in Tulia, thirty-nine African Americans
were arrested along with others who had ties to the African American community, all of whom, Coleman reported, had sold drugs to him.

Coleman had originally come to Tulia to clean up the small town by
working as an undercover agent, seeking out narcotics dealers. It was un-
usual, to say the least, for someone such as Coleman, with no experience
in narcotics, to do that well during his first time in the field. He claimed to
have made over one hundred drug purchases, using an alias, during his
eighteen-month undercover operation. He had long hair, drove a pickup
truck, and did odd jobs around Tulia while trying to set up drug buys.

From the beginning of the sting operation, there were questions about
everything, from how the evidence was gathered to why so many people
in Tulia were arrested. Many people wondered who was buying all the
drugs that were being sold by all the dealers who were arrested. It is hardly
a coincidence that Tulia's law enforcement officials targeted the town's
small African American population in this drug bust. Many African Americans in Tulia were unemployed and lived in public housing or trailer
courts, making them the "usual suspects."

As Coleman was making the alleged drug purchases, he claimed that
he wrote down important information on his leg or on scraps of paper

when nobody was watching. The small amount of evidence that Coleman was able to piece together during the trials was inconsistent and unreliable. Most of the arrests involved powdered cocaine, a substance most of the impoverished African Americans in Tulia could hardly afford. After making the arrests and claiming to have evidence on each person arrested, Coleman was unable to identify many of these same people in court. Because most of the defendants could not afford private legal counsel, they were dependent on court-appointed attorneys, who had little time or interest in their cases (Blakeslee 2000, 2002; Sherrer 2004; Stecklein 2009). A complete list of the Tulia sting docket appears in Table 5.1.

Joe Welton Moore

Joe Welton Moore, an African American, and Cash Love, a Caucasian married to Kizzie White, an African American, were among the first eight defendants who went to trial. Love, who fathered a mixed-race child, was accused of selling cocaine at least eight times to Coleman. He was sentenced to 361 years in prison, the longest of any of the Tulia defendants. Love had been in prison on two prior occasions for drug convictions, but he maintained that he was innocent this time. The arrest and sentence may have also been an attempt to send a message about getting too involved with the African American community in Tulia.

The other six defendants who went to trial also received sentences, ranging from twelve to sixty years. It was rapidly becoming apparent that anyone who went to trial would be sentenced to prison, often for the rest of their lives. This led many of the defendants to accept plea bargains, despite their innocence, rather than face the possibility of long prison sentences. In the end, twenty-seven people were convicted as a result of accepting a plea bargain, eleven more received jail sentences as a result of court trials, and the rest were placed on probation.

Coleman claimed that Moore, a diabetic hog farmer, was one of the kingpins of the drug operation in Tulia. Moore was known as a bootlegger and had been in trouble with the law before,[8] but the truth is that he was selling hogs, not cocaine. It is likely that all of the above factors worked against Moore, along with the fact that he was charged with selling cocaine within 1,000 feet of a school. Moore wanted to go to trial, believing that it would be the only way to prove his innocence. However, the jury accepted Coleman's testimony as authentic and Moore received a sentence of ninety-nine years (Blakeslee 2000). Moore eventually served four years of this sentence before being pardoned by Governor Rick Perry in 2005.

Table 5.1 Individuals Involved in the Tulia Sting

Name	Race	Age	Charge(s)	Sentence	Convicted	Cleared
Dennis Michael Allen	Black	34	Delivery of cocaine	18 years	1999	2003
James Ray Barrow	Black	31	Delivery of cocaine	10 years probation	1999	2003
Landis Barrow	Black	22	Delivery of cocaine and marijuana	20 years	2000	—
Leroy Barrow	Black	59	Delivery of cocaine, marijuana, and simulated controlled substance	10 years probation	2000	2003
Mandis Barrow	Black	22	Delivery of cocaine and marijuana	20 years	2000	—
Troy Benard	Black	29	Delivery of cocaine	10 years	2000	2003
Zury Bosset	Black	n/a	Delivery of cocaine	Pending	—	—
Fred Brookins, Jr.	Black	24	Delivery of cocaine	20 years	1999	2003
Yul Eugene Bryant	Black	31	Delivery of cocaine	Dismissed	—	—
Eddie Cardona	White	41	Delivery of marijuana	Dismissed	—	—
Marilyn Joyce Cooper	Black	39	Delivery of cocaine	3 days	2000	2003
Armenu Jerrod Ervin	Black	19	Delivery of cocaine	10 years probation	2000	2003
Michael Fowler	Black	28	Delivery of cocaine	5 years probation	2000	2003
Jason Paul Fry	Black	25	Delivery of cocaine	3 years	2000	2003
Vickie Fry	Black	27	Delivery of cocaine	5 years probation	2000	2003
Willie Hall	Black	38	Delivery of cocaine and marijuana	18 years	1999	2003
Cleveland J. Henderson	Black	25	Delivery of cocaine	5 years probation	2000	2003
Mandrell L. Henry	Black	24	Delivery of cocaine	2 years	2000	2003
Christopher Eugene Jackson	Black	18	Delivery of cocaine	20 years	1999	2003
Denise Kelly	Black	29	Delivery of cocaine	1 year	2000	2003
Eliga Kelly, Sr.	Black	62	Delivery of cocaine and marijuana	10 years probation	2000	2003
Etta Kelly	Black	23	Delivery of simulated controlled substance	3 years deferred adjudication	2000	2003
Calvin Kent Klein	White	22	Delivery of cocaine	10 years (probated to 5 years)	1999	2003
Jonathan Loftin	Black	16	Delinquent conduct	Juvenile boot camp	—	—
William Cash Love	White	25	Delivery of cocaine and marijuana	Multiple sentences 2 years to 99 years	2000	2003

Table 5.1 *continued*

Name	Race	Age	Charge(s)	Sentence	Convicted	Cleared
Joseph Corey Marshall	Black	23	Delivery of cocaine	10 years probation	2000	2003
Laura Ann Mata	Hispanic	23	Delivery of cocaine	5 years	2000	2003
Vincent Dwight McCray	Black	38	Delivery of cocaine	3 years	2000	2003
Joe Welton Moore	Black	58	Delivery of cocaine	90 years	1999	2003
James Moreno	White	n/a	Delivery of simulated and controlled substance	Charges dismissed	—	—
Daniel G. Olivarez	Hispanic	20	Delivery of cocaine and marijuana	12 years probation	2000	2003
Kenneth Ray Powell	Black	40	Delivery of cocaine	10 years probation	2000	2003
Benny Lee Robinson	Black	24	Delivery of cocaine	Deferred adjudication	2000	2003
Finaye Burnett Shelton	Black	25	Delivery of cocaine	5 years probation	2000	2003
Donald Wayne Smith	Black	31	Delivery of cocaine	12.5 years	2000	2003
Lawanda Smith	Black	25	Delivery of cocaine	3 years probation	2000	2003
Yolanda Yvonne Smith	Black	26	Delivery of cocaine	6 years	2000	2003
Romona Lynn Strickland	Black	26	Delivery of cocaine	$2,000 fine	2000	2003
Timothy Wayne Towery	Black	27	Delivery of cocaine	18 years	1999	2003
Billy Don Wafer	Black	42	Delivery of cocaine	Dismissed	—	—
Chandra White	Black	22	Delivery of cocaine	Dismissed	—	—
Kareem White	Black	24	Delivery of cocaine	60 years	2000	2003
Kizzie R. White	Black	22	Delivery of cocaine and marijuana	25 years	1999	2003
Tonya Michelle White	Black	30	Delivery of cocaine	Not indicted	—	—
Alberta Stell Williams	Black	n/a	Delivery of cocaine	n/a	n/a	2003
Jason Jerome Williams	Black	20	Delivery of cocaine	45 years	1999	2003
Michelle Williams	Black	23	Delivery of cocaine	2 years	2000	2003

Note: n/a = not available.

Freddie Brookins, Jr.

Things did not look very good for Freddie Brookins, Jr., before he went to trial either. The sentences that were being handed down to people such as Moore and Love were not good omens. One could surmise that the only reason that Freddie Brookins was arrested in the Tulia sting was because he had the wrong skin color. This former star athlete in high school was from a highly regarded family in Tulia's African American community. Brookins was always a hard worker, even after his girlfriend had a child and he lost his chance to obtain an athletic scholarship to college. Brookins continued to work and went to a trade school to qualify for a better job. He had not used or sold illicit drugs. Brookins knew that he was innocent of the charge of delivering cocaine, but he additionally knew that he could be sentenced up to twenty years for this alleged crime. He was offered a plea bargain that would significantly reduce this jail time to five years, but that would be tantamount to an admission of guilt, something he didn't want to do. He was confused. He had not been in trouble with the law before, had just successfully completed a job training program, and had never seen Coleman prior to his trial. Despite Brookins's insistence of his innocence during his trial, he received a twenty-year sentence.

Donald Wayne Smith

In 1989 Donald Wayne Smith was Tulia High School's Athlete of the Year. From that point forward, however, everything in his life would deteriorate. A failed marriage, which produced two children, and an unsuccessful college career were eventually followed by misdemeanor charges for fighting. He returned to Tulia disillusioned and prepared to accept whatever employment might be available. He took part-time employment at a local auction known locally as the Sale Barn. It was Eliga Kelly, another Tulia defendant, who introduced him to Coleman in the summer of 1998. Kelly, who was sixty-two years old, worked weekends at the local auction with Smith. The job involved feeding cows and handling livestock. Smith took the job because there was not much else he could get around Tulia and, because the work was on the weekend, he would get paid on Monday and could spend his money on drugs. Coleman told Kelly that if he would help him secure drug buys, that he would supply Kelly with alcohol. In Eliga Kelly, Coleman found a way to infiltrate Tulia's tight-knit African American community; and in Coleman, Kelly found a way to support his drinking habit. When Smith met Coleman for the first time, he was told by Kelly that he and Coleman had known each other for years. Smith would take the money that Coleman regularly gave him and would go to his crack dealer to purchase drugs for both of them, which they would then share in Coleman's truck. Tired of the drug life and wanting to reestablish his ties with his two children, Smith decided to attend a ninety-day rehabilitation program. After completing the program, he returned to Tulia and worked for a local farmer. He had been drug-free for six months when the Tulia drug sting occurred.

Although he had delivered small amounts of crack cocaine to Coleman when he was addicted, his overall criminal record was free of felony convictions, making him a possible candidate for probation. Coleman, however, contended that Smith had delivered between one to four grams of powder cocaine on six of the seven occasions, making his offense a second-degree felony. As a result, the district attorney initially sought a forty-five-year sentence. While awaiting his first trial, Smith was incarcerated in a jail in nearby Hale County, because the jail in Tulia was already full from the drug raid. In February 2000, during his first trial for delivery of less than a gram of crack cocaine, Smith openly admitted to the jury that he had purchased crack cocaine for Coleman on multiple occasions. Nevertheless, he vehemently denied having ever provided Coleman with powder cocaine. The jury responded by handing Smith the maximum sentence of two years in prison. Given the severe sentence for a relatively minor crime, his court-appointed attorney recommended that Smith plead guilty to the powder cocaine charges in the hopes of receiving some leniency. After reaching a plea bargain with the prosecution, Smith accepted a twelve-year sentence (Blakeslee 2000).

The Tulia Drug Sting: The Truth Prevails

Eventually a group of attorneys from around the country, working pro bono, secured new trials for the residents of Tulia accused of drug trafficking. Many of the accused had already served time in prison before anyone attempted to win their freedom. On August 22, 2003, Texas Governor Rick Perry issued a pardon for those wrongfully convicted. The wrongfully convicted citizens of Tulia have also sought monetary compensation for all of their suffering. At the same time, a lawsuit was filed on behalf of those charged in the Tulia drug operation. A settlement of $5 million was agreed upon as compensation for being falsely accused and, in many cases, sent to prison (Liptak 2004). Coleman was charged with perjury and went to trial. This charge, which ended his career in law enforcement, resulted in a sentence of ten years' probation (Lunsford 2005).

The War on Drugs and African Americans:
The Case of Hearne, Texas

An eerily similar event occurred in 2000 in Hearne, Texas, a small city approximately ninety miles east of Austin. Although African Americans comprised 44 percent of that city's population of 4,700 in 2000, there was a history of African Americans being singled out in drug raids in Hearne and nearby areas. According to an article in the *Texas Observer,* "African Americans accounted for 79 percent of all arrests by the South Central Texas Narcotics Task Force in surrounding Robertson and Limestone Counties in 2000" (Levy 2005). By comparison, African Americans comprised less than 40 percent of all task force arrests in other Texas jurisdictions. And much like the Tulia drug raid, the accusations of drug trafficking were largely based on a single informant, a troubled man named Derrick Megress, who had two prior convictions for theft, used marijuana and cocaine, and was mentally unstable and suicidal. Moreover, Megress was coerced into his role as informant. Faced with the possibility of going to prison on burglary charges if he failed to incriminate the list of African Americans that Robertson County District Attorney John Paschall had designated as targets of the drug task force, Megress felt that he had few options available to him (Levy 2005).[9]

On November 2, 2000, approximately thirty to forty armed law enforcement personnel were involved in the high-profile drug raid on the Columbus Village Apartments, a government-subsidized Hearne public housing project. According to the civil rights lawsuit brought on behalf of fifteen of the African American residents by the American Civil Liberties Union:

> The officers detained almost the entire African American community in Hearne, without provocation or cause, and demanded identification from the residents regardless of whether they remotely matched the gender, age, or physical description of those named by Megress. Young children playing on the street, individuals sitting in their cars, and elderly residents relaxing on their porches were all directed to remain still by defendants wielding guns. Each of the individual defendants possessed the names and addresses of the individuals whom they sought to arrest. Nonetheless, after demanding identification, the officers continued to detain many individuals who did not appear on their arrest list. (Civ. 02-A-02-CA-702JN 2002, 40-41)

Although only one case eventually went to trial, the sting had a lasting impact on many of those arrested during that raid. None of these cases showed up in our research on wrongful convictions of African American men, yet had the sting not captured the attention of the national media, it is likely that many of those arrested would have been wrongfully convicted. It is for that reason that a brief discussion of four of the cases is included in this chapter.

Regina Kelly

A black single mother of four, Regina Kelly was arrested by police officers on November 2, 2000, while she was working a double shift as a waitress. Kelly, who thought that the arrest was the result of unpaid parking tickets, was not informed of the reason for being taken into custody for almost two days. It came as quite a surprise to her when she learned that she was being held on felony drug distribution charges and found out that the judge had set her bail at $70,000, an amount that prevented her from being released from jail. Her arrest was based on a tape in which she was allegedly selling drugs to Megress, an informant. However, the voices on the recording appear to be male voices. Moreover, the indictment had her name misspelled and an incorrect address. Her court-appointed attorney recommended that she plead guilty in order to receive leniency, but a guilty plea was out of the question, because it would make her ineligible to remain in government-subsidized housing. As Thanksgiving approached and Kelly's case appeared to be weak, her bail was reduced to $10,000, whereupon her parents offered their land to a bond company to secure their daughter's release. Although the case against Kelly was eventually dismissed, she felt compelled to leave her waitress job, as other employees constantly gossiped about her being a drug trafficker. She had been accepted at a local college but had her acceptance revoked when the school learned that she had been arrested for selling illegal drugs. Her drug arrest also made her ineligible to serve as a teacher's aide at the local high school. Kelly's daughters were frequently harassed by other children at school who claimed that their mother was a "dope dealer." In 2005 she was fired from a job in Hearne after District Attorney Paschall had a discussion with her manager. Reluctantly, Kelly left Hearne in 2009 to begin a new life elsewhere ("'American Violet' Tells Story of Ill-Fated Hearne Drug Raids" 2009; Levy 2005; "Stories of ACLU Clients Swept Up in the Hearne Drug Bust of November 2000" 2002).

Erma Faye Stewart

Erma Faye Stewart was also a single black mother when she was arrested and charged with selling crack cocaine. She shared a jail cell with Regina

Kelly, whose case is discussed above. Like Kelly, Stewart had a court-appointed attorney, as she could not afford private counsel. Although she maintained her innocence, her attorney recommended that she accept a plea bargain in return for probation. Whereas Kelly was released from jail while awaiting trial, Stewart remained incarcerated. Because Stewart had no one to supervise her two young children, she agreed to plead guilty to delivery of a controlled substance of more than four grams in a drug-free zone. She was placed on probation for ten years and was required to pay $1,800 in fines. Because she had pleaded guilty, she became ineligible for food stamps or federal grant money for education. Stewart will not have her right to vote reinstated until she satisfies her ten-year probation. She was evicted from public housing due to her guilty plea and her inability to pay her rent. In 2004, when *Frontline* reported on this case, she was employed as a cook making only $5.25 per hour. At that time Stewart still owed a $1,000 fine, court costs, as well as late probation fees (Public Broadcasting System 2004).

Clifford Runoalds

Not all of those arrested for selling illegal drugs were captured on November 2, 2000. Clifford Runoalds, a thirty-three-year-old black father of seven, was arrested when he returned to Hearne to attend the funeral of his eighteen-month-old daughter. He was handcuffed prior to the funeral service and not permitted to view his daughter's body prior to her burial. After being taken into custody, he was informed that he was needed to testify against another black man who was arrested during the November raid. According to the district attorney, the police had an audiotape of the transaction in which his voice appeared. When Runoalds asked to hear the tape, his request was denied. Instead, he was told that if he didn't testify, he would be prosecuted for his involvement in the drug transaction. When Runoalds refused to accommodate the district attorney, he was indicted on felony drug charges and placed in jail for a month until the charges were dismissed. Runoalds, who as a young man had been in trouble with the law, had been trying to straighten out his life. He was employed at the time of the funeral and had an apartment in Silver Springs. Additionally, Runoalds was planning to have his five-year-old son come to live with him. But all of that changed after his arrest. He was fired from his job; he lost his apartment, furniture, and automobile. As of 2002, he was living in Bryan, Texas, and working at night with the Labor Ready program ("Stories of ACLU Clients Swept Up in the Hearne Drug Bust of November 2000" 2002).

Michael Wells

Another black man with a checkered past is Michael Wells. On probation for a crime he committed when he was young, in 1995 he made a conscious decision to turn his life around. But when he heard that the police were inquiring about him after the Hearne drug bust, he decided to turn himself into the authorities to clear up the misunderstanding. Wells was informed that his voice was present on an audio tape provided by Megress, the sole informant. It was later determined that his voice was not present on the tape because he was actually working at a local convenience store at the time of the alleged drug transaction and had time cards to substantiate his alibi. Although cleared of the charges, Wells spent five months in jail awaiting this outcome. Many of the local residents still distrust him, and he continues to struggle to rebuild his life. Despite his innocence in this matter, the arrest remains on his record, making it difficult for him to secure employment ("Stories of ACLU Clients Swept Up in the Hearne Drug Bust of November 2000" 2002).

The Mansfield, Ohio, Drug Bust

Not all drug busts targeting African Americans have occurred in the South. Another recent drug bust that resulted in the wrongful conviction of many African American men took place in Mansfield, Ohio, a city of approximately fifty thousand, on December 31, 2004, after Timothy Harris, a career criminal, was found dead in the snow. He had been stabbed in the stomach and had two gun shots in the neck. Authorities thought that this was a drug-related killing and, if they could apply some pressure on known drug dealers in the area, they might be successful in locating Harris's murderer. Sheriff's detectives, however, were unsuccessful in their attempts to arrest cocaine traffickers. After a few months and few leads, the local authorities requested help from the federal Drug Enforcement Administration in Cleveland and from Lee Lucas, a long-time veteran of the force. To gather information, Lucas turned to Jerrell Bray,[10] an informant with whom he had previously worked and who had connections within the drug world. This sting operation, which went by the name of Operation Turnaround, led to the arrest of twenty-six people on November 10, 2005. During the operation several drug deals were fabricated by Bray and Lucas to sound like evidence against those they were trying to convict. Bray named a number of Mansfield residents; some of the cases involved individuals with whom he had a personal grudge and against whom he was retaliating through the accusations (Kroll 2008; Love 2009; Simonich 2008). A complete list of those convicted in the Mansfield drug raid appears in Table 5.2.

Dwayne Nabors

After all the indictments were gathered, and despite the presence of weak evidence to support the indictments, prosecutors pressed forward to convict those thought to be selling illegal drugs in Mansfield. One victim of this sting operation was Dwayne Nabors, an ex-felon who now ran a successful car-detailing business. Bray was instructed to use Nabors as a contact to gain access to drug dealers who would have money available to pay for expensive automobiles and accessories. However, Bray never gained the access he sought, so instead he named Nabors as one of the drug dealers in Mansfield. Charged with being involved in a drug conspiracy, selling illegal drugs, and possessing illegal firearms, Nabors was acquitted of the first charge and the jury was deadlocked on the second charge. He was, however, convicted of possession of illegal firearms and served two years in prison before his conviction was overturned. As a result of his incarceration, he lost his business (Simonich 2008). Richland County Sheriff's Deputy Charles Metcalf, who assisted Lucas during the drug bust, pleaded guilty on May 14, 2009, to lying in the trial of Nabors in order to get a conviction. In February 2010 Metcalf was sentenced to twelve weekends in

Table 5.2 Mansfield, Ohio, Drug Bust

Name	Race	Charge	Sentence	Convicted	Cleared
Marlon Brooks	Black	Drug-related	3 years, 10 months	2006	2008
Tyron Brown	Black	Drug-related	8 years, 4 months	2006	2008
James Burton	Black	Drug-related	11 years, 8 months	2006	2008
Frank Douglas	Black	Drug-related	7 years	2006	2008
Geneva France	Black	Drug-related	10 years	2006	2007
Robert Harris	Black	Drug-related	5 years	2006	2008
Albert Lee	Black	Drug-related	10 years	2006	2008
Nolan Lovett	Black	Drug-related	5 years	2006	2008
Charles Matthews	Black	Drug-related	5 years, 3 months	2006	2008
Jerry Moton	Black	Drug-related	3 years, 1 month	2006	2008
Noel Mott	Black	Drug-related	4 years, 3 months	2006	2008
Dwayne Nabors	Black	Drug-related, firearms	5 years	2006	2008
Dametrese Ransaw	Black	Drug-related	3 years, 6 months	2006	2008
Johnny Robertson	Black	Drug-related	5 years, 10 months	2006	2008
Arrico Spires	Black	Drug-related	4 years, 9 months	2006	2008
Jim Williams	Black	Drug-related	5 years, 3 months	2006	2008

jail for his role in the botched drug bust. Bray eventually pleaded guilty to perjury and was sentenced to fifteen years in prison (Caniglia 2009; Krouse 2010, February 16).

Lowestco Ballard

A name that does not appear in Table 5.2 is that of Lowestco (Wes) Ballard. Because he was acquitted, it is easy to overlook his case. Yet his story is typical of many of the cases located in this research. A thirty-three-year-old black man, Ballard was not unlike many of the other defendants in the drug sting. He had prior felony convictions for drugs and openly admits that he occasionally committed small crimes. Nonetheless, he is adamant that he never sold the 4.5 ounces of crack cocaine to Agent Lucas as alleged by Bray. According to Ballard, "I messed around and sold a little pot, but was nothing on the magnitude of the FBI or DEA getting involved" (Simonich 2008). After being incarcerated for ten months while awaiting his trial in Akron, he was finally acquitted of the charges when the videotapes that supposedly showed him engaging in a drug transaction revealed that the drug seller was a heavyset man who was under 6' tall, whereas Ballard is extremely thin and 6'5" in height. Since his ordeal, Ballard has struggled to put his life back together. His wife, who was pregnant at the time, had a miscarriage. He works at a restaurant but has to contend with the problem that many of the town's inhabitants refuse to believe that he was innocent. According to Ballard, "Mansfield is a small town. There's a stigma on me" (Simonich 2008). Meanwhile, Gregory White, the US attorney who signed the indictments, was appointed a US magistrate in Detroit in February 2008 (Love 2009; Turner 2009).[11]

Geneva France

One of those accused of selling illegal drugs was an African American woman named Geneva France. Although this investigation focuses on wrongful convictions of African American men, her story is quite compelling and deserves at least a casual mention. After refusing to accept a plea bargain, France, a twenty-two-year-old mother of three who had no previous run-ins with the law, was convicted on drug charges largely based on the tainted testimony of Bray and DEA agent Lucas. She served sixteen months of her ten-year sentence before being released after Bray confessed to lying about her. France believes that the false accusations from Bray were the result of her refusal to date him. When she was released from prison, France discovered that her three-year-old daughter didn't recognize her, she had been evicted from her home, and her belongings had been discarded (Caniglia 2008; Simonich 2008; Sheeran 2008).

Joshawa Webb

All but one of those involved in the Mansfield drug investigation were African American. The lone white person to get caught in the botched drug investigation was Joshawa Webb, an ex-felon with two prior convictions. Nor was Webb entirely innocent. He openly admitted to selling powder cocaine and marijuana to a small number of customers. Webb vehemently denied, however, ever having sold crack cocaine, which is what was alleged by Lucas. Because of his prior convictions, a conviction for selling three ounces of crack cocaine would make him eligible for a life sentence. And given his prior record, Webb was denied bail and remained incarcerated in jail for twenty-one months while awaiting trial. When the audiotape implicating Webb was determined to be altered, the attorney representing him confronted Bray. It was at this time that Bray confessed that a friend of his, Jeremiah Conrad, was the actual drug dealer in the drug transaction. Bray additionally admitted that the Mansfield drug cases were an elaborate hoax and that those who were arrested had not committed the crimes for which they were charged. As noted earlier, Bray received a fifteen-year prison sentence for two counts of perjury and five charges of violating the civil rights of those falsely charged with drug crimes. DEA agent Lucas, who Bray alleges facilitated the drug hoax and whose testimony was instrumental in the prosecution of the Mansfield drug cases, was indicted on eighteen criminal charges related to the drug bust. On February 6, 2010, however, a federal court jury acquitted Lucas of all criminal charges (Krouse 2010, February 5; Simonich 2008).

The Rampart Division Scandal and Charles Harris

Charles Harris served nineteen months on a cocaine possession and sale that was part of the Rampart Division scandal involving the Los Angeles Police Department. Harris called the arrest a setup and a misunderstanding. When officers searched his car, he never consented, never received his Miranda rights when arrested, and had statements in the police report attributed to him that he never said. Harris claimed that the two officers searching his car planted rock cocaine and a stolen handgun. Harris was afraid that if he went to trial, a jury would believe the officers rather than him, and so he pleaded guilty. His conviction was overturned in 2000 after an investigation into corrupt practices in the Los Angeles Rampart Division. Plainclothes officer Rafael Perez had searched Harris's residence and, after taking three guns and $6,000, never entered them as evidence. The guns and money were returned to Mrs. Harris in exchange for information about other drug dealers.

Perez had additionally been accused of taking six pounds of cocaine, claiming that he needed it for evidence. His actual intent was to sell it for around $1 million. Perez was part of a Los Angeles Rampart scandal that involved more than seventy officers and included a variety of offenses, such as planting evidence, framing suspects, and dealing narcotics.

Conclusion

As the succinct review of drug prohibition at the beginning of this chapter suggests, drug legislation in the United States has frequently targeted groups that were seen as threatening to those who support the status quo. The Chinese during the latter part of the 1800s and Mexican immigrants during the Great Depression were adversely affected by legislation aimed primarily at drugs that were associated with those groups. As the US moved from a medical model to a criminal justice model to control drug use, stereotypes of drug abusers changed as well. When drugs could be purchased legally through outlets such as Sears Roebuck and drug addiction was viewed as a medical problem, the typical drug user was a middle-aged white woman from the middle or upper class because physicians frequently prescribed opium to alleviate gynecological and nervous "disorders" perceived to be common among women at that time (Berger, Free, and Searles 2009, 295). After the Harrison Narcotics Act of 1914 (and later the Marijuana Tax Act of 1937) made many drugs illegal, drug addiction was reconceptualized as a criminal justice problem, and the current criminal stereotype in which a minority group member became the new image associated with drug addiction emerged. Federal legislation in 1986 and 1988 focused on crack cocaine, a less expensive, smokeable form of cocaine, that was primarily associated with African Americans living in the inner city. And although there have been some recent modifications to the extreme measures passed during this time, law enforcement's preoccupation with drug control in these areas dramatically increased the proportion of African Americans in prison for drug offenses.

Cases in which drug violations were the most serious offense associated with the wrongful conviction numbered forty in this investigation. These cases represent almost 12 percent of the total cases uncovered during the study. Yet the cases undoubtedly represent only a small fraction of all drug-offense wrongful convictions, given law enforcement's preoccupation with crack cocaine that commenced during the mid-1980s. Human Rights Watch (2009, 1), using data obtained from the Federal Bureau of Investigation, reports that between 1980 and 2007 African Americans were arrested at rates relative to their population that were 2.8 to 5.5 times higher than their white counterparts. Yet African American and white rates for possession and drug sales are similar (Human Rights Watch 2008). While these disparities cannot be used to document the existence of wrongful drug convictions, they certainly enhance the probability that both innocent as well as guilty individuals will be charged with drug violations. Given that inhabitants living in the inner city typically lack the financial resources to obtain effective legal counsel if wrongfully accused, it is less likely that they will be able to avoid conviction. Because this study was able to locate only those cases in which a flagrant injustice had prevailed, individual examples of wrongful drug conviction that have not come to the attention of journalists and other interested parties are absent from this analysis.

Innocence projects and the Center on Wrongful Convictions, among others, tend to focus their limited resources on cases that involve extended sentences or capital punishment and those that can be successfully resolved through the analysis of DNA. For this reason wrongful convictions involving drug offenses are unlikely to become a priority unless they affect a large number of people, as the examples in this chapter illustrate. In each of these cases law enforcement abuse was so excessive that the injustices became apparent once an investigation was initiated. Because many wrongful drug convictions are not self-evident (especially if the accused has a prior criminal record), they are less likely than other offenses discussed here to come to light in an investigation that relies on known cases of wrongful conviction. It is thus prudent to avoid the inclination to excessively generalize from this limited sample of drug-related wrongful convictions.

Notes

1. It was not until 1909 that federal legislation made it illegal for other groups to import opium.

2. As early as 1906, pressure from various groups within and outside the government led to the passage of the Pure Food and Drug Act. This act required that substances such as marijuana and cocaine be clearly labeled. Concern about what would become known as the "gateway effect" was already being expressed. Many

believed that the use of marijuana could eventually lead to the use of stronger substances such as cocaine and heroin.

3. In the 1930s Harry Anslinger, the commissioner of the federal Department of Treasury's Bureau of Narcotics, began a national campaign against marijuana users and sellers (Becker 1963; Gray 1998). Under Anslinger's leadership, "educational" articles were released to the mass media to buttress the argument that immediate action was required to deal with the problems stemming from marijuana use. These stories often bordered on the outrageous, as indicated in the following article that appeared in 1937 in *American Magazine:*

> An entire family was murdered by a youthful (marijuana) addict in Florida. When officers arrived at the home they found the youth staggering about in a human slaughterhouse. With an ax he had killed his father, mother, two brothers, and a sister. He seemed to be in a daze. . . . He had no recollection of having committed the multiple crime. The officers knew him ordinarily as a sane, rather quiet young man; now he was pitifully crazed. They sought the reason. The boy said he had been in the habit of smoking something which youthful friends called "muggles," a childish name for marijuana. (cited by Becker 1963, 142)

4. Subsequent research on crack cocaine has questioned the veracity of the early claims of the damaging properties of crack versus powder cocaine. For example, a large study of drug users in the Northeast found that while almost all crack users had previously used other illegal drugs, their involvement with crack was for the most part unrelated to increased nondrug or violent criminality (Johnson, Golum, and Fagan 1995).

5. The street value of five grams of crack cocaine then was approximately $400, whereas the street value of 500 grams of powder cocaine was around $10,000 (Wallace 1993).

6. Although crack cocaine was thought to lead to greater violence among its users, there was a 12 percent *decline* in African Americans incarcerated in state prisons for violent offenses during this same five-year period. There was a corresponding 1 percent decrease among whites for the same offense during this time (US Department of Justice 1993, Figure 4).

7. The impact of the war on crack cocaine is particularly evident when examining data on youths. Florida represents an especially interesting case study. From 1982 through 1989 felony drug cases in Florida involving white male juveniles doubled (from 299 to 606). In contrast, felony drug cases increased 68 times (from 54 to 3,675) during this same period for black male juveniles (Tollett and Close 1991). Also difficult to explain is the finding of a single-day survey of juvenile drug offenders in Georgia's juvenile institutions during the spring of 1990. That survey disclosed that all of the juvenile drug offenders incarcerated in Georgia's juvenile correctional facilities were black ("Single-Day Study Finds" 1990).

8. In 1990 Moore was convicted for cocaine possession (Blakeslee 2000).

9. In a videotaped deposition Megress disclosed that District Attorney Paschall had threatened to incarcerate Megress's family members as well. Megress further revealed that "Paschall said that while I was in prison, he would make sure another inmate raped me every day" (Levy 2005).

10. Bray had served a thirteen-year stint in prison for the murder of a Cleveland drug dealer (Kroll 2008).

11. White claimed that he was tricked into authorizing the Mansfield prosecutions and, in fact, later recommended that the charges against the Mansfield defendants be dismissed. Prior to his appointment as a US attorney, he served for twenty-two years as the Lorain County prosecutor and was the prosecutor in the wrongful convictions of Nancy Smith and Joseph Allen, a couple incarcerated for fifteen years for the rape of a child before their convictions were overturned (Love 2009; Turner 2009).

6

Robbery and
Other Offenses

I feel that, perhaps due to some of my failing as an attorney,
maybe I didn't do as good a job as I . . . could have. There were
a number of alibi witnesses . . . that we could have called.
There was much mentioned . . . at the trial, much cross-examination
of the alibi witnesses; why didn't they go to the police right away?
I didn't tell them to, and that's why they didn't.

—*Comments of the defense counsel who represented Christopher Parish,
admitting his failure as an attorney during the sentencing hearing
in which his client received a thirty-year sentence for an
armed robbery that he didn't commit.*

The remaining wrongful convictions in this study are classified as either robbery or miscellaneous offenses that do not neatly fall into the crime categories previously outlined. There were fifteen cases in which the most serious charge was robbery and five additional cases in which the charges were sufficiently different from the charges discussed in earlier chapters to warrant a separate analysis. The first part of this chapter examines wrongful convictions in which robbery was the most serious charge, whereas the latter section examines five atypical offenses that culminated in a wrongful conviction.

Table 6.1 provides the reader with information on wrongful robbery convictions. The table includes the name of the wrongfully convicted individual, the state in which the wrongful conviction occurred, any additional charges, and factors associated with the wrongful conviction. When the states are organized geographically, it becomes apparent that almost half (seven out of fifteen) of the cases were from the South (Louisiana, North Carolina, Oklahoma, Texas, and Virginia). Although this statistic suggests that wrongful convictions in robbery cases are disproportionately found in

Southern locales, care should be exercised in generalizing this finding from so few cases. Additionally, it will be recalled that many of the earlier cases in which murder and sexual assault were the most serious offenses included robbery among the original charges. Table 6.1 further discloses that all of the cases in the sample involved some form of armed robbery. The most common factor contributing to the wrongful convictions was witness error, appearing in twelve of the cases. Police misconduct appeared in nine of the wrongful convictions, making it the second most frequent correlate. Ineffective assistance of counsel contributed to four of the wrongful convictions, and prosecutorial misconduct was a contributing factor in three wrongful conviction cases. The use of a snitch/informant, perjury by criminal justice officials, and insufficient evidence to support a conviction each appeared once.

An examination of some of the wrongful convictions in which robbery was the most serious charge is now in order. Because nearly half of the cases originated in Southern states, the first case under discussion comes from Virginia.

Teddy P. Thompson

Teddy Thompson was seventeen years old when he was convicted of two armed robberies in Hampton, Virginia, in 2000. Despite his contention that he was at a Virginia Beach recording studio when the first robbery was committed, he was sentenced to sixteen years in prison. When he agreed to plead guilty to the second robbery, he was given a ten-year suspended sentence. During the trial for the first robbery, one of the victims positively identified Thompson in a photographic lineup. A second victim of the robbery, however, did not believe that Thompson was the perpetrator and testified to this effect during a pretrial hearing. In September 2007 Hampton Circuit Court Judge Louis R. Lerner set aside Thompson's conviction and released him after hearing testimony from the first victim. That victim recanted his earlier statement that Thompson was the robber after the actual perpetrator apologized to him and offered to return his money.

Since his release Thompson has had minor run-ins with the law. Three misdemeanors (assault and battery, being abusive to a neighbor, and breach of the peace) and a possible violation of the terms of his ten-year suspended sentence have once again placed Thompson in the spotlight.[1] Despite these setbacks, Thompson was able to avoid getting sent back to prison in 2009, when his probation officer testified on his behalf.

The Commonwealth of Virginia recently awarded Thompson $270,000 for seven years of wrongful confinement. He anticipates using

Table 6.1 Factors in Wrongful Convictions in Robbery Cases (N=15)

Name	State	Additional Charge(s)	Contributing Factors
Jason Kindle	CA	Includes armed robbery	Police misconduct, witness error, ineffective assistance of counsel
Michael Glasper	IL	Includes armed robbery	Police misconduct, witness error
Keith Cooper	IN	Includes armed robbery	n/a
Christopher Parish	IN	Includes armed robbery	Prosecutorial misconduct, police misconduct, perjury by criminal justice officials, ineffective assistance of counsel
Kevin Williams	LA	Includes armed robbery	Prosecutorial misconduct, police misconduct, witness error
Leslie Vass	MD	Includes armed robbery	Witness error
Antonio Beaver	MO	Includes 1st degree robbery	Police misconduct, witness error
Derrick Bell	NY	Includes armed robbery, assault	Witness error, ineffective assistance of counsel
Erick Daniels	NC	Includes armed robbery	Prosecutorial misconduct, police misconduct, witness error, ineffective assistance of counsel
Terence Garner	NC	Includes armed robbery	Snitch/informant, prosecutorial misconduct, witness error
Marrio D'Shane Willis	OK	Includes armed robbery	Police misconduct, witness error, insufficient evidence to support a conviction
James Levi Byrd	TX	Includes armed robbery	Police misconduct
Lenell Geter	TX	Includes armed robbery	Witness error
Harry Miller	UT	Includes armed robbery	Witness error
Teddy Thompson	VA	Includes armed robbery	Police misconduct, witness error

Note: n/a = not available.

some of the money to become a sound engineer and to buy recording studio equipment. Thompson is part of the musical group Come Up Boyz and has recorded a hip-hop album that includes a song in which he mentions his wrongful incarceration. Additionally, he hopes to use some of his compensation to provide financial assistance to his two young daughters (Dujardin 2009a,b,c; Green 2009; Macaulay 2009).

Erick Daniels

Fourteen-year-old Erick Daniels lived in the now demolished Few Gardens housing project in Durham, North Carolina. The gang-infested housing project had Bloods on one side and Crips on the other. Shootouts were not uncommon and innocent bystanders had been killed periodically. Daniels, whose parents divorced when he was four years of age, was no stranger to law enforcement. At the age of twelve he was arrested for possession of marijuana. Although he received probation, he frequently violated the terms of his probation and repeatedly tested positive for marijuana. Daniels readily admits that he was infatuated with that lifestyle: "Marijuana smoking, music—I wanted to live that lifestyle. I wanted to sell drugs. It was mostly what the kids my age went through. [Rap] music came first, though. It gave me the concept of the life I wanted to live" (Secret 2007). Thus on September 21, 2000, when Ruth Brown, a Durham Police Department property room technician, was robbed at gunpoint of over $6,000 by two armed gunmen, Daniels's juvenile record made him a suspect.

Details regarding the stolen money have been called into question by Daniels's defense attorney. According to the victim, two masked gunmen entered her dwelling while she was braiding her seven-year-old daughter's hair and stole her purse, which contained $6,232, representing her savings.[2] However, Daniels's defense counsel found evidence suggesting that Brown frequently allowed illegal gambling in her house and commonly had large amounts of cash on hand. Doreal Henderson, once suspected of being the driver of the getaway car, noted, "Everyone knew she carried a lot of cash. A week before it even happened, everybody had been talking." If this scenario is correct, the list of possible perpetrators is much larger than originally envisioned.

Brown described the assailant, who was later identified as Daniels, as being a short, light-black male with cornrows. Although Daniels was short, he was dark-skinned and had hair too short to braid. On October 9, 2000, Brown identified Daniels after looking at seventh graders in a middle-school yearbook. Brown based her conclusion on the shape of his eyebrows, which she said she could see above his blue bandana. At the trial, Brown further testified that her assailant attacked her with a silver .22 revolver, yet the police failed to find a gun or the money after searching Daniels's house. Nor did fingerprints found on the front door of the victim's house match those of Daniels. And in an investigation of the case by the *Independent Weekly*, "the lead detective in the case, Delois West, wrote two chronologies of her investigation—one original, handwritten log and a subsequent typed report—and there are key discrepancies between the two that cast doubt on the legitimacy of Brown's identification. On top of that, police reports that should have been written and filed are either missing or were never made" (Secret 2007).

In 2001 Daniels was convicted of first-degree burglary and robbery with a firearm and sentenced to ten to fourteen years in an adult prison.[3] Freda Black, an assistant district attorney and friend of the victim, was the head prosecutor in the case. Although she was informed that another man was willing to confess to the crime, Black neglected to investigate this lead. With no witnesses to corroborate Brown's testimony and no physical evidence linking Daniels to the crime, Black relied largely on the victim's photographic identification of Daniels. Her cause was further strengthened by Daniels's incompetent defense counsel, Robert Harris, who allowed Daniels's juvenile history to be used against him and who allowed inadmissible evidence to be used during Black's cross-examination of Daniels. Although Harris contended that he didn't have enough time to prepare a strong defense, he first received the case in February 2001 and the trial did not begin until December of that year. Now fifteen years old, Daniels was one of the first juveniles to be tried as an adult under the Juvenile Justice Reform Act, which formalized the procedure for waiver to adult court.

An investigative exposé by the *Independent Weekly* in 2007 brought attention to new information that was eventually used to request a new trial. On September 19, 2008, Durham Superior Court Judge Orlando Hudson, after hearing the new evidence, declared Daniels innocent. Approximately four hours later, Daniels emerged from the Durham County jail a free man, having spent seven years in wrongful confinement. Daniels is currently employed at a used-car dealership. He continues to be under the watchful eye of Durham law enforcement. In December 2009 he was arrested on charges of carrying a concealed weapon and possessing illegal drugs. The gun was unloaded and the "illegal drugs" were prescription drugs that Daniels takes for pain. He is presently pursuing financial remuneration for his wrongful robbery conviction from the city of Durham (Khanna 2010; Secret 2007, 2008).

Christopher Parish and Keith Cooper

On October 29, 1996, at 9:30 p.m., two men allegedly broke into an apartment in Elkhart, Indiana, with the intention of robbing the inhabitants. During this alleged incident a struggle ensued after one of the victims, Michael Kershner, attempted to grab an assault rifle. He was shot in the hip by one of the intruders during the scuffle. As the two assailants quickly exited the apartment, a baseball cap worn by the assailant who shot Kershner fell off. The intruders took the assault rifle, a Taser gun, and $23 in cash with them. That is the story portrayed by the prosecution during the 1998 trial of Christopher Parish, one of the two men charged with the crime. The facts, however, suggest that this scenario never occurred.

Not disclosed during the trial was a report filed by crime technician Joel Bourdon, who was sent to investigate the crime. His report states, "Upon arrival, I walked inside looking for a crime scene, but one was never located." Officer M. DeJong, one of the first officers to arrive at the scene, further reported:

> Photographs were taken inside the apartment. I looked through the entire apartment looking for a shell casing or any type of bloodstain. I searched inside the apartment looking on the floor and looking up near the ceiling trying to find even a bullet hole in the plaster, but one was never found. I also looked down the stairwell since I was told the shooting took place near the inside of the front door, but a casing was never located. I did locate a SKS rifle that had a cylinder type belt that appeared to be loaded lying upright in the living room. When I was clearing the room, I unloaded the gun and removed the cylinder of bullets to make the weapon safe. No round was in the chamber. Photos were taken of everything I just got done talking about. (Parish 2005, 37)

Moreover, the prosecution neglected to mention during the trial that the baseball cap was examined for DNA and the results failed to match either Parish or Keith Cooper, the alleged second robber.[4]

At his trial, Parish was able to provide an alibi that he was in Chicago, 110 miles from Elkhart, Indiana, visiting his relatives with his wife and children when the alleged incident occurred. To cast doubt regarding his innocence, the prosecution suggested that Parish had threatened Jermaine Bradley, one of the inhabitants of the apartment, only moments prior to his testifying in court. However, all of the prosecution's witnesses were in a secure facility prior to testifying and no one in the courtroom had heard the alleged threat.[5] Yet the prosecutor referred to this threat during his closing argument and the judge used it to justify an enhanced sentence. In June 1998 Parish was sentenced to thirty years behind bars. The previous year Cooper had been sentenced to forty years in prison during a bench trial.

After the 1998 trial Mike Swanson, a private detective hired by the Parish family, found two witnesses to the crime. Stellana Neal and Bryant Wheeler, who claim to have been present at the shooting, contend that the shooting incident occurred in a laundromat parking lot across from the apartment. The witnesses also acknowledged that Kershner was a known drug dealer who operated his business out of his apartment. There is also evidence that one of the inhabitants of the apartment, Eddie Love, was coerced by the police to implicate Parish. Since the trials of Parish and Cooper, three Elkhart police detectives have been found to be involved in serious misconduct and two of them have been found to be involved in criminal activities.

The Indiana Court of Appeals vacated Parish's conviction on December 6, 2005, and ordered a new trial. Parish was released on bond while awaiting a retrial in July 2006. Cooper had been released on April 27, 2006, after serving ten years of his sentence. On December 1, 2006, Judge Evan Roberts of the Elkhart Superior Court finally dismissed all charges against Parish at the request of the prosecution ("Charges Dismissed Against Christopher Parish" 2006; Lechlitner 2006; Parish 2005; Sherrer 2005).

Harry Miller

On December 8, 2000, an elderly woman was robbed at gunpoint at a Stop-N-Go convenience store in the Salt Lake City area. Approximately $50 was taken during the robbery. Harry Miller, a native of Louisiana, was recovering from a stroke at the time of the incident some 1,900 miles away. According to Miller, "I was partially paralyzed. My whole right side went dead on me. I couldn't talk, I couldn't stand up, nothing." Shortly after moving back to Utah (he had previously lived there from 1989 to 1999), he was arrested for a 2003 robbery at Dee's restaurant. Although that case was eventually dismissed, police showed the photograph of Miller taken when he was a suspect to the victim of the armed robbery. She identified Miller as the assailant who had robbed her three years earlier.

During the trial Miller repeatedly brought up the alibi defense that he was in Louisiana at the time recovering from a stroke and would have been physically incapable of carrying out the crime. Unfortunately, his sister was unable to personally attend his trial to corroborate his statements. She did, however, compose a letter in which she said that she saw him on a daily basis after his stroke and that he was in Louisiana at the time of the robbery. With no other witnesses to corroborate his alibi, he was found guilty and sentenced to five years to life in prison for aggravated robbery.

While appealing his conviction to the Utah Court of Appeals, Miller's appellate attorney, Patrick Lindsay, uncovered new evidence to support his alibi. Medical reports from a nurse who treated Miller during his stroke and the testimony of a niece who lived with Miller at the time buttressed his contention that he was in Louisiana when the crime occurred and in a physically weakened state as a result of a stroke. Upon hearing the new evidence, Judge Pamela Greenwood of the Utah Court of Appeals wrote, "Because we determine that Miller's petition represents a 'bona fide issue as to whether (he) is factually innocent of the charges of which (he) was convicted,' we reverse and remand for a hearing to determine Miller's factual innocence." After prosecutors decided against a new trial and dismissed the charges, Miller was released from prison in July 2007. Miller currently lives in Arkansas, where he has difficulty locating steady work (Morgan 2009).

Kevin Williams

A Kenner, Louisiana, 7-Eleven convenience store was robbed on the night of October 6, 1985, by two black males in their late teens. A female cashier was held up at gunpoint and told to open her register, whereupon an unarmed robber took $15 in cash from the drawer. Immediately after the incident the cashier called the police, and the incident was officially logged in at 10:56 p.m. (Police estimate that the crime actually occurred at 10:54 p.m.) Two teenagers witnessed the robbers leaving the scene in a brown vehicle. At 11:06 p.m. the police stopped a brown 1976 Chevrolet Monte Carlo that matched the description provided by the eyewitnesses. Kevin Williams was driving the automobile, and a friend, Ernest Brown, was riding with him. The convenience store cashier was taken to the location where the two suspects were being detained by the police. With a bright spotlight shining to illuminate the area, the cashier identified Williams as the unarmed robber who took the money from the register.[6] She absolved Brown of any involvement in the crime. Consequently, Williams was charged with the robbery but Brown was released.

A search of the automobile failed to reveal any physical evidence linking Williams to the crime. Neither money nor a gun was found in a subsequent search of the vehicle. There were, however, two six-packs of Pepsi, which Brown admitted to stealing from an Exxon station earlier that night while Williams purchased gasoline.[7] Brown's statement was later corroborated by the cashier at the service station, who had called the police to report the theft. It was estimated by the Exxon cashier that the Pepsi theft occurred at 10:45 p.m., a mere nine minutes prior to the robbery of the 7-Eleven. Because the drive from the Exxon station to the 7-Eleven typically requires nine to eleven minutes, and Williams would have needed to pick up his accomplice along the route, it seems highly improbable that Williams could have been involved in the convenience store robbery.

While awaiting trial, Williams told the police that on the night of the crime he and Brown had seen a brown Oldsmobile Cutlass speed past them.[8] Williams also informed the police that he had heard that the owner of the Cutlass was bragging about the robbery. Unconvinced, the police did not pursue this lead. On October 16, 1986, Williams stood trial for the 7-Eleven robbery. The prosecution relied primarily on the cashier's eyewitness testimony and the testimony of the two teenaged witnesses who saw the fleeing vehicle. The cashier from the Exxon station was not called upon to testify in court. The one-day trial culminated in a fifty-year sentence for Williams.

An investigation of the circumstances of this case by Centurion Ministries (CM) commenced in 1988. Paul Henderson, a staff investigator with CM, discovered that exculpatory evidence had been ignored in the case. Further, the police had threatened one of the teenage witnesses with jail if he didn't testify against Williams. This new information, nonetheless, came too late, as Williams had already exhausted all of his appeals. His only avenue to freedom resided with the Louisiana Board of Parole. On October 12, 2006, the parole board heard Williams's case and released him on parole. Williams served twenty-one years of his sentence for a crime that he didn't commit.

Antonio Beaver

On August 15, 1996, a twenty-six-year-old white woman was approached by an African American man as she parked near the Gateway Arch in St. Louis. The man, whom the victim thought was a lot attendant, informed her that if she didn't move her car it would be towed. After she returned to her vehicle, she was told that she could leave it in its present location. As the woman began to exit the car, the man attacked her with a screwdriver and told her to give him her car keys and purse. A struggle ensued before the woman ran from the scene. As she was leaving, the woman noticed that her assailant had bled on the driver's side door. When she arrived at a nearby parking garage, the woman reported the incident to the police. She described her assailant as a 5'10" to 6' tall black man with no facial hair who wore a baseball cap and had a gap between his teeth. The victim further estimated the age of her assailant to be twenty-one. The following day, while the police drew a composite sketch of the perpetrator, the victim's vehicle was recovered in East St. Louis. Fingerprints and blood stains were collected from the automobile.

A police officer who thought that Antonio Beaver resembled the composite drawing arrested him six days after the incident. The thirty-one-year-old Beaver was 6'2" and had a mustache. He also had a chipped tooth, rather than a space between his teeth. There were no discernible cuts or injuries to his arm as alluded to by the victim during her description of the attack. A live lineup composed of two police officers, Beaver, and another nonofficer was assembled and shown to the victim. Only the two nonofficers wore baseball caps and only Beaver had any dental problems. After the victim identified Beaver from the lineup,[9] he was charged with first-degree burglary.

In April 1997 Beaver's case went to trial. During the trial, the prosecution had the victim testify that Beaver was the man who attacked her in August 1996. The defense counsel countered that the fingerprints taken from the victim's vehicle matched neither the victim nor Beaver. A jury convicted Beaver after a two-day trial, and he was sentenced to eighteen years in prison. There was no DNA testing of the blood stain on the driver's side door.

Without the benefit of an attorney, Beaver unsuccessfully requested DNA testing of the blood stain in 2001. Five years later the Innocence Project accepted his case and filed another brief on his behalf. DNA tests in October 2006 eliminated Beaver as the carjacker. Moreover, the DNA sample matched another man who was incarcerated at the time for an unrelated crime. After having served over a decade in prison, Beaver was exonerated on March 29, 2007 ("Antonio Beaver Exonerated in St. Louis" 2007; "Wrongly Convicted Man Freed from Jail after 11 Years" 2007).

Leslie Vass

Leslie Vass was a teenage high school basketball player with no prior criminal record when he was arrested and charged with armed robbery. Joseph Chester, a deliveryman for the Westport Pharmacy in Baltimore, Maryland, identified Vass in 1974 when Vass made one of his regular visits to the pharmacy to purchase a newspaper for his mother. According to Chester, Vass was one of three men who held him up four months earlier while making a delivery. His case was heard in a bench trial in the Baltimore City Circuit Court, in which he was tried as an adult. During the proceedings, the prosecutor relied exclusively on the eyewitness identification of Vass by Chester, despite inconsistencies in his testimony. Vass's defense counsel, in turn, focused upon his client's testimony that he was innocent. There was no pretrial investigation by the defense counsel. The judge pronounced Vass guilty of armed robbery and sentenced him to twenty years in prison. While incarcerated, Vass encountered an inmate who claimed that his brother, Bucky Nutt, was one of the perpetrators of the armed robbery for which Vass was serving time. The inmate provided Vass with a photograph of his brother, which Vass mailed to the Maryland Public Defender's Office (MPDO). The MPDO then sent an investigator to interview Chester. After viewing the photograph, Chester acknowledged that he had identified the wrong person and offered to testify to that effect. Vass had his conviction vacated on May 5, 1986, and on August 15, 1986, the Maryland governor granted a full and unconditional pardon to Vass.

At this juncture the story should be complete. However, the problems that Vass faced were only beginning. Seeking compensation for his wrongful confinement, Vass was awarded $250,000 from the state of Maryland in 1987. Despite multiple court orders that his criminal record be expunged, his conviction remained intact. In an attempt to get the felony removed, Vass sued the state in 1999 and received $50,000 in compensation. Again, though, the felony conviction remained on his criminal record. In 1999, after receiving a bachelor's degree in sociology and a certificate in paralegal studies, he was briefly successful in obtaining stable employment as a placement counselor with the Maryland Job Service. The position was eliminated in 2003, however, and steady employment again eluded him. In March 2004, Vass was arrested and charged with stabbing his estranged wife. Although Vass was eventually acquitted in 2005 of all charges, he was held in jail while awaiting trial because his conviction on armed robbery charges from 1975 convinced the judge that he was a dangerous felon. During that sixteen-month period, Vass lost his home and the custody of his children. Today Vass continues to pursue justice and attempts to have his wrongful conviction expunged from his criminal record. He remains optimistic while working with organizations such as the Mid-Atlantic Innocence Project to help others who have been wrongfully convicted (Arey 2006; "Still Struggling with Wrongful Conviction After 31 Years" 2006; "Wrongfully Convicted Maryland Man Gets Paid Again for State's Mistake" 1999).

Jason Kindle

In 1999 an armed African American man entered a Los Angeles Office Depot as it was opening for business. The robber gathered the store's employees together and demanded cash. Jason Kindle, a janitor at the store, was later arrested and charged with the crime. When the police searched his home, they found a list of store-cleaning instructions, which they construed to be a robbery "to do" list. However, the list actually contained notes that Kindle had written during a training course with Cover-All Cleaning, a fact noted by Kindle's supervisor during the trial. In addition to the list, the prosecution had five coworkers testify that they recognized the voice of the robber and identified Kindle as the perpetrator. Because Kindle had a previous criminal record, he was tried under California's "three strikes" law. Because this was his third "strike," Kindle was given a sentence of seventy years to life. At no time during the trial did Kindle's attorney call an expert on voice identification to raise questions about the accuracy of the coworkers' testimony. In 2003, after he had served two and a half years of his sentence, the California Innocence Project and a local attorney produced a videotape of the robbery revealing that the actual robber was 6'6" tall, six inches taller than Kindle, and the California Court of Appeals struck down his conviction. Ineffective assistance of counsel (failure to call an expert to question the voice identification), police misconduct (influencing the witnesses to erroneously implicate Kindle in the robbery), and witness error all contributed to this miscarriage of justice. Kindle was released that same year. The district attorney declined to retry the case ("Exonerated Men Tell Their Stories of Wrongful Conviction and Imprisonment" 2003; Martin 2004; "Stories of Wrongful Conviction from California" 2010).

Derrick Bell

At 2:30 a.m. on July 16, 1996, Brentonol Moriah was walking down a street in Brooklyn, New York, when he was robbed by a man with a shotgun. After he surrendered his money, the gunman became startled by some headlights from a passing vehicle. As the assailant fled, he shot Moriah in the thigh. Moriah almost bled to death before receiving treatment for his injury. Barely conscious when the police arrived, he described his assailant as a black male who was wearing a "lemon-colored shirt." At the time he gave no indication that he recognized his attacker. Shortly thereafter, Moriah fell into a comatose state for eleven days. When he emerged from his coma, still heavily medicated, he identified his attacker as Derrick Bell, a man that he knew because the two had lived in the same rooming house for over a year. Based solely on Moriah's testimony, Bell was found guilty of first-degree robbery and second-degree assault and sentenced to twelve and a half to twenty-five years in prison in 1997.

Bell appealed the decision based on an affidavit from Dr. Elkhonon Goldberg, a neuropsychologist, who questioned the accuracy of Moriah's eyewitness testimony. In that affidavit Goldberg noted that Moriah had suffered from retrograde amnesia, which was exacerbated by the medication he probably received at the hospital. Moreover, Goldberg observed, it was unlikely that Moriah was fully conscious when he first identified Bell as his assailant.[10] The failure of the defense to impeach the testimony of the only witness to the crime constituted ineffective assistance of counsel, according to the Second Circuit Court of Appeals. Chief Judge Dennis Jacobs, writing on behalf of the court, observed that

> where the only evidence identifying a criminal defendant as the perpetrator is the testimony of a single witness, and where the memory of that witness is obviously impacted by medical trauma and prolonged impairment of consciousness, and where the all-important identification is unaccountably altered after the administration of medical drugs, the failure of defense counsel to consider consulting an expert to ascertain the possible effects of trauma and pharmaceuticals on the memory of the witness is constitutionally ineffective. ("Federal Court Finds Lawyer Ineffective" 2007)[11]

As a result, in August 2007 the Second Circuit Court of Appeals overturned Bell's conviction and required that either he be retried within sixty days or released. Bell served eleven years of his sentence for a crime he didn't commit (Hamblett 2007).

Victim Characteristics and Wrongful Robbery Convictions

Generalizations from these cases should proceed with caution, given that many of the wrongful convictions for murder and rape/sexual assault also included robbery as one of the lesser charges. Further, information on the victims in the fifteen robbery cases was frequently inaccessible. With these caveats in place, an analysis of Table 6.2 is now in order.

Over half (eight of fifteen) of the robbery cases involved a single victim. The proportion of single-victim robberies would likely have been even greater if data on the four cases in which that information was missing could have been located.[12] Although victim age and race could not be ascertained with enough frequency to make any generalizations, victim gender was available for two-thirds of the robbery cases. An analysis of that data reveals only a slight preference for male victims. Of the twenty victims involved in the ten robberies, eleven involved male victims and nine involved female victims.[13]

Additional information contained in the table includes the sentence and dates of conviction, release, and exoneration. There was no typical sentence, because the circumstances (e.g., previous criminal record, cir-

Table 6.2 Victim and Case Characteristics in Robbery Cases (N=15)

Name	#	Victim Characteristics			Sentence	Convicted	Released	Cleared
		Age	Gender	Race				
CA								
Jason Kindle	n/a[a]	n/a	n/a	n/a	70 years to life	2000	2003	2003
IL								
Michael Glasper	1	n/a	n/a	n/a	Life	2006	2008	2008
IN								
Keith Cooper	6	15	Male	n/a	40 years	1998	2006	n/a
		n/a	Male	n/a				
		n/a	Male	n/a				
		n.a	Male	n/a				
		n/a	Female	n/a				
		n/a	Female	n/a				
Christopher Parish	6	15	Male	n/a	30 years	1998	2006	2006
		n/a	Male	n/a				
		n/a	Male	n/a				
		n/a	Male	n/a				
		n/a	Female	n/a				
		n/a	Female	n/a				
LA								
Kevin Williams	1	n/a	Female	n/a	50 years	1986	2006	—
MD								
Leslie Vass	1	n/a	Male	n/a	20 years	1975	1984	1984

Table 6.2 *continued*

Name	#	Victim Characteristics Age	Gender	Race	Sentence	Convicted	Released	Cleared
MO Antonio Beaver	1	26	Female	White	18 years	1997	2007	2007
NY Derrick Bell	1	n/a	Male	n/a	12.5 to 25 years	1996	2007	2007
NC Erick Daniels	1	n/a	Female	n/a	10–14 years	2001	2008	2008
Terence Garner	1	n/a	Female	White	32–43 years	1998	2002	2002
OK Marrio D'Shane Willis	n/a	n/a	n/a	n/a	10 years	2003	2006	2006
TX James Levi Byrd	n/a	n/a	n/a	n/a	30 years	1997	2002	2002
Lenell Geter	n/a	n/a	n/a	n/a	Life	1982	1984	1984
UT Harry Miller	1	Elderly	Female	n/a	5 years to life	2003	2007	2007
VA Teddy Thompson	2	n/a	Male	n/a	16 years	2001	2007	2007
		n/a	n/a	n/a				

Notes: n/a = not available.

a. The exact number of victims cannot be determined from the available literature, as the perpetrator gathered a number of store employees together before robbing a Los Angeles Office Depot.

cumstances specific to that case, applicability of three-strikes laws) surrounding each case varied. Nevertheless, there were four cases in which
the maximum sentence could include life (five cases if one considers a
fifty-year sentence as the equivalent of a life sentence). Only four cases involved a maximum sentence of less than twenty years. Generally, the fifteen robbery convictions occurred either during the last decade of the
twentieth century or early twenty-first century. More specifically, 40 percent of the convictions took place during the 1990s and an additional 40
percent of the convictions took place during the 2000s. Consequently, the
vast majority of the releases and exonerations transpired during the
twenty-first century. Approximately 87 percent of the releases occurred
during this time. Further, since 2000, over 70 percent of the wrongfully
convicted African American men in this table have been exonerated.

Other Wrongful Convictions
Involving African American Men

This section examines cases that fall outside the categories previously discussed. As revealed in Table 6.3, five cases are qualitatively distinct from
the wrongful convictions previously discussed in this book. All five
wrongful convictions are examined in this section.

Darrell Copeland

As a juvenile Darrell Copeland had been in trouble with the police. Arrested and convicted of robbery while a minor, Copeland was arrested
again in Chesapeake on November 26, 2006, after he wrecked his automobile while trying to elude the police. When the police approached his vehicle, Copeland refused to remove his hands from under the seat of the
vehicle. He acquiesced only after the police threatened him with pepper
spray. A weapon that appeared to be a semiautomatic pistol was confiscated from his automobile shortly thereafter. During his trial a state trooper
testified that the weapon found in Copeland's vehicle was an unloaded pistol. In 2007 Copeland was sentenced to five years in prison for being a
felon in possession of a firearm.

Three years prior to Copeland's conviction, the Virginia state legislature had enacted a law that allowed inmates to present newly discovered
evidence to prove their innocence. Using that law, Copeland filed a writ of
actual innocence based on the fact that the weapon was a "replica pistol
. . . not a functional firearm" (Glod 2008). Consequently, on August 12,

Table 6.3 Summary of Wrongful Convictions in Miscellaneous Cases (N=5)

Name	Charge(s)	Contributing Factors	Sentence	Convicted	Released	Cleared
AL						
William Ward	Manslaughter	Witness error	10 years	1975	1977	1977
FL						
Gary Siplin	Theft (including fraud, deception, and grand larceny)	Insufficient evidence	3 years probation	2006	not incarcerated	2007
Arthur Teele, Jr.	Threaten to assault or cause bodily harm	Insufficient evidence	n/a	2005	—[a]	2007
MA						
William Johnson	Assault	Prosecutorial misconduct, witness error	n/a	1981	1985	1985
VA						
Darrell A. Copeland	Firearm related (felon in possession of firearm)	Police misconduct	5 years	2007	2008	2008

Notes: n/a = not available.
a. Was not incarcerated during the time between his conviction and his suicide.

2008, the Virginia Court of Appeals overturned his conviction. Copeland's case represents the first time in which the 2004 Virginia law had been used to reverse a wrongful conviction.

Nevertheless, Copeland's freedom was only momentary, as he confessed to being involved in multiple robberies of 7-Eleven convenience stores in federal court. He additionally pleaded guilty to robbery and carjacking charges and is currently serving a ten-year sentence in federal prison.

William Ward

Another atypical case comes from Alabama, where in 1975 William Ward was given a ten-year sentence for first-degree manslaughter. His conviction was based on the erroneous belief of witnesses that the bullet that killed the victim came from his gun. The detective who originally investigated the case discovered in 1977 that Ward's gun had actually been fired into the air, making it impossible for him to have been the killer. When this evidence came to light, a new trial was ordered. Ward was subsequently released and his indictment was dismissed (Bedau and Radelet 1987, 167).

Gary Siplin and Arthur Teele, Jr.

The circumstances of Gary Siplin and Arthur Teele, Jr., share two common characteristics: (1) both wrongful convictions occurred in Florida and (2) both men were political officials at the time. Conversely, the former was a Democrat, whereas the latter was a prominent Republican. In wrongful convictions of this genre it is particularly difficult to ascertain objective information about the events leading up to the conviction, given the politically charged environment in which these types of accusations take place. With this caveat in place, this section begins with a discussion of Gary Siplin.

Gary Siplin, an attorney and Democratic state senator from Orlando, Florida, was accused of campaign misconduct during his 2004 reelection. According to the prosecution, "Siplin authorized and encouraged three state office workers to work on his 2004 reelection campaign. At least one of them drew both a state taxpayer paycheck and a Democratic Party paycheck at the same time" ("State Sen. Gary Siplin Found Guilty of Felony Grand Theft" 2006). After deliberating for less than three hours, the jury found him guilty in August 2006 of third-degree felony grand theft and a misdemeanor for improperly using state employees for campaign work. Eligible for a maximum sentence of five years in prison, Siplin received three years of supervised probation. The evidence used in his conviction, however, was circumstantial. His grand theft conviction was overturned on December 28, 2007, by the Florida Fifth Circuit Court of Appeals when it ruled that his conviction was based on insufficient evidence, thereby barring any possible retrial. According to the court, the state employee in question, Naomi Cooper, had previously taken a leave of absence to work on Siplin's reelection campaign, and Siplin may have been unaware that she had been reinstated as a state employee when she was asked to assist. The court additionally reversed his misdemeanor conviction of improperly using two other state employees ("Sen. Siplin Conviction Reversed" 2007).

The situation surrounding the wrongful conviction of Arthur Teele, Jr., is more complex and involves a number of unsubstantiated accusations. Because he took his own life on July 25, 2005, many aspects of his life will remain forever unknown. Unlike the vast majority of wrongfully convicted African American men, Teele was born into a wealthy family. As a private attorney he had provided pro bono services to defendants in the Wilmington Ten and was instrumental in gaining their freedom.[14] In addition to being a former President Reagan appointee to the Department of Transportation, he was elected Miami-Dade County commissioner in 1990 and the chairman of the commission three years later.

In August 2004 Teele was arrested and charged with aggravated assault with a motor vehicle and threatening a public official. The accusations stem from an incident in which Teele allegedly attacked a police officer who had been tailing him and his wife as part of undercover surveillance for possible corruption while Teele was the chair of Miami's Community Redevelopment Agency.[15] Then-Governor Jeb Bush removed Teele from office the following month. On March 2, 2005, a jury acquitted Teele of aggravated assault but found him guilty of threatening a public official. With an impending federal trial and a controversial cover story from the *Miami New Times*,[16] Teele became despondent and committed suicide in the *Miami Herald* building at around 6 p.m. on July 27, 2005. Less than two hours later, he was pronounced dead at the Ryder Trauma Center in Jackson Memorial Hospital. In a rare move, the Florida Third District Court of Appeals heard his case posthumously. On April 19, 2007, Teele's conviction for threatening a public official was vacated, based on the grounds that his attorney's motion for judgment of acquittal should have been granted by the trial court because Teele's behavior was not proven to be a criminal offense. The governor then retroactively reinstated him as commissioner of Miami ("Arthur Teele Remembered, Buried in Tallahassee" 2005; "Commissioner Arthur Teele Found Not Guilty" 2010; "Former Miami Commissioner Commits Suicide" 2005; "Verdict In for Former Commissioner" 2005; "Volatile Miami Commissioner Arrested" 2004).

William Johnson

Very little information is available on this case from Massachusetts. According to the Forejustice website, William Johnson was erroneously convicted of assault in 1981 based primarily on the testimony of one female witness. During the trial the prosecution asserted that the witness was credible, although there was evidence suggesting that the witness was lying. In 1985, after four years of wrongful confinement, the Massachusetts Court of Appeals overturned Johnson's conviction and publicly reprimanded the prosecutor for certifying the credibility of the witness who perjured herself at his trial.

Conclusion

The diversity of the cases in the last section of this chapter makes generalizing impractical. It is possible nevertheless to draw some generalizations from the fifteen wrongful robbery conviction cases. Before proceeding, however, a word of caution should be interjected. It should be noted that many murder and sexual assault wrongful convictions also included the lesser charge of robbery. Because this analysis is based on the most serious charge for which a defendant is wrongfully convicted, these earlier cases are not reviewed here.

Although wrongful robbery convictions were not limited to any one geographical area, a disproportionate number occurred in the South. Seven of the fifteen cases (47 percent) were from Southern states. When the factors associated with false convictions were analyzed, witness error again emerged as a major contributor.[17] Witness error was present in 80 percent of the wrongful robbery convictions. To the extent that the data permitted such an analysis, it appears that eyewitness testimony was the primary evidence used in many of the convictions. Moreover, in a number of witness error cases police complicity was evident. In the wrongful conviction of Jason Kindle from California, for instance, the five witnesses who identified him as the robber were unduly influenced by the police. Similar police influence was noted in the Illinois wrongful conviction of Michael Glasper. Police pressure was additionally used to get eyewitnesses to testify in cases in Louisiana (Kevin Williams) and Oklahoma (Marrio D'Shane Willis). In the wrongful conviction of Harry Miller in Utah the elderly victim who identified Miller as her assailant had been shown a mugshot that had been taken when he had been falsely arrested for an earlier robbery merely because he was observed walking in the vicinity of the crime. A flawed police lineup contributed to the misidentification of Antonio Beaver in this first-degree robbery case in St. Louis, Missouri.

As suggested by the preceding analysis, police misconduct was the second most common contributor to wrongful convictions for robbery. It was present in 60 percent of the robbery cases examined in this chapter. Ineffective assistance of counsel appeared in four cases (27 percent of the robbery cases). Given the flimsy evidence used to convict the clients in each of these cases, competent counsel could conceivably have prevented these four miscarriages of justice. Prosecutorial misconduct, the only other contributing factor that appeared more than once, was present in 20 percent of wrongful convictions for robbery.

Finally, many of the sentences imposed in the wrongful robbery convictions appear to be somewhat punitive. Although a number of factors enter into a sentencing decision, there were only four cases in which the maximum sentence was under twenty years in length. In contrast, there were five cases (one-third of the sample) in which the defendant received a maximum sentence of life or its equivalent.

Notes

1. Thompson had the assault-and-battery charge dropped in July 2009 when the alleged victim—the mother of one of Thompson's children—missed the hearing at the Juvenile and Domestic Relations District Court. He was charged with abuse to a neighbor after he verbally threatened Janet Parker, who asked Thompson to keep his girlfriend's children off her grass. He eventually received a year of probation for this misdemeanor. On May 27, 2009, Thompson was found guilty of a breach of the peace. Also in 2009 Thompson failed a drug screening test, thus placing him in jeopardy of being in violation of the terms of his probation.

2. The actual amount of money is also in dispute. Those who claim that the victim ran a gambling house suggested that the amount of cash could have been in the neighborhood of $10,000, because the house always kept a portion of the winnings.

3. Because Daniels was innocent of the charges, he previously declined a plea bargain in which he would receive a five-year sentence in return for a guilty plea.

4. In 2004 a match for the DNA found on the baseball cap was discovered after examining the FBI's National DNA Database. The DNA belonged to Johlanis Cortez Ervin, who was serving a sixty-two-year sentence in a Michigan prison for an unrelated crime.

5. It was later learned that Bradley was a former mental patient at Oaklawn Mental Hospital, where he had been treated for paranoid schizophrenia, and that he was taking medication for this problem at the time of the trial.

6. At the time of his arrest Williams was twenty-eight years old. The actual robbers were described as being much younger.

7. Williams was unaware of the theft by Brown until after they left the Exxon station.

8. The Chevrolet Monte Carlo and the Oldsmobile Cutlass are very similar in style, and because the incident occurred late at night, it would be easy for one to appear to be the other.

9. The victim initially was unable to positively identify her assailant from the lineup until they were asked to show their teeth. Because Beaver was the only one with any dental imperfections, the victim chose him.

10. One month after the incident, Moriah was still taking pain-killing drugs and suffered from memory loss and dizziness. He was also unable to remember the description he had given police of the attacker at the crime scene.

11. An earlier appeal to the state court had produced a different opinion. Judge Allyne Ross of the Eastern District of New York denied Bell's petition for a writ of habeas corpus, stating that defense counsel's failure to question Moriah's memory during the trial did not violate prevailing professional norms in 1997.

12. Although the case information often suggested that only one victim was involved, reading through the case scenarios of other robberies revealed that this was not always a correct assumption. Consequently, if there were insufficient data to definitively conclude that there was a lone victim, information on the number of victims was treated as missing data.

13. Two of the cases (Keith Cooper and Christopher Parish of Indiana) involve the same robbery. If this robbery is counted as a single case, then the number of male-to-female victims is identical.

14. A group of civil rights activists (nine African American men and one white woman) were convicted of arson and conspiracy in the firebombing of Mike's Grocery in Wilmington, North Carolina, on February 6, 1971, amid racial tensions stemming from an attempt to integrate the city's public schools. These defendants came to be known as the Wilmington Ten. Despite two witness recantations, a jury convicted them of the charges and sentenced them to a total of 282 years. In 1980, almost a decade later, the convictions were vacated by a federal appeals court.

15. Teele was under investigation for possible money laundering and fraud for allegedly assisting a minority-owned business to receive electrical contracts worth $20 million at Miami International Airport for work performed by another company. He faced a maximum period of incarceration of twenty years if found guilty of the federal charges.

16. Reporter Francisco Alvarado wrote in the introduction to the controversial cover story by the *Miami New Times* that "Art Teele is a man of very big appetites, and because of them he is now in very big trouble . . . the once-powerful politician is possessed of a seemingly insatiable craving for all things illicit—adulterous sex, illegal drugs, bribery, and extortion" (quoted in "Former Miami Commissioner Commits Suicide" 2005).

17. The researchers attempted to ascertain the race of the victim because the victim was usually the individual providing the eyewitness testimony. Because victim race could not be determined with any frequency, no generalizations regarding the extent to which cross-racial identification may have influenced the misidentification are possible.

7

Reducing Wrongful Convictions

> I looked around the courtroom. The judge was white. The prosecutor
> was white. My lawyer was white. The jury was white.
> Even though I was innocent, I knew I had no chance.
> —*Exonerated death row prisoner*

This exploratory investigation of known wrongful convictions involving
African American men reveals a number of intriguing findings. As anticipated, the most heavily populated states were typically the states with the
largest number of cases. Texas had the most wrongful convictions of
black men, followed by Illinois and Ohio. Florida and New York tied for
fourth place, while California was in sixth place. When the study focused
on the most serious offense that led to the wrongful conviction, mur-
der/attempted murder comprised slightly over half of the sample. The category of rape and sexual assault made up the second most common
offense. Drug offenses and robbery constituted the third and fourth most
common offense categories, respectively. Witness error was the most
common factor contributing to wrongful convictions for murder and attempted murder, rape and sexual assault, and robbery. Most alarming was
the fact that witness error was present in almost 93 percent of the rape and
sexual assault cases and was frequently the result of inaccurate cross-
racial identification. Forensic errors also played a major role in wrongful
convictions for rape and sexual assault. This factor appeared in over 30
percent of those cases. Further, police misconduct and prosecutorial misconduct were major contributing factors in murder/attempted murder and
rape and sexual assault. The primary factor in the wrongful drug convictions involving botched drug raids reviewed in this investigation was the
use of a questionable informant.

193

Reducing Wrongful Convictions: Areas of Concern

Given the sheer volume of cases processed through the criminal justice system, it is inevitable that some errors will occur. Nevertheless, as the quantity of known wrongful convictions accelerates, the legitimacy of the system is called into question, and its acceptance by those groups that disproportionately come under its control becomes more problematic. To enhance the legitimacy of the criminal justice system and to ensure that it is perceived as equitable by all citizens, it is necessary to examine ways in which wrongful convictions can be minimized. While the factors discussed in this section represent some of the more important areas of concern, the list should be viewed as suggestive rather than inclusive.

The Preoccupation of the War on Drugs with Crack Cocaine and Drug Use in the Inner City

As observed in Chapter 5, the mid-1980s witnessed a dramatic change in the racial composition of those in prison as a result of law enforcement's emphasis on eliminating crack cocaine in the inner city. African Americans, in particular, began to be incarcerated in increasing numbers relative to their size in the US population. As the failed drug busts in Tulia, Texas, Hearne, Texas, and Mansfield, Ohio, attest, the primary focus of much drug enforcement was on drug use and distribution in minority communities. When expediency took precedence over legally constituted arrests, excesses prevailed and many innocent individuals were caught up in drug sweeps. Many individual cases of wrongful drug convictions in minority communities never come to the attention of the various innocence projects and therefore have not been included in this study. Complicating many of the black drug convictions was the harsher punishment reserved for violations involving crack cocaine over powder cocaine. The Anti-Drug Abuse Act of 1988, for instance, mandated a minimum sentence of five years for a first-time drug offender with 5 grams of crack cocaine. Prior to this legislation, a first-time drug offender with 5 grams of crack cocaine would usually receive probation in lieu of a prison sentence. In contrast, 500 grams of the more expensive powder cocaine were required to invoke the mandatory five-year rule for first-time drug offenders. This sentencing disparity of 100:1 was finally reduced to 18:1 in August 2010 when President Obama signed into law the Fair Sentencing Act (S. 1789).[1] According to the new legislation, possession of 28 grams is now required for a five-year mandatory minimum sentence. Moreover, the amount of crack cocaine required to generate a ten-year mandatory sentence has increased from 50 to

280 grams. This change could affect up to three thousand defendants annually and could potentially reduce the average time spent in prison by over two years. The law as originally enacted is not retroactive and retains sentencing disparities between crack and powder cocaine despite the fact that the *Journal of the American Medical Association* found that the two types of cocaine produce the same physiological and psychological effects in their users (American Civil Liberties Union 2010; Protass and Harris 2010). To address this omission, on June 30, 2011, the US Sentencing Commission voted unanimously to make the law retroactive through a proposed amendment to the federal sentencing guidelines. If not acted upon unfavorably by Congress, the amendment takes effect on November 1, 2011. And while some inmates in federal prison for crack cocaine violations will not be eligible for a sentence reduction, the commission estimates that approximately twelve thousand inmates may eventually qualify, with an average sentence reduction of thirty-seven months. Despite these changes, the average sentence for a federal inmate previously convicted of a crack cocaine violation will remain in excess of ten and a half years. Implementation of this amendment is estimated to result in a $200 million savings (US Sentencing Commission 2011).

There is evidence to suggest that the potential number of drug convictions involving African Americans may be diminishing. A study published by the US Department of Health and Human Services (2010) found that the number of cocaine users had declined slightly from 2008 to 2009.[2] And, according to a report from the Sentencing Project that appeared in the *Washington Post,* the number of African American inmates residing in state prisons for drug offenses declined by 22 percent from 1999 to 2005, whereas the number of white inmates in state prisons for drug offenses increased by 43 percent.[3] Several factors were attributed to this change, including the expansion of prison alternatives and a shift in the drug war to methamphetamines, an illegal substance that is more likely to be associated with whites than African Americans.

Racial Profiling by the Police

Although there is no single, universally agreed-upon definition of racial profiling, the term generally refers to "police targeting of particular groups for more intrusive law enforcement because of their race, ethnicity, or national origin" (Berger, Free, and Searles 2009, 418).[4] The practice is derived from the use of criminal profiles to determine those individuals whose traits make them of greater interest to the police "because they fit the profile of someone who *might* commit a crime" (Berger, Free, and

Searles 2009, 418). Hence racial profiling may lead to police intervention with little to no evidence to support the intrusion. Research reveals that African American males in particular are more likely than their white counterparts to have their vehicles stopped (Brazil and Berry 1992; Curtis 1992; Kocieniewski and Hanley 2000; Robinson 2000). Nor is racial profiling confined to traffic stops. In the late 1990s in New York City, over half the pedestrians stopped by the police were black, a figure that is double their representation in the city (Spitzer 1999). Yet black stops are less likely to result in the discovery of contraband than stops involving whites (Harris 2003). A consequence of racial profiling is the potential for a wrongful arrest and ultimately the possibility of a wrongful conviction.

Reducing racial profiling should help to reduce some of the miscarriages of justice identified in this investigation. However, proving the existence of racial profiling can be problematic, because other justifications can be made for making a stop (e.g., the license plate of the car was obstructed, the driver turned without using a signal, the car looked out of place in that neighborhood, etc.). Nevertheless, the use of racially diverse citizen boards to oversee police practices might serve to dissuade this practice in local communities. Although unlikely to completely eliminate racial profiling by the police, the greater visibility of possible cases of racial profiling may reduce some of the excesses of this practice.

Inadequate Black Representation in Decisionmaking Positions in the Criminal Justice System

The lack of diversity among actors in the criminal justice system makes it easier for nonwhites to be processed through the system without the necessary safeguards to minimize the probability of a wrongful conviction. An absence of minorities is especially problematic for nonwhites accused of murder and facing the possibility of the death penalty, given the added pressure on criminal justice personnel to locate and prosecute the alleged perpetrator. Yet a 1998 study of states with the death penalty revealed that only 1.2 percent of the district attorneys in those jurisdictions were black.[5] Furthermore, twenty-five of the thirty-eight states with capital punishment statutes had *no* black prosecutors whatsoever (Dieter 1998). Nationally, 90 percent of all state and federal judges are white, despite the fact that over 25 percent of the US population is nonwhite (Equal Justice Initiative 2010, 42). While inadequate black representation does not guarantee a failure to dispense justice, it does make the possibility of its occurrence more probable. For instance, the presence of white prosecutors may increase the likelihood of prospective jurors from nonwhite groups being rejected, thereby increasing the possibility of a race-based jury decision. Investigations of jurisdictions without an adequate minority presence bear this out. In Philadelphia from 1983 to 1993 prosecutors used peremptory strikes to dismiss over half of all potential black jurors. In contrast, only 23 percent of potential jurors from other groups were removed from jury service (cited in Dieter 1998). Moreover, a study of prosecutors in the Chattahoochee Judicial District of Georgia found that 83 percent of the peremptory strikes were used to dismiss prospective black jurors (cited in Dieter 1998). Most recently, an investigation of jury selection in eight Southern states[6] found evidence of racial discrimination in jury selection in some jurisdictions despite the fact that *Batson v. Kentucky* (1986) had reduced the use of racially discriminatory peremptory strikes in other jurisdictions. However, 80 percent of all qualified blacks were excluded from capital cases in Houston County, Alabama. Additionally, "the high rate of exclusion of racial minorities in Jefferson Parish, Louisiana, has meant that in 80 percent of criminal trials, there is no effective black representation on the jury" (Equal Justice Initiative 2010, 5). Because research suggests that all-white juries deliberate for shorter periods of time, are more prone to make mistakes, and consider fewer perspectives than racially diverse juries, the significance of the racial composition of the jury should not be dismissed lightly (see Equal Justice Initiative 2010, 40–41). Toward this end, the criminal defense bar should be more proactive in addressing the problem of racially biased jury selection practices.

An underrepresentation of African Americans in positions of authority within the courtroom is likely to continue into the immediate future, as the number of African Americans accepted into law school has declined. According to a study by Conrad Johnson at the Columbia University School of Law, although law schools from 1993 to 2008 increased their enrollment by almost 3,000 students, the number of African Americans entering these law schools dwindled from 3,432 African Americans (7.9 percent of those who matriculated) in 1993 to 3,392 African Americans (7.3 percent of those who matriculated) in fall 2008. These figures belie the fact that for the last two decades the number of African Americans applying to law school has remained constant or grown slightly. However, 61 percent of all African American applicants were rejected from 2003 to 2008. This occurred despite the fact that in 2003 the US Supreme Court ruled that race could be a factor used in the law school admission process (see *Grutter v. Bollinger* 2003). In contrast, only 34 percent of the white applicants were rejected (Johnson 2009, Lewin 2010). John Nussbaumer, associate dean of the Thomas M. Cooley Law School in Auburn Hills, Michigan, attributes this disparity to the concern over ratings: "A big part of it is that many schools base their admissions criteria not on whether students have a reasonable chance of success, but how those LSAT [Law School Admission Test] numbers are going to affect their rankings in the *US News and World Report.* . . . Deans get fired if the rankings drop, so they set their LSAT requirements very high" (Lewin 2010). Until such time as rankings assume a subordinate role to the need for a diverse student body, it is unlikely this issue will be resolved. Remedying this disparity will require a concerted effort from a number of professional organizations such as the National Black Prosecutors Association.

Use of Questionable Practices in Policing and the Courts

A number of concerns revolve around common police and prosecutorial practices that were associated with wrongful convictions in this investigation. As noted earlier, the use of informants led to wrongful convictions in drug busts in Tulia, Texas, Hearne, Texas, and Mansfield, Ohio. An investigation of 111 death row exonerations by the Center on Wrongful Convictions (CWC) (2005, 3) additionally revealed that the use of questionable informants was a factor in 46 percent of the wrongful capital convictions. While these findings are not suggesting that informants should never be used to secure a conviction, more supervision over, and greater care in the selection of, informants is necessary at a minimum. The results of the research also suggest that convicting a defendant based solely on the statements of an informant should be avoided if wrongful convictions are to be minimized.

Incorrect identification of perpetrators by eyewitnesses was also problematic in numerous cases examined in this study. It was present in nearly 93 percent of the wrongful convictions in which rape or sexual assault was the most serious offense. In many of those cases the misidentification involved a white witness. The CWC study mentioned above also found that erroneous eyewitness identification was the second most common cause of wrongful convictions in capital cases. Misidentification by eyewitnesses was present in 25 percent of the wrongful capital convictions that the CWC analyzed (p. 3). Although the police and courts will undoubtedly continue to rely on eyewitness testimony in their daily activities, a greater recognition of the fallibility of these eyewitness accounts should be recognized and duly noted in the arrest and conviction of alleged offenders.

Of special significance is the potential problem that results when a white eyewitness is attempting to accurately identify an African American suspect. In a testament to this problem, an American Psychological Association journal, *Psychology, Public Policy, and Law,* devoted an entire issue in 2001 to the phenomenon known as own-race bias (ORB) in eye-witness identification. An article from that journal reports on a meta-analy-sis of thirty-nine empirical studies of ORB published from the 1970s through the 1990s (Meissner and Brigham 2001). The investigation in-cludes over ninety independent samples and almost five thousand subjects. As expected, the "results indicated a 'mirror effect' pattern in which own-race faces yielded a higher proportion of hits and a lower proportion of false alarms compared with other-race faces." The researchers additionally observed that whites are more likely than nonwhites to exhibit a tendency to incorrectly identify individuals who are not of their own race, and that the higher proportion of false identifications is unrelated to racial attitudes. False identifications, moreover, appear to be more pronounced in the newer studies than in the older studies. The authors also note that as the amount of elapsed time increased between the subject's observation of the individual and the subject's identification of said individual, the likelihood of a false identification was greater.

Although it is beyond the scope of this book to articulate a complete set of procedures to address this problem, police lineups should be sensi-tive to possible misidentification and should be developed so as to mini-mize this possibility. Gary Wells and Elizabeth Olson (2001) offer several suggestions to reduce the likelihood of false eyewitness identifications in cross-racial identifications. They recommend that more "fillers" (persons inserted into the lineup who resemble the suspect and whose presence re-duces the probability of the witness choosing an innocent suspect) should be used in lineups in which the eyewitness and the suspect are of different races. Wells and Olson further suggest that a blank lineup control proce-dure should be employed in these circumstances. Thus, the eyewitness would first be exposed to a lineup in which none of the individuals is the actual suspect. If no one was selected from the first lineup, the eyewitness would then be shown a second lineup in which the suspect and appropri-ate fillers appear. The purpose of the two lineups is to prevent a false iden-tification should the eyewitness be prone to pick anyone who resembles the actual suspect because the actual suspect would not be present in the initial lineup.[7] Although the use of increasing numbers of fillers and blank lineups would add to the cost of locating the perpetrator, the dividends to be received through the reduction in false eyewitness identifications would help to offset the additional expenditure of time and money and potentially reduce the number of appeals due to wrongful convictions.

Prosecutors and defense counsel should be made aware of the possi-bility of inaccurate eyewitness accounts in the courtroom, and the exclu-sive reliance on eyewitness testimony to secure a conviction should be avoided if at all possible. Whereas cross-examination of an eyewitness is of limited usefulness in helping jurors to ascertain the accuracy of the eyewitness account, cautionary jury instructions, if accurate, show some potential for reducing wrongful convictions in cases of eyewitness error (Meissner and Brigham 2001).[8] Experts on eyewitness fallibility could also be utilized, especially in cases involving disputed eyewitness accounts. Finally, when a conviction is based solely on eyewitness testimony the results of the trial should be immediately subject to legal review.

Cases involving juvenile and mentally impaired suspects require special attention as well. Interrogation procedures should be reexamined by all police departments to ensure that these individuals do not wrongly confess to crimes that they did not commit or feel compelled to implicate others in order to avoid prosecution. Restrictions on the length of the interrogation as well as limitations on interrogation techniques must take precedence over getting a confession if wrongful convictions are to be avoided in cases where the suspects lack maturity or the mental comprehension to effectively endure a police interrogation. And interrogations of *all* suspects should be videotaped to permit their reanalysis by defense counsel.

Inadequate Defense Counsel

One of the factors in wrongful convictions examined in this study was ineffective assistance of counsel. When detailed accounts of the trial were available, evidence of at least some inadequacies on the part of the defense counsel was present in a number of wrongful convictions. Unless the ineffective assistance of counsel was self-evident, however, it was not listed among the causes of the miscarriage of justice. Hence, the presence of a sloppy legal defense in wrongful convictions tends to be understated. Because a lack of financial resources by those accused of legal improprieties increases the probability of receiving inadequate legal advice, the social class of the defendant figures strongly in cases such as these. The disparity in outcome by social class is especially unacceptable in cases involving extended periods of incarceration or loss of life. Mandatory reviews of convictions involving indigent defendants should be conducted looking for evidence of ineffective assistance of counsel. Court-appointed attorneys should receive adequate remuneration to permit the full investigation of all charges against their clients. Defense attorneys who refuse to provide their clients with effective legal representation should face punitive measures if it can be shown that their failure to provide adequate counsel contributed to a miscarriage of justice. And if DNA evidence is present at the crime scene, defense counsel should insist that it be sent to a crime laboratory for testing.

Issues Raised by Research on Wrongful Convictions

As researchers continue to investigate the factors associated with false convictions, questions regarding the use of capital punishment have inevitably arisen. Because a wrongful conviction involving the death penalty cannot be reversed once the sentence has been carried out, opponents of capital punishment have been quick to condemn this sanction. Death penalty statistics in the United States suggest that the criminal justice system is responding to this concern over the possible execution of innocents. The annual number of executions has declined since its peak in 1999. In that year the US executed ninety-eight individuals, the most since the reinstatement of the death penalty in 1976. Although the decrease in executions has been uneven, the general trend is in the direction of fewer executions. In 2010, for example, the number of executions had diminished to forty-six (Death Penalty Information Center 2011). Moreover, the annual number of death sentences has dropped since the late twentieth century. In 1998 courts handed out 294 death sentences. In contrast, in 2009 there were only 112 death sentences (Death Penalty Information Center 2011).

Information on wrongful convictions appears to have influenced the public's acceptance of capital punishment as well. A 2010 poll conducted by Lake Research Partners found dwindling support for the death penalty in murder cases when other options were available. In that study only one-third of the respondents favored the death penalty. The most popular option was life without parole (LWOP) and restitution to the victim's family, which was favored by almost four of every ten respondents. An additional 13 percent favored LWOP with no restitution, whereas 9 percent opted for life with the chance of parole (reported by the Death Penalty Information Center 2011).

Data on wrongful convictions also raise concerns over the use of informants or snitches. As mentioned earlier, the Innocence Project found that over 15 percent of the wrongful convictions overturned through DNA evidence were attributed to the use of informants (Innocence Project 2009e), and a study of death row exonerations by Northwestern University's Center on Wrongful Convictions (2005) revealed that the use of informants was the most common factor in false capital convictions. Informants were used in 46 percent of the wrongful convictions examined in the CWC report.[9]

As noted earlier, the study of wrongful convictions has additionally cast a dark cloud over the reliability of eyewitness identifications. Although some witnesses may deliberately lie to deflect their own guilt or to protect the actual perpetrator, these eyewitness identifications apparently are a numerical minority. Of greater concern are those eyewitness identifications from well-intentioned individuals who wrongly select an innocent person. Some reduction in eyewitness error can be expected by modifications to the lineup mentioned previously in this chapter. Nonetheless, social scientists have repeatedly documented an identification problem when the eyewitness and the suspect are of different races. Of paramount importance to this study is the difficulty whites have in properly identifying blacks. Although length of exposure to the suspect, the amount of light during the encounter, as well as other variables may affect the accuracy of any identification, other things being equal, white witnesses are more likely to misidentify black suspects than they are to misidentify someone of their own race. This phenomenon is of greatest concern when the main evidence against the suspect comes from a positive identification made from an eyewitness. Moreover, the longer the time span between the initial encounter and the identification of the suspect, the more likely that the identification will be inaccurate. Until such time as the criminal justice system openly acknowledges this problem and develops guidelines to minimize it, wrongful convictions based on positive identifications from eyewitnesses will continue to proliferate.

Recommendations for Improving Research Data on Wrongful Convictions

During the data collection for this investigation, it became evident that much of the information on wrongful convictions is fragmented and at times contradictory. Particularly frustrating was the dearth of information on many of the older cases and on some of the less publicized recent cases. Some cases initially found in the databases were fraught with inaccuracies, including the incorrect racial classification of the defendant. The absence of data on race in numerous cases additionally made this research cumbersome and time-consuming. Multiple attempts were made to bring each file up to date and as free of errors as possible given the limitations of the research methodology. Based on the problems noted above, three recommendations seem warranted.

Recommendation 1:
A Need for a Centralized Data Collection Source

While the Center on Wrongful Convictions, the various innocence projects, the Forejustice website, and the Death Penalty Information Center do admirable work in this area, it is inadequate to the task. A centralized depository where all the information on wrongful convictions can be stored and preserved is necessary if research in this area is to be encouraged. The hundreds of hours that each of the researchers of this study devoted to developing a list of wrongfully convicted African American men would have been substantially shortened if such a database had been available. Furthermore, the centralization of the data would permit a more complete account of each case to be developed and inconsistencies to be resolved before the case becomes a cold file.

Although a centralized depository is desirable, universities and innocence projects, the most likely venues for centralized data collection, may not have the resources in a time of financial austerity to establish a single database. Even in the best of economic times, the cost for such a venture may be prohibitive for an individual institution. To reduce the expenditure required to establish a centralized data source, perhaps a consortium of interested universities and other groups could be assembled to accomplish this task. Given the capability of modern computers, actual storage space for paper documents could be minimized, so that the physical demands for such an undertaking could be made more manageable.

Recommendation 2:
A Need to Preserve Data on Older Wrongful Convictions

Older cases (1970s and 1980s in particular) were frequently incomplete and contained limited information on the events that resulted in the wrongful conviction. Because criminologists were not cognizant of the dimensions of the wrongful conviction problem during much of this time period, information on these cases was not systematically retained. However, even when the authors of this book contacted the Center on Wrongful Convictions and various innocence projects, data on some of the more recent wrongful convictions were unavailable. While all of the contacts were cooperative and courteous, data retrieval was unfortunately sporadic. Although some of the earliest data on wrongful convictions are undoubtedly lost forever, the preservation of relevant data is imperative if this field is to progress. Toward this end, the presence of a centralized data source suggested earlier would facilitate proper record keeping and facilitate the development of a historical database.

Recommendation 3: A Need to Expand
Wrongful Convictions to Include Less Serious Offenses

Typically overlooked in investigations such as this are wrongful convictions involving less serious offenses. These cases tend to be ignored in favor of the more serious offenses because convictions involving serious crimes typically lead to extended incarceration or, in some jurisdictions, the loss of life. Nevertheless, given that convictions for less serious offenses far exceed those of the more serious offenses, the potential number of unidentified wrongful convictions is staggering. Yet resources limit the number of cases that innocence projects and the CWC can pursue, making the inclusion of minor crimes unlikely. To increase the number of cases examined, law schools need to take a more proactive stance in locating wrongful convictions in jurisdictions in proximity to them. In this study, for instance, there were nineteen states with *no* known cases of wrongful convictions involving African American men. If law schools in those states more diligently pursued potential wrongful convictions, undoubtedly some of these convictions would have been reported. To facilitate this process, incentives such as release time, research funding, and sabbaticals could be awarded to faculty interested in researching potential wrongful conviction cases. Law schools could additionally create credit and noncredit courses for students interested in pursuing this field of study. Conferences could also be sponsored by these law schools to increase the visibility of wrongful convictions. Finally, ways to increase the number and size of state innocence projects throughout the US should be examined to expand the number of cases under review. While some wrongful convictions are inevitable, the heightened visibility of wrongful convictions is a necessary ingredient if remedial action is to be forthcoming.

Recommendation 4: A Need to Examine Wrongful Convictions Involving African American Women

Due to the labor-intensive nature of this research, the investigators of this study chose to limit their investigation to African American men. Although the sheer volume of such wrongful convictions justified such an endeavor, one should not conclude that many of the discriminatory practices investigated in this study are absent when examining black women. In a 2005 study of forty-two wrongfully convicted women, for instance, significant racial differences appeared when black women were compared to their white cohorts. African American women were more likely to be falsely convicted of murder and drug offenses, whereas white women were more likely to be falsely convicted of child abuse. More telling, perhaps, was the finding that two-thirds of the wrongful black female convictions occurred in the South. And while perjury by criminal justice officials was present in over half of the black cases, it had a negligible effect on the outcome of white women (Ruesink and Free 2005). Although the small sample size

(N=42) and limited database suggest the need to approach these results with some caution, the presence of racial differences reveals a need for further investigation of this area.

Concluding Remarks: Some Personal Observations

Before concluding our research on wrongfully convicted African American men, some personal remarks are warranted. As we examined the available information on each of the cases, we began to sense that ineffective assistance of counsel tends to be understated in the literature. The degree to which incompetency of legal counsel contributed to false convictions often could not be directly ascertained and therefore was not included in our list of factors. Yet the latitude of behavior that the prosecution was frequently allowed during the trial, the failure of defense counsel to investigate possible defense alibi witnesses, the failure to object to potentially misleading statements by the prosecution, and the failure to adequately cross-examine hostile witnesses and raise other relevant legal issues seemed to suggest an all-too-common pattern of legal incompetence. Although some of these issues might not qualify in the strictest sense as ineffective assistance of counsel, it seemed that defense counsel was too complacent, given the seriousness of the accusations against the client, in many of the cases where such information was obtained.

As our study began to unfold, the extent to which we found evidence of overt racism was limited to a relatively small subsample of cases. However, that does not necessarily preclude the presence of institutionalized racism. It became evident, for instance, that even if the defendant had a number of black alibi witnesses placing him at a different location during the crime, their testimony was viewed as less credible than that of white witnesses. An exception to this statement occurs when a black witness is testifying *against* the defendant. At that juncture the testimony is commonly treated as credible. Thus, a double standard making it difficult for a black man to prove his innocence frequently prevailed in the courtroom. Part of the reluctance to accept the testimony of the defendant's alibi witness undoubtedly stems from the prior criminal background that a number of the wrongfully convicted individuals possessed. However, even when the defendant had no prior record, the information available to us seemed to suggest that testimony from nonwhites was seen as less convincing than testimony from whites. Because this represents a subjective interpretation of the data, however, we did not broach this issue in our earlier discussions.

A problem that we discussed in various wrongful conviction cases involves the use of jailhouse snitches or informants. Frequently there was an incentive for someone such as a jailhouse snitch to testify against the person being tried. As we examined the various cases, however, it was not always evident to what extent this arrangement had been utilized. Because some of the less-well-documented cases were reticent regarding the witnesses used in the trials, it was impossible to fully assess the role of snitches in wrongful convictions, particularly in some of the older cases.

A perusal of the various tables immediately reveals that wrongful convictions are seldom the result of a single factor. Some form of prosecutorial and/or police misconduct is present in many of the cases. Although evidence was found to support a climate of tolerance for abuse in some prosecutorial offices and some police departments, information such as this was generally unavailable. Nevertheless, the extent to which police departments tolerate and possibly encourage unethical and legally impermissible practices to secure an arrest, and the extent to which prosecutors are wantonly encouraged to aggressively seek a conviction regardless of the guilt of the defendant, represent areas worthy of the attention of future research in this area.

The role of social class in wrongful convictions was obvious from the outset. With few exceptions, those who were wrongfully convicted were from the lower and working classes. It could thus be argued that many of the known wrongful convictions involving African American men are attributable to their limited financial resources. While this interpretation may have some merit, it neglects to explain *why* African Americans are disproportionately found at the lowest socioeconomic status in American society. An alternate explanation could focus on the role of prejudice and discrimination as factors that impede the movement of many African Americans from the lower stratum of society. Residing in lower-class communities, in turn, increases their surveillance by the police and enhances their probability of arrest and possible wrongful conviction. Whatever the reason for their continued overrepresentation in the lower stratum of society, the inclusion of many African Americans in that social class places them at a distinct disadvantage in the American criminal justice system, as this investigation clearly reveals.

Notes

1. The original bill introduced in the Senate would have established identical penalties for crack and powder cocaine under federal law. However, to ensure pas-

sage, a compromise with the Republican Senate Judiciary Committee was necessary, resulting in an 18:1 ratio being established (American Civil Liberties Union 2010).

2. The study estimates that in 2008 there were 1.9 million current cocaine users aged twelve or older. In 2009 this figure was estimated to be 1.6 million users (US Department of Health and Human Services 2010).

3. The study was confined to the period from 1999 to 2005 because 2005 was the last year that the Bureau of Justice Statistics divided the state prison inmate population by race and drug offense (Fears 2009).

4. Although this section discusses racial profiling as it pertains to the unlawful intrusion of the police against black men, racial profiling is a more pervasive problem than the discussion would suggest. The War on Terrorism, for instance, makes people of Middle Eastern descent potentially subject to undue police scrutiny. Moreover, the recent concern with undocumented workers and the related legislation that has accompanied this focus suggests the potential for greater police intrusion among all individuals who appear to be Hispanic, whether in the country legally or not. To the extent that undocumented workers have few constitutional safeguards, they are even more vulnerable to the whims of the police than other groups.

5. The study further disclosed that only 1.2 percent of the district attorneys in death penalty states were Hispanic (Dieter 1998).

6. The eight states included in the investigation were Alabama, Arkansas, Florida, Georgia, Louisiana, Mississippi, South Carolina, and Tennessee.

7. In addition, the fillers should be selected by individuals of the same race as the suspect. Research has shown that when the individuals constructing the lineup are from a different race than the suspect, the fillers do not as closely resemble the suspect as in situations when the constructors of the lineup are from the same race as the suspect (Brigham and Ready 1985).

8. In 1999 in *State v. Cromedy* the Supreme Court of New Jersey held that when the eyewitness and the defendant are of different races, the defendant is entitled to jury instructions that include information on the potential for misidentification in cross-race situations.

9. Apparently concern over the use of informants has not trickled down to the state of Nebraska. As of April 2011, a bill designed to reduce gang violence that is being considered by the Nebraska legislature contains a provision that would repeal a ban on the use of prison inmates and probationers and parolees as informants ("Bill Supporting Use of Snitches Advances" 2011).

Appendix A: Methods

Although the Forejustice website contains the most extensive enumeration of miscarriages of justice, the database did not lend itself to the easy identification of appropriate cases, given the quantity of the data. Moreover, the database includes wrongful convictions dating back to the fifth century, and many of the cases are from foreign countries. Because the data could be accessed by state, however, it was possible to identify some relevant cases, although the amount of usable information fluctuated from case to case. In particular, information on "ethnicity/race" was frequently absent and occasionally incorrect. Computer searches were conducted to determine the race of the offender in those cases where this information was absent. Names of individuals were additionally cross-checked with other databases for accuracy. Older entries were somewhat problematic, as many of the links to other web pages proved to be futile. Google was used to identify other web-based sources to augment the case data.

Also appearing on the Forejustice website is a link to *Justice: Denied*, a magazine founded in 1998 by the Justice Institute, a nonprofit organization. According to its website, this magazine "publicizes cases of wrongful conviction, and exposes how and why they occur." Contributors are volunteers from the United States and abroad. Available in both print and electronic formats, current and back issues of *Justice: Denied* were examined for articles containing additional information on the cases identified in the Forejustice database.

The list of convicted innocents contained on the Center on Wrongful Convictions website was used to supplement information on previously identified cases as well as to locate wrongful convictions that escaped detection by the earlier website. With an annual budget approaching half a million dollars, the Center on Wrongful Convictions (CWC) at the Northwestern University School of Law has a paid staff of five, including Larry Marshall, the legal director, and Rob Warden, a noted journalist in the area of wrongful convictions. Since the center's inception during the 1999–2000 academic year, its mission has been threefold: to investigate potential wrongful convictions and represent incarcerated clients; to engage in research; and to educate the public regarding the causes, prevalence, and social costs of wrongful convictions. The CWC additionally actively promotes reforms within the criminal justice system. In December 2000 the CWC began collaborating with the Innocence Project to further the development of innocence projects in other jurisdictions.

Although the database identifies exonerations by state and the District of Columbia, the information is frequently incomplete. Some names do not contain exoneration dates, and individual records for many of those listed are not provided. Hence, ascertaining the race of wrongfully convicted individuals was often problematic. Cross-checks with other known databases and computer searches by subject name were conducted to ensure the inclusion of as many African American men as possible.

The Innocence Project (IP), a nonprofit legal clinic, consists of full-time attorneys and students from the Cardozo School of Law at Yeshiva University who provide legal assistance or representation to individuals whose innocence can be validated through DNA testing. In addition to providing legal counsel to wrongfully convicted individuals, the IP strives to reform the criminal justice system so that future wrongful convictions will be minimized. It is a founding member of the Innocence Network, a combination of law and journalism schools and public defender offices throughout the United States, whose goal is to assist incarcerated individuals who have been wrongfully convicted. According to its website, innocence projects are currently located in forty-two states, the District of Columbia, Canada, the United Kingdom, Australia, and New Zealand.

As of March 2011, the IP database contained 267 exonerations in the United States that resulted from DNA testing. Each profiled individual contains a link with information on that case. A picture commonly accompanies the report, thereby enhancing the probability of ascertaining the racial identity of the wrongfully convicted individual. Again, the information obtained from this website was cross-checked with information obtained from other websites to ensure accuracy of its data. Although this database facilitated the enumeration of wrongfully convicted African American men, its exclusive focus on cases in which DNA was successfully employed to demonstrate innocence limited its scope.

The Death Penalty Information Center (DPIC) was founded in 1990 as a nonprofit organization that focuses on various issues surrounding the use of capital punishment. This site contains an enumeration of death row inmates exonerated since the *Furman v. Georgia* (1972) decision, which temporarily suspended executions in the United States. The DPIC's list includes convicted death row inmates who have had their convictions overturned and were subsequently acquitted at retrial or had all their charges dropped. It additionally includes those individuals who have received gubernatorial pardons as a result of new evidence of innocence. The list identifies the race of each inmate and provides a short narrative of each case. Because the DPIC excludes noncapital cases, only the most egregious offenses that culminated in a wrongful conviction are contained in the database. As with other data sets, this information was cross-checked to verify the accuracy of the data.

Other sources of information were utilized in the compilation of wrongful conviction cases. In particular, special attention was paid to overturned cases from the district attorney's office in Dallas, Texas, given its checkered past. *The Dallas Morning News* and its online counterpart, dallasnews.com, were especially helpful in identifying cases for inclusion in this study. Where necessary, personal correspondence with individuals familiar with these as well as other cases augmented information available electronically.

As operationalized in this study, wrongful convictions include only those individuals whose innocence has been established through the disclosure of new evidence or through DNA testing procedures. It does *not* include those individuals whose convictions were overturned as a result of technical irregularities. This study further limits its investigation to known cases of African American men who were convicted since 1970 and whose wrongful convictions were detected by 2008. The year 1970 was chosen as a beginning point, albeit somewhat arbitrarily, in part because published accounts of wrongful convictions seldom included individuals convicted prior to this date. Although much time and effort was expended in identifying known cases of wrongfully convicted African American men, it is inevitable that some less-high-profile cases are not readily accessible using this approach. For example, because the Center on Wrongful Convictions and the various innocence projects are more likely to concentrate their limited resources on cases involving extended sentences or the death penalty, wrongful convictions involving short sentences are less likely to be championed by these organizations. Consequently, the conviction of innocents in cases involving less serious felonies and misdemeanors is unlikely to surface in searches such as this one. Even less likely to be reported by the media are those cases in which an individual is given a suspended sentence or probation in return for a guilty verdict despite innocence. Because it is impossible to sample the full range of possible wrongful convictions, the results of this research should be viewed as suggestive rather than definitive.

The variables chosen for inclusion in the study were based on availability of the data and the extent to which prior empirical research had implicated these variables in the conviction of innocent defendants. Nine criminal justice system variables were chosen for analysis. *Witness error*, the first of these variables, has been identified as a major source of the conviction of innocents since the early work of Borchard (1932). It has additionally been attributed as a factor in a majority of DNA exonerations (Innocence Project 2009c). The second and third variables—*police misconduct* and *prosecutorial misconduct*—are also frequently mentioned factors in the research (see, for example, Gershman 1991; Huff et al. 1996; Scheck et al. 2000; Weinberg 2003). Yet another factor that contributes to wrongful convictions is *false confessions*. As observed in Chapter 1, false confessions were present in one-fourth of the DNA exonerations reported by the Innocence Project (2009d) and in 60 percent of the wrongful murder convictions in Illinois since 1970 (Warden et al. 2003).

Because the *use of informants/snitches* is one of the most controversial practices in the criminal justice system, it represents the fifth variable examined in the study. Although this practice has been associated with wrongful convictions in much of the literature, the extent to which it contributes to this problem is subject to debate. Whereas only slightly over 15 percent of all wrongfully convicted cases later exonerated through DNA testing were based at least in part on testimony from informants or jailhouse snitches (Innocence Project 2009e), nearly half of the death row wrongful convictions reported by Warden (2004, 3) resulted from testimony by snitches.

Three additional contributors to wrongful convictions are examined in the study. These variables include *forensic errors, perjury by criminal justice officials,* and *insufficient evidence to support a conviction.* Forensic errors, in particular, represent a potential problem of considerable magnitude in wrongful convictions. While many cases probably go undetected, a study conducted in 2003 by the Federal Bureau of Investigation revealed that forensic errors may have been present in three thousand federal cases tried before 1997 ("Errors at F.B.I." 2003). In 2008 an investigation of possible forensic errors by the Detroit Police Department Forensic Services division was initiated. Although the full impact of this investigation may not be known for three or more years, it is estimated that forensic errors may have been present in thousands of cases (Lundberg 2008).

Other case-specific data collected include the state in which the case was tried, charge(s), sentence, year of conviction, year of release (if applicable), and year cleared (if applicable). This information was obtained primarily from the four major databases identified earlier. If any of this information was unavailable at the primary databases, additional computer searches were conducted to secure the missing data. A comparison of the databases revealed some discrepancies regarding the offenses for which the defendant was charged. Where possible, discrepancies were reconciled through additional computer searches.

Victim characteristics included in the study comprise race, age, and gender of the victim. In addition, the number of victims was ascertained. The availability of this information varied from case to case. Again, when the information was unavailable on the four main websites, additional computer searches were conducted to locate the missing data. Personal correspondence was also used to obtain some of this information.

Appendix B: Case Histories

_____

Alabama

Medell Banks, Jr.

Medell Banks, Jr., was wrongfully convicted of the murder of a nonexistent newborn baby. Banks was part of the Choctaw Three, along with his former wife, Victoria Banks, and her sister, Diane Bell Tucker. Victoria Banks, who had had a tubal ligation five years earlier, falsely claimed to be pregnant to get out of jail. She was released on bond based on a rushed exam by a doctor who believed that he might have heard a fetal heartbeat. After her release authorities wanted to know what happened to the child. Victoria claimed that she had miscarried, but when an exam was finally performed, there was no evidence that she had ever been pregnant. All three were charged in the crime.

Banks, who did not have money for an attorney, was assigned a court-appointed attorney who had never practiced criminal law. Banks's conviction was based on no physical evidence and a false confession. Banks, who has the mental age of a child, admitted to the charges after several hours of intense interrogation. He was released from prison after serving three years when the capital murder charge was dropped in exchange for a guilty plea on a misdemeanor charge.

Melvin Todd Beamon

Melvin Todd Beamon was convicted in 1988 of murder in Montgomery, Alabama, and was sentenced to twenty-five years in prison. During his seventeen hours of interrogation, police officers beat Beamon and threatened him with shooting if he did not confess to the crime. During the trial, police officers and witnesses, who had also been threatened, gave false testimony to help secure Beamon's conviction. He was imprisoned for one year after being convicted on the basis of the false testimony of witnesses who were also threatened by police.

James "Bo" Cochran

James "Bo" Cochran had been previously convicted of manslaughter and had served a lengthy prison term; then he was tried three times before being convicted in 1982 of the murder of the assistant manager of a grocery store. Police claimed that they saw him running from the scene of the crime, even though he did not commit the murder. Cochran claimed that he had been beaten by police when he was a teen and had been avoiding them since that time. His first trial was a mistrial; the second trial, which resulted in a verdict of death, was overturned; and the third trial put him on death row for twenty years. In each of these trials the juries comprised eleven whites and one black. Cochran was convicted after the prosecutor used his peremptory challenges to strike black jurors because of their race.

Freddie Lee Gaines

The Reverend Freddie Lee Gaines was nineteen when he was arrested and charged for two murders he did not commit. He spent thirteen years in prison before being released in 1985. The cause of his conviction was a mistaken identity. Five years after Gaines was released, Larry Dennis Cohan, who bears a resemblance to Gaines, was arrested on a drug charge and confessed to both killings.

Dale Mahan

Dale Mahan and his brother, Ronnie Mahan, were charged with raping and kidnapping an eighteen-year-old woman. The two men gave the alibi that they were at a birthday party when the incident occurred. The victim identified both brothers as the perpetrators of the crime. Dale Mahan was convicted of committing the rape and sentenced to thirty-five years in prison. He was denied parole three times because he was unwilling to admit his involvement in the crime. Ronnie Mahan, who had been previously convicted of burglary as well as other crimes, was sentenced to life without parole under Alabama's habitual offender statute. After serving thirteen years, ten months, and twelve days in prison, both men were released when

DNA tests revealed that the semen found in the victim's vagina and on her clothes did not match either man.

Ronnie Mahan

See Dale Mahan.

Walter McMillian

Walter McMillian was convicted of the murder and rape of a store clerk in 1988. The jury recommended a life sentence but the judge imposed a death sentence. McMillian ended up spending six years in prison. He believed that he had been framed from the beginning of the case. McMillian had been in trouble with the law previously for selling marijuana and for assault, so after this crime was committed, police looked at him as a suspect. The causes of the wrongful conviction included the suppression of exculpatory evidence by the prosecutor, police misconduct, and false eyewitness testimony resulting from the coerced testimony of a career criminal and two other witnesses who later admitted they had lied. McMillian's trial lasted a little over a day; then he was sent to a facility in Atmore, Alabama, that was the home of most of the state's death row inmates. He served his entire six-year sentence there.

William Ward

In 1975 William Ward was charged with first-degree manslaughter and sentenced to ten years in prison. Ward, who had fired his gun into the air, was thought to be responsible for the death of the victim. In 1977, however, it was determined that the bullet that killed the victim came from a different weapon. After a new trial, his indictment was dismissed, and Ward was released from prison after having served two years of his sentence.

Freddie Lee Wright

Freddie Lee Wright was sentenced to death after being charged with a double murder. Ironically, the man who was originally arrested for the crime and whose gun had been identified as the murder weapon was never put on trial. Wright spent twenty-two years in prison before being executed. Wright's wrongful conviction was the result of prosecutorial misconduct, police misconduct, and ineffective assistance of counsel. His attorney was later disbarred.

Arizona

Christopher McCrimmon

After a triple murder at the El Grande Market in 1992, Christopher Mc-Crimmon was sentenced to death, along with Andre Minnitt and Martin Soto-Fong, a juvenile. Other charges included armed and aggravated robbery. The Arizona Supreme Court eventually overturned the conviction when it was discovered that the judge had influenced the jury's decision. McCrimmon remains in prison on an unrelated charge.

Andre Minnitt

Andre Minnitt spent nine years in prison after being charged with murder. His conviction rested on the word of a jailhouse snitch and various forms of misconduct from the prosecutor and police officials. Despite three trials, Minnitt remains in prison on an unrelated charge.

California

Eugene Allen

In 1976 Eugene Allen, along with his codefendant Ernest Graham, received a death sentence for the murder of a white prison guard. He was cleared in 1981 after it was revealed that the prosecutor intentionally used peremptory challenges to exclude jurors who were African American. *See Ernest (Shuhaa) Graham.*

Herman Atkins

Herman Atkins was sentenced to forty-seven years in prison for the crimes of rape and robbery and spent eleven years in prison before being released. The cause of his wrongful conviction was false eyewitness testimony. The victim, who was white, was raped in a shoe store. She was not able to identify the assailant until she saw a wanted poster. Atkins's picture was on this wanted poster because he had injured three people, including two police officers, while trying to protect a friend who was being robbed. Later she erroneously identified Atkins from among seven prisoners, six of whom were white. He fled to Texas and then to Arizona before being apprehended. During the trial, Atkins took the stand in his own defense saying that he had been in Los Angeles when the crime took place, a claim his wife also testified to in court.

Timothy Atkins

Timothy Atkins was convicted in 1987 of murder and robbery and spent twenty years in prison before being released. At the time, Atkins was seventeen years old and in a gang. A friend, Denise Powell, claimed that Atkins and Ricky Evans had bragged about the killing to her. She admitted later that she had lied after police put pressure on her. Atkins was also implicated by Melvin Moore, a jailhouse snitch, who claimed that Atkins had confessed to him. Moore did this so that he could be released on a robbery charge. Both Atkins and Evans were assaulted while they were in jail, and only Atkins survived. The victim's wife had identified Atkins in a lineup, describing the assailant as 5'4", whereas Atkins is six feet tall.

Damon Auguste

Damon Auguste was convicted of rape and sodomy and sentenced to eighteen years in prison. He spent seven years in prison before being judicially exonerated. He was wrongfully convicted based on the withholding of exculpatory evidence at trial, forensic errors, and false eyewitness testimony by the woman accusing him of rape, despite the claims of nearly twenty other witnesses who contradicted her. Auguste claimed that the intercourse was voluntary.

Clarence Chance

Clarence Chance and Benny Powell were charged with the murder of a sheriff's deputy in 1975. The conviction rested on the false testimony of witnesses coerced by police. Eventually it came to light that the jailhouse informant who had implicated the two men had also accused two other men of the same crime, as well as failing two polygraphs. Chance spent eighteen years in prison before being released. *See Benny Powell.*

Tony Cooks

Tony Cooks was imprisoned for five years after being charged with second-degree murder in 1981. When the victim was identifying the assailant, Cooks was the only person who fit the description of a "light-skinned black" in the police lineup. Other factors in the case include false eyewitness testimony by an informant.

Frederick Daye

Frederick Daye served ten years after being convicted of two counts of rape and one count each of kidnapping and vehicle theft. Daye had been stopped by police for a routine traffic violation and, fifteen days later, due to his matching the description of the assailant, had a photograph taken of him. The victim identified Daye from a photograph lineup and, along with another witness, from a regular lineup. Daye was convicted, in spite of the fact that he had several witnesses that said he was attending a birthday party when the crime was committed. He was sentenced to life in prison and was released in 1994 based on DNA evidence.

Antoine Goff

Antoine Goff was imprisoned for thirteen years as the result of the gang murder of Roderick Shannon. Police felt pressure to convict Goff, even though there was no evidence that he had committed the crime. It was later discovered that prosecutors withheld evidence that would have freed Goff. Instead of doing a thorough investigation of what had happened, the case was built around the testimony of two young girls.

Ernest (Shuhaa) Graham

Ernest Graham spent his youth in and out of juvenile institutions and was incarcerated when he was framed for the murder of a white prison guard. His first trial was a mistrial after the jury could not decide on a verdict. Graham's second trial, in front of an all-white jury after the district attorney eliminated all black jurors, led to a death sentence. Graham spent three years on death row before a third trial resulted in a hung jury, and a fourth trial found him innocent and won him his freedom.

Willie Earl Green

Willie Earl Green was convicted of murder in 1983 and sentenced to thirty-three years to life based on the testimony of a witness who was high on cocaine, had impaired vision after being attacked, and was fed information by police. Even after the witness admitted that he did not get a good look at the murderer, he was assisted and pressured by police to identify the suspect. Green was imprisoned for twenty-five years before being released.

Harold Hall

Harold Hall was held in custody for five years before being convicted of a double murder and rape and sentenced to life, based on false testimony of a jailhouse informant and a false confession. Hill spent another fourteen years in prison before being released. Hill admitted to the crimes after the police put intense pressure on him to confess, despite a complete lack of evidence.

Charles Harris

Charles Harris was imprisoned for a year and a half after being found guilty on charges of cocaine possession and sale. Harris was framed by police after they searched his vehicle, failed to notify him of his rights, and falsely quoted him. Harris was exonerated as part of an investigation related to corruption in the LAPD's Rampart Unit.

Albert Johnson

Albert Johnson was convicted of two counts of sexual assault and sentenced to thirty-nine years. The first sexual assault involved a young white woman. The first victim was escorted to the intersection where Johnson was stopped for speeding, where she identified him as the perpetrator. The second victim, who was raped, was shown photographs of suspects. When she saw a picture of Johnson, she immediately stated that her attacker had lighter skin. She was told that Johnson had little exposure to the sun in prison. She also claimed that detectives pressured her to make the identification in the rape. Another factor was defense counsel ineptitude, including failing to request DNA testing, to consult eyewitness identification experts, and to file a petition to preserve the rape kit.

Troy Lee Jones

Troy Lee Jones was convicted of the murder of a woman with whom he had had an ongoing relationship. He was sentenced to death and imprisoned for fourteen years. The charges were dismissed after the California Supreme Court declared that Jones was not adequately defended and should have a new trial. Factors included the fact that the defense attorney did not conduct an adequate pretrial investigation and did not talk to possible witnesses. Furthermore, the defense counsel elicited damaging testimony against his own client during cross-examination of a witness.

Jason Kindle

In 1999 a Los Angeles Office Depot was robbed by a black man who eyewitnesses thought was Jason Kindle, a janitor at the store. He was convicted under California's three-strikes law and sentenced to seventy years to life. It was later determined that the witnesses had been improperly influenced by the police in their identification of Kindle as the perpetrator. Further, a videotape of the robbery disclosed that the actual robber was 6'6" tall and Kindle is only six feet tall. His conviction was reversed in 2003, and the district attorney dropped the charges based on the new evidence.

Dwayne McKinney

Dwayne McKinney was imprisoned for nineteen years and charged with the murder of a Burger King manager in 1981. After the crime, a sloppy police investigation and poor handling of the four white witnesses, along with erroneous eyewitness testimony, led to the conviction. Evidence of the defendant's innocence was ignored. The witnesses stated that the killer had no limp and, at the time of the murder, McKinney had a leg injury that required crutches. Due to his leg injury, he would not have been able to leap over the counter, as witnesses claimed the man who committed the killing did. McKinney, who had gang ties, insisted that he was innocent, even producing witnesses claiming that he was elsewhere when the crime was committed. The jury did not believe him, and he was sentenced to life in prison without parole. While he was in prison, he was attacked several times. Nineteen years later, new details surfaced about the crime; McKinney was eventually released from prison when law enforcement officials realized that they had locked up the wrong person. McKinney received a settlement of over $1,000,000 and was ready to start a new life as a successful businessman. McKinney died in 2008 in a moped accident.

Oscar Lee Morris

Oscar Lee Morris was initially charged with murder and robbery and sentenced to death in 1983, in spite of the fact that there was no motive for the murder. He spent seventeen years imprisoned before being released. His conviction was based on the testimony of a jailhouse snitch who was arrested while on parole and given special treatment for his testimony. Eventually the snitch confessed that he had fabricated the entire story.

Aaron Lee Owens

Aaron Lee Owens was convicted of a double murder in 1973 and sentenced to life in prison. He was sent to prison by one of his best friends, John Taylor, who prosecuted him in this case. Owens was released in 1982 after spending eight years in prison. His conviction was due to false eyewitness testimony by a witness who mistook Owens for the murderer, who closely resembled Owens. After spending ten years in prison, he was released due to the efforts of John Taylor who, realizing the error, worked to free Owens.

Benny Powell

Benny Powell received a life sentence for the murder of a sheriff's deputy in 1975. He was imprisoned for eighteen years before being released in 1992. *See Clarence Chance.*

Elmer "Geronimo" Pratt

In 1970 Elmer Pratt was charged with the murder of a white couple, Kenneth and Caroline Olsen, who were waiting to play tennis with some friends. Kenneth Olsen survived the attack and Caroline did not. According to Mr. Olsen, two black men told them to lie down on the tennis court and then began firing at them. He would later identify Pratt as one of the gunmen. Pratt was convicted and sentenced to life. He was imprisoned for twenty-seven years before being released. This was a police frame-up; the defendant was the leader of the Los Angeles Black Panther party, and the FBI had vowed to "neutralize" him. Julius Butler, a fellow Black Panther who served as an FBI and LAPD informant, lied, fingering Pratt as the killer.

John Tennison

John Tennison faced a charge of a gang-related murder and was sentenced to twenty-five years to life. He spent thirteen years in prison. The causes included concealing exculpatory evidence, prosecutorial and police misconduct, prosecution witness perjury, and attorney error.

Connecticut

Mark Reid

Mark Reid was charged and convicted of sexual assault and kidnapping in 1997 based on a comparison of three pubic hairs that were recovered from the victim. The hairs, originally believed to be from a Negro, were actually discovered to be from a Caucasian. Reid was released, based on this discovery, and deported to Jamaica because he had a prior conviction.

James Tillman

James Tillman was convicted of sexual assault, kidnapping, robbery, assault, and larceny and sentenced to forty-five years in prison. The victim, a white woman, was in her car when a black man entered and proceeded to rape, rob, and beat her. The semen that was recovered could have been from Tillman, but also fit a common profile for 20 percent of the male population. The female victim of the crime mistakenly identified Tillman as the perpetrator of the crime. Tillman was exonerated after spending eighteen years in prison.

District of Columbia

Bradford Brown

Bradford Brown was sentenced to eighteen years to life in 1975 for the murder of Rodney Frazier. A witness to the crime claimed that she saw Brown's face and would never forget what he looked like. This identification was backed up by others who lived in the same neighborhood as Frazier. Brown was imprisoned for four years due to eyewitness error before being judicially exonerated.

Florida

James Adams

James Adams was convicted and sentenced in 1974. He was imprisoned for ten years and executed in 1974. Adams had escaped from a Tennessee prison after being convicted of raping a white woman. His wrongful conviction was the result of a delayed release of hair analysis. Three days after sentencing, the Florida crime lab reported that the attacker's hairs found in the victim's hand did not match the defendant's.

Larry Bostic

Larry Bostic was arrested and charged with sexual battery and robbery in 1989. The victim picked Bostic as the perpetrator out of several photos that she was shown. He pleaded guilty to the crime and received a sentence of eight years, believing from both attorneys that if he did not, he would receive a life sentence. Bostic was released after three years, but was later arrested on a battery charge and sentenced to twelve years in prison.

Anthony Brown

Anthony Brown was charged with the murder of a gas company delivery man, James Dasinger, based on the word of a jailhouse snitch in 1983. Brown was implicated in the crime when another man was arrested and named Brown as an accomplice. In return for his perjured testimony this codefendant received a deal from law enforcement officials. After hearing the testimony, the jury recommended that Brown receive life in prison, but the judge decided that he should receive the death sentence. When the verdict was appealed, it was determined that Brown did not receive a fair trial. He spent three years in jail before being released.

Joseph Green (Shabaka) Brown

Joseph Green Brown was charged with rape, robbery, and first-degree murder and given a death sentence in 1974. He spent thirteen years and nine months in prison before being judicially exonerated. In this case the prosecution falsely told the jury that Brown's handgun had been used in the crime. The main witness in the trial had been granted leniency in an unrelated crime for testifying. Brown was defended by a court-appointed attorney who was paid $2,800 for the case and was only thiry years old. Brown was within fifteen hours of being executed when the court of appeals ruled that the conviction was based on false testimony.

Timothy Brown

Timothy Brown was fourteen years old at the time of the crime and charged with murder of a sheriff's deputy. In 1991 he was sentenced to life in prison. Brown spent twelve years in prison after giving a false confession under interrogation. His conviction was later vacated on the grounds that he did not have the mental capacity to waive his constitutional rights prior to confession.

Willie Brown

A jailhouse snitch, Frank Wise, admitted that he had perjured himself after Willie Brown was charged with murder and sentenced to death in 1983, along with Larry Troy, for murder of a fellow inmate in Florida's Union Correctional Institution. Brown spent five years in prison before being released in 1988. The Florida Supreme Court reversed the conviction of Brown and Troy when it was discovered that information important to the trial had been withheld. Both men are back in prison on unrelated charges, Troy for selling cocaine and Brown for robbery.

Kevin Coleman

Kevin Coleman was charged with murdering a nightclub patron and convicted in 1992. Coleman originally turned down a deal to plead guilty to manslaughter and to serve a little over a year because he knew he was innocent. Despite the lack of any physical evidence and eight witnesses providing alibis for Coleman, he was found guilty. His wrongful conviction was the result of prosecutorial misconduct (concealing statements that could have exonerated Coleman) and false eyewitness testimony by two witnesses.

Alan Crotzer

Alan Crotzer spent twenty-four years in prison after being arrested in 1981, along with Douglas James and Corlenzo James, and charged with a variety of crimes including sexual battery, kidnapping, burglary, aggravated assault, and robbery. Contributing to Crotzer's conviction were false eyewitness testimony by multiple witnesses who identified Crotzer as the assailant and questionable blood typing that could have included the defendant as well as the adult female victim. Crotzer was exonerated when more sophisticated DNA testing became available.

Johnny Frederick

Johnny Frederick spent two years in prison after being charged with murder in 1971. He was convicted after five witnesses said that he had committed the crime. The coerced confession of two defendants also contributed to his conviction.

Joseph Nahume Green

Joseph Green spent seven years in prison after being charged with murder and receiving a death sentence in 1993. Green was released in 2000. The victim, a white woman who was the society editor of a local newspaper, described the perpetrator as a skinny black man. The only other witness who saw anything was Lonnie Thompson, who became the main witness in the trial. He suffers from head trauma and has a reported IQ of 67. He initially described the killer as a white man, but later identified Green in a single-person lineup. It was on the basis of his testimony that Green was convicted. During retrial it was determined by the Florida Supreme Court that the main witness, Thompson, was incompetent and the charges against Green were dropped.

Robert Earl Hayes

Robert Earl Hayes was charged with rape and murder in the first degree. He spent seven and a half years in prison before being released in 1997. The victim, a fellow race track worker, was white. During the trial, the prosecution presented evidence that Hayes had been with the victim around the time of the murder. Faulty DNA evidence was also presented that was supposedly linked to Hayes. Hayes was later exonerated by DNA evidence. It was disclosed that the hairs in the victim's hands were from a Caucasian.

Rudolph Holton

Rudolph Holton was convicted of rape and murder after the FBI Crime Lab misidentified hair samples from the crime scene as Holton's. He spent sixteen years on Florida's death row before being released in 2003, when it was discovered that exculpatory evidence pointing toward another person was withheld. In addition, a jailhouse snitch falsely claimed that Holton had made incriminating statements to him about committing the crime. Holton was judicially exonerated when it was determined that the evidence presented against him failed to prove that he had committed the crime. It was also stated that this case represented one of the strongest cases of innocence that has come to the attention of the Florida Supreme Court.

David Keaton

David Keaton spent two years in jail after being charged with armed robbery and the murder of a police officer. After three days of intense interrogation, Keaton confessed to the crime, even though his version of a confession included several details that did not match the facts that investigators already had pieced together about the crime. There were five defendants charged in the crime, yet only two were sentenced: Keaton, who received a death sentence, and Johnny Frederick, who received a life sentence. When Keaton finally went to trial, an all-white jury heard his case and convicted him of the crime. He was exonerated when it was determined that a combination of false eyewitness testimony and a false confession had contributed to his conviction. After his trial, it was discovered that the polygraph operator in this case had elicited several prior false confessions and, after a tip from an informant, fingerprints discovered at the crime scene proved the guilt of three other suspects. This new evidence led to the judicial exoneration of Keaton.

Anthony Ray Peek

In spite of the fact that Anthony Ray Peek had witnesses to support his alibi, he was convicted of the murder of an elderly woman in her home in 1987. Peek lived in a halfway house within a mile of where the murder was committed. Investigators also found Peek's fingerprints on the window of the victim's car. Peek claimed that he was trying to break into her car at the time. Peek was convicted mainly on the strength of hair identification that was later shown to be false. Peek spent nine years in prison before being judicially exonerated. He remains in prison on an unrelated rape charge.

Derrick Robinson

Derrick Robinson originally pleaded guilty to a crime that he didn't commit to avoid the possibility of execution. He was convicted in 1989 and charged with second-degree murder, which carried with it a seven-year sentence. Both eyewitness error and his false confession contributed to his wrongful imprisonment. In 1992 two witnesses testified that someone else had committed the murder, and Robinson was released.

Gary Siplin

In 2006 Florida Senator Gary Siplin was found guilty of campaign misconduct. He was convicted of both third-degree felony grand theft and a misdemeanor involving the improper use of staff members during his 2004 reelection campaign. Eligible for up to five years in prison, Siplin received three years of supervised probation before the Florida Fifth Circuit Court of Appeals overturned his felony conviction based on insufficient evidence. His misdemeanor was overturned by the appeals court as well when it determined that the prosecution failed to provide evidence that Siplin had intended to violate the law.

Frank Lee Smith

Frank Lee Smith was convicted of the murder and rape of an eight-year-old girl and received a death sentence. Officials based their case on the identification of Smith as the murderer by the girl's mother and other eyewitnesses, because there was no physical evidence linking Smith to the crime. He spent fourteen years in prison before dying on death row. He was posthumously exonerated when it was discovered that the conviction was caused by witness error. Pressure from police and friends to identify the killer, as well as his past criminal record, had led to Smith's arrest. DNA testing after Smith died proved that he was not the person who had committed the crime.

Gilbert Stokes

Gilbert Stokes was sentenced to life in 2002 after a murder involving an eighteen-year-old black male victim. Ironically, the state's star witness, Leon Harrell, had named Stokes as the killer after Harrell himself had been charged with the crime. After the trial two jailhouse snitches claimed that Harrell had told them he had committed the murder. Their testimony, however, was considered unreliable. At Stokes's trial, it was also determined that the prosecution prejudiced the jury by implying that Stokes had committed the crime because he was a gang member and his victim was not. Although an article in the fall 2005 issue of *Justice Denied* notes that as of mid-December 2005 Stokes remained incarcerated pending action by the prosecutor, the Forejustice website states that Stokes was judicially exonerated and released in 2005.

Arthur Teele, Jr.

In 2005 Arthur Teele, Jr., was wrongfully convicted of threatening an undercover police officer while he was a Miami councilman. His conviction was overturned on appeal in 2007.

Delbert Lee Tibbs

The charges against Delbert Lee Tibbs included the rape of a sixteen-year-old white girl and first-degree murder of her twenty-seven-year-old white companion. The victims were hitchhiking when the crime occurred. Tibbs did not match the initial eyewitness description and was initially released. The police mailed a picture of Tibbs to the rape victim, and she later identified him as the assailant. Tibbs, who was a theological student, had an alibi and did not have a prior criminal record. His conviction also rested on the made-up testimony of a jailhouse snitch to fit the case and to gain leniency in his own trial. Tibbs, who was tried before an all-white jury, spent three years in prison before being released in 1977. In 1982 the prosecution finally dropped all the charges.

Jerry Frank Townsend

Jerry Frank Townsend, who has the mental capacity of an eight-year-old, was convicted after falsely confessing to murdering and raping a pregnant woman on a downtown Miami street. Officers did not have a difficult time obtaining a confession. He received seven life sentences in 1975 and spent twenty-two years in prison until DNA tests absolved him of any wrongdoing in 2001.

Larry Troy

See Willie Brown.

Georgia

Jerry Banks

Jerry Banks was found guilty of five counts of murder and sentenced to death in 1975. Shotgun shells discovered at the scene were believed to be from the gun Banks had been hunting with in the area that day. Police talked to a witness who corroborated the fact that Banks only discovered the bodies, but this was never brought out in court. Banks had a second trial and was represented by an attorney who was later disbarred. Banks was again sentenced to death. Banks remained in prison for five years before new evidence pointed to someone else who was observed arguing with one of the victims before the murders.

Earl Patrick Charles

Earl Patrick Charles was charged with two counts of murder and sentenced to death in 1975. Charles was convicted after an eyewitness identified him as the murderer and a jailhouse snitch claimed to have heard Charles confess to the killing. Charles contended that he was working at a gasoline station in Tampa at the time of the crime, a long way from the Savannah crime scene. Despite the testimony of his boss and time sheets to prove that he was working, Charles was convicted on the basis of an eyewitness who had been coached by a detective. Charles spent three years in prison before the motion for a new trial was supported by the prosecution and the charges were dropped. Charles received $75,000 in compensation.

Robert Clark

In 1982 Robert Clark was sentenced to life in prison for the charges of rape, kidnapping, and armed robbery. The victim was abducted in her car while in a parking lot in Atlanta. She described her attacker as a short black male. Being 6'2", Clark did not fit this description. Nonetheless, he was linked to the crime because he was driving a stolen car that belonged to the victim. Police failed to investigate another suspect identified as the possible perpetrator, who, as it turns out, actually committed the crime. Clark spent twenty-four years in prison before the Innocence Project in New York took his case and, after DNA testing, was exonerated of all charges. He was released in 2005. Clark received over $1 million in compensation for his years spent in prison.

Douglas Echols

Douglas Echols was convicted in 1987 of rape, kidnapping, and robbery. The victim was leaving a Savannah nightclub when three men approached her and took her to a house. The victim was able to escape and led police to Samuel Scott's house, which she believed to be the location of the rape. Echols and Scott were in the house at the time. Both men had alibis and witnesses to testify that they were at a restaurant when the crime took place. The victim claimed that Scott committed the rape while Echols held her down. Both men were convicted: Scott received a life sentence and Echols spent five years in prison before being judicially exonerated. DNA testing later showed that neither man could have committed the crime.

Clarence Harrison

Clarence Harrison was convicted in 1987 of rape, robbery, and kidnapping and sentenced to life in prison. Harrison was suspected of the crime because he lived in close proximity to the crime scene. During the rape, the assailant took the woman's wristwatch, and it was believed that someone at Harrison's house was trying to sell that watch. Although law enforcement officials could not find any evidence linking Harrison to the crime, he was convicted. In 2003 the Georgia Innocence Project took over his case and, using DNA testing, proved that Harrison was innocent.

Calvin Johnson, Jr.

Calvin Johnson, Jr., was convicted in 1983 based on false eyewitness testimony. Authorities believed that he broke into a white woman's apartment in College Park to rape and burglarize the victim. Two evenings earlier another woman in that vicinity had also been raped. Believing that the two rapes were similar to a 1981 rape that Johnson had been charged with (although not found guilty of), police suspected that he was the perpetrator. The prosecution based its case on victim identification and others who had experienced run-ins with someone who looked like Johnson. He was convicted of rape, aggravated sodomy, and burglary and given a life sentence and two concurrent terms of fifteen years each. Johnson was exonerated in 1999 after DNA testing of the rape kit revealed that he was not the contributor of the semen.

Walter McIntosh

Walter McIntosh was suspected of the murder of his niece and Jimmy Drinkard when their bodies were found inside his house. McIntosh, who was a World War II veteran with mental problems, later falsely confessed to the crime. He was found guilty and sentenced to life in prison in 1980 based solely on his confession. He died four months after being in prison. Another niece, Emma Heard McIntosh, who lived nearby, admitted that she had committed the crime along with a friend, Dorothy Mae Rucker. McIntosh received twenty years in prison for voluntary manslaughter while Rucker received a two-year sentence for lesser charges.

Gary Nelson

Gary Nelson was convicted of the rape and murder of a six-year-old child in 1980 and sentenced to death although he had an alibi. Nelson spent eleven years in prison before being released in 1991. Nelson happened to be one of the suspects in the neighborhood where the police concentrated their search. They searched the apartment where Nelson and his roommate lived. Nelson also had an attorney who was not experienced in trying death penalty cases and, due to his inexperience, made several legal errors during the course of the trial. This same attorney was later disbarred.

Samuel Scott

Convicted of rape, kidnapping, and robbery, Samuel Scott was sentenced to life plus twenty years in 1987. The victim identified the house that was the scene of the crime and Scott as the perpetrator. His alibi was that he was with another woman. Scott served five years of his sentence. He was released on parole in September 2001 when DNA test results excluded Scott from committing the crimes. Two days later he was rearrested for failing to register as a sex offender. After spending a month in prison, he was released again, this time on electronic monitoring. In April 2002 he was imprisoned for a third time for failure to pay the expenses associated with his required electronic monitoring. *See Douglas Echols.*

Robert Wallace

In 1980 Robert Wallace was sentenced to death for the killing of a police officer. Wallace claimed that the shooting was accidental because he was being beaten by police officers at the time. The Eleventh Circuit Court determined that Wallace had not been competent to stand trial and ordered a retrial. At the second trial he was acquitted when evidence suggested that the shooting was indeed accidental.

John Jerome White

John Jerome White faced a sentence of life plus forty years in 1980 after he was charged with the rape, aggravated assault, burglary, and robbery of a seventy-four-year-old woman. The victim picked White out as her attacker even though the lighting was bad and she was not wearing her glasses. Based on this testimony and questionable forensic evidence, White was convicted of the crimes and spent ten years in prison. He was released but then charged with possession of drugs and robbery and sent back to prison to complete his sentence. White served an additional twelve years before being exonerated.

Willie "Pete" Williams

Willie "Pete" Williams was charged with rape, kidnapping, and sodomy and spent twenty-two years in prison. Williams was misidentified by the rape victim and another woman who was attacked five days later. Williams was in jail when a similar rape occurred in the same area. The perpetrator had also been mentioned at Williams's trial as a possible suspect. Eventually, DNA tests proved that Williams did not commit the crime.

Illinois

Kenneth Adams

Kenneth Adams, one of the Ford Heights Four, was found guilty of a double murder and rape and sentenced to seventy-five years in prison. The prosecutor's case against Adams relied on his identification by a witness, Charles McCraney, who supposedly saw the defendants near the crime scene when the crime was being committed. Based on this information, police questioned Paula Gray, seventeen, who was borderline mentally retarded. She told a grand jury that she had been present when the murders had been committed and saw Adams, Verneal Jimerson, Willie Rainge, and Denise Williams commit the crime. Prosecutorial misconduct, police misconduct, witness error, and forensic errors contributed to this miscarriage of justice. Adams spent eighteen years in prison before being judicially exonerated.

Randy Boss

In 1993 Randy Boss and his brother, Revell Boss, were charged with the murder of Eugene Oliver, a fifty-two-year-old neighbor. The state's sole witness was a teenager, Robert McAfee, who said that he saw the Boss brothers and two other individuals standing across the street from the senior citizens' home drinking beer. McAfee said that Randy Boss took his bicycle from him and followed the victim to Central Park in Chicago. After catching up with Randy Boss, McAfee observed both Boss brothers and two other individuals kick Oliver in the face and on his side. During the trial defense counsel noted that the witness for the state was on probation for juvenile manslaughter and that the witness may have himself initially been a suspect in Oliver's murder. The defense counsel also called four witnesses who provided alibis for both men. Despite these revelations Randy Boss received a fifty-year sentence and Revell Boss received a forty-year sentence in 1994. They were both exonerated in 2001 when it was determined that the prosecutor withheld exculpatory evidence. According to the Forejustice website, neither Randy nor Revell was released, and their cases remain active.

Revell Boss

See Randy Boss.

Marcellius Bradford

Marcellius Bradford, along with Larry Ollins, Calvin Ollins, and Omar Saunders, were convicted in 1988 of the rape and murder of Lorri Roscetti, a twenty-three-year-old white female. In order to receive a lighter sentence, Bradford falsely confessed and testified against his codefendants, even though the blood type of the actual perpetrator did not match that of the four accused men. As a result of his testimony his three codefendants received life sentences. Bradford received a twelve-year sentence for his cooperation in the case. In 2001 the convictions of all four defendants were overturned when DNA tests, not available at the time of the trial, excluded them as the possible assailants. Bradford later served six and a half years in prison for an unrelated burglary conviction.

Robert Brown

Robert Brown was charged along with Elton Houston with what was assumed to be a gang-related murder in 1984 and sentenced to thirty-five years. A witness identified Brown as the perpetrator and two other witnesses identified Houston as the perpetrator. Brown spent five years in prison before being judicially exonerated when two other men confessed to the crime. *See Elton Houston.*

Ronnie Bullock

Even though he did not commit the crime, Ronnie Bullock was a natural suspect in the sexual assault and kidnapping of two little girls. Bullock had previously been convicted for rape. In addition, he resembled the man who committed the crime. Both victims, ages nine and twelve, identified Bullock as their assailant. He was sentenced to sixty years in prison for his alleged sexual assault and kidnapping of the nine-year-old child. After Bullock spent over ten years in prison, DNA tests revealed that he did not commit the crime, and he was released in 1994.

LaVale Burt

LaVale Burt was convicted but not sentenced in 1986. A judge vacated his conviction when it was discovered that police misconduct during his interrogation led to his false confession. Burt confessed to killing two-year-old Charles Gregory, not because he was slapped around by detectives, but because he was scared. Gregory's mother was initially a suspect after residue from the gun was discovered on her hands. Her story quickly changed from not seeing anything to saying that a young man fired at two girls and hit her son. Burt was arrested after one of the two girls hesitantly said that he was the one who shot the gun. Police theorized that Burt had wounded the girl's brother in an earlier gang-related shooting that day and shot at the girls to keep them quiet. Burt was declared innocent when Gregory's grandmother found the pistol that had been used to shoot him in her daughter's possession, and the shooting was declared accidental.

Dean Cage

Convicted of the 1993 rape of a fifteen-year-old female and sentenced to forty years, Dean Cage spent almost twelve years in prison and two years in jail while awaiting his bench trial before being released. In 2005 the Innocence Project began investigating his case. DNA tests excluded Cage as the assailant. On May 27, 2008, Cage was finally reunited with his family in Chicago.

Perry Cobb

Perry Cobb was charged with the murder of two white men that took place during an armed robbery. He was convicted in 1979 and sentenced to death. Cobb and Darby Tillis were arrested three weeks after the crime when a witness, Phyllis Santini, went to police with a story implicating the two men. Both men claimed that they were innocent, but when police found a watch belonging to one of the victims in Cobb's possession, it seemed that the police had found the right man. (Cobb had bought the watch from Santini's boyfriend.) It took three trials to convict the two men after the first two trials ended in hung juries. Cobb spent eight years in prison before being released in 1987.

Michael Evans

Michael Evans's conviction, along with that of Paul Terry, was based solely on lineup identifications. The Cook County State Attorney's Office obtained indictments charging Terry and Evans with the rape, kidnapping, and murder of a nine-year-old child. A friend of Evans, Keith Jones, made a statement to police that implicated Evans and James Davis. Later, Jones claimed that the statement had been fabricated. Evans received 200–400 years for the murder and 15–150 years for the rape and kidnapping. The lead prosecutor in the case, Thomas Breen, began having doubts about the prosecution of Evans and Terry and asked the Center on Wrongful Convictions to look into the case. Evans was incarcerated for twenty-seven years before Cook County prosecutors dropped all charges, after DNA testing excluded him as the perpetrator.

Sammie Garrett

Sammie Garrett was sentenced to twenty to forty years for the murder of a Caucasian woman, Karen Thompson, who was having an affair with Garrett. They met in a college class and had checked into a motel. They drank and smoked marijuana and Garrett eventually fell asleep. When he woke up, Thompson was dead, lying in a pool of blood with a shotgun nearby. The coroner could not find any powder burns on Thompson's body, so it was assumed that Garrett had fired the fatal shot. Even though Thompson left a suicide note, it was assumed that Garrett had committed the murder. Garrett was judicially exonerated based on ineffective defense counsel. His attorney failed to challenge inconsistencies in the coroner's report or to adequately defend Garrett against the murder charges.

Hubert Geralds

Convicted of the murder of a twenty-four-year-old African American woman named Rhonda King, Hubert Geralds was sentenced to death in 1997. Geralds, who has an estimated IQ of 59 to 71, falsely confessed to the crime. His sentence was later commuted to life. In 2000 he was exonerated for the murder of King. As of 2000 Geralds remained incarcerated for five homicides, which he may or may not have committed.

Michael Glasper

Wrongfully convicted in 2006 of robbery, Michael Glasper received a life sentence. The robbery victim, whom Glasper's attorney contends was manipulated by the police to identify Glasper, initially described the robber as an individual seven inches shorter than Glasper. Moreover, although a gun had been used during the crime, police never searched Glasper's home for a weapon. Upon retrial Glasper was acquitted after having served two years of his sentence.

Harold Hill

When Harold Hill was arrested for murder and rape in 1992, Chicago police detectives used physical and mental coercion to get Hill, Dan Young, Jr., who has an IQ of 56, and another man, who was incarcerated at the time of the crime, to confess to killing thirty-nine-year-old Kathy Morgan. Once detectives realized that nineteen-year-old Peter Williams had been in jail when the crime was committed, charges were dropped against him. Hill was sixteen at the time of the crime and was tried as an adult. He was sentenced to life in prison. Hill was exonerated based on DNA testing in 2005 after spending fifteen years in prison. Hill is still in prison on an unrelated armed robbery conviction.

Madison Hobley

Madison Hobley was sentenced to death in 1990 on multiple charges of felony murder and aggravated arson in a fire that killed his wife, his infant son, and five others in 1987. Hobley claimed that his false confession occurred while he was handcuffed to a chair and being kicked by Sgt. Patrick Garrity. His conviction was based on the testimony of four officers who claimed that Hobley voluntarily confessed to the crime. When Hobley was on trial, the main evidence against him was the testimony of Andre Council, who was suspected of arson. Council said that he saw Hobley buying a can of gasoline. Additionally, a gas station employee thought that Hobley might be the man who purchased the gasoline. The trial was riddled with judicial mistakes, including two pieces of evidence that were never disclosed to the defense. When the gas can that supposedly started the fire was introduced at the trial, it was never disclosed that Hobley's fingerprints were not on the can. A second gas can found at the scene was destroyed. In addition, jury members felt pressured by some nonjurors and by the jury foreman, who was certain that Hobley was guilty. Hobley was incarcerated for sixteen years before being cleared in 2003.

Dana Holland

Dana Holland was tried on charges of attempted murder and aggravated criminal sexual assault and sentenced to 118 years in prison. Holland spent ten years in prison before being cleared in 2003 by DNA testing. Holland was only a suspect in the attempted murder case because of his false conviction in a rape case. Holland was convicted on the basis of false eyewitness testimony and the testimony from police crime laboratory technician Pamela Fish, who lied about the amount of semen needed to perform DNA testing.

Elton Houston

Elton Houston was sentenced in 1984 to thirty-five years on a murder charge, along with Robert Brown. Houston spent five years in prison before being cleared and released in 1989. He was convicted on the basis of false eyewitness testimony and prosecutorial misconduct. *See Robert Brown.*

Stanley Howard

In 1984 Stanley Howard was sentenced to death after being charged with the murder of Oliver Ridgell, a forty-one-year-old African American, and attempted robbery. Ridgell was shot while in a parked car with Tecora Mullen. She identified Howard as the murderer but also mentioned that it was dark and raining, making it more difficult to be certain of the identification. Howard was arrested as a suspect in the armed robbery of two police officers that had occurred fourteen months earlier. He confessed during the interrogation after being tortured by criminal justice officials. Howard remains in prison until 2023 on the armed robbery charge but was pardoned in 2003 by Governor George Ryan on the murder charge.

Verneal Jimerson

Verneal Jimerson, one of the Ford Heights Four, received a death sentence in 1985 for the charges of murder, robbery, and kidnapping. Both of his victims were white. His conviction was caused by a combination of police and prosecutorial misconduct, witness error, and ineffective assistance of counsel. *See Kenneth Adams.*

Henry Johnson

Henry Johnson was convicted of murder in 1991 and sentenced to life in prison. He was picked out of a lineup, along with his brother, Juan, by witnesses who were coerced by the police to select the Johnson brothers as the murderers. Eyewitnesses claimed that the victim had been beaten by Hispanics, thereby eliminating the Johnson brothers as suspects. Johnson was released in 2002 on bail when he took a plea bargain for time served with no probation.

Juan Johnson

Along with Henry Johnson, Juan Johnson was sentenced to life in prison in 1991 after Chicago police directed witnesses to pick Johnson out of a lineup. He spent over eleven years in prison before being released in 2002. Johnson was represented pro bono and was exonerated during a trial in 2004.

Richard Johnson

Richard Johnson was charged with the rape and robbery of a twenty-one-year-old white woman in 1991. He was exonerated in 1995 by DNA testing that proved that the eyewitness testimony presented at the trial was not accurate. The judge, who had found Johnson guilty five years earlier, reversed his decision.

Ronald Jones

Ronald Jones was homeless when he was convicted of murdering and raping an African American woman in 1989. His main connection to the crime was that he lived in the area where the crime occurred. Jones claimed that his confession was coerced by police detectives. His confession also asserted that the woman who had been killed was a prostitute, although she wasn't known to engage in such activity. The state's case claimed that Jones had engaged in sex with the victim and then, while in a struggle about payment, stabbed the woman in self-defense. Jones was found guilty despite an absence of any physical evidence tying Jones to the crime. He was judicially exonerated when DNA testing proved that he did not commit the crime.

Carl Lawson

Carl Lawson spent six years in prison after being charged with the murder of eight-year-old Terrence Jones. He was sentenced to death in 1990. Lawson's footprint was found at the church where the body was discovered. However, Lawson claimed to have arrived at the church after the crime had been committed. Lawson was tried three times for the murder. After the first trial, the conviction was overturned partly due to the fact that Lawson's appointed attorney had been working for the state attorney's office at the time of Lawson's arrest. His second trial ended in a hung jury, with eleven members voting to acquit Lawson. Lawson was tried a third time and the death penalty was sought. Instead, Lawson was acquitted. He was released from prison in 1996. In 2002 Lawson was pardoned by Governor George Ryan.

Lloyd Lindsey

Lloyd Lindsey was convicted in 1975 after being accused of murdering four children—three little girls and their brother—and raping one of the girls. A brother of the victims claimed that Lindsey, along with two others, had strangled the children and then set the home on fire. Lindsey, who was seventeen, was arrested and questioned by the police and confessed to committing the crime. It was later determined that the children died from smoke inhalation rather than from being strangled. Lindsey was convicted on the basis of his false confession and witness error, while his two codefendants went free. Lindsey was incarcerated for four years before having his sentence reversed.

Alton Logan

Alton Logan was charged with the murder of security guard Lloyd Wickliffe, an African American, during a robbery at a McDonald's in 1982. His conviction was based on eyewitness testimony that was later proven to be incorrect. Another man, Andrew Wilson, who had already been convicted of killing a police officer, also admitted to his attorneys to killing Wickliffe, but this information was bound by attorney-client privilege. The confession was revealed only after Wilson had passed away and Logan had spent twenty-four years in prison. Logan filed for a new trial based on the confession and was released in 2008.

Marcus Lyons

After a twenty-nine-year-old white neighbor was sexually assaulted in 1988, Lyons was charged with the crime in part because he was the only black man in the apartment complex. The victim gave police a composite description and neighbors said that the attacker bore a strong resemblance to Lyons. At the time Lyons, who had served in the naval reserves, was working for AT&T and was taking courses at a local college. The victim identified Lyons in court as the attacker, and he was convicted and sentenced to six years in prison. He was released when it was determined through DNA testing that he did not commit the crime. After being released, Lyons, dressed in his naval uniform, took a wooden cross back to the outside of the courtroom where he was wrongfully convicted. He proceeded to try to nail himself to the cross as a protest of his wrongful conviction. Lyons spent a week in a mental hospital for making this symbolic gesture.

Jerry Miller

Jerry Miller was convicted of the rape, kidnapping, and robbery of a white woman in Chicago and sentenced to forty-five years in prison. Miller was tentatively identified as the perpetrator by the victim and by two parking lot employees. He remained in prison for over twenty-four years before DNA testing revealed that he did not commit the crime.

James Newsome

In 1979 James Newsome was stopped by police officers near Wrigley Field and taken into the station, although he was taller and younger than the described suspect in the murder, robbery, with armed violence, of a seventy-two-year-old white man. Newsome was charged with these crimes and sentenced to life. Newsome spent fifteen years in prison due to police misconduct and false eyewitness testimony before being released in 1994 and being pardoned the following year. Police later admitted that the fingerprints from the crime scene matched those of Dennis Emerson, who was already on death row for another crime.

Calvin Ollins

See Marcellius Bradford.

Larry Ollins

See Marcellius Bradford.

Leroy Orange

Leroy Orange was convicted of four counts of murder and sentenced to death in 1984. His conviction rested primarily on his confession, which he contended had been extracted by torture, including beating, suffocation, and electroshock. Orange's half brother, Leonard Kidd, also arrested for the crime, testified that Orange had been at the apartment that night, but had left before the murders had taken place. Orange spent nineteen years in prison before being pardoned by Governor George Ryan in 2003.

Aaron Patterson

Despite a lack of evidence, Aaron Patterson spent seventeen years on death row before being released. His conviction was based on evidence tying him to the crime. Patterson tried to have his false confession thrown out on the grounds that it was obtained by torture. The only other evidence linking Patterson to the crime was testimony from Marva Hall, who is the cousin of another suspect in the case. Hall, sixteen, claimed that Patterson had told her that he committed the crime. Patterson's girlfriend testified that he was with her on the night of the crime. The evidence that convicted Patterson is now missing. In 2003 Governor George Ryan pardoned Patterson.

Marlon Pendleton

Marlon Pendleton was convicted in 1992 of the rape and robbery of a home health care worker. The victim originally reported that her attacker weighed at least 175 pounds, which is at least forty pounds more than Pendleton weighed at the time. Pendleton also claimed that he was home at the time of the crime, and his statement was corroborated by his parents. He was cleared and released in 2006. His conviction was based on false eyewitness testimony and forensic errors. During his trial Pendleton had requested DNA testing to prove his innocence, but police crime laboratory technician Pamela Fish incorrectly claimed that the amount of semen recovered was not sufficient to be tested.

Anthony Porter

A Chicago gang member, Anthony Porter was charged in 1982 with two counts of murder along with one count of armed robbery, one count of unlawful restraint, and two counts of unlawful use of weapons. Porter was fifty hours away from being executed when he received a reprieve from the Illinois Supreme Court. The court was more concerned with Porter's inability to comprehend the charges against him and less concerned about whether or not he committed the crime. Porter was defended by Alan Gursel, who fell asleep during the trial and stopped investigating the crime after being paid only a quarter of his fee. The case was investigated further and Porter was released in 1999. As is often the case, there was not any physical evidence tying Porter to the crime. A year later, the actual murderer was caught and sentenced to nearly forty years in prison.

Willie Rainge

Willie Rainge was convicted with three others known as the Ford Heights Four. Rainge spent eighteen years in prison after being wrongfully convicted of the murder of a young couple and rape of the woman. *See Kenneth Adams.*

Donald Reynolds

Donald Reynolds, along with Billy Wardell, was sentenced to fifty-five years (reduced from sixty-nine years) for the sexual assault and robbery of two white female college students in 1988. Reynolds spent eleven years in prison before being released. He was convicted due in part to his resemblance to the actual perpetrator. Reynolds filed for DNA testing after the trial, but this request was rejected. His motion was not granted until 1997. Reynolds was also convicted based on the testimony of crime laboratory technician Pamela Fish, who exaggerated her findings to help convict Reynolds and Wardell.

Lafonso Rollins

Lafonso Rollins, a seventeen-year-old special education student, was sentenced in 1994 to seventy-five years after signing a confession that he may not have been able to read and that was coerced by police. He was represented by a lawyer who was later disbarred. Rollins spent ten years in prison before DNA testing revealed that he did not commit the crime. He was later awarded $9 million as a settlement.

Omar Saunders

See Marcellius Bradford.

Steven Smith

Steven Smith was charged with the murder of Virdeen Willis, Jr., an off-duty assistant warden at an Illinois penitentiary, and sentenced to death in 1985. Smith was charged with the crime after Debrah Caraway identified him as the man who had killed Willis. Her testimony, however, was tainted, as she had been smoking crack cocaine at the time. Further, Caraway claimed that the victim was alone when he was killed, yet two other witnesses stated that they were next to the victim when the fatal shot was fired. Moreover, Caraway had an incentive to lie about Smith's involvement in the crime because her boyfriend was also a suspect in the case. Smith spent fourteen years in prison before being pardoned.

Paul Terry

Paul Terry and Michael Evans were convicted in the 1976 murder of Lisa Cabassa, a nine-year-old female. Terry was incarcerated for twenty-seven years before DNA testing exonerated him in 2003. *See Michael Evans.*

Franklin Thompson

Franklin Thompson, a war veteran who was addicted to narcotics, was convicted in 1997 of first-degree murder and sentenced to twenty-four years for the death of a forty-one-year-old African American woman. Thompson signed a confession that stated he was at the murder scene and he had accidentally killed the victim, Jacquel Oaki, a known prostitute in the area. Thompson claimed that it was a coerced confession, as a police officer during the interrogation claimed to have overwhelming evidence that Thompson had committed the crime. Thompson was convicted despite a lack of physical evidence that tied him to the murder. Thompson spent six years in prison before being released in 2003, after Governor George Ryan pardoned him.

Darby Tillis

Darby Tillis spent ten years in prison after being convicted of two murders and armed robbery in 1977. He was released in 1987 and pardoned in 2001 by Governor George Ryan. *See Perry Cobb.*

Billy Wardell

See Donald Reynolds.

Dennis Williams

Dennis Williams was one of the Ford Heights Four, convicted of the murder of a white couple. He was sentenced to death in 1979 and spent eighteen years in prison before being released. Williams died five years later. *See Kenneth Adams.*

John Willis

Forty-two-year-old John Willis was charged with five counts of robbery and two counts of sexual assault. While Willis was awaiting trial, five similar crimes took place on the south side of Chicago. Despite this and the fact that another man, Dennis McGruder, was arrested and charged with the additional crimes, Willis was still put on trial. He was convicted in 1992 based in part on the victim's identification and other eyewitnesses. Prosecutorial and police misconduct additionally contributed to this miscarriage of justice. Willis received a sentence of one hundred years. After DNA testing revealed that he was not the perpetrator, he was released from custody in 1999 and officially exonerated later that same year.

Dan Young, Jr.

Along with Harold Hill, Dan Young, Jr., was convicted of the murder and rape of a thirty-nine-year-old woman and sentenced to life in prison. Peter Williams confessed to the crime and implicated Young and Hill, even though he had been in jail at the time. Young and Hill were still charged with the crime, despite questionable evidence. Unable to read or write, Young confessed to the crime after being beaten by police. In 2008 Governor Rod Blagojevich officially pardoned Young of any wrongdoing. *See Harold Hill.*

Indiana

Harold Buntin

When Harold Buntin was fifteen years old, a dry cleaning store clerk was raped and robbed. The victim, who initially identified another person as her assailant, later identified Buntin as the man responsible for the crime. Panicked, Buntin fled the state prior to the conclusion of his trial in 1986. He was sentenced to fifty years in absentia. When he was finally arrested in 1994 in Florida, he was extradited to Indiana to begin serving his sentence. Although DNA tests in 2004 excluded him as the rapist, he wasn't released until 2007 because of judicial error.

Keith Cooper

In 1998 Keith Cooper and Christopher Parish were wrongfully convicted of an alleged robbery and shooting in Elkhart, Indiana. According to police reports, two intruders entered an apartment building, whereupon one of the individuals shot Michael Kershner while both intruders proceeded to rob him. When the police arrived, they failed to find any evidence suggesting that a crime had occurred. The "shooter" supposedly left behind a baseball cap while fleeing the crime scene. Although DNA tests on the cap excluded Cooper, he was charged with attempted murder and armed robbery. Acquitted of the attempted murder, Cooper was convicted of armed robbery and given a forty-year prison sentence. Parish, who was 110 miles away visiting relatives in Chicago at the time of the robbery, was eventually sentenced to thirty years in prison. In 2006, one year after Parish's conviction was overturned by an appeals court, Cooper was given an early release from prison. *See Christopher Parish.*

Larry Hicks

In 1978 nineteen-year-old Larry Hicks was convicted of stabbing to death two African American men in Gary, Indiana. Unable to afford his own legal counsel, Hicks was given the services of a public defender who, until a week before the trial, was unaware that his client faced the death penalty. Nor did his public defender adequately prepare a defense for his client. After a day-and-a-half-long trial, Hicks was sentenced to death by the electric chair. Two weeks before he was scheduled to die, he received a stay of execution. Upon retrial in 1980, Hicks was acquitted and released after it was determined that the eyewitness testimony used to convict him was perjured.

Larry Mayes

Larry Mayes spent twenty-one years in prison after being convicted for the rape and robbery of a white woman in 1982. He received an eighty-year sentence. The victim was not able to identify Mayes in a police lineup, but she had stated that the person who raped her had a gold tooth, and Mayes did have a gold tooth. It later came out that police had somehow hypnotized the victim prior to her identifying him from a photographic lineup. DNA testing in 2001 eliminated Mayes as the rapist.

Christopher Parish

Christopher Parish and Keith Cooper were wrongfully convicted in 1998 of a robbery that never took place. Parish claimed that he was with his family over 100 miles away in Chicago when the crime occurred. He was convicted and sentenced to thirty years in prison. Parish spent over nine years in prison before it was discovered that the prosecution failed to disclose that DNA tests proved that a hat worn by one of the alleged perpetrators was not from either Parish or Cooper. In 2005 Parish was awarded a new trial based on ineffective assistance of counsel. Then, in 2006, the district attorney dismissed the charges and Parish was released. *See Keith Cooper.*

Charles Smith

Charles Smith, Briddie Johnson, and Phillip Lee were planning to rob individuals leaving the Elegant Farmer, a restaurant in Fort Wayne, Indiana, on December 10, 1982. During the botched attempt a twenty-year-old white woman was shot and killed. Smith was convicted and sentenced to death in 1983 for the incident. The primary witness for the state was Phillip Lee, who claimed to be the getaway driver. Based on his testimony Smith was found guilty of murder and robbery. In exchange for his testimony, Lee had his charges dropped. In 1989 the Indiana Supreme Court overturned Smith's conviction when it was determined that he had received ineffective assistance of counsel. Upon retrial in 1991, he was acquitted and released when it was shown that the witnesses testifying against him in his original trial had perjured themselves.

Iowa

James Hall

James Hall was sentenced to fifty years behind bars for second-degree murder in 1974. An appeal of his conviction was unsuccessful. In 1983, after new evidence emerged that exculpatory evidence had been concealed, Hall's conviction was vacated. One year later, the original indictment against Hall was dismissed based on several grounds, including racial slurs by the prosecutor when the case was presented to the grand jury, the failure of the prosecutor to present evidence that pointed to the possibility of other suspects, and the misrepresentation of comments Hall allegedly made during an interview by a state investigator.

Terry Harrington

Terry Harrington, along with Curtis McGhee, Jr., faced life in prison for the charge of murder in 1978. Both men were convicted of killing a white man. In 2003 the Iowa Supreme Court finally reviewed the decision and concluded that police reports indicating the possibility of a different suspect had been withheld. The court further noted that a witness later testified he had lied during the trial after feeling pressure from the police and prosecution to testify against Harrington. Additionally, fingerprints found at the crime scene tended to suggest that Harrington was not responsible for the crime. Harrington was incarcerated for twenty-five years before winning his freedom in 2003, when Governor Tom Vilsack signed a reprieve after the Iowa Supreme Court overturned his initial conviction. *See Curtis McGhee, Jr.*

Curtis McGhee, Jr.

Curtis McGhee, Jr., and Terry Harrington were convicted in separate trials of first-degree murder and received life sentences in 1978 for the murder of a white man. In 2003 the Iowa Supreme Court overturned Harrington's conviction, and he received a reprieve from Governor Tom Vilsack and was released from prison. However, the prosecutor refused to dismiss the charges against McGhee, and he was convicted largely on the same discredited evidence as his codefendant. In September 2003 McGhee won his release from prison in return for pleading guilty to second-degree murder. *See Terry Harrington.*

Kentucky

William Gregory

Convicted of rape, attempted rape, and burglary in 1993, William Gregory was sentenced to seventy years in prison. He was a suspect mainly because he lived in the same apartment complex as the victims, and forensic evidence indicated that an African American had committed the crime. One of the victims claimed that she had not had any African Americans in her apartment. Gregory spent seven years in prison before being judicially exonerated, after DNA testing of hairs found at the crime scene excluded him.

Louisiana

David Alexander

David Alexander was convicted in 1976 of the robbery and murder of Louis Gladu, the proprietor of Hasty Mart in New Iberia, Louisiana.

Alexander received a life sentence for the crimes. His original conviction was the result of testimony provided by a career criminal headed for prison after being charged with trying to pass multiple bad checks. The informant may also have been offered money by the sheriff's department to testify against the defendant. This case was further complicated when the sheriff convinced the real killers to retract their confessions because he had already indicted David Alexander and others and could not admit that he had made a mistake. Alexander was released by the Louisiana parole board after the board heard testimony from a former sheriff and a former deputy sheriff.

Gene Bibbins

Gene Bibbins was charged with the rape and burglary of a thirteen-year-old girl in a south Baton Rouge housing project. In 1987 he received a life sentence for the crime. Bibbins lived in the same housing project as the victim and had become the prime suspect when police found him in possession of a radio that had been taken from the victim. He claimed that he found the radio between buildings and didn't know that it was stolen. While Bibbins sat inside the squad car and the police shined a flashlight on his face, the victim identified him as her assailant. During the trial, the testimony of the victim played heavily in the jury's decision to convict. Although the victim had identified him as her attacker, her original description of her assailant did not match that of Bibbins. In 2002, biological evidence from the rape kit was subjected to DNA testing at two different laboratories. Both laboratories excluded Bibbins as the perpetrator. Bibbins was finally released from prison in March 2003.

Dan L. Bright

Dan L. Bright was charged with first-degree murder in 1995 and sentenced to death in 1996. This sentence was later commuted to life. During the trial his attorney was often intoxicated. Also, the FBI had information indicating that another person had committed the crime, but this information, which could have led to Bright's exoneration, was withheld. Bright tried to have the information released, but the FBI refused, claiming a right to privacy. Eventually, the Louisiana Supreme Court overturned Bright's conviction. He spent eight years in prison before being judicially exonerated.

Dennis Brown

Dennis Brown was sentenced to life in prison in 1985 after being charged with the rape and burglary of a white woman. He was convicted after being picked out of a lineup by the victim. Brown also falsely confessed to the crime after having been threatened by police at knifepoint. Further, forensic evidence pointed to the perpetrator being a type O blood and secretor, which was true of Brown but also of 40 percent of the African American population. Brown was released in 2004 after DNA evidence cleared him of any wrongdoing.

Clyde Charles

Clyde Charles was convicted of raping a young white nurse near Houma, Louisiana. The victim identified him as the perpetrator although he did not look like the person who committed the crime. An all-white jury found him guilty in 1982. He was sentenced to life in prison and spent eighteen years there before DNA testing led to his conviction being overturned. He received between $100,000 and $200,000 in compensation for his wrongful conviction. Charles died in 2009 of natural causes at the age of fifty-five.

Allen Coco

Allen Coco faced aggravated rape and aggravated burglary charges from an incident that occurred during the early morning hours of May 26, 1995. The victim awoke that morning to find a black man standing over her bed. After raping the woman both anally and vaginally, the perpetrator was stabbed in the buttocks by the victim. Although the victim identified Coco as her assailant during the trial, her initial description did not match Coco and failed to mention the large tattoos that Coco has. Nevertheless, Coco had the same blood type as the bloodstains found at the crime scene, and this blood type is found in only 5.8 percent of all African Americans. Consequently, he was found guilty in a bench trial on November 7, 1997, and sentenced to life without parole. Six years later, the Innocence Project of New Orleans agreed to investigate Coco's case. After DNA tests excluded Coco as the perpetrator, an appeals court overturned his conviction and ordered a new trial. Finally, in 2006 the district attorney dropped the charges and Coco was released.

Shareef Cousin

Shareef Cousin was charged with murder and sentenced to death in 1996. Although a video showed him playing basketball at the time of the murder and his coach testified that he gave him a ride home after the game, he was still put on trial. The suppression of this tape as evidence was the reason for Cousin's conviction being overturned after he spent three years in prison.

Harry Granger

Harry Granger was released from prison in 2006 after having been incarcerated for thirty years for a wrongful conviction. The sheriff in the case convinced the actual killers to recant their confessions because he had already charged several innocent people, including David Alexander. *See David Alexander.*

Travis Hayes

This conviction, along with that of Ryan Matthews, was based on Hayes's false confession, police misconduct, and erroneous eyewitness identification. Police detectives wore Hayes down, and eventually he confessed to the crime even though he was innocent. DNA testing of a ski mask found at the scene did not match Hayes or Matthews. The perpetrator was also described as much shorter than Matthews, who is 6'1". Further, DNA testing proved conclusively that Hayes did not commit the murder. He was released after spending nine years in prison.

Willie Jackson

Willie Jackson was charged with attempted aggravated rape and robbery and sentenced to forty years in prison in 1989. He was put on trial even though he was nearly two hundred miles away at the time of the crime. He was convicted on the basis of a note that was written to the victim on the back of one of his bank receipts and testimony that he was the one who bit the woman. Shortly after Willie Jackson was convicted, his brother Milton Jackson confessed, but Willie wasn't released. The case was eventually investigated by the Innocence Project of New Orleans, and further DNA testing proved that Willie Jackson's brother Milton Jackson had indeed committed the crime. After seventeen years behind bars, Willie was finally released. Milton Jackson is currently serving a life sentence for an unrelated rape.

Rickey Johnson

Rickey Johnson was charged with the aggravated rape of a twenty-two-year-old black woman in 1982 and received a life sentence in 1983. He remained incarcerated for over twenty-five years before being judicially exonerated. His conviction was largely based on the victim's identification of Johnson from an old photograph. DNA tests excluded him as a suspect in 2008, and he was awarded $150,000 as compensation.

Curtis Kyles

Curtis Kyles received the death penalty in 1984 for the murder of a sixty-year-old white woman in a store parking lot. He spent fourteen years in prison after evidence that was important to the case was withheld. Kyles was convicted based on testimony that he sold the victim's automobile, on a murder weapon that was found near Kyles's home, and on witnesses' claims that Kyles was near the scene of the crime. His conviction was overturned by the US Supreme Court in 1995, when it was determined that the prosecution's main witness was a paid informant who may have been the actual perpetrator. In 1998, after a series of hung juries, the charges against Kyles were dropped and he became a free man. During his time in prison Kyles came within thirty days of being executed for a crime that he did not commit.

Dwight Labran

Dwight Labran was sent to prison for life in 1997 after being convicted of the murder of Martin Hubbard. The main eyewitness was Hubbard's cousin, Kevin Watson. He was the owner of the automobile where the victim was found. Watson avoided being arrested for his own warrants by not using his own name and was also not a suspect in the crime. Labran was released in 2001 after his conviction was reversed because of eyewitness perjury.

Ryan Matthews

See Travis Hayes.

Johnny Ross

At the age of sixteen, Johnny Ross was sentenced to death on a rape conviction involving a white woman in 1975. Police misconduct, false eyewit-

ness testimony, and a false confession contributed to his wrongful conviction. Ross spent six years as the youngest person on death row before
being judicially exonerated in 1981. He was released after his blood type
was compared with that of the rapist and they did not match.

John Thompson

John Thompson was convicted in 1985 of a New Orleans murder and received the death penalty. In 2001 Judge Patrick Quinlan vacated his death
sentence and gave Thompson a sentence of life without parole. Thompson
spent nineteen years in prison prior to being exonerated. He was sent to
prison after the prosecution had concealed the fact that the murderer had a
different blood type than Thompson. In 2003 Thompson was released from
prison after being acquitted at his retrial.

Calvin Williams

Calvin Williams was sent to prison for murder in 1977 and sentenced to
life. He remained in prison until 1992, when he was granted a new trial. In
1996 the murder charge was dismissed after it was discovered that the
prosecutor failed to give the defense counsel potentially exculpatory evidence. In 2007 Williams was awarded compensation for his wrongful conviction from the state of Louisiana, making him the first person to receive
such compensation under a 2005 Louisiana statute.

Kevin Williams

Kevin Williams was found guilty in 1986 of robbing a convenience store.
During the investigation police stopped Williams and a friend about a half
mile from the crime scene because he was driving a car that resembled the
getaway car. The main eyewitness had doubts about her identification of
Williams but did not say so in court. Prosecutorial misconduct, police misconduct, and false eyewitness testimony contributed to the wrongful conviction. Williams was sentenced to fifty years in prison for participating in
a fifteen-dollar robbery. He was paroled in October 2006, when Louisiana
Parole Board members expressed their belief that Williams had been
wrongfully convicted.

Michael Williams

Michael Williams was sixteen years of age when he was charged with the
aggravated rape of a twenty-two-year-old woman in 1981 and sentenced

to life without parole. The victim of the attack knew Williams from tutoring him. Williams became infatuated with the victim, often dropping by her place of employment. At one point he refused to leave, broke a window, and was arrested by the police. Williams asserted that he was at home during the crime, a claim backed up by his grandmother and cousin. All of the physical evidence, including clothes, shoes, and a footprint, failed to point to Williams as the rapist. When the police drove Williams to the victim's house, he attempted to take off, a fact later used to prove his guilt. Williams spent twenty-four years in prison before DNA testing exonerated him.

Calvin Willis

Calvin Willis was convicted of a 1981 rape in Shreveport, Louisiana, and sentenced to life in prison. He remained incarcerated for twenty-two years before finally being released in 2003. False eyewitness testimony and forensic errors contributed to his wrongful conviction. Willis was exonerated after DNA testing excluded him as the perpetrator.

Maryland

Ronald Addison

Ronald Addison was charged with second-degree murder and gun possession and sentenced to thirty years in prison. He was found guilty of shooting thirty-four-year-old Lewis Jackson in 1996. Addison was awarded a new trial in October 2005 because the prosecutor had withheld the names of three eyewitnesses who would have testified on behalf of Addison. The charges against him were dropped later that same year due to a lack of evidence to convict. Addison spent nine years in prison before being judicially exonerated.

Michael Austin

False eyewitness testimony from a lifelong drug addict sent Michael Austin to prison with a life sentence for murder and robbery in 1975. Austin provided proof that he had clocked out of his factory job a short time before the murder. The location of the factory would have made it impossible for him to be at the murder scene at the time of the crime. Also, Austin is 6'5" and the killer was no more than 5'9" according to a robbery victim. Austin spent 27 years in prison prior to his release. It was later revealed that police had withheld evidence and failed to check other leads. Austin received $1.4 million in compensation.

Cornell Avery Estes

Cornell Avery Estes was sentenced to twenty years in prison in 1979 after being convicted of murder at the age of fifteen. Estes spent a year in prison before being judicially exonerated when another person confessed to the crime. He received $16,500 in compensation for his wrongful conviction.

Anthony Gray, Jr.

Anthony Gray, Jr., was convicted in Calvert County, Maryland, in 1991 of first-degree murder and first-degree rape and sentenced to two concurrent life terms. Gray's conviction resulted from a combination of factors including a jailhouse snitch, a false confession, and ineffective assistance of counsel. Gray remained in prison until DNA testing implicated a man arrested on a burglary charge. He was released from prison in 1999.

Eric D. Lynn

Eric D. Lynn was convicted in 1994 of murder due to prosecutorial misconduct and the use of a snitch. The prosecution did not inform anyone that their only witness was a paid police informant. Lynn's conviction was vacated in 2003 and he was released on bail while awaiting his retrial. On October 31, 2007, he was acquitted of the charges, and in August 2008 he filed a lawsuit against Montgomery County, Maryland, for his wrongful incarceration.

Leslie Vass

In 1975, at the age of seventeen, Leslie Vass was found guilty of armed robbery and received a sentence of twenty years. A witness came forward in 1984 with evidence that Vass was innocent, and he was subsequently released. Vass received $250,000 in compensation from the state of Maryland in 1987 for his wrongful conviction. Disregarding two court orders, the state refused to expunge Vass's armed robbery charge from his criminal record. Consequently, when in 2004 he was accused of a stabbing, he was denied bail and remained in jail until he was finally acquitted of the charge.

Bernard Webster

In 1983 Bernard Webster was found guilty of rape and daytime house-breaking in Towson, Maryland. The female victim, who is white, described her assailant as a black male with a dark complexion and closely cropped hair. Several items left by the attacker were also found in the apartment where the rape occurred. Three additional witnesses reported seeing a black man matching that description. Although two of the witnesses described the suspect as light skinned and 5'8" tall (Webster is 5' tall), all three witnesses picked Webster's picture from a photograph lineup. Webster was subsequently placed in a physical lineup where two of the three witnesses and the victim identified him as the perpetrator. His attorney produced two witnesses placing Webster at a basketball court at the time of the crime. However, questionable forensics and witness testimony ruled the day and Webster was sentenced to thirty years in prison. In 2002 the prosecution vacated Webster's conviction, when two separate DNA tests excluded him as the donor of the spermatozoa found in the rape kit.

Massachusetts

Laurence Adams

In 1974, at the age of nineteen, Laurence Adams was convicted of murdering and robbing a Boston subway worker and sentenced to death in the electric chair. This sentence was later commuted to life in prison, when Massachusetts abolished capital punishment. During his trial, two informants implicated Adams in the crime. As a result of their testimony both had unrelated charges against them dropped. The state's star witness, who testified that Adams had confessed to the crime, was actually incarcerated at the time. A second witness recanted her testimony just before her death. In 2004, after Adams had served thirty years of his sentence, Superior Court Judge Robert Milligan vacated the conviction. The judge determined that the police had withheld exculpatory evidence and ordered that Adams be released on his own recognizance. Later that same year charges against him were formally dropped.

Christian Amado

Twenty-one-year-old Christian Amado was sentenced to life in prison after being convicted of murder in 1980. The victim, a twenty-eight-year-old African American man named George Sneed, was killed in an apartment building in Boston. One week subsequent to the crime, Frederick Johnson, the lone eyewitness, was shown eight photographs of possible suspects, one of which included Amado. Although Johnson said he knew one of the men (Amado), he didn't say that Amado was the assailant. Yet two months later and absent any evidence linking him to the incident, Amado was indicted on first-degree murder charges. During the trial Johnson testified that Amado was not the person he saw murder Sneed. Without any evidence directly linking Amado to the crime, the jury still found him guilty as charged, and Judge Herbert Abrams sentenced him to life. After Amado had spent almost two years behind bars, the Supreme Judicial Court of Massachusetts unanimously vacated his conviction, determining that Judge Abrams was in error in denying the defense counsel's motion for a not-guilty finding. Further, the court argued that to retry Amado's case would violate the double-jeopardy clause.

Ulysses Rodriguez Charles

Ulysses Rodriguez Charles was accused of raping three white women in a Brighton, Massachusetts, apartment building in separate incidents in 1984. He was charged with aggravated rape, robbery, unlawful confinement, and entering a dwelling with intent to commit a felony and was sentenced to seventy-two to eighty years in prison. His wrongful conviction was the result of prosecutorial misconduct, police misconduct, and eyewitness error. When DNA tests of semen found on a robe and bedsheet matched those of two other men, Charles was finally released from prison in 2001, having spent eighteen years behind bars. Recently he received $3.25 million in compensation from the city of Boston for his wrongful conviction.

Stephan Cowans

An incorrect fingerprint analysis led to the arrest and conviction of Stephan Cowans in 1998. Charged with armed assault with intent to murder, home invasion, assault and battery by means of a dangerous weapon, armed robbery, assault and battery of a police officer, assault by means of a dangerous weapon, and the unlicensed possession of a firearm, Cowans was sentenced to prison for thirty to forty-five years. In 2004 he was exonerated, when DNA tests and a reanalysis of the fingerprint used to convict him excluded Cowans as the perpetrator.

Shawn Drumgold

Shawn Drumgold spent fifteen years in prison after being charged with the murder of a twelve-year-old black child named Darlene Tiffany Moore and sentenced to life without parole in 1989. Moore was killed the year before when she was hit by a stray bullet from gunfire between rival gangs in her neighborhood in Roxbury, Massachusetts. According to Drumgold's lawsuit over his wrongful conviction after his release in 2003, police officers withheld exculpatory evidence and pressured a key witness to commit perjury during his trial. An investigation by the *Boston Globe* revealed that the key witness against Drumgold suffered from brain cancer at the time of his trial, and that other witnesses used by the prosecution had recanted their testimonies. Drumgold further contends that the police officers provided false testimony at his trial.

Frank Grace

Police had already targeted Frank Grace, a former Black Panther and activist, as someone who was dangerous and a troublemaker. Grace was charged with the murder of Marvin Morgan in New Bedford, Massachusetts, and sentenced to life in prison in 1974 after police coaxed a witness to falsely testify against him. He spent eleven years in prison before being judicially exonerated in 1985, when another man confessed to the murder and evidence of police misconduct in the case was uncovered.

Donnell Johnson

After the police concealed evidence of his innocence, Donnell Johnson was convicted of a 1995 murder and sent to prison for life. The victim, nine-year-old Jermaine Goffigan, was fatally shot while he was examining his Halloween candy. Criminal justice officials also committed perjury on the stand to secure a conviction. Johnson remained in prison for five years before being released in 2000, after an unrelated federal drug investigation uncovered evidence of his innocence.

Lawyer Johnson

Lawyer Johnson was charged with murdering James Christian, a thirty-year-old white man. He was tried by an all-white jury and was sentenced to death in 1971. Johnson was released after spending eleven years in prison, when an eyewitness came forward and identified the killer as the main witness for the state.

William Johnson

William Johnson was convicted of assault in 1981 on the basis of a witness who was later determined to not be credible. During the trial the prosecutor vouched for the credibility of the witness, albeit there was reason to believe that she was lying. Johnson spent four years in prison before being exonerated in 1985 by the Massachusetts Court of Appeals.

Bobby Joe Leaster

Bobby Joe Leaster was charged with murdering Levi Whiteside, a white man, during a holdup in Roxbury, Massachusetts, on September 27, 1970. Despite any physical evidence linking him to the crime, Leaster was convicted and sentenced to life that same year. Two attorneys, convinced that Leaster had been wrongfully convicted, spent long hours examining the case and eventually proved his innocence. An erroneous eyewitness identification from the hysterical and sedated wife of the victim and ineffective assistance of counsel contributed to his wrongful conviction. Leaster spent fifteen years in prison before being judicially exonerated.

Neil Miller

Neil Miller was charged in 1990 with the rape and robbery of a nineteen-year-old white woman. The perpetrator had forced his way into the woman's apartment and forced her to have vaginal and oral sex. He also robbed her before exiting the apartment. The prosecution's case rested primarily on the victim's identification of Miller during a review of mug shots. Miller was found guilty and given a sentence ranging from twenty-six to forty-five years in prison. After ten years in prison, he was exonerated on the basis of DNA testing.

Marvin Mitchell

In 1988 a Suffolk County grand jury indicted Marvin Mitchell on two counts of forcible sexual intercourse with a minor and two counts of unnatural sexual intercourse, even though he did not match the description given by the eleven-year-old female victim. He was sentenced to nine to twenty-five years in prison in 1990. Mitchell was incarcerated for seven years before his case was retried, and he was released based on DNA evidence that proved he did not commit the crime.

Marlon Passley

Marlon Passley received a life sentence in 1996 after being convicted of shooting a teenager and two other men in Boston. During the trial four witnesses claimed to have seen him shoot the victims while riding past on a motorcycle. The defense presented seven witnesses who claimed that Passley was at a cousin's graduation ceremony in a different section of the city when the crimes occurred. Passley was released on April 18, 1999, when prosecutors admitted that there was a "substantial likelihood of a miscarriage of justice" and that there was evidence to prove that someone else committed the crime.

Guy Randolph

Guy Randolph was charged in 1991 with the aggravated sexual assault of a six-year-old child. Although there was no physical evidence linking Randolph to the crime, only the identification of him by the victim (the victim had initially told the police that Randolph was not her attacker), he received a ten-year suspended sentence. The charges were finally dismissed in 2008 when the prosecution admitted that Randolph was not the perpetrator. However, Randolph had spent four months in prison after failing to show up for an alcohol counseling session as a result of the wrongful conviction.

Louis Santos

Louis Santos was convicted of murdering Colleen Maxwell, a thirty-two-year-old white social worker, and sentenced to life in 1985. In 1988 his conviction was overturned by the Massachusetts Supreme Judicial Court, when it was determined that a witness was unduly influenced by the police to testify against Santos. While awaiting his retrial, Santos was released on bail. His 1990 retrial resulted in an acquittal. Santos spent three years behind bars.

Michigan

Nathaniel Hatchett

In 1996, at the age of seventeen, Nathaniel Hatchett was charged with rape, carjacking, armed robbery, and criminal sexual conduct of a twenty-three-year-old woman. The incident occurred in a parking lot outside a Super K-Mart store in Sterling Heights, Michigan. When he was arrested by the police, Hatchett allegedly waived his Miranda rights and confessed to the crimes after a seven-hour interrogation. Hatchett contends that he was told that he could go home if he would tell the police what they wanted to hear. In a bench trial in March 1998 Hatchett was found guilty and sentenced to twenty-five to forty years in prison based on false eyewitness identification, prosecutorial misconduct, police misconduct, and his own false confession. He spent over eleven years in prison before DNA tests excluded him as the perpetrator.

Eddie Joe Lloyd

Eddie Joe Lloyd faced life in prison without parole after being convicted in 1985 of brutally murdering sixteen-year-old Michelle Jackson in Detroit. Lloyd, who was mentally ill, was tricked by the police into confessing to the crime in order to help them "smoke out" the actual killer. After deliberating for less than one hour, the jury found him guilty of first-degree murder. After all of his appeals failed to vacate his conviction, he turned to the Innocence Project in 1995. Forensic testing of the biological evidence from the crime scene by multiple laboratories disclosed that Lloyd was not the perpetrator. He was eventually released in 2002, after having served seventeen years of a sentence for a crime that he didn't commit. In 2004 Lloyd died at the age of fifty-six.

Dwight Love

In 1981 Dwight Love was convicted of murdering James Connelly after police hid evidence that could have set him free. Love was sentenced to four life terms without parole. In 1995 a convict named Dannelle Fisher confessed that he and another man had murdered Connelly. Two years later Love's conviction was overturned, and he was released on October 15, 1998, when the state declined to retry him. Love spent seventeen years behind bars for a crime of which he was innocent.

Claude McCollum

After a robust interrogation by police that led to a false confession, Claude McCollum was charged with the rape and murder of sixty-year-old Carolyn Kronenberg, a white professor from Lansing Community College. In 2005 McCollum was sentenced to life in prison. Two years later his conviction was overturned when a video from the college showed that McCollum was in another part of the campus when the crime occurred. The prosecutor dropped all charges against him the following month. In 2008 the prosecutor from McCollum's original trial was released from the office of the Ingham County District Attorney for failure to disclose exculpatory evidence to the defense.

Vidale McDowell

Eighteen-year-old Vidale McDowell faced a murder charge in 2002 for the death of Janice Williams, a thirty-seven-year-old black woman. Dowell was eventually sentenced to life in prison. Contributing to his wrongful conviction was a police informant (a thirteen-year-old friend who had been badgered by the police to implicate Dowell in return for leniency) and police misconduct associated with the case. As a result of investigative journalism by Erika Beras, which uncovered faulty police work by the Detroit Police Department, McDowell's conviction was overturned in 2004 by the Michigan Court of Appeals, and his case was not retried. McDowell spent two years in prison before being judicially exonerated.

Walter Swift

Walter Swift was convicted in 1982 of raping and robbing a pregnant thirty-five-year-old white woman during a home invasion, based in part on the victim's erroneous identification of him. Forensic tests conducted prior to his trial, which would have supported his contention that he was innocent, were withheld from the trial. Moreover, his court-appointed attorney, Lawrence Greene, failed to adequately prepare a defense for his client. (Greene has been suspended from practicing law in Michigan several times since Swift's trial because of misconduct and ineffective assistance of counsel.) Swift was denied parole on five occasions because he was unwilling to admit his guilt. Finally, on May 22, 2008, Swift was released after his conviction was overturned on the basis of new evidence of his innocence.

Minnesota

David Brian Sutherlin

Sutherlin was charged with rape in 1985 and sentenced to forty-three months. He is currently serving time on two unrelated murder convictions.

In 2002 Sutherlin was exonerated from the rape charge when it was determined from DNA tests that he was not the perpetrator. His case is atypical, as most exonerated convicts do not commit other serious crimes.

Mississippi

Kennedy Brewer

Forensic errors led to the conviction of Kennedy Brewer in 1995 for the rape and murder of three-year-old Christine Jackson. Brewer was dating the victim's mother when the crime occurred and had been babysitting the night of the assault. The body of the victim was discovered in a creek. Sentenced to death, Brewer remained incarcerated until 2007, when he was released on bail after the arrest of Justin Albert Johnson, who confessed to raping and strangling Jackson. In 2008 Brewer was officially exonerated of any wrongdoing in the case.

Levon Brooks

In circumstances strikingly similar to that of the Brewer case, Levon Brooks was charged with murdering and raping his ex-girl friend's three-year-old daughter in 1992 in Noxubee County, Mississippi. According to the Innocence Project, "The same sheriff's officer investigated both crimes, the same district attorney prosecuted both crimes, and the same discredited forensic dentist and same controversial pathologist conducted the post mortems and misled juries in both cases with false testimony implicating Brooks and Brewer." The one difference in the two cases was the outcome of the trial: Brewer was sentenced to death, whereas Brooks was sentenced to life in prison. Brooks was released from prison in 2008 when Justin Albert Johnson, who had been an initial suspect in both the Brewer and Brooks cases, confessed to both crimes.

Arthur Johnson

Johnson was charged with burglary and rape in 1993 and sentenced to fifty-five years in prison based on eyewitness error. In August 2005 the Innocence Project of New Orleans sought to have the DNA evidence tested. DNA tests in November 2007 excluded Johnson as the contributor. In September 2008 the DNA profile was found to match that of an inmate in prison on a sexual assault charge in Colorado. Moreover, the Colorado inmate had been convicted of burglary and sexual assault in Mississippi during the same year the crime was committed for which Johnson had been convicted. When Johnson was released in 2008, he had spent sixteen years behind bars since his arrest.

Cedric Willis

In 1994 Cedric Willis was nineteen years old when he was arrested in Jackson, Mississippi. He was convicted in 1997 on multiple charges, including murder, robbery, rape, and aggravated assault. (The charge of rape was later dropped.) Willis received a life sentence for the murder plus ninety years (thirty years for each robbery). Released in 2006, Willis spent twelve years behind bars before being judicially exonerated. His wrongful conviction resulted from a combination of prosecutorial misconduct and eyewitness error. DNA testing was used to exonerate Willis.

Missouri

Joseph Amrine

On October 30, 1986, an all-white jury found Joseph Amrine guilty of murdering Gary "Fox" Barber, a fellow inmate in one of Missouri's "Supermax" penitentiaries. At the time, Amrine was serving a prison sentence for robbery, burglary, and forgery. Despite the absence of any physical evidence connecting him to the murder, Amrine was sentenced to death on the basis of the testimony of three inmates who provided inconsistent statements. His state-appointed defense counsel neither presented any mitigating evidence nor questioned the incongruent statements made by the prosecution's witnesses against his client. Moreover, his attorney failed to object to false statements made regarding an alleged stabbing by Amrine. Consequently, Amrine was convicted of the murder. When the Missouri Supreme Court overturned his murder conviction in April 2003, Amrine, having lost four previous appeals, had already chosen his funeral music. The court, ordering that Amrine be released within thirty days, based its decision on the recantations of the three informants and testimony by a prison correctional officer who witnessed the murder. Three months later the local district attorney announced that he would not attempt to retry the case, and Amrine was released on July 28, 2003. If Amrine had not been wrongfully convicted of murder, he would have been released in 1992 for his previous convictions.

Antonio Beaver

The testimony of an eyewitness led to Beaver's conviction for first-degree robbery in 1997. The victim, a white woman, had been accosted in a parking lot in St. Louis, Missouri, near the Gateway Arch. A black man, whom she described as 5'10" and approximately twenty-one years of age, then drove off with her vehicle. Beaver was stopped by a detective who thought he resembled the victim's description, although Beaver is taller and older than the alleged perpetrator. The composite sketch provided by the victim revealed an assailant without facial hair and with a gap between his front teeth, yet Beaver had a moustache and no space between his teeth. However, the victim later identified Beaver in a flawed police lineup. Fingerprints taken from the recovered automobile were analyzed but failed to match those of Beaver. The jury, relying primarily on the victim's testimony, found him guilty, and he received an eighteen-year sentence. In 2006 the Innocence Project agreed to pursue his case and requested that blood found inside the vehicle, which was assumed to be that of the assailant, be tested for DNA. The results of that test excluded Beaver as the perpetrator. He was exonerated on March 29, 2007.

Johnny Briscoe

Johnny Briscoe faced a variety of charges, including rape, sodomy, burglary, robbery, stealing, and armed criminal action, stemming from an incident involving a twenty-eight-year-old white woman in a suburb of St. Louis. The victim was robbed in her apartment and sexually assaulted at least three times, with the perpetrator ejaculating each time. According to the victim, at one point her assailant identified himself as Johnny Briscoe. The perpetrator telephoned her three times after the encounter and again identified himself as "John." The call was traced to a public telephone in the vicinity of Briscoe's apartment. The victim identified Briscoe in two lineups. Despite the presence of blood at the crime scene, no blood typing was conducted and Briscoe's defense attorney did not request any. Flawed forensic testimony involving a Negroid hair found in the apartment was also used by the prosecution to secure a conviction, and in 1982 Briscoe was sentenced to forty-five years in prison.

In 2000 Centurion Ministries accepted Briscoe's case and requested that the St. Louis Crime Laboratory search for biological evidence from the case. Until 2004 the evidence was presumed to be destroyed. It was at this time that cigarette butts from the assailant were discovered in a freezer, although DNA testing of the evidence did not begin until 2006.

DNA taken from the cigarettes matched a man who was currently serving a prison sentence in Missouri. The actual perpetrator of the crime knew Briscoe and may have used Briscoe's name to avoid being captured. On July 29, 2006, Briscoe was released from prison.

Darryl Burton

Darryl Burton spent twenty-four years in prison after being convicted in 1985 of murdering a twenty-six-year-old black man in St. Louis. The jury's decision was based on the testimony of two eyewitnesses. Burton received a life sentence. After the trial it was learned that the prosecution failed to provide information that would have called into question the testimony provided by the state's two witnesses. One of the witnesses later recanted his testimony, and the other witness, who was now dead, had a long criminal history. After filing a writ of habeas corpus, Burton's conviction was overturned in 2008. He was released when the prosecutor informed the judge that he had no intention to retry Burton's case.

Eric Clemmons

Eric Clemmons was convicted of the 1985 murder of a prison inmate and sentenced to death in 1987. After repeated unsuccessful attempts to have his conviction vacated, Clemmons asked his mother to make funeral arrangements for him. However, Clemmons was eventually granted a new trial, when new evidence emerged that the eyewitness testimony of a correctional officer who identified Clemmons as the killer was perjured. Further, an internal Missouri Department of Corrections document identified another inmate as the actual perpetrator. Within three hours of his new trial, a jury acquitted him of the murder charge. Clemmons remains incarcerated on other charges, which he is also challenging.

Lonnie Erby

Lonnie Erby faced multiple charges, including kidnapping, forcible rape, sodomy, robbery, armed criminal action, felonious restraint, stealing, attempted rape, attempted robbery, and sexual abuse in 1986 and was sentenced to 115 years in prison. Although there was no physical evidence directly linking Erby to the crimes, he was considered a likely suspect because he (and half of the male population) fit the profile of the biological evidence collected in the case. Erby spent seventeen years in prison before being judicially exonerated through DNA testing.

Larry Johnson

Larry Johnson was charged with the rape, kidnapping, sodomy, and robbery of a white woman in 1984 and received a sentence of life plus fifteen
years. The victim, who initially described her attacker as a clean-shaven
black man, identified Johnson in both photograph and physical lineups in
spite of the fact that he had facial hair. No fingerprints were found on the
victim's automobile where the attack occurred. Defense counsel was not
allowed to request information regarding the sperm found on the victim's
clothing. Johnson's conviction resulted primarily from the victim's identification of him as her assailant. When his appeal process proved unsuccessful, Johnson requested assistance from the Innocence Project in 1995.
After the Innocence Project encountered resistance in obtaining the biological evidence from the case, it filed a civil rights suit in 2000. In 2002, testing of the evidence finally excluded Johnson as the contributor of the
sperm. On July 30, 2002, he was exonerated and released after having
served eighteen years in prison for crimes that he didn't commit.

Steven Toney

Steven Toney faced charges of rape and sodomy of a white woman in 1983
and received a sentence of two life terms in prison. The victim, who identified Toney in both a photograph and a physical lineup, was "100 percent"
certain that he was the perpetrator even though he didn't resemble the description that the victim and a witness (a gasoline station attendant) gave
to the police. Both prosecutorial misconduct and eyewitness error contributed to this wrongful conviction. In 1996, DNA testing of biological
evidence from the crime scene excluded Toney as the perpetrator. He spent
over thirteen years in prison before being judicially exonerated.

New Jersey

Earl Berryman

Earl Berryman, along with Michael Bunch, was charged with raping and
kidnapping a Hispanic woman in Irvington, New Jersey, in 1983. He was
sentenced in 1985 to twenty-five to fifty years at New Jersey State Prison,
the state's maximum security prison, for his alleged involvement in the
crime. In July 1995 Berryman was released from prison after a federal district court judge in Newark, New Jersey, vacated his conviction. Ineffective assistance of counsel and an erroneous identification of him by the

victim contributed to his wrongful conviction. His codefendant, Michael Bunch, died in prison before he could have his conviction reversed.

Michael Bunch

See Earl Berryman.

McKinley Cromedy

McKinley Cromedy, who was charged with sexual assault, robbery, burglary, criminal sexual contact, and terrorist threats, was sentenced to sixty years in prison in 1994. The victim, a white woman, erroneously identified him as her attacker eight months after the incident. His defense attorney didn't request DNA testing at the trial even though biological evidence had been collected. During his retrial a jury composed of eleven whites and one African American again pronounced him guilty. When DNA tests were finally conducted on December 8, 1999, the results excluded Cromedy as the perpetrator. He was released six days later.

Byron Halsey

Byron Halsey was charged with two counts each of felony murder, aggravated manslaughter, aggravated sexual assault, and child abuse. He was additionally charged with one count of possession of a weapon in a case involving the murder and rape of two young children in 1985. Halsey was convicted in 1988 and sentenced to two life sentences plus twenty years. He was cleared and released in 2007 when DNA tests revealed that he was not the perpetrator. As a result of these tests a neighbor, Clifton Hall, has been charged with two counts of murder and one count of aggravated sexual assault in the case. Halsey was wrongfully incarcerated for twenty-two years.

Clarence Moore

Clarence Moore received a life sentence in 1985 after being convicted of the rape of a white woman in Atlantic City, New Jersey. After the rapist broke into the victim's apartment, he instructed her to keep her eyes closed. Consequently, the victim had only one brief glance at her assailant while he was still in her dark bedroom. Yet she later identified Moore as the man who had raped her. During the trial summation the prosecutor told the jury that because Moore's wife and the victim were both white, Moore had a predilection for white women. On July 25, 2001, after fifteen years in prison, Moore was exonerated by the Third Circuit US Court of Appeals.

Larry Peterson

Larry Peterson received a sentence of forty years in 1989 for the 1987 murder and aggravated sexual assault of a twenty-five-year-old black woman. The victim, a mother of two, had been brutally raped and strangled, and a stick had been shoved down her throat. The victim had been using crack cocaine and had previously had sex with multiple partners. Hair samples found at the crime scene seemed to point to Peterson as the perpetrator. Using a microscope, the forensic scientist from the New Jersey State Police crime laboratory testified that the hairs "compared" to those of Peterson. Peterson's case was also weakened by testimony from a friend and two other passengers riding with him in an automobile, who claimed to have heard him describe in detail how he raped and murdered the victim. The evidence against him was so compelling that Peterson himself later commented, "If I was sitting on the jury, I would be inclined to convict the person also."

In 2005 the Innocence Project agreed to represent him. Sophisticated DNA tests of the hairs found at the crime scene revealed that the hairs actually belonged to the victim. Moreover, the tests revealed that semen and tissue failed to match Peterson's. The conviction was overturned in July 2005, but the prosecution wasn't through with Peterson. He was rearrested and moved from the Trenton State Prison to a county jail. In April 2008 the key witness for the prosecution, a chronic drunk and drug addict, recanted his story. He had lied in order to get released from a three-day police interrogation. The witness later admitted that he overheard the police discussing Peterson's case and used that information to testify against Peterson. Finally, in June 2006 the Burlington County, New Jersey, prosecutor announced that he would no longer pursue the case against Peterson.

David Shepard

In 1984 David Shepard faced a variety of charges, including rape, robbery, weapons violations, and terrorist threats in a case involving a white woman. The prosecution relied heavily on the victim's identification of Shepard. Personal items taken from the victim were also found near the airport where Shepard worked. Sentenced to thirty years in prison, Shepard spent ten years in prison before being judicially exonerated by DNA testing.

Damaso Vega

Witness error by three people testifying for the state led to the conviction of Damaso Vega in 1982 for the Monmouth County, New Jersey, murder of the sixteen-year-old daughter of his best friend. In 1989 Vega was released after all three witnesses recanted their statements. Centurion Ministries was responsible for helping Vega clear his name. He was wrongfully incarcerated for seven years.

Nathaniel Walker

Nathaniel Walker was convicted of rape, kidnapping, and sodomy in 1975 and sentenced to life plus fifty years. The twenty-one-year-old victim was brutally attacked while in her automobile outside a Newark housing project. During the trial the victim's testimony was inconsistent with the account that she had previously given to the police. When Centurion Ministries accepted Walker's case, it insisted that the semen taken from the victim be tested. A DNA analysis of the semen disclosed that Walker wasn't the contributor. He was released on November 5, 1986, after having served eight years in Trenton State penitentiary and spent three years as a fugitive in California.

New Mexico

Van Bering Robinson

On September 10, 1980, off-duty Albuquerque, New Mexico, police officer Phil Chacon was killed while attempting to respond to a call about an armed robbery in progress. Van Bering Robinson was convicted in 1981 of first-degree murder of the police officer and sentenced to life imprisonment. His conviction was the result of testimony given by three other police officers who were later found to have falsified the information. Robinson was released in 1983, and in 1985 he received $75,000 in damages against the three police officers.

Terry Seaton

In 1973 Terry Seaton was convicted of first-degree murder in Hobbs, New Mexico, and given a life sentence. Seaton, who was committing a burglary when the murder occurred, was convicted on the basis of testimony from an informant and prosecutorial misconduct resulting from the withholding of exculpatory evidence. In 1979 the conviction was overturned and Seaton was awarded $150,000 for punitive damages.

New York

Derrick Bell

Derrick Bell was wrongfully convicted in 1996 of robbery and assault and sentenced to twelve and a half to twenty-five years in prison. His conviction was based on the eyewitness testimony of the victim. The case was overturned in 2007 on the basis of ineffective assistance of counsel at the time of trial. His attorney had failed to present testimony that would have shown that the victim was not able to make a positive identification of the perpetrator at the time.

Kareem Bellamy

Bellamy was convicted in 1994 of the murder of James Abbott, who had been stabbed to death outside a grocery store in Queens. Six weeks after the murder Bellamy was stopped by the police outside his home for being in violation of the "open container" law and placed in handcuffs. According to one of the police officers, Bellamy said, "This must be a mistake—someone must have accused me of murdering someone." If, indeed, this is what Bellamy said, it was prophetic, given that the police had been sent to his address because a cashier from the grocery store told them that the man who was with the victim before he was killed was drinking a beer on Beach Channel Drive. Although Bellamy had no motive for the killing and the only eyewitness to the crime was not certain if it was Bellamy, he was sentenced to twenty-five years to life in prison. His conviction was vacated in June 2008 by a Queens Supreme Court judge. Bellamy was released on bail on August 14, 2008, after a former FBI agent used his condominium as security.

Lamont Branch

Lamont Branch spent thirteen years in prison after being convicted in 1990 of the murder of Danny Josephs, a reputed drug dealer and friend of the family. He received a life sentence based on the testimony of two drug addicts, who later admitted to lying in order to receive between $100 and $150 from New York Police Department police officers. Branch was released on September 20, 2002.

Lazaro Burt

Lazaro Burt was charged in 1992 with murdering a man who had claimed that Burt was fondling his girlfriend. His wrongful conviction was the result of witness error. Burt spent ten years in prison before being judicially exonerated in 2002, after another man was charged with the crime.

Nathaniel Carter

Nathaniel Carter was charged with second-degree murder in the killing of his former mother-in-law, an elderly woman who lived in the Cambria Heights district of Queens. Carter was sentenced to twenty-five years to life. He spent two years in prison before being judicially exonerated in 1984. His wrongful conviction was the result of the false testimony of an informant.

Marion Coakley

Marion Coakley was wrongly convicted of raping and robbing a white woman in 1985 and sentenced to fifteen years in prison. He was able to produce at least three witnesses, including a minister, who testified that Coakley was attending a Bible study meeting near his home at the time of the rape. He spent four years in prison before a blood test revealed that the blood type of the rapist and his blood type were not the same.

Charles Dabbs

Charles Dabbs spent nine years in prison for a 1982 rape that he did not commit. In 1984 Dabbs was sentenced to twelve and a half to twenty years for the crime. As in many other wrongful conviction cases, the cause of his conviction was incorrect identification by the victim. In 1991, DNA testing proved that he was not the rapist and he was released.

John Duval

John Duval was convicted in 1973 of the murder of a fifty-two-year-old white man and sentenced to twenty-five years to life. Duval, a transvestite prostitute, falsely confessed to murdering his client after police threatened him. His conviction was due to a combination of many factors, including prosecutorial and police misconduct, perjury by criminal justice officials, coerced eyewitness testimony, and his own false confession. Duval's conviction was overturned in 1999 and he was acquitted in 2000.

Anthony Faison

Anthony Faison was convicted in 1988 of second-degree murder in the death of Jean Ulysses, a forty-six-year-old black cab driver. Faison was wrongfully incarcerated for fourteen years. His conviction was the result of an informant who perjured herself in order to split the reward with her boyfriend, the actual murderer. Faison was exonerated when his fingerprints didn't match those of the confessed killer. In 2003 he was awarded $1,650,000 in compensation for his wrongful incarceration.

Edmond Jackson

Edmond Jackson was put on trial in 1971 for the murder of Harold Dixon, a Queens bartender. At that time he was sentenced to twenty years to life. In 1978 a federal court vacated his conviction on the basis of unreliable witness testimony and the lack of any evidence connecting him with the crime. The US Court of Appeals upheld the ruling and chastised the prosecutor for trying the case with insufficient evidence and ignoring evidence that suggested a different perpetrator. Jackson was wrongfully imprisoned for seven years of his life.

Vincent Jenkins (aka Habib Wahir Abdal)

In 1982 Vincent Jenkins was convicted of raping a young white woman in Buffalo, New York. The victim had been raped in a nature preserve after getting lost from her spouse. Her assailant, who had blindfolded her, was described as a black man with a hooded jacket. Four months after the rape Jenkins was picked up by the police and identified by the victim. Jenkins didn't match the woman's description, and forensic analysis of hairs found at the crime scene did not produce a match with him either. Yet he was convicted and sentenced to twenty years to life by a jury. Eventually, DNA testing of the sperm from the sexual encounter excluded Jenkins as the contributor and he was released in 1999, having served seventeen years for a crime that he didn't commit.

Lee Long

In 1995 Lee Long was convicted of rape and robbery based on the victim's tentative identification (she "felt" that he was the attacker) of him as her assailant. Moreover, the prosecutor failed to provide to his defense counsel the information that a police officer had contacted Long's girlfriend and verified his alibi. Long was sentenced to two concurrent terms of eight to twenty-four years. Upon appeal, his conviction was affirmed in 1997. In 2000 a New York Supreme Court justice vacated his conviction and declared, "The wrong man was convicted."

William Maynard

Black activist William Maynard was sentenced to ten to twenty years in prison after being convicted of first-degree murder in 1971. Two previous trials had resulted in hung juries. Although an appellate court affirmed his conviction, the New York State Supreme Court vacated his conviction based on its finding that the prosecution suppressed information on the unreliability of the state's key witness against Maynard. (The witness had an extensive history of hospitalization for a mental disorder.) After having served almost seven years, Maynard was released in 1978.

Antron McCray

Antron McCray, a fifteen-year-old ninth grader with an IQ of 87, was one of five defendants charged in 1989 with brutally raping a twenty-eight-year-old white woman, a wealthy investment banker, who was jogging in New York's Central Park. With no memory of the incident after emerging from a coma twelve days later, the victim could not identify her attackers. McCray was charged with rape and assault and sentenced to five to ten years. Despite a lack of evidence, the youths were coerced into confessing to the crime after undergoing interrogations lasting from fourteen to twenty-eight hours. The five youths had been at the park at the time of the crime, but could not have been at the crime scene based on their location in the park. In 1995 McCray was released from prison. In 2002 he was finally exonerated when the actual perpetrator confessed to the crime and DNA testing corroborated his story. *See Kevin Richardson, Yuself Salaam, Raymond Santana, and Kharey Wise.*

Alan Newton

Alan Newton was convicted of rape, robbery, and assault in 1985 after the twenty-five-year-old victim and a convenience store clerk where the victim was abducted identified him. He was sentenced to thirteen and one-third to forty years in prison. He was imprisoned for twenty-one years before being released in 2006, when DNA tests proved that he wasn't the assailant.

Kevin Richardson

Kevin Richardson faced multiple charges, including the attempted murder, robbery, rape, and sodomy of a twenty-eight-year-old white female Central Park jogger. Richardson, along with four other black teens believed to be responsible for the crime, was interrogated for fourteen to twenty-eight hours. He received a sentence of five to ten years in 1990 and spent six and a half years in prison before being released. In 2002 the actual perpetrator confessed to the crime and DNA evidence corroborated his story. *See Antron McCray, Yuself Salaam, Raymond Santana, and Kharey Wise.*

Yuself Salaam

When a twenty-eight-year-old white female jogger was brutally attacked in New York's Central Park on April 19, 1989, fifteen-year-old Yuself Salaam and four other black youths were immediately suspected of the crime. With no memory of the incident, the victim could not identify her attackers. Consequently, the prosecution relied on false confessions obtained after fourteen to twenty-eight hours of police interrogation. After serving six and a half years of his sentence, Salaam was released. The actual perpetrator confessed to the crime in 2002. *See Antron McCray, Kevin Richardson, Raymond Santana, and Kharey Wise.*

Raymond Santana

Fourteen-year-old Raymond Santana was one of five black teenagers who were charged with the brutal rape and assault of a twenty-eight-year-old white female jogger in New York's Central Park. With no recollection of the assault, the victim was unable to identify her attackers. But police interrogations lasting from fourteen to twenty-eight hours provided the prosecution with confessions from each of the youths. However, the youths were in a different section of the park when the incident occurred. Convicted in 1989, Santana spent eight years in prison before being released. Finally, in 2002, the actual perpetrator confessed to the crime, thereby clearing Santana and his four acquaintances. *See Antron McCray, Kevin Richardson, Yuself Salaam, and Kharey Wise.*

Charles Shepard

See Anthony Faison.

Dhoruba al-Mujahid bin Wahad (aka Richard Moore)

Dhoruba al-Mujahid bin Wahad was charged with the attempted murder of two white New York City police officers, Thomas Curry and Nick Binetti. An informant testified that Wahad shot at the officers as they were attempting to give someone a ticket for a traffic violation. In 1973 he was sentenced to twenty-five years to life. In 1990 the conviction was vacated when it was determined that exculpatory evidence obtained from FBI documents was not turned over to his defense attorney. After nineteen years of incarceration, Wahad was released. Finally, in 1995 the charges against him were dismissed when Manhattan District Attorney Robert Morgenthau announced that he wouldn't pursue the case. That same year Wahad was awarded $400,000 from a civil rights lawsuit against the FBI. In 2000 he was awarded $490,000 from a lawsuit against the city of New York and the New York Police Department.

Kharey Wise

Kharey Wise, who at age sixteen had a second-grade reading level and an IQ of 73, was one of five black teenagers charged in the brutal assault of a white female jogger in New York's Central Park in 1989. After police interrogations lasting from fourteen to twenty-eight hours in length, all five youths falsely confessed to the crime. Convicted of assault, sexual abuse, and riot, Wise spent eleven and a half years in prison before being released. The actual perpetrator confessed to the crime in 2002. His account of the events of that night was corroborated through DNA tests. *See Antron McCray, Kevin Richardson, Yuset Salaam, and Raymond Santana.*

North Carolina

Glen Chapman

In 1994 Glen Chapman was convicted and sentenced to death for the 1992 murders of Betty Jean Ramseur and Tenene Yvette Conley. According to the Death Penalty Information Center, the North Carolina Superior Court in 2007 granted him a new trial on the basis of "withheld evidence, 'lost, misplaced, or destroyed' documents, the use of weak, circumstantial evidence, false testimony by the lead investigator, and ineffective assistance of counsel." Forensic evidence also suggested the possibility that Conley may have died from a drug overdose. One of Chapman's defense attorneys was later disciplined by the North Carolina State Bar, while the other confessed to using alcohol while representing a different client, who was given the death penalty and executed in 2001. On April 2, 2008, Chapman was finally released when prosecutors agreed to drop all charges against him.

Ronald Cotton

After a 1985 conviction was overturned, Ronald Cotton was convicted in 1987 of two rapes and burglaries that occurred in 1984. He received a sentence of life plus fifty-four years for these crimes. Mistaken eyewitness testimony by one of the two victims was partially responsible for his conviction. In 1995 Cotton was released when DNA from one of the rapes excluded him as the perpetrator. (DNA from the other rape was too deteriorated to be analyzed.) That same year the governor of North Carolina officially pardoned him of any wrongdoing. Before his release from prison, Cotton had been wrongfully incarcerated for ten and a half years.

Erick Daniels

Fourteen-year-old Erick Daniels was convicted in 2001 as the member of a gang who allegedly robbed a police department employee of over $6,000. Despite a lack of physical evidence linking Daniels to the crime, he was tried as an adult and sentenced to prison for ten to fourteen years. Prosecutorial and police misconduct, false eyewitness testimony, and ineffective assistance of counsel contributed to his wrongful conviction. In 2007 Daniels won a new trial, when a reinvestigation of his case revealed that his defense counsel had failed to adequately represent him. He was released in 2008 after the judge declared Cotton innocent of the crime.

Terence Garner

In 1998 Terence Garner was convicted of armed robbery and sentenced to thirty-two to forty-three years behind bars. The white victim, who had lost eyesight from one of her eyes and had experienced brain damage as a result of being shot in the eye during the holdup, incorrectly identified Garner as one of her assailants. However, one of the two codefendants in this case testified that Terence Garner was not the "Terence" who was their accomplice. Garner also had four witnesses who testified that he was twenty-five miles away at the time of incident. Although two days after Garner's conviction a man confessed to being the third robber, the trial judge refused to grant Garner a new trial and the North Carolina Supreme Court refused to review the case. His conviction was not overturned until Public Broadcasting System's *Frontline* television series ran a program that highlighted his legal situation. On June 11, 2002, charges were dismissed after Garner passed a polygraph test.

Jonathon Hoffman

In 1995 an all-white jury found Jonathon Hoffman guilty in the murder of Danny Cook, a white jewelry store owner. Sentenced to death for the crime, Hoffman was convicted primarily on the basis of testimony provided by Johnell Porter, Hoffman's cousin. When it was later revealed that Porter had received immunity from federal charges in exchange for his testimony and that this fact had not been conveyed to defense counsel, jury, or judge, the General Court of Justice Superior Court Division awarded Hoffman a new trial. In 2007 the charges against him were dropped. Porter later admitted to lying in order to punish his cousin who had taken money from him.

Darryl Hunt

Darryl Hunt was accused of brutally raping and murdering Deborah Sykes, a twenty-five-year-old white woman, on August 10, 1984. The victim had been stabbed sixteen times. Hunt was wrongfully convicted twice of the crime. Although the first conviction in 1985 was overturned, he was reconvicted in 1990 and sentenced to life. Despite a DNA test that excluded him as the perpetrator in 1994, the prosecutor would not release him, claiming that Hunt still could have played some role in the crime. When on December 22, 2003, Willard E. Brown confessed to the crime, Hunt was released two days later on bail pending a hearing. His conviction was finally vacated on February 6, 2004, after Hunt had served over eighteen years in prison. Hunt received a full pardon on April 15, 2004, from North Carolina Governor Mike Easley.

Levon "Bo" Jones

Levon "Bo" Jones was accused of killing a sixty-seven-year-old white bootlegger named Leamon Grady. The prosecutor charged him with murder, robbery, and conspiracy. A jury found him guilty and a judge sentenced Jones to death in 1993. The key witness for the state was Lovely Lorden, a career snitch who was paid for testifying against Jones and who later recanted her story. And an individual with a motive to kill Grady was never charged with the crime. Although US District Court Judge Terrence Boyle vacated the conviction in 2006 after criticizing the "constitutionally deficient" performance of Jones's attorneys, Jones remained incarcerated until Duplin County District Attorney Dewey Hudson announced in 2008 that he was dropping all charges.

Charles Munsey

Charles Munsey was convicted of murdering sixty-six-year-old Shirley Weaver in 1996 and sentenced to death. Munson was convicted after the prosecution concealed the fact that the jailhouse snitch had never been in prison with the defendant and thus could not have heard Munsey's "confession." Moreover, the jury disregarded three witnesses who testified that Munsey was with them at a softball game and a fourth witness who testified that a man seen with Weaver just prior to the murder was not Munsey. A year after his conviction, the actual perpetrator—Munsey's ex-brother-in-law—signed a written confession admitting to the murder. Then, in 1998, a judge ordered the prosecutor to give Munsey's legal counsel access to files that had been concealed during his trial. The following week the prosecutor who was responsible for Munsey's incarceration hanged himself. The previously hidden files revealed that the jailhouse snitch had lied about being in prison with Munsey. Although the snitch recanted his story, the new prosecutor refused to release Munsey. In September 2001, while still wrongfully imprisoned, Munsey died of lung cancer.

Samuel A. Poole

Samuel Poole spent a year in prison after being convicted of first-degree murder and sentenced to death in 1973. His case was overturned when it was determined that there was not enough evidence to support a conviction.

Sylvester Smith

Sylvester Smith was convicted in 1984 of raping two girls, ages four and six. Smith was living with one of the girls' mothers at the time. There was evidence that the girls had been abused and that a grandmother had pressured the two children to say that Smith had committed the crime to protect a cousin. The cousin, who was nine years of age at the time, is now serving a life sentence for murder. Smith spent twenty years in prison prior to being exonerated, when the girls admitted that Smith had not had sexual contact with them when they were young.

Christopher Spicer

Christopher Spicer was convicted in 1973 of murder and sentenced to death. Spicer's conviction was overturned in 1974 by the North Carolina Supreme Court. A jailhouse snitch, Charles Pennington, claimed that Spicer confessed to the crime while they were in a jail cell together. In return for his testimony, Pennington received a reduced bail bond and was released from prison. Two other witnesses said that Spicer and Pennington had never shared a jail cell. The judge refused to allow the defense to cross-examine Pennington. When Spicer was tried again in 1975, the jury acquitted him after deliberating for only fifteen minutes.

Ohio

Donte Booker

Donte Booker was convicted in 1987 of rape, robbery, kidnapping, and sexual imposition and sentenced to ten to twenty-five years in prison. After the crime had been committed, police officers noticed that a toy gun was missing from the victim's automobile where the assault had taken place. The victim of the crime, a white woman, identified Booker as the assailant after he was arrested on an unrelated charge involving a toy gun. After the arrest, police searched Booker's home and found clothing similar to the description that the victim had given. Booker was paroled in 2002, after spending fifteen years in prison and refusing a chance at an earlier parole in return for admitting guilt. He was exonerated in 2005 through DNA testing that was not available at the time of his conviction. Booker received over $600,000 in compensation for this wrongful incarceration.

Marlon Brooks

Marlon Brooks was one of seventeen people convicted in the Mansfield, Ohio, drug bust discussed in greater detail in Chapter 5. He received a sentence of three years and ten months. Brooks spent eighteen months in prison before being released.

Daniel Brown

Daniel Brown spent nineteen years in prison after being convicted of the 1981 murder and rape of Bobbie Russell in Toledo, Ohio. Brown's conviction was based on the erroneous eyewitness testimony of the victim's six-year-old son, who only briefly saw his mother's assailant. Moreover, the trial judge admitted that the eyewitness testimony contained "glaring inconsistencies." DNA tests in 2001 identified the actual perpetrator who was already serving a life sentence for an unrelated crime. On April 9, 2001, Brown became a free man.

Tyron Brown

Tyron Brown was one of seventeen people convicted in the Mansfield, Ohio, drug bust discussed in greater detail in Chapter 5. He received a sentence of eight years and four months. Brown was incarcerated for eighteen months before being released.

James Burton

One of seventeen people convicted in the Mansfield, Ohio, drug bust, James Burton was sentenced to eleven years and eight months in prison. After eighteen months in prison he was released. More about the Mansfield, Ohio, drug bust can be found in Chapter 5.

Frank Douglas

Frank Douglas was one of seventeen people convicted in the Mansfield, Ohio, drug bust. He received a sentence of seven years in prison but was released after serving eighteen months. More about the Mansfield, Ohio, drug bust can be found in Chapter 5.

Anthony Michael Green

Anthony Michael Green was charged with rape and aggravated robbery in an incident involving a white woman. On October 26, 1988, he was sentenced to twenty to fifty years in prison. His conviction was primarily the result of the erroneous identification of him by the victim, who was attacked in her room at the Cleveland Clinic Inn, where she had been undergoing treatment for cancer. DNA testing of the semen collected after the incident was done in 2001, and Green was released in October of the same year, when the results excluded him as the donor. He served thirteen years behind bars for a crime that he didn't commit.

Robert Harris

Robert Harris was one of seventeen people convicted in the Mansfield, Ohio, drug bust discussed in Chapter 5. He received a sentence of five years in prison. Harris was released after serving eighteen months.

Timothy Howard

Timothy Howard and codefendant Gary Lamar James were accused of a bank robbery that resulted in the death of a seventy-four-year-old bank guard. In 1976 they both received death sentences, which were changed to life in 1978 after Ohio's death penalty was determined to be unconstitutional. Howard and James spent twenty-six years in prison before evidence that had been concealed from their defense attorneys was discovered. Both men were released from prison in 2003. In compensation for their wrongful imprisonment Howard received $2 million and James received $1.5 million.

Gary Lamar James

See Timothy Howard.

Derrick Jamison

Derrick Jamison was charged with robbing and murdering a Cincinnati bartender. In 1985 he was convicted and sentenced to death. During the trial the prosecution withheld exculpatory evidence, including information regarding Charles Howell, a codefendant who had received a more lenient sentence in exchange for testifying against Jamison. The prosecution additionally withheld statements that contradicted Howell's testimony. In 2005 the Ohio Common Pleas Court vacated the charges against Jamison and prosecutors decided not to retry the case. Jamison remains in prison on unrelated charges.

Harllel Jones

In 1972 Harllel Jones, the leader of a black nationalist organization, was convicted of second-degree murder and kidnapping in an incident involving the death of a rival black nationalist. The chief witness was an FBI informant, who was rewarded with dismissal of charges against him for testifying. Jones spent five years in prison before being judicially exonerated.

Albert Lee

One of seventeen people convicted in the Mansfield, Ohio, drug bust discussed in Chapter 5, Albert Lee received a sentence of ten years in prison. After eighteen months of incarceration, he was released.

Nolan Lovett

Nolan Lovett was one of seventeen people convicted in the Mansfield, Ohio, drug bust. He was sentenced to five years behind bars. Lovett was released after serving eighteen months. More about the Mansfield, Ohio, drug bust can be found in Chapter 5.

Rasheem Matthew

Rasheem Matthew was convicted of the murder of Wayne Price, who was killed at a housing project while trying to purchase cocaine. Matthew was sentenced to forty-five years to life in 1990. In ordering a retrial for the 1989 murder, a federal judge noted that the prosecution had failed to inform the jury that the state's main witnesses against Matthew had been given lesser sentences in exchange for their testimony. The behavior of the prosecutor of this case, Carmen Marino, has been the subject of at least fifteen Ohio criminal appeals. The retired prosecutor has had five of his convictions overturned by the Ohio Supreme Court. Although Matthew was exonerated in 2006, he remains in prison because of two convictions for murder during a prison riot in 1993. Ironically, he would not have been an inmate at the Southern Ohio Correctional Facility when the riot occurred if he hadn't been wrongfully convicted.

Charles Matthews

Charles Matthews was one of seventeen persons convicted in the Mansfield, Ohio, drug bust discussed in Chapter 5. He received a sentence of five years and three months. Matthews spent eighteen months in prison before being released.

Robert McClendon

Robert McClendon was charged with raping and kidnapping his ten-year-old daughter. At his trial McClendon's daughter testified that her father had raped her. This claim was made even though his daughter had been with him only one other time in her life. Further evidence against him included a failed polygraph test. McClendon contended that he was driving around with friends when the crime occurred. Rejecting a jury trial, McClendon opted for a bench trial with Judge David L. Johnson. He was convicted and sentenced to fifteen years to life in 1991. McClendon filed for DNA testing in 2004 but did not have his request granted until 2008, after the Ohio Innocence Project had accepted his case. DNA tests of the semen found in the girl's underwear excluded him as the perpetrator, and he was freed on bail on August 12, 2008, while awaiting a hearing to dismiss the charges.

Jerry Moton

One of seventeen people convicted in the Mansfield, Ohio, drug bust, Jerry Moton received a sentence of three years and one month. Moton spent eighteen months in prison before being released. More about the Mansfield, Ohio, drug bust can be found in Chapter 5.

Noel Mott

Noel Mott was one of seventeen persons convicted in the Mansfield, Ohio, drug bust discussed in Chapter 5. He received a sentence of four years and three months but was released after serving eighteen months in prison.

Dwayne Nabors

Yet another person who was wrongfully convicted during the Mansfield, Ohio, drug bust based on the false testimony of an informant, Nabors was convicted of illegally possessing two handguns. The handguns were discovered during a search of his premises based on the informant's statements that he had purchased drugs from Nabors. Although no drugs were found, Nabors received a five-year sentence for the handguns. Because the search warrant leading to the discovery of the weapons was obtained through perjured testimony, the search warrant was invalid. Nabors spent sixteen months in prison prior to his release. More about the Mansfield, Ohio, drug cases can be found in Chapter 5.

Dametrese Ransaw

Dametrese Ransaw was one of seventeen people convicted in the Mansfield, Ohio, drug bust. He received a sentence of three and a half years. Ransaw spent eighteen months in prison before being released. Chapter 5 contains more information on the Mansfield, Ohio, drug bust.

Johnny Robertson

One of seventeen people convicted in the Mansfield, Ohio, drug bust, Johnny Robertson was sentenced to five years and ten months in prison. He was incarcerated for eighteen months before being released. More information on the Mansfield, Ohio, drug bust can be found in Chapter 5.

Walter D. Smith

Walter D. Smith was already scheduled to go on trial for robbery when three women claimed that he had raped them. Smith admitted to the robbery, which he committed to support his cocaine habit, but denied any involvement with the rapes. The trial came down to his word against several eyewitnesses, and Smith was convicted in 1986 of two of the rapes and sentenced to 78 to 190 years behind bars. In 1996 DNA tests excluded him as the rapist. While in prison Smith successfully completed a drug rehabilitation program and earned an associate degree from Wilmington College.

Arrico Spires

Arrico Spires was one of seventeen people convicted in the Mansfield, Ohio, drug bust. He received a sentence of four years and nine months. Spires spent eighteen months in prison before being released. More information about these drug cases is available in Chapter 5.

Allan Thrower

Allan Thrower was charged with the 1972 murder of Joseph Edwards, a white Columbus, Ohio, police officer who was ambushed while out on patrol. In 1973 Thrower received a life sentence. He was released from prison in 1979 after the Internal Affairs Bureau ascertained that Thrower had been framed for the murder.

Jim Williams

Jim Williams was one of seventeen individuals convicted in the Mansfield, Ohio, drug bust discussed in Chapter 5. He was sentenced to five years and three months in prison. Williams was released after being incarcerated for eighteen months.

Oklahoma

Charles Ray Giddens

Eighteen-year-old Charles Ray Giddens was charged with murdering Beulah Fay Tapley, an Idabel, Oklahoma, grocery store cashier. He was sentenced to death in 1978 by an all-white jury after they had deliberated for fifteen minutes. Johnnie Gray, who was never indicted, testified that he accompanied Giddens to the murder. Giddens's conviction was vacated in 1981, when the Oklahoma Court of Appeals determined that Gray was an unreliable witness and the evidence used to convict Giddens was insufficient.

Arvin McGee

After three trials, Arvin McGee was convicted in 1989 of the kidnapping, rape, robbery, and forced sodomy of a twenty-year-old Tulsa woman in a laundry. He was subsequently sentenced to 365 years in prison. (The sentence was later reduced to 298 years.) His conviction was based largely on the victim's identification of him as the perpetrator, although she was not sure what her attacker looked like. The prosecution also presented serological evidence that included McGee as a possible attacker. McGee served over fourteen years in prison before DNA tests showed that another man, who was being held in an Oklahoma prison, had committed the crime.

Robert Lee Miller, Jr.

Robert Lee Miller, Jr., was accused of three robberies in 1986, and of raping two elderly white women during the robberies. The main clues that Oklahoma police officers had to go on were that the suspect was a black man and that he was a type A secretor. Miller was brought in and, after police talked with him about the crime, he was charged, even though he was delusional at the time of the confession, claiming to be various heroes such as the Lone Ranger. He was tried and convicted of the crimes and sentenced to death in 1988 for the murders. Miller was incarcerated for over nine years before prosecutors agreed to drop all charges, three years after DNA testing had exonerated him.

Adolph Munson

Adolph Munson was convicted of the kidnapping and murder of Alma Hall in 1985 and was sentenced to death. During the trial the prosecution withheld exculpatory information. Dr. Ralph Erdmann, a discredited forensic specialist who was later convicted of seven felony counts for misrepresenting facts in other cases, testified at his trial. Munson spent ten years in prison before being acquitted at retrial in 1995.

Calvin Lee Scott

Calvin Lee Scott was in a county jail for a larceny conviction when police received an anonymous telephone call that Scott was responsible for an earlier rape involving a young mother. The woman, a widow with a four-month-old son, was attacked in her bed as she slept. Because the rapist kept a pillow over her face, the victim was unable to identify her attacker. In 1983 Scott was convicted of the rape and sentenced to twenty-five years in prison based on faulty forensics. He was imprisoned for twenty years before DNA testing using the rape kit collected after the crime exonerated him of any wrongdoing.

Marrio D'Shane Willis

Marrio D'Shane Willis was convicted in 2003 of robbing an E-Z Mart in Tulsa, Oklahoma, where he had been employed. He was sentenced to ten years behind bars for the armed robbery. Willis was identified by a manager using a surveillance video and then by a clerk, who was pressured by the police to make the identification. At a hearing in 2005, the clerk recanted his testimony and identified another man as the perpetrator. In 2006 the Oklahoma Court of Criminal Appeals reversed Willis's conviction because of insufficient evidence. That same year the prosecutor dropped the charges against Willis, and he became a free man.

Pennsylvania

Edward Baker

Edward Baker was accused of robbery and the 1973 murder of seventy-five-year-old Shane Gibbons in Philadelphia. Although Baker had passed a polygraph test and had twelve witnesses to corroborate his alibi, he was convicted and sentenced to life in prison in 1974. Twenty-two years later the state's main witness admitted that he had killed Gibbons and that he had implicated Baker to avoid a life sentence. He additionally identified his accomplices in the crime, facts that were corroborated by Centurion Ministries. In December 1999 Baker was released after a judge ruled that "there is evidence pointing to perpetrators other than the petitioner" and vacated the conviction. It was not until February 2002, however, that the district attorney formally announced that he would not retry the case, thereby bringing this twenty-eight-year-old miscarriage of justice to an end.

Matthew Connor

In 1978 Matthew Connor was sentenced to life in prison after being convicted of raping and murdering eleven-year-old Corinthea Fields in his North Philadelphia housing project. The young girl had died from repeated stab wounds from an ice pick. Connor was convicted when the prosecution presented false testimony and the police hid reports that contradicted this testimony. Centurion Ministries began investigating the case in 1984 and uncovered evidence suggesting the victim had been killed by her now deceased half-brother. In 1990 Connor was exonerated of any wrongdoing in the crime.

Thomas Doswell

In 1986 Thomas Doswell was convicted of raping a white woman in Pittsburgh as she entered the hospital where she was employed. The victim was shown photographs of possible suspects. She chose his photograph, in part, because it was the only one marked with an R, which indicates a rapist. The victim and a coworker identified Doswell in court, and this, along with the photograph identification, led to his conviction and sentence of thirteen to twenty-six years in prison. Doswell spent nineteen years in prison before DNA tests that were not available when he was convicted proved his innocence. On August 1, 2005, Doswell was released from prison.

Riky Jackson

Riky Jackson spent over two years in prison after being convicted in 1997 of killing his friend and sometimes lover, Alvin Davis, in Upper Darby, Pennsylvania. The victim was brutally stabbed and strangled. Jackson was sentenced to life without parole in prison. He was released in 1999 after it was determined that his fingerprints were not those found at the crime scene.

Vincent Moto

Vincent Moto was charged with rape, robbery, involuntary deviate sexual intercourse, and criminal conspiracy and sentenced to twelve to twenty-four years in prison in 1987. Five months after the crime occurred, the victim identified Moto as one of the two rapists when she saw him walking down the street. Moto and his parents testified that he was at home when the crime was committed. During cross-examination Moto's mother also admitted that her son had been convicted previously for crimes against his girlfriend. Moto spent eight years in prison before being judicially exonerated by DNA tests.

Edward Ryder

In 1974 Edward Ryder was convicted of a jailhouse murder in Philadelphia and sentenced to life. He was in jail awaiting trial on a robbery charge that was eventually dismissed. Ryder tried to break up a fight among Muslims in his cell and then had an argument with Samuel Molton, who didn't like Muslims. When Molton was murdered two days later, Ryder was charged with the crime along with three others. His public defender failed to investigate his case before the trial and fell asleep several times. Ryder's two co-defendants had testified against him, as well as two jailhouse informants. Further investigation led to another witness, Kenneth Webb, who refuted the previous testimony and claimed that Ryder was not involved in the murder. Ryder was released in 1993 after nineteen years in prison. In 1996 his conviction was vacated on the grounds of prosecutorial misconduct.

Drew Whitley

Drew Whitley was convicted in 1988 of murdering a twenty-two-year-old white McDonald's night manager in Duquesne, Pennsylvania. The victim, who was completing her shift around 3 a.m. on August 17, 1988, was shot in the back as she fled to her automobile. During the trial, mistaken identification by a coworker and testimony from a death row inmate, who claimed that the defendant confessed while they were incarcerated together, were used to obtain a conviction. And, during the closing arguments, the prosecutor argued that the hairs found on the killer's mask were "positively" those of the defendant, although the crime laboratory had only confirmed that the hairs were "similar." DNA testing in 2006 proved that Whitley was not the perpetrator. In 2006, after eighteen years in prison, Whitley was finally exonerated.

Harold Wilson

In 1989 Harold Wilson, who faced three counts of murder, received three death sentences. In 1999 his death sentences were overturned due to ineffective assistance of counsel. His attorney failed to investigate and present mitigating evidence. Finally, in 2003 Wilson won a new trial when it was determined that the prosecution used racial bias to exclude black jurors. After a mistrial, Wilson's third trial included DNA evidence that acquitted him of the crimes. He was exonerated in 2005 after spending seventeen years in prison.

South Carolina

Tyrone James

Tyrone James and Winfred Peterson were convicted of shooting a state highway trooper and sentenced to life in prison in 1982. The prosecution's conviction rested largely on the testimony of a police officer who claimed that the two men had been overheard making incriminating remarks while they were in police custody. Two months later, after a new witness implicated four other men in the shooting, a new trial was ordered. As a result of the new evidence, a grand jury dismissed the charges against James and Peterson, as well as two other men who had yet to go on trial. The police subsequently arrested the new suspects. At least one of the new suspects was found guilty and given a life sentence.

Warren Douglas Manning

Warren Douglas Manning was convicted of shooting to death George T. Radford, a white state highway trooper, and was sentenced to death in 1989. Manning escaped when the trooper, who had stopped Manning for driving with a suspended license, stopped a second automobile. His attorney argued that if Manning had shot the officer, then he would have blood stains. Yet witnesses who saw Manning a short time later said he didn't have any blood on him. Manning was tried again and this trial resulted in a hung jury. A third trial resulted in Manning being convicted again, but a fourth trial was declared a mistrial. Finally, at a fifth trial, Manning was acquitted of all charges after having spent ten years behind bars.

Perry Mitchell

Perry Mitchell was convicted of the sexual assault of a seventeen-year-old white girl at gunpoint near his house. In 1984 he was sentenced to thirty years in prison. Mitchell was arrested because he resembled the description of the attacker that was provided by the victim. He claimed that he was at a neighbor's house and then went to a nearby party. Mitchell was convicted after the victim picked him out of a lineup, and after the presentation of forensic evidence that could not exclude him as the assailant. DNA testing eventually exonerated him after he had been incarcerated for over fourteen years of his life.

Winfred Peterson

See Tyrone James.

Tennessee

Clark McMillan

Clark McMillan was charged with raping a sixteen-year-old white girl and robbing her boyfriend at knifepoint. McMillan had a leg brace and an obvious limp that was not mentioned by either victim. At the trial he was identified by both victims, although his sister and girlfriend provided alibis. In 1980 McMillan was convicted and sentenced to 119 years in prison. In 2002, after spending twenty-two years in prison, he was exonerated on the basis of DNA evidence that excluded him as the perpetrator. On May 2, 2002, his conviction was overturned and the charges against him were dismissed. He remained incarcerated in prison on an unrelated gun possession charge until he was finally released on May 15, 2002. He was awarded over $800,000 in compensation in 2004.

Texas

Dennis Michael Allen

In 1999 Dennis Michael Allen was sentenced to eighteen years in prison for delivery of cocaine in the Tulia, Texas, drug bust discussed in Chapter 5. His conviction was the result of perjured testimony from an undercover sheriff's deputy. Allen was pardoned in 2003.

James Ray Barrow

James Ray Barrow was convicted in 1999 in the Tulia, Texas, drug bust for delivery of cocaine. Barrow's conviction was the result of perjured testimony from an undercover sheriff's deputy. He was sentenced to ten years on probation. Barrow was pardoned in 2003. More about the Tulia, Texas, drug bust can be found in Chapter 5.

Landis Barrow

In 2000 Landis Barrow was sentenced to twenty years in prison for delivery of cocaine and marijuana in the Tulia, Texas, drug bust discussed in Chapter 5. His conviction was the result of perjured testimony from an undercover sheriff's deputy.

Leroy Barrow

This wrongful conviction was part of the Tulia, Texas, drug scandal. Barrow was convicted in 2000 of delivery of cocaine, marijuana, and a simulated controlled substance on the basis of perjured testimony from an undercover sheriff's deputy. He was placed on ten years' probation as a result. More about the Tulia, Texas, drug bust appears in Chapter 5.

Mandis Barrow

Mandis Barrow was another victim of the perjured testimony of an undercover sheriff's deputy in the Tulia, Texas, drug scandal. He was charged with delivery of cocaine and marijuana and received a twenty-year sentence in 2000. More information about this drug bust can be found in Chapter 5.

Troy Benard

Troy Benard was sentenced to ten years in prison in 2000 on the basis of the perjured testimony of an undercover sheriff's deputy in the Tulia, Texas, drug bust. In 2003 he was pardoned. This drug scandal is discussed in greater detail in Chapter 5.

Clarence Lee Brandley

A janitor at a Conroe, Texas, high school, Clarence Lee Brandley was convicted of raping and murdering Cheryl Dee Ferguson, a sixteen-year-old white student. He was the only African American janitor at the school, and when the janitors were investigated by Wesley Styles, a Texas Ranger, Styles informed Brandley, "One of you is going to have to hang for this. Since you're the nigger, you're elected." Witnesses claimed that Brandley had followed Ferguson into a restroom and that he was the only one with a key to the area where she was found. His conviction was based on witness error and intimidation of witnesses by the police. In 1981 Brandley was convicted and sentenced to death. He spent nine years on death row before being judicially exonerated in 1990.

Fred Brookins, Jr.

Twenty-four-year-old Fred Brookins, Jr., was charged with the delivery of cocaine in the Tulia, Texas, drug scandal discussed in Chapter 5. In 1999 he was convicted based on the perjured testimony of an undercover sheriff's deputy and received a twenty-year prison sentence. He was pardoned in 2003.

A. B. Butler

In 1983 A. B. Butler was convicted of kidnapping and raping a twenty-five-year-old white woman. Although Butler had alibi witnesses at his trial, the victim identified him as the perpetrator and he was sentenced to ninety-nine years in prison. Butler was issued a full pardon in 2000 after spending sixteen years in prison for a crime he didn't commit. DNA testing was used to prove his innocence.

James Levi Byrd

James Levi Byrd was arrested and convicted of robbery. Byrd was sentenced to thirty years in prison in 1997. He spent five years in prison before a new investigation revealed that his brother, Donnie Johnson, who had confessed to the crime in 1997, was the actual perpetrator. Byrd was released from prison on December 23, 2002.

Kevin Byrd

Kevin Byrd was convicted of the rape of a twenty-five-year-old pregnant black woman and sentenced to life in 1985. His conviction was based on the victim's testimony that he had committed the crime in spite of the fact that she had previously claimed her attacker was white. Byrd spent twelve years behind bars before DNA tests unavailable at the time of his conviction excluded him as the donor of the semen found at the crime scene. After he was released from prison, Texas Governor George Bush officially pardoned him of any wrongdoing.

Charles Allen Chatman

In 1981 Charles Allen Chatman was convicted, after the victim identified him as the perpetrator, of raping a white woman. He received a ninety-nine-year sentence for aggravated rape. Chatman claimed that he was at work at the time of the rape, and his employer corroborated that story. His attorney also presented evidence that Chatman didn't know how to drive and didn't have a valid driver's license. DNA testing eventually proved his innocence, and he was released in 2008 after spending almost twenty-seven years in wrongful confinement.

Tim Cole

Tim Cole was convicted in 1985 of raping a female student at Texas Tech University, where he was also a student. He was convicted based on eyewitness testimony from the white victim, who picked him out of photograph and physical lineups. Cole was sentenced to twenty-five years behind bars. He was wrongfully imprisoned for fourteen years before another man, Jerry Wayne Johnson, confessed to the rape. Cole died in prison of complications from asthma before authorities acted on the confession. He was posthumously exonerated in 2009. Although Johnson admitted to the female student's rape, he was not charged due to the statute of limitations. However, Johnson is currently in prison on two unrelated rapes.

Armenu Jerrod Ervin

In 2000 Armenu Jerrod Ervin received ten years' probation for the alleged delivery of cocaine in the Tulia, Texas, drug bust. His conviction resulted from the perjured testimony of an undercover sheriff's deputy. In 2003 he was officially pardoned on any wrongdoing. Chapter 5 contains more information on this scandal.

Wiley Fountain

Wiley Fountain, who at the time of his conviction was on parole for a 1983 burglary conviction, received a forty-year sentence for the rape of a preg-

nant black woman in 1986. His conviction was based on the victim's identification of him as the perpetrator. After serving fifteen years of his sentence, he was paroled in 2001. However, Fountain returned to prison
because he had not found employment and had failed to register as a sex
offender. In 2002 he was released after DNA tests proved that he wasn't
the rapist. He received $190,000 for his wrongful imprisonment, much of
which he used to procure drugs, cigarettes, and women. After becoming
homeless, he began selling aluminum cans to make money. In 2008 he was
arrested again, this time on theft charges. He was subsequently released.

Michael Fowler

In 2000 Michael Fowler was placed on five years' probation for the alleged
delivery of cocaine in the Tulia, Texas, drug scandal reported in Chapter 5.
His conviction resulted from the perjured testimony of an undercover sheriff's deputy. He was pardoned in 2003.

Jason Paul Fry

Jason Paul Fry was convicted in 2000 in the Tulia, Texas, drug scandal and
sentenced to three years in prison for delivery of cocaine, based on the perjured testimony of an undercover sheriff's deputy. He was pardoned in
2003.

Larry Fuller

Convicted of the rape of a white woman in 1981, Larry Fuller was sentenced to fifty years in prison. Fuller's conviction was based on the victim's identification of him as the assailant. He spent eighteen years
wrongfully imprisoned before being paroled in 1999. However, Fuller
went back to prison in 2005 after a parole violation. Texas Governor Rick
Perry officially pardoned Fuller in 2007 on the basis of DNA tests, which
revealed that he was not the perpetrator.

Lenell Geter

Five people claimed that they saw Lenell Geter commit an armed robbery
in Balch Springs, Texas. However, at the time of the crime Geter was
working fifty miles away in Greenville, Texas. This alibi notwithstanding,
the jury convicted him of armed robbery and sentenced him to life in
prison in 1982. Geter spent two years in prison before the person who had

committed the robbery was caught and confessed to that robbery and six others.

James Curtis Giles

James Curtis Giles was convicted in 1983 of being part of the gang rape of a pregnant white woman. The victim identified Giles from a photograph, but it later was disclosed that he should not have been included in the photograph lineup. Police had confused him with someone who had the same name. Giles was wrongfully imprisoned for ten years before being paroled in 1993. In 2007 he was exonerated when DNA evidence excluded him as the assailant.

Willie Hall

In 1999 Willie Hall was convicted of delivering cocaine and marijuana and sentenced to eighteen years in prison in a drug raid in Tulia, Texas. His conviction was achieved through the perjured testimony of an undercover sheriff's deputy. In 2003 he was cleared of the crime. More information on the Tulia drug bust can be found in Chapter 5.

Cleveland J. Henderson

Twenty-five-year-old Cleveland J. Henderson was convicted in 2000 in the Tulia, Texas, drug bust and sentenced to five years' probation for delivery of cocaine. His wrongful conviction resulted from the perjured testimony of an undercover sheriff's deputy. He was exonerated in 2003. This drug scandal is discussed in greater detail in Chapter 5.

Mandrell L. Henry

Convicted in 2000 of delivering cocaine in the Tulia, Texas, drug scandal discussed in Chapter 5, Mandrell L. Henry was given a two-year sentence. The perjured testimony of an undercover sheriff's deputy was responsible for his wrongful conviction. Henry was exonerated in 2003.

Eugene Henton

Eugene Henton spent two years in prison after being convicted of sexual assault in 1984 and being released on parole in 1986. He returned to prison in 1995 on drug and assault charges after being sentenced to forty years.

DNA tests in 2006 excluded him as the perpetrator of the sexual assault, and his second conviction was thrown out because the sentence was based on the first conviction. Henton was released from prison in 2007.

Christopher Jackson

Eighteen-year-old Christopher Jackson was convicted of delivery of cocaine in 1999 during the Tulia, Texas, drug bust and sentenced to twenty years. He was convicted based on perjured testimony from an undercover sheriff's deputy. In 2003 he was cleared of any wrongdoing. More information on this drug scandal is available in Chapter 5.

Antrone Lynelle Johnson

Antrone Lynelle Johnson was twice convicted of rape while a student in high school. He received a life sentence in 1995 as a result of the two sexual assaults. Prosecutorial misconduct contributed to his wrongful incarceration. Although one of the victims told the prosecutor that Johnson had not sexually assaulted her and the other gave conflicting statements regarding the alleged incident, this information was not conveyed to Johnson's defense attorney. In 2008 Johnson was cleared when a Dallas County judge vacated his conviction and ordered that Johnson be released on his own recognizance. The prosecutor in the case had been fired in 2007 when a new district attorney took office. Johnson was wrongfully incarcerated for thirteen years.

Eliga Kelly, Sr.

Sixty-two-year-old Eliga Kelly, Sr., was convicted of delivery of cocaine and marijuana in 2000 during the Tulia, Texas, drug bust. He received ten years' probation. The case against Kelly was based on the perjured testimony of an undercover sheriff's deputy. Kelly was exonerated in 2003. More about this drug scandal can be found in Chapter 5.

Johnnie Earl Lindsey

Johnnie Earl Lindsey was convicted in 1983 of a rape charge and sentenced to life in prison. The victim identified Lindsey as the perpetrator nearly a year after the attack. Lindsey said that he was at work when the crime occurred. His boss also testified that Lindsey was at work at the time, and his time card corroborated this. Nevertheless, Lindsey was convicted and spent almost twenty-six years in prison before being pardoned by Governor Rick Perry based on DNA evidence.

Joseph Corey Marshall

Twenty-three-year-old Joseph Corey Marshall was sentenced to ten years' probation in 2000 for the delivery of cocaine in the Tulia, Texas, drug bust discussed in greater detail in Chapter 5. His conviction was the result of perjured testimony by an undercover sheriff's deputy. He was exonerated in 2003.

Vincent Dwight McCray

Vincent Dwight McCray was convicted in 2000 in the Tulia, Texas, drug bust and sentenced to three years in prison for delivery of cocaine. His conviction was based on perjured testimony by an undercover sheriff's deputy. McCray was pardoned in 2003. More information about this drug bust is available in Chapter 5.

Thomas Clifford McGowan

Accused of aggravated sexual assault and burglary of a habitation, Thomas Clifford McGowan was given two consecutive life sentences in two separate trials in 1985 and 1986. McGowan spent twenty-three years in prison before DNA testing, which was not available at the time of the convictions, proved that he was innocent.

Billy Wayne Miller

Billy Wayne Miller was convicted in 1984 of raping a woman after the victim had identified him as the perpetrator. At the time of incident he was on parole for assault to commit murder and robbery. Police misconduct and mistaken eyewitness identification contributed to his wrongful conviction. He was released in 2006 after DNA testing exonerated him of the rape.

Joe Welton Moore

Joe Welton Moore was convicted in 1999 in the Tulia, Texas, drug raid discussed in Chapter 5. He was sentenced to ninety years in prison for delivery of cocaine based on the perjured testimony of an undercover sheriff's deputy. He received a pardon in 2003.

Arthur Mumphrey

Arthur Mumphrey was convicted in 1986 of raping a thirteen-year-old girl and was sentenced to thirty-five years behind bars. He served fourteen years of his sentence before being released on parole. Mumphrey received a pardon from Governor Rick Perry in 2006 when DNA tests excluded him as the perpetrator. He additionally received over $400,000 in compensation for his wrongful incarceration.

Kenneth Ray Powell

In 2000 forty-year-old Kenneth Ray Powell was given ten years' probation for delivery of cocaine in the Tulia, Texas, drug bust discussed in Chapter 5. Perjured testimony from an undercover sheriff's deputy led to his conviction. In 2003 he was exonerated.

Ricardo Rachell

Ricardo Rachell was convicted in 2003 of the sexual assault of an eight-year-old boy and sentenced to forty years in prison. The boy said that the man who committed the crime had a scar, and Rachell's face is disfigured from a shotgun blast. The victim and another child identified Rachell as the assailant. Prosecutorial misconduct, police misconduct, erroneous eyewitness testimony, and ineffective assistance of counsel contributed to this miscarriage of justice. Rachell spent over five years in prison before DNA testing exonerated him of the crime.

Anthony Robinson

Anthony Robinson was convicted in 1987 of sexual assault and sentenced to twenty-seven years in prison. He was originally a suspect because he matched the victim's description. The case was based on the victim's identification of Robinson as the attacker in a lineup. He spent ten years behind bars before being released on parole in 1997. DNA testing excluded Robinson as the assailant in 2000, and in 2007 he received a pardon.

Benny Lee Robinson

In 1999 twenty-four-year-old Benny Lee Robinson was accused of the delivery of cocaine during the Tulia, Texas, drug bust discussed in Chapter 5.

Perjured testimony from an undercover sheriff's deputy contributed to this accusation. In 2003 he was exonerated of any wrongdoing.

Billy James Smith

Billy James Smith was sentenced to life in prison in 1987 for a 1986 sexual assault that occurred in his apartment building. The victim knew Smith and identified him as the assailant. Smith's sister testified that she was with him in his apartment during the time of the crime. Smith was wrongfully incarcerated for nineteen years before DNA testing led to his exoneration in 2006.

Donald Wayne Smith

Thirty-one-year-old Donald Wayne Smith was convicted in 2000 of the delivery of cocaine in the Tulia, Texas, drug bust. His sentence of twelve and a half years in prison was based on perjured testimony from an undercover sheriff's deputy. In 2003 Smith was cleared of the crime. Chapter 5 contains additional information about this drug scandal.

Ben Spencer

Ben Spencer was charged with the 1987 robbery and murder of a thirty-three-year-old white Dallas businessman. In 1988 he was sentenced to life in prison. With no physical evidence connecting Spencer with the murder, the prosecution relied on the testimony of three witnesses who said they saw Spencer abandon the stolen automobile. Their identification was used to convict Spencer despite very poor lighting and a considerable distance of at least 100 feet. In 2008 a judge, reviewing the evidence, ordered a new trial for Spencer. Eyewitness error and the use of an informant contributed to this miscarriage of justice.

Josiah Sutton

In 1999 Sutton was convicted of a rape and carjacking that occurred when he was sixteen years old. He was sentenced to twenty-five years behind bars. The jury convicted Sutton based on DNA evidence that was reported as a positive match and identification from the forty-one-year-old victim. He served over four years before the DNA was retested and he was excluded as the attacker. Sutton received a settlement of over $100,000.

Ronald Gene Taylor

Ronald Gene Taylor was convicted of aggravated sexual assault in 1995 and sentenced to sixty years in prison. The police brought Taylor in as a suspect because he lived near the victim and he vaguely resembled the victim's description of the attacker. The victim identified Taylor after viewing a video lineup, which was later challenged in court. Forensic evidence was not tested after it was determined that there wasn't enough to have a reliable test. Taylor's conviction was based on the victim's identification. He spent fourteen years in prison before the forensic evidence was retested and he was found innocent of the rape.

Timothy Wayne Towery

Timothy Wayne Towery was sentenced to eighteen years in prison in 1999 as a result of the Tulia, Texas, drug bust. He was convicted of delivery of cocaine. The verdict rested on the perjured testimony of an undercover sheriff's deputy. In 2003 Towery was exonerated. More information on this drug scandal can be found in Chapter 5.

Keith Turner

Keith Turner was convicted in 1983 of rape and sentenced to twenty years in prison. Turner and the victim worked for the same company at different locations until Turner was transferred. Turner had an alibi but was convicted based on the victim's identification of Turner's appearance and voice. He was wrongfully incarcerated for four years before being paroled in 1987. In 2005 Texas Governor Rick Perry pardoned Turner based on exclusionary DNA evidence.

James Waller

In 1983 James Waller was convicted of the rape of a twelve-year-old white boy in his apartment complex after the boy identified Waller as the perpetrator. Waller was sentenced to thirty years behind bars despite his claim that he was asleep when the crime took place. His alibi was confirmed by his girlfriend and roommate. Waller spent ten years in prison before being paroled in 1993. DNA tests in 2007 cleared him of any involvement in the crime.

Patrick Waller

A kidnapping, robbery, and rape led to the conviction of Patrick Waller in 1992. He received a sentence of thirty years in prison for the crimes. The white victims identified Waller as one of the perpetrators, and Waller, who was already on probation for cocaine possession, was charged with the offenses. Forensic evidence presented at his trial could not exclude him as a possible suspect. Waller spent over fifteen years in prison before DNA testing exonerated him.

Calvin Washington

Calvin Washington was sentenced to life in prison in 1987 for the murder and rape of a fifty-four-year-old Waco woman. Washington and his codefendant, Joe Sidney Williams, were both convicted of the crime in separate trials. An informant claimed to have overheard Washington admitting to the crime. At the trial, the prosecution stated that Washington and Williams had the victim's automobile and tried to sell various items belonging to the victim. Washington had blood on his shirt that was originally assumed to be from the victim. Further DNA tests showed that the blood came from Washington. Bite marks found on the victim were used at the trial to secure the conviction of Williams. Washington spent fourteen years behind bars before being exonerated through DNA testing. He received over $100,000 in compensation in 2007. *See Joe Sidney Williams.*

Kareem White

In 2000 Kareem White was convicted of delivery of cocaine in the Tulia, Texas, drug bust and sentenced to sixty years in prison. His conviction rested on the perjured testimony of an undercover sheriff's deputy. White was exonerated in 2003. More detailed information on this drug scandal can be found in Chapter 5.

Jason Jerome Williams

In 1999 twenty-year-old Jason Jerome Williams received a forty-five-year sentence for delivery of cocaine resulting from the Tulia, Texas, drug bust. His conviction was obtained through perjured testimony from an undercover sheriff's deputy. Williams was cleared in 2003. Chapter 5 contains additional information on this drug scandal.

Joe Sidney Williams

In 1987 Joe Sidney Williams was convicted of the murder and rape of a fifty-four-year-old Waco woman. In a separate trial, his codefendant, Calvin Washington, was also convicted of this crime. His conviction was overturned in 1993 on the grounds of improper testimony. Williams was released the same year, after the prosecution dismissed all charges against him. He was wrongfully imprisoned for over six years. *See Calvin Washington.*

James Lee Woodard

In 1981 James Lee Woodard was convicted of raping and murdering his twenty-one-year-old girlfriend and sentenced to life in prison. Prosecutorial misconduct, police misconduct (failing to investigate other possible suspects), and eyewitness error contributed to this wrongful conviction. After twenty-seven years in prison Woodard was released in 2008, after DNA evidence cleared him of any wrongdoing.

Utah

Harry Miller

Harry Miller was convicted in 2003 of robbing at gunpoint an elderly woman in Salt Lake City. He was sentenced to five years behind bars. Miller's conviction was the result of the victim's identification of him as the perpetrator from a photograph. The police had a photograph of Miller that was taken earlier, when he had been falsely arrested for an unrelated robbery. Miller had been incarcerated for over four years when it was discovered that he had been in Baton Rouge, Louisiana, recovering from a stroke when the elderly woman had been robbed. He was released in 2007 after the prosecution dismissed the charges against him.

Virginia

Marvin Anderson

Charged with the rape, abduction, sodomy, and robbery of a twenty-four-year-old white woman, Marvin Anderson was sentenced to 210 years in prison in 1982. Anderson was identified by the victim as her attacker. In addition, the prosecution withheld important evidence. John Otis Lincoln admitted to the crime in 1988, but the judge who presided over Anderson's trial didn't believe Lincoln and refused to overturn the conviction. Anderson was paroled in 1997 and exonerated in 2001, after forensic tests excluded him as the predator. Governor Mark Warner in April 2002 pardoned him. The next year the Virginia General Assembly approved a $750,000 compensation package for Anderson.

Darrell A. Copeland

Darrell A. Copeland, a felon, was convicted in 2007 of being in possession of a firearm and sentenced to five years in prison. He appealed the sentence and it was shown that the item in question was not a functional firearm. Copeland was imprisoned for over a year before gaining his release.

Russell Leon Gray

Russell Leon Gray was convicted of first-degree murder in 1987 and sentenced to fifty-two years in prison. Gray was identified by a witness as the murderer. The witness eventually changed his identification to another man. A second witness, who did not appear in court, had already identified the other man as the killer. Gray spent three years in prison before being judicially exonerated in 1990.

Troy D. Hopkins

Charged with murdering a thirty-seven-year-old man, Troy D. Hopkins was sentenced to twenty-eight years behind bars in 1990. Hopkins's conviction was the result of false eyewitness testimony involving a drunk witness who thought that she heard someone call the perpetrator "Squeaky." His conviction was overturned in 1992 after another man confessed, but the decision was reversed by a higher court. Hopkins spent eleven years in prison before being paroled in 2001. Four years later he received an official pardon.

Julius Earl Ruffin

Julius Earl Ruffin was convicted in 1981 of the rape and sodomy of a thirty-two-year-old white nurse and sentenced to five life terms in prison after two hung juries. Although Ruffin claimed that he was with his girlfriend at the time of the crime, the victim believed that Ruffin was her attacker. Forensic evidence that might have shown him to be innocent was excluded at the trial. Ruffin was released in 2003 on parole because it was faster than waiting for a court to exonerate him. DNA tests identified another incarcerated man as the actual assailant.

Lindsey Scott

In 1983 Private Lindsey Scott, a marine, was convicted by a military court of raping a thirty-five-year-old white woman. The victim identified him as the perpetrator. Scott remained incarcerated until 1988, when he was acquitted in a retrial in a civilian court. An investigation later uncovered evidence that the prosecution had not divulged a medical report that would have eliminated him as the attacker. The report had additionally verified Scott's alibi that he was at a department store when the attack took place.

Teddy Thompson

Seventeen-year-old Teddy Thompson was convicted in 2001 of two armed robberies and sentenced to sixteen years in prison. He was identified by one of the two victims as the man who had committed the crime. Thompson finally received a new trial when the eyewitness acknowledged that he had mistakenly identified Thompson as the perpetrator. When his conviction was vacated and he was released in 2007, Thompson had been incarcerated for seven years. Thompson received in excess of $250,000 in compensation for his wrongful imprisonment. In 2009 he had three run-ins with the law: one involved a breach of the peace, the second involved an assault-and-battery charge, and a third involved a probation violation. None of these violations resulted in his being returned to prison.

Phillip Leon Thurman

Phillip Leon Thurman was convicted of rape, abduction, and assault in 1985 stemming from a 1984 incident involving a thirty-seven-year-old woman. He was sentenced to thirty-one years behind bars. Thurman, who matched the victim's description of her attacker, was arrested near the crime scene. Forensic evidence found on the victim's underwear was tested but, due to limited testing capabilities, only the assailant's blood type could be ascertained. (The attacker and Thurman shared the same blood type.) After twenty years in prison, Thurman was paroled in 2004. In 2005 Thurman received a pardon when DNA tests not available at the time of his conviction provided proof of his innocence. Thurman received an undisclosed amount as compensation for his wrongful imprisonment.

Earl Washington, Jr.

In 1984 Earl Washington, Jr., was convicted of the murder and rape of Rebecca Lynn Williams, a nineteen-year-old white mother of three. He was sentenced to death. He was originally detained by the police after a robbery. Washington, who has a low IQ, falsely confessed to four other crimes as well as the one involving Williams. It is believed that Washington confessed to the crimes to please authorities and to tell them what they wanted to hear. Despite several inconsistencies in Washington's confession, including not knowing where the murder occurred, he was charged with the crime. Forensic evidence suggested that Washington was not the assailant, as the attacker had a rare plasma protein that Washington didn't possess. Washington spent eighteen years in prison before DNA testing that was unavailable at the time of his arrest excluded him as the perpetrator. Washington received almost $2 million in compensation for his wrongful incarceration.

Troy Webb

In 1989 Troy Webb was convicted of rape, kidnapping, and robbery and sentenced to forty-seven years in prison. He was convicted on the basis of the victim's identification, because DNA evidence seemed to suggest that Webb didn't commit the crime. Webb was incarcerated for seven years before being released in 1996. DNA testing eventually proved that he was not the perpetrator.

Arthur Lee Whitfield

The rape of two women in 1981 led to Arthur Lee Whitfield's conviction in 1982. His conviction was based on the victims' identification of him as the attacker. Although Whitfield didn't match the initial description and his family testified that he was with them during the time of the rapes, he was sentenced to sixty-three years in prison. He was incarcerated for almost twenty-three of those years when DNA tests that were not available when he was convicted excluded him as the perpetrator. Four years later he received a full pardon. Whitfield received over $600,000 in compensation for his wrongful imprisonment.

Washington

Benjamin J. Harris III

Benjamin J. Harris III was convicted of the murder of Tacoma, Washington, automobile mechanic Jimmie Lee Turner and was sentenced to death in 1985. Although Harris confessed to the crime, he was mentally unstable when he made the confession. Twice Harris came very close to being executed, and both times he was given a stay of execution. At his trial the prosecution implied that Harris had paid another man, Gregory Lee Bonds, to help him murder Turner. Harris was also represented by an incompetent attorney who failed to interview potential witnesses and to challenge the decision to go for the death penalty. In 1994 a federal judge found that Harris's legal representation was so flawed that his guilt had never been established. The judge ordered that Harris be released or given a new trial. This decision was upheld by the Ninth Circuit Court of Appeals in 1995. After deciding not to retry Harris, the prosecutor attempted to have Washington committed to a mental hospital (although he had previously argued that Washington was competent to stand trial). In 1997 a jury determined that Washington should not be held in a mental facility. In 2003, after being held at Western State Hospital contrary to a court decision, Washington was finally released. He died a short time later.

Wisconsin

Jarrett Adams

Jarrett Adams and Dimitri Henley, both from Chicago and students at the University of Wisconsin–Whitewater, were sentenced to twenty-eight years in prison in 2000 for sexual assault. The white victim, Shawn Stratton, was also a student at Whitewater. Additionally, a third man, Rovaughn Hill, was tried for the crime, but after a hung jury and the dismissal of charges when new evidence came to light, he was released. The conviction of both men was based on the victim's testimony. Both men faced all-white juries and, despite the lack of proof that force was used, were convicted of second-degree sexual assault. Both Adams and Henley appealed the decision. After seven years Adams had his decision reversed by the US Court of Appeals for the seventh district. In 2008 a new trial was ordered for Henley, and he was released on bond two weeks later.

Dimitri Henley

See Jarrett Adams.

Anthony Hicks

Anthony Hicks was convicted of raping and robbing a white woman in 1991 and was sentenced to twenty years in prison. Five hairs recovered from the bedroom where the rape occurred were examined after the victim testified that she had never had an African American man in her apartment and the last African American woman in her apartment was over a year ago. The hairs from the crime scene were consistent with hairs taken from Hicks. Hicks spent five years in prison before he was released. Further DNA testing eventually ruled out Hicks as the perpetrator of the crime.

Bibliography

Abel, D. (2005, August 5). "Man Jailed in 3 Rapes; Earlier Suspect Is Freed." *Boston Globe*. Available online at: http://www.boston.com/news/local /massachusetts/articles/2005/08/05/man_jailed_in_3_rapes_earlier_suspect _is_freed/.

American Civil Liberties Union. (2010, August 3). "President Obama Signs Bill Reducing Cocaine Sentencing Disparity." Press release. Available online at: http://www.aclu.org/print/drug-law-reform/president-obama-signs-bill -reducing-cocaine-sentencing-disparity.

"'American Violet' Tells Story of Ill-Fated Hearne Drug Raids." (2009, March 13). *Dallas Morning News*. Available online at: http://www.dallasnews.com.

"Antonio Beaver Exonerated in St. Louis." (2007, April 1). Wrongful-Convictions website. Available online at: http://wrongful-convictions.blogspot.com/2007 /04/antonio-beaver-exonerated-in-st-louis.html.

Arey, D. (2006, Fall). "Leslie Vass Haunted by Unexpunged 1975 Wrongful Conviction." *Justice Denied* 34, p. 5.

Arizona Supreme Court oral argument case summary. (2002, May 23). *State v. Minnitt* (CR-99-0243-AP). Phoenix, AZ: Arizona Supreme Court Administrative Office of the Courts.

"Arthur Teele Remembered, Buried in Tallahassee." (2005, August 1). Local10.com (Miami, FL). Available online at: http://www.justnews.com /news/4796170/detail.html.

Associated Press. (1999, September 6). "Man Serving Life May Be Innocent." Truth in Justice. Available online at: http://truthinjustice.org/mckinney.htm.

Associated Press. (2001, July 6). "DNA Evidence Frees Man Convicted of Murder." *Lubbock Avalanche-Journal*. Available online at: http://www.lubbock online.com/stories/070601/upd_075-4495.shtml.

Associated Press. (2004, November 5). "Man's 1984 Child Molestation Charges Nixed." Available online at: http://www.injusticebusters.com/04/Smith _Sylvester.shtml.

Associated Press. (2007, July 10). "They Won't Retry Innocent Man." Available online at: http://www.nydailynews.com/news/ny_crime/2007/07/10/2007-07 -10_they_wont_retry_innocent_man.html.

Associated Press. (2008, February 20). "Man Once on Miss. Death Row Exonerated in 1992 Murder Case." Available online at: http://www.ncadp.org/news /cfm?articleID=208andaffID=46.

Balko, R. (2007, August 2). "'Indeed, and Without a Doubt': How a Mississippi Dentist May Be Sending Innocent People to Jail." *Reason.* Available online at: http://reason.com/archives/2007/08/02/indeed-and-without-a-doubt.

Balko, R. (2008, February 20). "The Bite-Marks Men: Mississippi's Criminal Forensics Disaster." *Slate.* Available online at: http://www.slate.com/id /2184798/pagenum/all/.

Baran, M. (2009, October 21). "Minnesota Receives $859,000 Grant to Review DNA Cases." Minnesota Public Radio. Available online at: http://www.nlada .org/DMS/Documents/1256218329.57/index.html.

Barksdale, T. (2008, May 3). "Death Row Ordeal Behind Him: With a Murder Charge Dismissed, Levon 'Bo' Jones Steps into Freedom After 15 Years." *Raleigh News and Observer.* Available online at: http://www.newsobserver .com/news/story/1059361.html.

Barrett, B. (2004, November 6). "Falsely Accused Man Freed." *Raleigh News and Observer.* Available online at: http://www.injusticebusters.com/04/Smith _Sylvester.shtml.

Barta, C. (2008, May 2). "*60 Minutes* to Feature Dallas DA's Office." Available online at: http://www.dallasblog.com.

Batson v. Kentucky, 476 U.S. 79, 106 S. Ct. 1712 (1986).

Bean, A. (2004, April 9). "Twin Tragedy in Tulia." *Texas Observer.* Available online at: http://www.november.org/stayinfo/breaking2/Tulia4-30.html.

Bean, A. (2009, October 29). "Twins Tragedy in Tulia." Friends of Justice. Available online at: http://friendsofjustice.wordpress.com/2009/10/29/twins -tragedy-in-tulia/.

Becker, H. (1963). *Outsiders: Studies in the Sociology of Deviance.* New York: Free Press.

Bedau, H., and Radelet, M. (1987). "Miscarriages of Justice in Potentially Capital Cases." *Stanford Law Review* 40, pp. 21–179.

Berger, R., Free, M., and Searles, P. (2009). *Crime, Justice, and Society: An Introduction to Criminology* (3rd ed.). Boulder, CO: Lynne Rienner.

Bernhard, A. (2001). "Effective Assistance of Counsel." In S. Westervelt and J. Humphrey (eds.), *Wrongly Convicted: Perspectives on Failed Justice.* New Brunswick, NJ: Rutgers University Press.

"Bill Supporting Use of Snitches Advances." (2011, April 7). WOWT News. Available online at: http://www.wowt.com/news/headlines/44829477.html ?storySection=story.

Blackburn, E. (2008, June 30). "Hope Deferred: Tim Cole's Family Gets DNA Report Proving What They Always Knew." *Lubbock Avalanche-Journal.* Available online at: http://www.lubbockonline.com/stories/063008/loc_297531088.shtml.

Blackburn, E. (2009, April 7). "Judge Exonerates Timothy Cole." *Lubbock Avalanche-Journal.* Available online at: http://lubbockonline.com/stories/040709 /loc_426805642.shtml.

Blakeslee, N. (2000, July 28). "Color of Justice: An Undercover Drug Bust Opens Old Wounds in Tulia, Texas." *Austin Chronicle.* Available online at: http://www.austinchronicle.com/gyrobase/Issue/story?oid=oid%A78058.

Blakeslee, N. (2002, November). "Bust Town." *Texas Monthly.* Available online at: http://www.texasmonthly.com/cms/printthis.php?file=reporter.phpand issue=2002-11-01.

Blueline Radio. (nd). "Smith Set Free." Available online at: http://www.blueline radio.com/smithsetfree.html.

Blumberg, A. (1967). "The Practice of Law as a Confidence Game." *Law and Society Review* 1, pp. 15–39.

Blumstein, A. (1982). "On the Racial Disproportionality of US Prison Populations." *Journal of Criminal Law and Criminology* 73, pp. 1259–1281.

Blumstein, A. (1993). "Racial Disproportionality of US Prison Populations Revisited." *University of Colorado Law Review* 64, pp. 743–760.

Borchard, E. (1932). *Convicting the Innocent: Sixty-five Actual Errors of Criminal Justice*. Garden City, NY: Doubleday.

Bowers, J. (2008). "Punishing the Innocent." *University of Pennsylvania Law Review* 156, pp. 1117–1179.

Brady v. Maryland, 373 US 83 (1963).

Brandley v. Texas, 691 S.W.2d 699 (1985).

Brandon, R., and Davies, C. (1973). *Wrongful Imprisonment: Mistaken Convictions and their Consequences*. London: Archon Books.

Brazil, J., and Berry, S. (1992, August 23). "Color of Driver Is Key to Stops in I-95 Videos." *Orlando Sentinel*, p. A1.

Breecher, E. (1972). *Licit and Illicit Drugs*. Boston: Little, Brown.

Brigham, J., and Ready, D. (1985). "Own-Race Bias in Lineup Construction." *Law and Human Behavior* 9, pp. 415–424.

Bright, T. (2001a, August). "Fighting for Another Chance" (Execution of Justice series). *Birmingham Post-Herald*. Available online at: http://www.patrick crusade.org/execution_2_5.htm.

Bright, T. (2001b, August). "Love Letters Almost Fatal" (Execution of Justice series). *Birmingham Post-Herald*. Available online at: http://www.patrick crusade.org/execution_2_5.htm.

Brownstein, H. (1996). *The Rise and Fall of a Violent Crime Wave: Crack Cocaine and the Social Construction of a Crime Problem*. Guilderland, NY: Harrow and Heston.

Buckley, J. (2007, June 12). "The Exoneration of Larry Peterson." National Public Radio. Available online at: http://ww.npr.org/templates/story/story.php ?storyId=10961075.

Buckley, J. (2007, June 13). "Larry Peterson: Life After Exoneration." National Public Radio. Available online at: http://www.npr.org/templates/story/story .php?storyId=10974437andps=rs.

Burnett, C. (2010). *Wrongful Death Sentences: Rethinking Justice in Capital Cases*. Boulder, CO: Lynne Rienner.

Byrd, S. (2008, August 5). "Miss. State Pathologist's Contract Is Terminated." *USA Today*. Available online at: http://www.usatoday.com/news/nation/2008 -08-05-389476708_x.htm.

Byrd, S. (2008, August 12). "Man May Be Exonerated in Child Murder." *USA Today*. Available online at: http://www.usatoday.com/news/nation/2008-02 -12-1859933072_x.htm.

Campaign to End the Death Penalty. (2009). "Former Death Row Prisoners." Available online at: http://www.nodeathpenalty.org/content/page.php?cat_id =7andcontent_id=9.

Canadian Coalition Against the Death Penalty. (2001, June 2). "News About Freddie's Execution, March 3rd, 2000." Available online at: http://ccadp.org/freddiewrightnews.htm.

Caniglia, J. (2008, January 22). "Feds to Release 15 More People in Botched Mansfield Drug Case." *Plain Dealer*. Available online at: http://blog.cleveland.com/metro/2008/01/feds_to_release_15_more_people.html.

Caniglia, J. (2009, May 14). "Deputy Charles Metcalf, Who Worked with DEA Agent Lee Lucas, Pleads Guilty to Lying at Trial." *Plain Dealer*. Available online at: http://blog.cleveland.com/metro//print.html.

Castano, C. (2009, February 6). "Austin Judge Reverses Cole Conviction." KXAN.com. Available online at: http://www.kxan.com/dpp/news/texas/Tim_Cole_exoneration_hearing_continues.

CBS News. (2001, July 6). "DNA Test Opens Prison Door." Available online at: http://www.cbsnews.com/stories/2001/07/06/national/main300157.shtml.

CBS News. (2009, November 23). "Man Accused of Killing 2 Children Dies in Prison." Available online at: http://wcbstv.com/local/murder.suspect.dead.2.1329563.html.

Center on Wrongful Convictions. (2005). *The Snitch System: How Snitch Testimony Sent Randy Steidl and Other Innocent Americans to Death Row.* Chicago: Northwestern University School of Law.

Center on Wrongful Convictions. (2009a). "Exonerations in Illinois Capital Cases." Available online at: http://www.law.northwestern.edu/wrongfulconvictions/exonerations/ilIndexdp.html.

Center on Wrongful Convictions. (2009b). "Our Mission." Available online at: http://www.law.northwestern.edu/wrongfulconvictions/aboutus/mission.html.

Centurion Ministries. (2007). "Cases: Edward Baker." Available online at: http://www.centurionministries.org/cases.html.

"Charges Dismissed Against Christopher Parish." (2006, Fall). *Justice Denied* 34, p. 19.

Chiricos, T. (1996). "Moral Panic as Ideology: Drugs, Violence, Race, and Punishment in America." In M. Lynch and E. Patterson (eds.), *Justice with Prejudice*. Guilderland, NY: Harrow and Heston.

Christianson, S. (2004). *Innocent: Inside Wrongful Conviction Cases*. New York: New York University Press.

Civ. 02-A-02-CA-702JN (2002). ACLU Lawsuit Brought in US District Court for the Western District of Texas on Behalf of 15 of the Individuals Involved in the Hearne, Texas, Drug Bust.

Clements, C. (2007, October 5). "A Gentle Soul, Unbroken by Injustice." *Texas Observer*. Available online at: http://www.texasobserver.org/article.php?aid=2602andprint=true.

Coffey, J. (2010). "DNA Evidence Set Clear Two Noxubee County Men Convicted of Rape and Murder." *Commercial Dispatch*. Available online at: http://www.truthinjustice.org/kennedy-brewer2.htm.

Cohen, S. (2003). *The Wrong Men: America's Epidemic of Wrongful Death Row Convictions*. New York: Carroll and Graf.

"Commissioner Arthur Teele Found Not Guilty." (2010). David M. Garvin, Miami Criminal Defense Attorney. Available online at: http://www.davidmgarvin.com/commissioner-arthur-teele-found-not-guilty/.

Conti, R. (1999). "The Psychology of False Confessions." *Journal of Credibility Assessment and Witness Psychology* 2, pp. 14–36.

Corella, H., and Duarte, C. (1992, June 26). "Triple Murder Has Police Puzzled." *Arizona Daily Star*. Available online at: http://www.swtraffic.com/ths/Gee.htm.

Crimmins, J. (2004, July 15). "Conviction 'an Outrage,' Probe Warranted: Attorney." *Chicago Daily Law Bulletin* 150 (138). Available online at: http://www.truthinjustice.org/rollins.htm.

Curtis, H. (1992, August 23). "Statistics Show Pattern of Discrimination." *Orlando Sentinel*, p. A11.

Davis, A. (2007). *Arbitrary Justice: The Power of the American Prosecutor*. New York: Oxford University Press.

Death Penalty Focus. (2008, March 28). "Wrongful Convictions in California Capital Cases." Available online at: http://deathpenalty.org.

Death Penalty Information Center. (2011). "Fact Sheet." Available online at: http://www.deathpenaltyinfo.org/documents/FactSheet.pdf.

Dewan, S. (2007, September 6). "Despite DNA Test, a Case Is Retried." *New York Times*. Available online at: http://www.truthinjustice.org/Kennedy-Brewer.htm.

Dewan, S. (2008, February 8). "New Suspect Is Arrested in 2 Mississippi Killings." *New York Times*. Available online at: http://www.nytimes.com/2008/02/08/us/08dna.html?r=2andoref=slogin.

Dieter, R. (1998). *The Death Penalty in Black and White: Who Lives, Who Dies, Who Decides*. Washington, DC: Death Penalty Information Center. Available online at: http://www.deathpenaltyinfo.org/death-penalty-black-and-white-who-lives-who-dies-who-decides.

"DNA Frees Another: Joshua Sutton Exonerated." (2003, March 10). TalkLeft.com. Available online at: http://www.talkleft.com/story/2003/03/11/947/87209.

Dobbin, B. (2000, February 3). "Duval Acquitted After 25 Years in Jail." Associated Press. Available online at: http://www.truthinjustice.org/duvalupdate.htm.

Dujardin, P. (2009a, February 24). "Wrongfully Jailed Man Wants to 'Move Forward.'" *Daily Press* (Newport News, Virginia). Available online at: http://www.dailypress.com/news/dp-thompson-archive5,0,5844413,printstory.

Dujardin, P. (2009b, July 24). "Assault Charge Against Thompson Dropped." *Daily Press* (Newport News, Virginia). Available online at: http://www.dailypress.com/news/dp-thompson-archive3,0,5057979,printstory.

Dujardin, P. (2009c, August 18). "Ex-prisoner Awarded $270K Avoids Jail." *Daily Press* (Newport News, Virginia). Available online at: http://www.dailypress.com/news/dp-thompson-archive2,0,4664762,printstory.

Dunn, D. (1987, March 28). "Capital Murder Hearings Held." *Waco Tribune-Herald*, pp. 1B, 2B.

Earley, P. (1996). *Circumstantial Evidence: Death, Life, and Justice in a Southern Town*. New York: Bantam.

Edds, M. (2003). *An Expendable Man: The Near-Execution of Earl Washington, Jr.* New York: New York University Press.

"El Grande Murder Conviction Tossed Out: The State Supreme Court Finds Misconduct by a Pima County Prosecutor and Calls a 3rd Trial a Violation of the Double-Jeopardy Law." (2002, October 12). *Tucson Citizen*, on Canadian Coalition Against the Death Penalty website. Available online at: http://www.ccadp.org/andreminnitt-news.htm.

Emily, J. (2009, January 12). "TV Show About Dallas County's DA Conviction Integrity Unit Will Air in April." *Dallas Morning News*. Available online at: http://crimeblog.dallasnews.com.

Equal Justice Initiative. (nd). "Alabama's Exonerated." Available online at: http://eji.org/eji/files/alabamasexonerated.pdf.

Equal Justice Initiative. (2009, April 7). "EJI Honors Kenneth Frazier and Randy Hertz and Celebrates the Release of Bo Cochran and Phillip Shaw." Available online at: http://eji.org/eji/node/289.

Equal Justice Initiative. (2010, June). *Illegal Racial Discrimination in Jury Selection: A Continuing Legacy*. Montgomery, Alabama: Equal Justice Initiative.

"Errors at F.B.I. May Be Issue in 3,000 Cases." (2003, March 17). *New York Times*, p. A18.

"The Exonerated." (2008, November). *Texas Monthly*. Available online at: http://www.texasmonthly.com/2008-11-01/feature2-1.php.

"Exonerated Men Tell Their Stories of Wrongful Conviction and Imprisonment." (2003, February 26). California Western School of Law press release. Available online at: http://www.cwsl.edu/main/default.asp?nav=news.aspandbody =news/March6Event.asp.

"Expert Testimony: Educators in the Courtroom: Alabama vs. Victoria Banks." (2009). University of Alabama at Birmingham website. Available online at: http://main.uab.edu/show.asp?durki=68032.

Farish, J. (2008, July 15). "Free at Last." *UM Lawyer*. Available online at: http://www.law.olemiss.edu/UMLAWSpr08/umlawyer/news_free.html.

Fears, D. (2009, April 15). "A Racial Shift in Drug-Crime Prisoners." *Washington Post*. Available online at: http://www.washingtonpost.com/wp-dyn/content /article/2009/04/14/AR2009041401775.html.

Federal Bureau of Investigation. (2009). *Crime in the United States 2008*. Washington, DC: US Department of Justice. Available online at: http://www.fbi.gov/ucr/cius2008/index.html.

Federal Bureau of Investigation. (2010). *Crime in the United States 2009*. Washington, DC: US Department of Justice. Available online at: http://www.fbi.gov/ucr/cius2009/index.html.

"Federal Court Finds Lawyer Ineffective for Failure to Call Expert on Effects of Blood Loss and Sedation on Witness's Memory." (2007, September 10). Eyewitness Identification Reform Blog. Available online at: http://eyeid.word press.com/2007/09/.

Fergus, M. (2004a, March 6). "Josiah Sutton: One Year Later." *Houston Chronicle*. Available online at: http://www.chron.com/disp/story.mpl/life/2434872.html.

Fergus, M. (2004b, March 7). "Josiah Sutton Still Waits for Legal Exoneration." *Houston Chronicle*. Available online at: http://www.truthinjustice.org/sutton -waiting.htm.

Forejustice. (2011). "Forejustice." Available online at: http://forejustice.org.

"Former Miami Commissioner Commits Suicide." (2005, July 28). Local10.com (Miami, FL). Available online at: http://www.justnews.com/news/4778148 /detail.html.

Frank, J., and Frank, B. (1957). *Not Guilty*. New York: Da Capo.

"Freddie Lee Wright: Executed March 3, 2000, by Electric Chair in Alabama." (2009). Prosecuting Attorney, Clark County, Indiana, website. Available online at: http://www.clarkprosecutor.org/html/death/US/wright618.htm.

"Freddie Lee Wright: Petition for a Writ of Certiorari." (1999, July 20). Canadian Coalition Against the Death Penalty. Available online at: http://ccadp.org /wrightcert.htm.

Freedberg, S. (1999, July 4). "The 13 Other Survivors and Their Stories." *St. Petersburg Times*. Available online at: http://www.deathpenaltyinfo.org/node/1916.

Fulginiti, M., Redmond, L., and Johnson, S. (2008, May 22). ABC News. "From Prison to Prosperity, Against All Odds." Available online at: http://abcnews.go.com/print?id=3748603.

Gaertner, S. (Ramsey County [Minnesota] Attorney). (2010). "Resources for Criminal Justice Professionals." Available online at: http://www.co.ramsey.mn.us/attorney/SPDNA.htm.

Gardner, E. (1952). *Court of Last Resort*. New York: Pocket Books.

Garrett, B., and Neufeld, P. (2009). "Invalid Forensic Science Testimony and Wrongful Convictions." *Virginia Law Review* 95, pp. 1–97.

Gershman, B. (1991, June). "Abuse of Power in the Prosecutor's Office. *The World and I*, pp. 477–487.

Glod, M. (2007, March 28). "Former Death-Row Inmate Would Get $1.9 Million." *Washington Post*. Available online at: www.washingtonpost.com/wp-dyn/content/article/2007/03/27/AR2007032702240.html.

Glod, M. (2008, August 13). "Va. Court Grants First-Ever Innocence Writ." *Washington Post*. Available online at: http://www.washingtonpost.com/wp-dyn/content/article/2008/08/12/AR2008081202842.html.

Gold, J. (2007, May 15). "New DNA Test Frees Man Jailed for 2 Decades." Associated Press. Available online at: http://abclocal.go.com/wpvi/story?section=news/localandid=5297873.

Goode, E. (2002). "Drug Legislation." In *Encyclopedia of Crime and Punishment* (vol. 1), D. Levison (ed.). Thousand Oaks, CA: Sage.

Goodin, D. (1996, June 28). "California Death Sentence Reversed Due to Incompetence." *The Recorder* (an affiliate publication of Court TV). Available online at: http://www.deathpenaltyinfo.org/node/1893.

Goodman, A. (2005, December 20). "The Story of Harold Wilson: Convicted of Triple Murder, Sentenced to Die, Exonerated After 17 Years in Prison." *Democracy Now!* Available online at: http://www.democracynow.org/2005/12/20/the_story_of_harold_wilson_convicted.

"Governor Signs Tim Cole Act After Wrongful Lubbock Conviction." (2009, May 27). KCBD Television. Available online at: http://www.kcbd.com/Global/story.asp?s=10435107andclienttype=printable.

Gray, M. (1998). *Drug Crazy: How We Got into This Mess and How We Can Get Out*. New York: Random House.

Green, F. (2000, October 3). "DNA Clears Washington: Once Condemned to Die, He Is Pardoned but Remains Imprisoned in Unrelated Case." *Richmond (VA) Times-Dispatch*. Available online at: http://truthinjustice.org/washington_pardon.htm.

Green, F. (2009, April 23). "Freed Man from Hampton Might Go Back to Jail." *Richmond (VA) Times-Dispatch*. Available online at: http://www2.timesdispatch.com/member-center/share-this/print/ar/45634.

Gross, S., Jacoby, K., Matheson, D., Montgomery, N., and Patil, S. (2005). "Exonerations in the United States 1989 Through 2003." *Journal of Criminal Law and Criminology* 95, pp. 523–560.

Grutter v. Bollinger, 539 US 306 (2003).

Gutierrez, T. (2006, November 30). "Man Wrongly Imprisoned for 11 Years Donates to Pilgrim Baptist Church." WLS-TV, Chicago. Available online at: http://www.abclocal.go.com/wls/story?section=news/local&id=4811741.

Hall, M. (2008, November). "The Exonerated." *Texas Monthly.* Available online at: http://www.texasmonthly.com/2008-11-01/feature2-6.php.

Hamblett, M. (2007, September 6). "2nd Circuit Upsets Conviction over Defense Failure to Test Victim's Memory." *New York Law Journal.* Available online at: http://truthinjustice.org/Derrick-bell.htm.

Hancock, L. (2003). "Wolf Pack: The Press and the Central Park Jogger." *Columbia Journalism Review,* issue 1. Available online at: http://cjrarchives.org /issues/2003/1/rapist-hancock.asp?printerfriendly=yes.

Harmon, T. (2004). "Race for Your Life: An Analysis of the Role of Race in Erroneous Capital Convictions." *Criminal Justice Review* 29, pp. 76–96.

Harris, D. (2003). "The Reality of Racial Disparity in Criminal Justice: The Significance of Data Collection." *Law and Contemporary Problems* 66, pp. 71–98.

Harris, J. (2011, March 17). "Notorious Chicago Cop Reports to Prison." *Courthouse News Service.* Available online at: http://www.courthousenews.com /2011/03/17/34993.htm.

Helmer, J. (1975). *Drugs and Minority Oppression.* New York: Seabury.

Hester, T. (1995, July 22). "Cleared Con Begins Life Outside Prison." *Star-Ledger,* Newark, NJ, pp. 1, 6.

Hollingsworth, H. (2004, December 2). "Freed Missouri Death Row Inmate Sues Prosecution, Law Enforcement." Associated Press. Available online at: http://signonsandiego.com/news/nation/20041202-1756-freed -deathrow.html.

Holmes, W. (2001). "Who Are the Wrongly Convicted on Death Row?" In S. Westervelt and J. Humphrey (eds.), *Wrongly Convicted: Perspectives on Failed Justice.* New Brunswick, NJ: Rutgers University Press.

"Houston Crime Lab Scandal: After DNA Proves Innocence." (2003, March 16). TalkLeft.com. Available online at: http://www.talkleft.com/story/2003/03/16 /856/52154.

Huff, C. R. (2002). "Wrongful Conviction and Public Policy: The American Society of Criminology 2001 Presidential Address." *Criminology* 40, pp. 1–18.

Huff, C. R., Rattner, A., and Sagarin, E. (1996). *Convicted but Innocent: Wrongful Conviction and Public Policy.* Thousand Oaks, CA: Sage.

Human Rights Watch. (2008, May). *Targeting Blacks: Drug Law Enforcement and Race in the United States.* New York: Human Rights Watch.

Human Rights Watch. (2009, March). *Decades of Disparity: Drug Arrests and Race in the United States.* New York: Human Rights Watch.

Humphrey, J., and Westervelt, S. (2001). "Introduction." In S. Westervelt and J. Humphrey (eds.), *Wrongly Convicted: Perspectives on Failed Justice.* New Brunswick, NJ: Rutgers University Press.

"Illinois Governor Signs Bill Ending Death Penalty, Marking the Fewest States with Capital Punishment Since 1978." (2011, March 9). Death Penalty Information Center. Available online at: http://www.deathpenaltyinfo.org /document/ILRepealPR.pdf.

Innocence Project. (2009a). "Innocence Project Case Profiles." Available online at: http://www.innocenceproject.org/know/.

Innocence Project. (2009b). "Mission Statement." Available online at: http://www.innocenceproject.org/about/.

Innocence Project. (2009c). "Understanding the Causes: Eyewitness Misidentification." Available online at: http://www.innocenceproject.org/understand/Eyewitness-Misidentification.php.

Innocence Project. (2009d). "Understanding the Causes: False Confessions." Available online at: http://www.innocenceproject.org/understand/False-Confessions.php.

Innocence Project. (2009e). "Understanding the Causes: Informants/Snitches." Available online at: http://www.innocenceproject.org/understand/Snitches-Informants.php.

Innocence Project. (2009f). *Wrongful Convictions Involving Unvalidated or Improper Forensic Science That Were Later Overturned Through DNA Testing.* New York: Innocence Project.

Innocence Project. (2011). "Innocence Project Case Files." Available online at: http://www.innocenceproject.org/know/.

Innocence Project of New Orleans. (2009a). "Exoneree Profiles: Dan Bright." Available online at: http://www.ip-no.org/exoneree-profiles/dan-bright.

Innocence Project of New Orleans. (2009b). "Non-IPNO Exonerees: Willie Jackson." Available online at: http://www.ip-no.org/exoneree-profiles/non-ipno-exonerees/willie-jackson.

Innocence Project of New Orleans. (2010). "Exoneree Profiles: Travis Hayes." Available online at: http://www.ip-no.org/exoneree-profiles/travis-hayes.

Johnson, B., Golum, A., and Fagan, J. (1995). "Careers in Crack, Drug Use, Drug Distribution, and Nondrug Criminality." *Crime and Delinquency* 41, pp. 275–295.

Johnson, C. (2009). *A Disturbing Trend in Law School Diversity.* Available online at: http://blogs.law.columbia.edu/salt/.

"Jon Burge to Begin Prison Term." (2011, March 16). *Huffington Post.* Available online at: http://www.huffingtonpost.com/2011/03/16/jon-burge-to-begin-prison_n_836435.html.

"Joseph Amrine." (2005). Available online at: http://ccjr.policy.net/proactive/newsroom/release.vtml?id=34361.

"Josiah Sutton Back in Jail." (2007, October 26). KHOU.com, Houston, TX. Available online at: http://www.khou.com/topstories/stories/khou071026%20tj%20josiahsutton.1ad6a3466.html#%2010/1/09.

Journey of Hope. (2004). "Shujja Graham." Available online at: http://www.journeyofhope.org/pages/shujja_graham.htm.

"Justice for Josiah Sutton." (2004, April 12). Available online at: http://www.talkleft.com/story/2004/04/12/906/85824.

Justice Project. (2009a). "Darby Tillis and Perry Cobb." Available online at: http://www.thejusticeproject.org/profiles/darby-tillis-and-perry-cobb/.

Justice Project. (2009b). "Earl Washington, Jr." Available online at: http://www.thejusticeproject.org/profiles/earl-washington-jr/.

Kamionski, A. (2009, January 21). "Clark McMillan, Exonerated on DNA Evidence in 2002, Has Yet to Receive His Cash Settlement." Available online at: http://www.wrongfulconvictionlawsuitdefense.com/2009/01/.

Kassin, S. M., and Wrightsman, L. S. (1985). "Confession Evidence." In S. M. Kassin and L. S. Wrightsman (eds.), *The Psychology of Evidence and Trial Procedure.* Thousand Oaks, CA: Sage.

Kelley, T. (2007, May 16). "DNA in Murders Frees Inmate After 19 Years." *New*

York Times. Available online at: http://www.nytimes.com/2007/05/16/ny region/16dna.html.

Kennedy, J. (2003). "Drug Wars in Black and White." *Law and Contemporary Problems* 66, pp. 153–181.

Khanna, R. (2008, December 18). "Attacks on Kids Continued After Rachell Was Jailed." *Houston Chronicle.* Available online at: http://www.chron.com/disp /story.mpl/metropolitan/6170602.html.

Khanna, R., and McVicker, S. (2003, March 10). "New DNA Test Casts Doubt on Man's 1999 Rape Conviction." *Houston Chronicle.* Available online at: http://www.truthinjustice.org/sutton.htm.

Khanna, R., Olsen, L., and Schiller, D. (2008, December 13). "Cleared on Child Sex Assault, Houston Man Is Free." *Houston Chronicle.* Available online at: http://www.chron.com/disp/story.mpl/chronicle/6159775.html.

Khanna, S. (2010, January 5). "City of Durham and Erick Daniels Could Reach Settlement in Wrongful Conviction Case." *Independent Weekly.* Available online at: http://www.indyweek.com/indyweek/city-of-durham-and-erick -daniels-could-reach-settlement-in-wrongful-conviction-case/content ?oid=1299580.

Klein, M. (2002, February 12). "With Murder Case Dismissed, S. Phila. Man Finally Is Freed." *Philadelphia Inquirer,* p. B10.

Kocieniewski, D., and Hanley, R. (2000, November 28). "Racial Profiling Was the Routine, New Jersey Finds." *New York Times.* Available online at: http://www.nytimes.com/2000/11/28/nyregion/racial-profiling-was-the -routine-new-jersey-finds.html?pagewanted=all.

Kroll, J. (2008, June 22). "Mansfield Drug Case Gone Wrong: The Inside Story." *Plain Dealer.* Available online at: http://blog.cleveland.com/metro/2008/06 /drug_prosecutions_gone_wrong_t.html.

Kroll, M. (1991). *Chattahoochee Judicial District: Buckle of the Death Belt.* Washington, DC: Death Penalty Information Center.

Krouse, P. (2010, February 5). "Jury Acquits DEA Agent Lee Lucas on All 18 Charges Related to Drug Investigation." *Plain Dealer.* Available online at: http://blog.cleveland.com/metro/2010/02/dea_agent_lee_lucas_acquitted.html.

Krouse, P. (2010, February 16). "Richland County Deputy Sheriff Sentenced to 12 Weekends in Jail." *Plain Dealer.* Available online at: http://blog.cleveland .com/metro/2010/02/richland_county_deputy_sheriff.html.

Lechlitner, E. (2006, December 18). "Not Where He Left Off." *The Truth* (Elkhart, IN).

Lee, R. (2006, November 10). "Wrongful Conviction Amounts to $450,000." *Houston Chronicle.* Available online at: http://www.chron.com/disp/story.mpl /4324803.html.

Leo, R. (2005). "Rethinking the Study of Miscarriages of Justice: Developing a Criminology of Wrongful Conviction." *Journal of Contemporary Criminal Justice* 21, 201–223.

Leo, R., and Gould, J. (2009). "Studying Wrongful Convictions: Learning from Social Science." *Ohio State Journal of Criminal Law* 7, pp. 7–30.

Levy, N. (2005, April 29). "Bringing Justice to Hearne." *Texas Observer.* Available online at: http://www.texasobserver.org/article.php?aid=1935.

Levy, N. (2006, March 28). "Freed by DNA Test, Texas Man Cautiously Returns to Society." *New York Times.* Available online at: http://www.nytimes.com /2006/03/28/national/28mumphrey.html.

Lewin, T. (2010, January 7). "Law School Admissions Lag Among Minorities." *New York Times.* Available online at: http://www.nytimes.com/2010/01/07 /education/07law.html?_r=1andpagewanted=print.

Liptak, A. (2003, March 16). "You Think DNA Evidence Is Foolproof? Try Again." *New York Times.* Available online at: http://www.nytimes.com/2003 /03/16/weekinreview/16LIPT.html?pagewanted=printandposition=top.

Liptak, A. (2004, March 11). "5 Million Settlement Ends Case of Tainted Texas Sting." *New York Times.* Available online at: http://www.mapinc.org/news csdp/v04/n418/a09.html.

Locke, M. (2008, May 2). "Death Row Inmate to Go Free: Levon 'Bo' Jones Won't Be Retried in the 1987 Slaying of a Duplin County Bootlegger." *Raleigh News and Observer.* Available online at: http://www.newsobserver .com/news/crime_safety/story/1057974.html.

Lohr, D. (2009, April 30). "Dallas DNA." *The Criminal Report Daily.* Available online at: http://blogs.discovery.com/criminal_report/2009/04/dallas-dna.html.

Love, J. (2009, July). "Mansfield, Ohio, DEA Drug Sting Self-Destructs When Informant Admits Manufacturing Evidence." *Justice Denied.* Available online at: http://justicedenied.org/wordpress/archives/344.

Lundberg, C. (2008, December 22). "Plan to Retest Forensic Evidence for Mich. Prisoners Will Take at Least 3 Years." *Michigan Lawyers Weekly.* Available online at: http://www.correctionsone.com/pc_print.asp?vid=1768052.

Lunsford, D. (2005, January 15). "Coleman Convicted of Perjury." *Lubbock Avalanche-Journal.* Available online at: http://www.mapinc.org/newscsdp/v05 /n091/a06.html.

Luo, M. (2002, July 7). "Small Town Justice: The Accused Was Mentally Retarded; The Victim May Never Have Existed" (Part 1 of a series). Press release (2002 George Polk Awards at a Glance). Available online at: http://www.brooklyn.liu.edu/polk/press/small_town_justice1.html.

Lydersen, K. (nd). "Harold Hill Versus Burge Protégées at Area Three." News Photography Network. Available online at: http://www.newsphotography network.com/html/showcase.php?showcase=7.

Macaulay, D. (2009, June 5). "Man Freed on Wrongful Conviction Gets Probation for New Crime." *Daily Press* (Newport News, VA). Available online at: http://ww.dailypress.com/news/dp-thompson-archive4,0,5451196,printstory.

Macdonald, J., and Michaud, D. (1987). *The Confession: Interrogation and Criminal Profiles for Police Officers.* Denver, CO: Apache.

Markman, S., and Cassell, P. (1988). "Protecting the Innocent: A Response to the Bedau-Radelet Study." *Stanford Law Review* 41, pp. 121–160.

Martin, N. (2004, November). "Innocence Lost." *San Francisco* magazine.

Mauer, M. (1999). *Race to Incarcerate.* New York: New Press.

Mauer, M., and King, R. (2007, July). *Uneven Justice: State Rates of Incarceration by Race and Ethnicity.* Washington, DC: Sentencing Project.

McFadden, R., and S. Saulny. (2002, December 6). "Prosecutor Seeks the Reversal of Convictions in Jogger Case." *New York Times.* Available online at: http://www.nytimes.com/2002/12/06/nyregion/06JOGG.html.

McGonigle, S. (2007, January 22). "Old Cases Back to Haunt County: Why Were Exonerated Convicts Found Guilty to Begin With?" *Dallas Morning News.* Available online at: http://www.dallasnews.com.

McGonigle, S., and Emily, J. (2008, October 12). "18 Dallas County Cases Overturned by DNA Relied on Heavily Eyewitness Testimony." *Dallas Morning News*. Available online at: http://truthinjustice.org/dallas-eyewitness.htm.

McIntyre, L. (1987). *The Public Defender: The Practice of Law in the Shadows of Repute*. Chicago: University of Chicago Press.

Meincke, P. (2006, January 27). "City Settles for $9 Million in Rape Conviction Suit." WLS-TV, Chicago. Available online at: http://abclocal.go.com/wls /story?section=news/localandid=3853040.

Meissner, C., and Brigham, J. (2001). "Thirty Years of Investigating the Own-Race-Bias in Memory for Faces: A Meta-Analytic Review." *Psychology, Public Policy, and Law* 7, pp. 3–35.

Mills, S., and Coen, J. (2005, January 31). "2 Men Exonerated in 1990 Murder." *Chicago Tribune*. Available online at: http://truthinjustice.org/young-hill.htm.

Mississippi Innocence Project. (2010a). "Kennedy Brewer." University of Mississippi School of Law. Available online at: http://www.mississippiinnocence .org/casefile_KennedyBrewer.html.

Mississippi Innocence Project. (2010b). "Levon Brooks." University of Mississippi School of Law. Available online at: http://www.mississippiinnocence .org/casefile_LevonBrooks.html.

Morales, T. (2005, August 25). "Innocent Man Free to Dream Again." CBS News. Available online at: http://cbsnews.com/stories/2005/08/25/earlyshow/living /main795001.shtml.

Morgan, E. (2009, November 20). "Freed Inmate Struggling to Prove His Innocence in Salt Lake City Robbery." *Deseret News*. Available online at: http://truthinjustice.org/harry-miller.htm.

Mott, R. (2008, March 13). "'The Nightmare Is Over': Levon Brooks Finally Free." *Jackson Free Press*. Available online at: http://www.jacksonfreepress.com /index.php/site/comments/the_nightmare_is_over_levon_brooks_finally_free/.

Murphy, S., and Ellement, J. (2000, March 28). "DA Will Seek to Vacate '96 Murder Conviction." *Boston Globe*. Available online at: http://www.nodp.org/ma /stacks/d_johnson.html.

Musto, D. (1987). *The American Disease: Origins of Narcotic Control*. New York: Oxford University Press.

Myers, M. (2000). "The Social World of America's Courts." In J. Sheley (ed.), *Criminology*. Belmont, CA: Wadsworth.

Natapoff, A. (2009). *Snitching: Criminal Informants and the Erosion of American Justice*. New York: New York University Press.

National Association of Criminal Defense Lawyers. (2010). "True Stories of Injustice … Earl Berryman and Michael Bunch—New Jersey, 1985." Available online at: http://www.nacdl.org/PUBLIC/INJUST/true0008.htm.

National Public Radio. (nd). *Testing DNA and the Death Penalty (Part I: Fatal Flaws: The Case of Earl Washington)*. Boston: Inside Out Documentaries. Available online at: http://www.insideout.org/documentaries/dna/radioprogram.asp.

Nellis, A., and King, R. (2009, July). *No Exit: The Expanding Use of Life Sentences in America*. Washington, DC: Sentencing Project.

O'Hagan, M. (2003, March 31). "Exonerated but Never Set Free." *Seattle Times*. Available online at: http://www.deathpenaltyinfo.org/node/1899.

O'Hagan, M. (2009, December 23). Personal correspondence (email).

Olsen, L., Schiller, D., and Khanna, R. (2008, December 14). "Man Freed by DNA Wonders What to Do Next." *Houston Chronicle*. Available online at: http://www.chron.com/disp/story.mpl/metropolitan/6163477.html.

Orcutt, J., and Turner, J. (1993). "Shocking Numbers and Graphic Accounts: Quantified Images of Drug Problems in Print Media." *Social Problems* 40, pp. 190–212.

Parish, C. (2005, Fall). "Phantom Robbery and Fake Crime Scene Leads to 30-Year Prison Sentence—the Christopher Parish Story." *Justice Denied* 30, no. 7, pp. 37–39.

Paternoster, R. (1991). *Capital Punishment in America.* New York: Lexington Books.

People v. Allen, 590 P.2d 30, 34 (Cal. 1979).

Perlstein, M. (2004, October 10). "A Forgotten Man: Prosecutors Refuse to Reconsider Inmate's Case Despite Evidence Supporting His Claim." *Times-Picayune,* New Orleans, LA, Available online at: http://truthinjustice.org /travis-hayes.htm.

Peters, A. (2000, May 10). "New Jersey Conference Exposes Cases of Wrongful Conviction and Imprisonment." World Socialist Web Site. Available online at: http://www.wsws.org/articles/2000/may2000/conv-m10.shtml.

Pfeifer, S. (2008, October 8). "Millionaire Ex-inmate Dies in Crash." *Los Angeles Times.* Available online at: http://articles.latimes.com/2008/oct08/local /me-mckinney8.

Pirro, J. (2006, September 14–20). "The Exoneree: A One-Time Convicted Axe Murderer Becomes the Local Death-Penalty-Abolitionist's Frontman." *Philadelphia City Paper.* Available online at: http://citypaper.net/articles /2006-09-14/cb.shtml.

Possley, M., and Mills, S. (2003, October 26). "Crimes Go Unsolved as DNA Tool Ignored." *Chicago Tribune.* Available online at: http://truthinjustice.org /unsolved-crimes.htm.

Protass, H., and Harris, M. (2010, September 27). "Make New Crack Law Retroactive." *National Law Journal.* Available online at: http://www.law.com /jsp/nlj/index.jsp.

Public Broadcasting System. (2000). *Frontline.* "Interview: Clyde Charles." Available online at: http://www.pbs.org/wgbh/pages/frontline/shows/case /interviews/charles.html.

Public Broadcasting System. (2003, May 1). *Frontline.* "Burden of Innocence: Neil Miller." Available online at: http://www.pbs.org/wgbh/pages/frontline /shows/burden/profiles/miller.html.

Public Broadcasting System. (2004, June 17). *Frontline.* "Erma Faye Stewart and Regina Kelly." Available online at: http://www.pbs.org/wgbh/pages/frontline /shows/plea/four/stewart.html.

Radelet, M., Bedau, H., and Putnam, C. (1992). *In Spite of Innocence: Erroneous Convictions in Capital Cases.* Boston: Northeastern University Press.

Radin, E. (1964). *The Innocents.* New York: William Morrow.

Rampart Independent Review Panel. (2002). "The Los Angeles Police Department Rampart Division Scandal: Exposing Police Misconduct and Responding To It." In M. Ermann and R. Lundman (eds.), *Corporate and Governmental Deviance.* New York: Oxford University Press.

Ramsey, R. (2007). "Wrongful Conviction: Perceptions of Criminal Justice Professionals Regarding the Frequency of Wrongful Conviction and the Extent of System Errors." *Crime and Delinquency* 53, pp. 436–470.

Reeves, J., and Campbell, R. (1994). *Cracked Coverage: Television News, the Anti-Cocaine Crusade, and the Reagan Legacy.* Durham, NC: Duke University Press.

Regoli, R., and Hewitt, J. (1997). *Delinquency in Society*. New York: McGraw-Hill.

Reiman, J., and Leighton, P. (2010). *The Rich Get Richer and the Poor Get Prison: Ideology, Class, and Criminal Justice* (9th ed.). Boston: Pearson.

Reinarman, C., and Levine, H. (1989). "The Crack Attack: Politics and Media in America's Latest Drug Scare." In J. Best (ed.), *Images of Issues*. New York: Aldine de Gruyter.

Reynolds, J. (2003, July 31). "Pardons Urged in Drug Cases." *Lubbock Avalanche-Journal*. Available online at: http://lubbockonline.com/stories/073103/reg_073103064.shtml.

Richardson, F., and Mulvihill, M. (2004, May 5). "22 Bay State Men Wrongfully Jailed: Overzealous Cops, Shoddy Investigations, Lying Witnesses—How the System Failed." *Boston Herald* (Special Report: Justice Denied). Available online at: http://www.nodp.org/ma/stacks/herald_050504a.html.

Riley, S. (2002, February 21). "Free and Clear." *South Philly Review* (West Edition), pp. 1, 7, and 12.

Risinger, D. M. (2007). "Innocents Convicted: An Empirically Justified Factual Wrongful Conviction Rate." *Journal of Criminal Law and Criminology* 97, pp. 761–806.

Robinson, M. (2000). "The Construction and Reinforcement of Myths of Race and Crime." *Journal of Contemporary Criminal Justice* 16, pp. 133–156.

Rogge, O. (1959). *Why Men Confess*. New York: Da Capo Press.

Ruesink, M., and Free, M. (2005). "Wrongful Convictions Among Women: An Exploratory Study of a Neglected Topic. *Women and Criminal Justice* 16, 1–23.

Rutledge, J. (2001). "They All Look Alike: The Inaccuracy of Cross-Racial Identifications." *American Journal of Criminal Law* 28, pp. 207–228.

Ryan, J. (2007, May 15). "Man Released from Prison After DNA Wins Him New Trial in Killings of Two Children." *Star-Ledger,* Newark, NJ. Available online at: http:blog.nj.com/ledgerupdates/2007/05/dna_could_free_man_convicted_o.html.

Sack, K. (1997, December 24). "Brothers Freed in Rape Case Are Likely to Face Retrial." *New York Times,* p. A10.

Scheck, B., Neufeld, P., and Dwyer, J. (2000). *Actual Innocence: Five Days to Execution and Other Dispatches from the Wrongly Convicted*. New York: Doubleday.

Secret, M. (2007, May 23). "Stolen Youth: How Durham's Criminal Justice System Sent Erick Daniels to Prison for 10 Years Based on the Shape of His Eyebrows." *Independent Weekly*, Durham, NC. Available online at: http://www.indyweekly.com/indyweek/stolen-youth/Content?oid=1201791.

Secret, M. (2008, September 24). "Finally Free: Wrongly Convicted of Robbery, Erick Daniels Served Seven Years Before He Was Exonerated." *Independent Weekly,* Durham, NC. Available online at: http://www.indyweek.com/indyweek/finally-free/Content?oid=1211101.

"Sen. Siplin Conviction Reversed." (2007, December 28). *Orlando Sentinel*. Available online at: http://blogs.orlandosentinel.com/news_politics/2007/12/sen-siplin-conv.html.

Sheeran, T. (2008, February 10). "Ohio Drug Probe Left in Shambles by Lies Informant Concocted." *Decatur Daily*. Available online at: http://www.decaturdaily.com/stories/Ohio-drug-probe-left-in-shambles-by-lies-informant-concocted,4874.

Sherrer, H. (2000, March). "The 19-Year Ordeal of Dwayne McKinney: Injured and on Crutches 30 Miles Away from a Murder Is Finally Recognized as an

Alibi." Available online at: http://www.forejustice.org/wc/dwayne_mckinney _v1_i11.htm.

Sherrer, H. (2003, February 12). "Choctaw Three Saga Continues—Medell Banks, Jr. Walks Free When the Murder Charge Against Him Is Dismissed." Available online at: http:www.forejustice.org/wc/choctaw_three_update21403.htm.

Sherrer, H. (2003, March). "Medell Banks Jr.'s Conviction for Killing a Non-existent Child Is Thrown Out as a 'Manifest Injustice.'" *Justice Denied* 2 (9). Available online at: http://forejustice.org/wc/choctaw_three_92602.htm.

Sherrer, H. (2004, Winter). "Travesty in Tulia, Texas: Frame-up of 38 Innocent People Orchestrated by a County Sheriff, Prosecutor, and Judge." *Justice Denied* 23, pp. 3–5. Available online at: http://justicedenied.org/issue/issue_23/tulia _travesty.html.

Sherrer, H. (2005, Fall). "Parish's Conviction Vacated; New Trial Ordered." *Justice Denied* 30, no. 7, p. 39.

Simonich, M. (2008, February 24). "A Frame-up Falls Apart." *Pittsburgh Post-Gazette*. Available online at: http://www.mapinc.org/newscsdp/v08/n217 /a07.html.

"Single-Day Study Finds All Blacks in State Youth Prisons." (1990, July 4). *Juvenile Justice Digest* 18, pp. 5–6.

"6 More Convictions Overturned in LAPD Corruption Scandal." (2000, March 23). Los Angeles, CNN. Available online at: http://archives.cnn.com/2000/US /03/23/lapd.probe/.

Smith, G. (2007, October 22). "Rape Conviction Gone, Stigma Isn't." *Chicago Tribune*. Available online at: http://truthinjustice.org/marcus-lyons.htm.

Spitzer, E. (1999). *The New York City Police Department's "Stop and Frisk" Practices*. New York: Civil Rights Bureau.

Spohn, C., and Spears, J. (1996). "The Effect of Offender and Victim Characteristics on Sexual Assault Case Processing Decisions." *Justice Quarterly* 13, pp. 649–679.

"State, City to Pay $4M for Wrongful Murder Conviction." (2006, May 8). *USA Today*. Available online at: http://www.usatoday.com/news/nation/2006-05-08-wrong-conviction_x.htm?csp=34.

"State Sen. Gary Siplin Found Guilty of Felony Grand Theft." (2006, August 15). WESH 2 News. Available online at: http://www.wesh.com/print/9676954 /detail.html.

State v. Cromedy, 727 A.2d 457 (NJ 1999).

Stecklein, J. (2009, July 19). "Decade After Notorious Tulia Drug Raid, Subject Still Taboo in Town." *Lubbock Avalanche-Journal*. Available online at: http://www.lubbockonline.com/stories/071909/loc_465634283.shtml.

Stern, R. (2000, June 1). "Princeton Ministry Helps Man Prove Innocence." *Trenton Times*. Available online at: http://www.centurionministries.org/cases.html.

"Still Struggling with Wrongful Conviction After 31 Years." (2006, January 31). *Washington Post* and WJZ-TV (Baltimore, MD). Available online at: http://truthinjustice.org/vass.htm.

"Sting Docket." (2001, March 20). Amarillo.com. Available online at: http://www.amarillo.com/stories/032001/spe_sting.shtml.

"Stories of ACLU Clients Swept Up in the Hearne Drug Bust of November 2000." (2002, November 1). American Civil Liberties Union. Available online at: http://www.aclu.org/drug-law-reform/stories-aclu-clients-swept-hearne-drug -bust-november-2000?tab=legaldoc.

"Stories of Wrongful Conviction from California." (2010). *Death Penalty Focus.* Available online at: http://www.deathpenalty.org/article.php?id=407.

Strickland v. Washington, 466 US 668, 104 S. Ct. 2052 (1984).

Swanson, D. (2000, March). "Duval Was Freed, Retried, Then Finally Acquitted." *Justice Denied* 1 (11). Available online at: www.justicedenied.org/v1issue11.htm.

Tanner, R. (2003, July 7). "Forensic Scientists Under Scrutiny After Rash of Errors." *Wisconsin State Journal,* p. A3.

Taylor, M., and Doyle, M. (2011, March 20). "Investigation Rips Army's Crime Lab, Analyst." *Wisconsin State Journal,* p. B1.

"Texan Who Died in Prison Cleared of Rape Conviction." (2009, February 6). CNN. Available online at: http://www.cnn.com/2009/CRIME/02/06/texas .exoneration/index.html.

"Texas Awards $450,000 to Man Who Spent 18 Years in Prison on Wrongful Conviction." (2006, November 11). *Strange Justice.* Available online at: http://stju.blogspot.com/2006/11/texas-awards-450000-to-man-who -spent.html.

Texas Wesleyan University School of Law. (2007, February 2). "Dallas County Exonerees to Share Their Story at WIP Luncheon." Press release.

Tillis, D. (2009). "Darby Tillis: The First Illinois Death Row Exoneree." Darby Tillis website. Available online at: http://www.darbytillis.com/index.htm.

Tollett, T., and Close, B. (1991). "The Overrepresentation of Blacks in Florida's Juvenile Justice System." In M. Lynch and E. Patterson (eds.), *Race and Criminal Justice.* Albany, NY: Harrow and Heston.

Tonry, M., and Melewski, M. (2008). "The Malign Effects of Drug and Crime Control Policies on Black Americans." *Crime and Justice* 37, pp. 1–44.

Toobin, J. (2005, January 17). "Killer Instincts: Did a Famous Prosecutor Put the Wrong Man on Death Row?" *New Yorker,* pp. 54–63.

Truthinjustice. (2009). *Innocence Projects.* Available online at: http://www.truthin justice.org/ips.htm.

Turner, K. (2009, May 13). "Key Players in the 2005 Mansfield Drug Case." *Plain Dealer.* Available online at: http://blog.cleveland.com/pdextra//print.html.

United Press International. (2004, November 5). "Man Freed from Prison, Victims Admit Lying." Injusticebusters.com. Available online at: http://www.injustice busters.com/04/Smith_Sylvester.shtml.

US Census Bureau. (2009). *USA Quick Facts from the US Census Bureau.* Available online at: http://quickfacts.census.gov/qfd/states/.

US Department of Health and Human Services. (2010, September). *Results from the 2009 National Survey on Drug Use and Health: Volume I. Summary of National Findings.* Rockville, MD: Office of Applied Studies.

US Department of Justice. (1993). *Survey of State Prison Inmates, 1991.* Washington, DC: Bureau of Justice Statistics.

US Department of Justice. (1996). *Convicted by Juries, Exonerated by Science: Case Studies in the Use of DNA Evidence to Establish Innocence After Trial.* Washington, DC: National Institution of Justice.

US Department of Justice. (2006, December). *Capital Punishment, 2005.* Washington, DC: Bureau of Justice Statistics.

US Department of Justice. (2007, July). *Felony Sentences in State Courts, 2004.* Washington, DC: Bureau of Justice Statistics.

US Sentencing Commission. (2011, June 30). *US Sentencing Commission Votes*

Unanimously to Apply Fair Sentencing Act of 2010 Amendment to the Federal Sentencing Guidelines Retroactively (News Release). Washington, DC: US Sentencing Commission.

"Verdict In for Former Commissioner." (2005, March 2). Local10.com (Miami, FL). Available online at: http://www.justnews.com/4247135/detail.html.

Victims of the State. (2009). "Louisiana Victims of the State." Victims of the State. Available online at: http://www.victimsofthestate.org/LA/index.html.

"Volatile Miami Commissioner Arrested." (2004, August 27). Local10.com (Miami, FL). Available online at: http://www.justnews.com/news/3685406/detail.html.

Wallace, H. (1993). "Mandatory Minimums and the Betrayal of Sentencing Reform: A Legislative Dr. Jekyll and Mr. Hyde." *Federal Probation* 57, pp. 9–19.

Walsh, A. (1987). "The Sexual Stratification Hypothesis and Sexual Assault in Light of the Changing Conceptions of Race." *Criminology* 25, pp. 153–173.

Warden, R. (2004). *The Snitch System: How Snitch Testimony Sent Randy Steidl and Other Innocent Americans to Death Row.* Chicago: Center on Wrongful Convictions.

Warden, R., and Drizin, S. (eds.) (2009). *True Stories of False Confessions.* Chicago: Northwestern University Press.

Warden, R., Linzer, J., Lively, S., Royal, J., and Smith, B. (2003, May 12). *The Role of False Confessions in Illinois Wrongful Murder Convictions Since 1970.* Chicago: Center on Wrongful Convictions. Available online at: http://www.law.northwestern.edu/wrongfulconvictions/issues/causes andremedies/falseconfessions/FalseConfessionsStudy.html.

Webb, J. (2009). "Black Case Stirs Unease in Alabama." BBC News. Available online at: http://news.bbc.co.uk/2/hi/americas/2226855.stm.

Webster, R. (2007, May 25). "Louisiana Slow to Clear Imprisoned Innocents." *Journal of Jefferson Parish.* Available online at: http://www.nacdl.org/public.nsf /PrinterFriendly/Louisiana241?opendocument.

Weinberg, S. (2003a, June 26). *Breaking the Rules: Who Suffers When a Prosecutor Is Cited for Misconduct?* Washington, DC: Center for Public Integrity. Available online at: http://www.publicintegrity.org/pm/default.aspx?s ID=main.

Weinberg, S. (2003b, August 3). "Trials and Errors." TheAge.com. Available online at: http://www.theage.com.au/articles/2003/08/03/1059849267718.html?oneclick =true.

Wells, G., and Olson, E. (2001). "The Other-Race Effect in Eyewitness Identification: What Do We Do About It?" *Psychology, Public Policy, and Law* 7, pp. 230–246.

Wells, T., and Leo, R. (2009). *The Wrong Guys.* New York: New Press.

Westervelt, S., and Humphrey, J. (eds.). (2001). *Wrongly Convicted: Perspectives on Failed Justice.* New Brunswick, NJ: Rutgers University Press.

Westling, W. (2001). "Something Is Rotten in the Interrogation Room: Let's Try Video Oversight." *John Marshall Law Review* 34, pp. 537–555.

Wilgoren, J. (2002a, August 26). "Confession Had His Signature; DNA Did Not." *New York Times.* Available online at: http://www.nytimes.com/2002/08/26 /national/26DNA.html?todaysheadlines.

Wilgoren, J. (2002b, August 27). "Man Freed After DNA Clears Him of Murder." *New York Times.* Available online at: http://www.nytimes.com/2002/08/27/us /man-freed-after-dna-clears-him-of-murder.html.

Wilonsky, R. (2007, August 16). "No Doubt the First Lawsuit of Many." *Dallas Observer*. Available online at: http://blogs.dallasobserver.com/unfairpark/2007 /08/no_doubt_the_first_lawsuit_of.php.

Wilson, H. (2000, July 24). "Philadelphia Spotlight 2000." Canadian Coalition Against the Death Penalty. Available online at: http://ccadp.org/haroldwilson -spotlight.htm.

Wright, F. (1999). "Running Out of Time." *Justice Denied* 1 (5). Available online at: http://justicedenied.org/v1/issue5.htm#Running%20Out%20Of%20Time.

"Wrongfully Convicted Maryland Man Gets Paid Again for State's Mistake." (1999, January 18). *Jet*. Available online at: http://findarticles.com/p/articles /mi_m1355/is_7_95/ai_54724669/?tag=content;coll.

"Wrongly Convicted Man Freed from Jail After 11 Years." (2007, March 30). *Digital Journal*. Available online at: http://www.digitaljournal.com/article/153396.

Yant, M. (1991). *Presumed Guilty: When Innocent People Are Wrongly Convicted*. Buffalo, NY: Prometheus Books.

Zalman, M. (2006). "Criminal Justice System Reform and Wrongful Conviction: A Research Agenda." *Criminal Justice Policy Review* 17, pp. 468–492.

Zalman, M., Smith, B., and Kiger, A. (2008). "Officials' Estimates of the Incidence of 'Actual Innocence' Convictions." *Justice Quarterly* 25, pp. 72–100.

Zerwick, P. (2003). "Room for Doubt: Nineteen Years Later, a Brutal Crime Downtown Remains a Study in Contradictions and Uncertainty." *Winston-Salem Journal* (Part I of series titled "Murder, Race, Justice: The State v. Darryl Hunt"). Available online at: http://darrylhunt.journalnow.com/stories /printstory1.html.

Index

329

Witness error: as a factor in wrongful convictions, 6–7; conviction of innocents and, 31–33

Wright, Freddie Lee, 78–79

Wrongful convictions: African Americans and, 11–12; DNA exonerations and, 5; estimates from criminal justice professionals, 5–6; organizational culture and, 7; poverty and, 57; prevalence and incidence of, 4–6; problems estimating prevalence and incidence of, 4; social class and, 206; 4–5; states with largest number of, 30, 193; summary of findings of, 193

Wrongful murder convictions: case characteristics and, 103–104; factors associated with, 61–62, 104; false confessions and, 83–86; forensic errors and, 88–91; ineffective assistance of counsel and, 86–88; informants/snitches and, 80–83; police and prosecutorial misconduct and, 76–80; victim characteristics and, 91, 103; witness error and, 62, 72–76

Wrongful rape and sexual assault convictions: case characteristics and, 137; factors associated with, 107, 137, 146; factors other than witness error in, 132–136; victim characteristics and, 136–137; witness error as a factor in, 125–132; witness error as the primary factor in, 115–125

Wrongful robbery convictions: factors associated with, 172, 190–191; geographical distribution of, 171, 190; victim characteristics and, 183

The Wrong Guys, 58n

Wrongly Convicted: Perspectives on Failed Justice, 4

The Wrong Men: America's Epidemic of Wrongful Death Row Convictions, 4

Young, Dan, Jr., 51–53

About the Book

In this investigation of some 350 wrongful convictions of African American men, Marvin Free and Mitch Ruesink critically examine how issues of race undercut the larger goals of our criminal justice system.

Free and Ruesink expand the focus of wrongful conviction studies to include not only homicide, but also sexual assault, drug dealing, and non-violent crime. Their careful analysis reveals that black men accused of crimes against white victims account for a disproportionate number of wrongful convictions. They also uncover other disturbing failings on the part of prosecutors, police, witnesses, and informants. Highlighting the systemic role of race, the authors challenge us to move past the "just a few bad apples" explanation and to instead examine what it is about our criminal justice system that allows the innocent to be judged guilty.

Marvin D. Free, Jr., is professor of sociology at the University of Wisconsin–Whitewater. He is coauthor of *Crime, Justice, and Society* and editor of *Racial Issues in Criminal Justice: The Case of African Americans.* **Mitch Ruesink** teaches psychology at Waukesha County Technical College.